to Mike

♥

♥ Pat + Robyn 2006 ♥

VOYAGES OF DELUSION

Capt. James Cook
of the Endeavour.

Captain James Cook, the celebrated navigator whose third and final voyage
took him on a vain search for the Pacific entrance of the Northwest Passage.
This recently rediscovered portrait by William Hodges, which shows Cook
in a captain's undress uniform, seems to have been painted in 1775 or 1776,
between Cook's second and third voyages.
National Maritime Museum.

VOYAGES OF DELUSION

The Quest for
the Northwest Passage

GLYN WILLIAMS

Yale University Press
New Haven and London

Published with assistance from the Annie Burr Lewis Fund.

First published in the United States in 2003 by Yale University Press.

First published in Great Britain in 2002 by HarperCollins Publishers.

Set in PostScript Linotype Janson with Castellar and Spectrum display
by Rowland Phototypesetting Ltd.,
Bury St. Edmunds, Suffolk.

Printed in the United States of America.

Library of Congress Control Number: 2002109284

ISBN 0-300-09866-9 (cloth : alk. paper)

A catalogue record for this book is available from the British Library.

The paper in this book meets the guidelines for permanence and durability
of the Committee on Production Guidelines for Book Longevity of the
Council on Library Resources.

10 9 8 7 6 5 4 3 2 1

For Bill

CONTENTS

ILLUSTRATIONS

MAPS
(Drawn by John Gilkes)

INTRODUCTION

The European Enlightenment of the eighteenth century represented a determined attempt to dispel myth, superstition and ignorance. Those reminders of a darker age were replaced by a more rational and scientific approach, shown in the proliferation of learned societies, the systematic classifications of Linnaeus, the writings of the *encyclopédists* in France, the economic theories of Adam Smith and his contemporaries. Across the oceans of the world European navigators used new techniques and instruments to explore, survey and chart with a precision that would have amazed their predecessors. It is paradoxical then that the period since known as the Age of Reason witnessed a revival of hopes, often based on evidence that was little more than an expression of blind faith, that a navigable Northwest Passage might yet exist.

The quest for a sea route through or around America had begun in the sixteenth century when the successors of Columbus slowly realised the massive, continental dimensions of the new lands across the Atlantic. Seamen sailed along thousands of miles of coastline looking for a gap in the barrier through which they could reach the lands of the Orient and their fabulous riches, but they found only the tortuous Strait of Magellan far to the south. Whether there was a waterway through or round North America remained a matter for conjecture, although rumours about the little-known region north of Mexico hinted at golden cities and a strait linking the Pacific and Atlantic oceans. By the middle of the sixteenth century the strait had a name, Anian, but repeated Spanish efforts to find it failed. Nor did French expeditions probing along the eastern shores of North America have any more success, although they followed the St Lawrence River deep into the continent. For their part English seamen sailed even farther north, where they searched for the route they called the Northwest Passage, a name that in time would carry emotive implications, of men and ships battling against hopeless odds in a frozen wilderness. In the late Tudor and early Stuart period small vessels entered the eastern fringes of the Arctic archipelago in search of an open strait. The main features of this vast region were named after these explorers: Davis Strait, Baffin Island and Baffin Bay, Frobisher Bay, Hudson Strait and Hudson Bay, Foxe Basin, James Bay. Once those names stood like hopeful signposts on the maps, pointing the way to the Pacific; but for all the endurance and bravery of the navigators there was no way through. In Hudson Bay they reached their farthest west, only to be blocked by icebound shores. After the expeditions of Luke Foxe and Thomas James in 1631 failed to find an opening no other ship entered Hudson Bay for almost forty years.

The published narratives of the voyages were a reminder of what the crews had endured. Mountainous icebergs towered over the tiny vessels, and pack ice bore down to grip them as in a vice. The ice blurred the distinction between land and sea, and its shifts could be sudden and capricious. A clear channel one day might be solid with ice the next. Wooden hulls could be crushed, pierced, or overset as heavy floes smashed into them until, as William Baffin wrote of one moment, 'unless the Lord himselfe had been on our side we had shurely perished'. Nor was ice the only danger, for the tides were so violent that they spun the ships around as in a whirlpool. Variation of the compass, little understood and unpredictable, added to the difficulties of navigation, while fog and snow often prevented for weeks at a time the taking of sun-sights to establish latitude. And always there was the cold, so extreme that even in the summer months sails and rigging froze solid. However, amid the hazards lessons were learned. Seamen became expert in spotting leads from the masthead, and in taking their ships through them. They cut channels through the ice with long saws, fended off floes with ice-poles and boat-hooks, and slowly winched or towed their vessels forward. They gained experience that would allow later adventurers to exploit the resources of a region where the first explorers had suffered hardship and death.

Not until 1668 did another vessel from Europe sail through the 'furious overfall' of Hudson Strait and into Hudson Bay. The voyage of the *Nonsuch* ketch was for trade rather than exploration. Although the captain was ordered by the venture's London investors 'to have in your thoughts the discovery of the Passage into the South Sea and to attempt it as occasion shall offer', this directive was more a public relations exercise than a serious intention. The voyage was a commercial enterprise to obtain furs, and the crew established their base as far south as possible, at Rupert River in James Bay (the name given to the southern part of Hudson Bay), where they survived the winter in good health. In the spring Cree Indians came down the river from the interior to trade, and when the ketch returned to England it did so with a cargo of furs and the news that 'Beaver is very plenty.' In 1670 the Hudson's Bay Company was established by royal charter to exploit this newfound trade, and was given monopoly rights over the seas, straits and lands within the entrance of Hudson Strait. In the following decades the Company established posts along the shores of James Bay and of Hudson Bay proper, and built up a steady if small-scale trade in furs. As in other parts of the world, commerce had followed exploration; and for the London directors of the Hudson's Bay Company this seemed a logical and natural sequence. To be allowed to trade in comfortable obscurity was the height of their ambition, and risky, costly discovery ventures played no part in their calculations. It was with consternation, then, that in the eighteenth century they saw their half-hidden world in Hudson Bay once again coming into public view, for against all expectation the search for the Northwest Passage was resumed.

Whatever the attitude of the Hudson's Bay Company towards attempts to find a passage through its territories, the existence of trading posts in Hudson Bay reassured outsiders that conditions there were not as hazardous as the old accounts suggested. The commercial advantages of a short sea-route to the East remained as compelling as ever – it would cut a twelve-month voyage to six weeks, one optimist estimated – and evidence was shaped to fit the thesis. Projectors and publicists seized upon fragments of tidal observations from past voyages, concocted pseudo-scientific theories about the formation of ice, and resurrected reports of voyages claimed to have been made through the passage in earlier centuries. At the time of their first appearance these reports had been discounted as fanciful inventions, but in an age that prided itself on its dispassionate approach they were reinstated. The story of the search for a passage in the eighteenth century is one of credulity and some duplicity, of hopes raised and dashed, of the misdirection of practical seamen by those 'closet navigators' or armchair geographers much reviled in the explorers' journals. It has a rhythm similar to that of the tides on whose rise and fall believers in the existence of a passage pinned their hopes. Slowly a surge of support for a discovery voyage gathered momentum, only to break and collapse as the venture failed; but before long a groundswell gathered once more, and the process was repeated. Rather like generals in some endless war of attrition, those projectors who sent expeditions to find the Northwest Passage were always convinced that the next 'push' would pass through all obstacles to reach its objective. This book is as concerned with the intervals between the voyages as with the voyages themselves; for the arguments and intrigues of those quieter years tell us something about the ways in which men can delude themselves that the objects of their desires are easily attainable.

The first draft of this book was completed in the year 2000, when the voyage of the Royal Canadian Mounted Police vessel

St Roch II suggested that global warming might have trans-
formed the idea of a navigable Northwest Passage from a
chimera into a reality. In the early 1940s the original *St Roch*
had taken twenty-seven months to complete the first traverse
of the Northwest Passage from west to east. By contrast, her
successor, leaving Vancouver in July 2000, sailed through the
Arctic Ocean to Baffin Bay in little more than a month, and
encountered none of the feared pack ice that had defeated
earlier expeditions. It is too soon to say whether this is a sign
of things to come, or whether 2000 was one of those freakish
ice-free years across parts of the Arctic archipelago that have
been reported at intervals since the sixteenth century. To read
the account of the commander of the *St Roch II*, reporting
only a few icebergs and some small floes, is to be reminded
of those apocryphal voyages through the Northwest Passage
that once so excited enthusiasts for its discovery. It was the
contrast between those effortless voyages of the imagination
and the daunting experiences of the eighteenth-century
explorers that prompted my original interest in the subject
and my first book many years ago. Much has changed in the
world of historical scholarship since then. The journals of the
major British and French navigators involved in the search
during the eighteenth century are now available in critical
editions. An impressive amount of work has been done on
the Russian and Spanish voyages. The superb archives of the
Hudson's Bay Company have become a treasure-house of
information for increasing numbers of researchers. The maps
of the period, both European and Native American, have
yielded much to the probings of historical cartographers and
anthropologists. Archaeological investigations in Hudson Bay
have shown the fallibility of both written and oral evidence
about one failed voyage. In a rather broader way, scholars have
become more interested in the part that preconceptions play
in exploration, and how those preconceptions are formed.

My own researches have been helped by a succession of
dedicated archivists: at the Public Record Office, Kew; the

British Library; the National Maritime Museum; the Public Record Office of Northern Ireland, Belfast; the Hudson's Bay Company Archives (now part of the Provincial Archives of Manitoba), Winnipeg; and the Museo Naval, Madrid, among others. I also owe much to the work of scholars from many different countries and disciplines, and I hope that these debts are properly acknowledged in my section on sources. In a more personal way I would like to thank that fine geographer and good friend, William Barr, who a few years ago persuaded me to return to the Northwest Passage – in our studies, where we worked on the documents, and in Hudson Bay, where we saw those places where hopeful explorers wintered before setting out to find their promised strait. For much help and encouragement in the making of this book I must once again thank Giles Gordon, and at HarperCollins Michael Fishwick and Arabella Pike.

GLYN WILLIAMS
1 July 2001

I

To Hudson Bay

'There seems to be strong Reasons to believe there is a Passage to Northwestwards of Hudsons Bay, and that Passage no way Difficult by being pester'd with Ice.'

ARTHUR DOBBS, Memorial on the
Northwest Passage, 1731

1

Dead Man's Island: The Doomed Voyage of James Knight

> 'You are with the first Opertunity of Wind and Weathr to Depart Gravesend in your intended Voyage by Gods Permission to find out the Streight of Annian in Order to Discover Gold and Other Valuable Comodities to the Northward.'
>
> Instructions to Captain James Knight, 4 June 1719

ON 5 JUNE 1719 three small merchantmen and a sloop sailed in company from Gravesend on the Thames estuary, bearing the wishes of their owners for 'a prosperous voyage and safe'. Two of the four vessels were setting out on their annual voyage across the Atlantic and through Hudson Strait to supply the fur-trading posts of the Hudson's Bay Company. The other two, the *Albany* and *Discovery*, were also bound for Hudson Bay, but on a different mission. They were headed for the Strait of Anian, that legendary sea-route known to the English as the Northwest Passage, and carried on board iron-bound chests to bring back gold. Even by the standards of a turbulent year in which the country was swept by South Sea fever as investors risked their money in madcap schemes at home and overseas, the venture was an extraordinary one; as was the personality of the leader of the treasure seekers, James Knight.

Knight had served the Hudson's Bay Company for more than forty years. He had first gone to Hudson Bay as a shipwright in 1676, only six years after the Company was established, and he soon rose to be chief factor at one of its Bayside posts. In 1692, during the war with France that spread to Hudson Bay, he was appointed 'Governor in the Bay', and was involved in the tit-for-tat operations that saw frequent captures and recaptures of the main trading posts. On his return to England in 1700 he became a substantial shareholder in the Company and a member of its London Committee which served under the direction of the Governor of the Company (in modern terms, its chief executive). During these years Knight acquired a double-edged reputation. He was 'able and dexterouse in business', but a sturdy, often truculent individualist whose attention to 'severall Concernes of his owne', as he once put it, often set him at odds with his superiors in the Company. Even so, he formed part of a delegation that was sent to Holland in 1710 to represent the Company's interests in the long drawn-out peace negotiations with France. These reached a successful conclusion as far as the Company was concerned when the Treaty of Utrecht in 1713 returned to it all the Bay posts. By now Knight was well into his sixties, a man of some substance who was described in the records as 'Merchant, London'. He was ready, it might be thought, for retirement. Instead, after hard bargaining, he was once more appointed Governor in the Bay, with orders to receive from the French the surrender of their gains in Hudson Bay. His demands were considerable: the highest salary ever paid to a Company servant, a ten per cent share in any new trade, the right to decide on all operational matters, and perquisites ranging from a fur coat to a beaver covering for his bed. With all this settled, on 6 July 1714 Governor James Knight sailed for Hudson Bay, with Henry Kelsey as his Deputy. He carried with him commissions from the Queen and the Company, a cargo of trading goods – and a secret that would slowly be revealed in the following years.

Hudson Bay was no place for a man of Knight's age and infirmities. (Three months before he was due to sail an anxious Committee member checked 'in what Condition of Health' he was.) To gain entrance to the Bay through the bottleneck of Hudson Strait was struggle enough, for it was navigable only for about three or four months of the year, usually from the middle of July to some time in October. Even then, ships could take several weeks to force a way through the ice of its two-hundred-mile length, and once they reached the more open waters of the Bay those that stayed too long ran the risk of being trapped. At the Bay posts winter came early and finished late, with extremes of cold well beyond the experience of anyone in Britain. To the first European newcomers, Hudson Bay was a frozen wilderness. In the published narratives it loomed as a scene of desolation and calamity: of Henry Hudson being cast adrift with a handful of loyal crew members, of privation and death for the later crews that wintered there.

Knight's own lifetime had seen a less apocalyptic view emerging as the commercial possibilities of Hudson Bay were exploited, especially the trade in beaver pelts. The best supplies came from the Cree Indians who lived and trapped along the rivers inland from Hudson Bay, and to encourage this trade the Hudson's Bay Company built wooden forts at Albany, York and Moose, where the main rivers of the interior ran north to the shores of James Bay and Hudson Bay. The forts were two-storey buildings protected by four flankers or bastions to carry cannon, surrounded by an outer stockade pierced by a single gate. In them small garrisons learned to survive the rigours of the winter, their seasonal routine dominated in general terms by the climate, and in detail by the weather from day to day. The garrisons remained perilously dependent on the annual supply ships from England, which during their brief stay in July or August unloaded an assortment of trade goods, stores and provisions. A few weeks earlier, Indians from the interior would have come downstream with their canoes full of furs, and many would still be waiting at the fort to be paid in the trade goods from the ship when it arrived. These goods varied from the familiar staples of the fur trade – guns, powder, kettles, tobacco, brandy – to the more exotic such as

Hudson Bay and Strait

Boothia
Peninsula

BAFFIN ISLAND

Davis Strait

70°

70°

Arctic Circle

Melville
Peninsula

Foxe

Basin

Cumberland Sound

65°

65°

Repulse Bay

Cape Hope

Wager Bay

Frozen Strait

Baker Lake

Cape Dobbs

Roes Welcome

Foxe Channel

Chesterfield Inlet

Cape Fullerton

Southampton
Island

Frobisher Bay

Rankin Inlet
Corbett Inlet

Hudson Strait

Marble Island

Resolution
Island

Whale Cove

Coats Island

Cape
Chidley

Eskimo Point

60°

60°

Ungava
Bay

Prince of Wales Fort

*Hudson
Bay*

Cape Churchill

Churchill River

York Fort

Nelson River

Hayes River

55°

Fort Severn

55°

*James
Bay*

50°

Fort Albany

Moose
Factory

Rupert River

50°

0   100   200   300 Miles

ostrich feathers and hawks' bells. The list of stores was even longer. Together with food, ammunition, tools and the like were items which seem trivial – sealing wax, a salt cellar, a flag, table napkins – but whose inclusion is a reminder of the reliance of the garrison on the annual cargo. A Company post was as self-contained, and in many ways as isolated, as a lone ship on an oceanic voyage. What the factor held in his warehouse, supplemented by hunting, trapping and fishing, had to last not only the garrison for twelve months but also the 'Home Indians' (the Company's name for the Crees who lived near the Company posts, and hunted and fished for the garrison). If the next ship lost its passage, then that period would stretch to two long years.

Knight's destination in 1714 was York Fort, the most important and northerly of the Company posts, which had been built on the swampy point of land between the mouths of the Hayes and Nelson rivers. There, Knight's official priority was to re-establish trading relations with the inland tribes after the long interruption of the French occupation of the fort. This task, however important it was in the Company's eyes, was not the main incentive that had tempted the ageing Governor back to Hudson Bay. During his wartime years in England, Knight had heard rumours about rich mineral deposits somewhere west of Hudson Bay, and with him on the ship he took crucibles and other items to test for minerals. What evidence Knight had come across in England (or possibly on the Continent during his diplomatic mission) to reawaken his interest is not known, but it was enough to dominate the last years of his life. First, though, there was the matter of survival, and Knight's early months back at York were hard. On taking over the fort from the French he found it 'nothing but a Confusd heap of old rotten Houses' which gave little shelter from the ice and snow of winter. Spring brought new dangers, for the thaw led to a deluge that flooded the fort to its second storey, and sent its garrison scrambling into the nearest trees. Knight described how great slabs of ice rumbling down on the torrential flood waters of the Hayes River crashed against the buildings with such force that even the walls of Christopher Wren's newly-built St Paul's Cathedral would have collapsed. None of this diverted the Governor from his determination to explore and exploit the unknown country to the northwest. We can follow the story in his journals, never published, but still preserved among the records of the Hudson's Bay Company. Most Company factors were reluctant journal-keepers, content with sparse entries about the post's daily routine, but Knight treated his journals as a trusted confidant. They are full of long entries in which the Governor expressed his fears, his frustrations, and above all his hopes.

As a first step in his expansionist policy Knight needed to end the destructive hostilities between the Crees who lived near the shores of Hudson Bay, and the more distant 'Northern Indians' (Chipewyans) who ranged across the Barrens far to the northwest of York Fort. No European had ever seen that country, but in the summer of 1715 Knight persuaded a large group of the fort's Home Indians to head inland to the country of the Northern Indians in an attempt to make peace. They were accompanied by a Cree-speaking Company servant, William Stuart, and by a Chipewyan woman, Thanadelthur, who played a central part in the drama that now unfolded. In Knight's journal she was called 'the slave woman' because she had been captured and enslaved by a Cree war party, but Chipewyan oral tradition recalls her name as Thanadelthur or 'marten shake'. She had shown enterprise and courage in escaping from her Cree captors and reaching York Fort the previous winter, and so impressed Knight that he engaged her as an interpreter for the northern expedition. Meanwhile, he became increasingly intrigued by what she had to say about her country, where, Knight noted in his journal, 'there is a Large River or Streights and that the tides Ebbs & flows at a great rate & it hardly freezes some Winters'. In time Knight would return to this, but for the moment he pinned his hopes on Stuart and his overland party. His instructions to Stuart ordered him to make peace between the warring Indian groups, to look for furs, and above all to inquire about minerals. The Governor wanted information about the copper deposits of which there had been rumours among the Company servants in Hudson Bay for some time, but his real quest was for a far more valuable and enticing mineral. Now for the first time references appear in Knight's journal to the 'yellow mettle' or gold that he was convinced existed far inland. Thanadelthur's answers to Knight confirmed his belief that somewhere west of Hudson Bay lay another El Dorado, which he thought might be located on the Pacific coast of North America, for if Stuart sighted sea-going ships or heard cannon he was to 'make a Smoak for a Signall [that] it is ye English comeing to trade'.

During the winter that followed Stuart's departure Knight was desperately ill with gout, fever, ague and colds. 'I must have gone if Nature had not been very strong,' he reflected. Life was not made easier when the annual supply ship from England, commanded by Captain Joseph Davis, and carrying essential provisions and trade goods, turned away from York when almost within sight of the fort. 'None but a Sott or a Madman would have done it,' Knight raged in his journal as he agonised over the damage done to his plans by this 'thoughtless, Ignorant, obstinate fooll'. In April 1716 a few members of the peace party straggled back to York Fort with a grim story of sickness and starvation. Their last sight of Stuart and Thanadelthur had been as they slowly plodded north across a frozen landscape, accompanied by only a handful of Home Indians. Those who had turned back gave Knight a harrowing description of the crossing of the Barrens where, in conditions of bitter cold, with drifting snow piled high above their shelters, they had neither fuel nor food. Some killed their dogs, others lived on moss. A few days later other Indians came into the fort with a note from Stuart, dated the previous October. It made worrying reading for the anxious Governor.

'Wee are in a Starving Condition at this time ... Wee have eat nothing this 8 days. I do not think as I shall see you any more but I have a good heart.' Then, on 7 May, to the garrison's surprise and delight, Stuart returned, accompanied by Thanadelthur, the survivors from among the Home Indians – and ten Northern Indians.

'Experiencing a world of hardship', Stuart estimated that his party had travelled a thousand miles northwest from York. They had started their journey across a windswept terrain where the only trees were dwarf spruce, growing a few feet high in sheltered hollows. Soon even these disappeared, and as winter set in Stuart's party found itself in the 'Baren Desarts' of a frozen and featureless landscape. Apart from a compass, Stuart had none of those instruments that later explorers would take for granted, nor did he keep a journal; and although he claimed to have reached latitude 67°N. Knight suspected that this was too far north. From Stuart's description of the terrain, he seems to have reached the region just southeast of Great Slave Lake, about seven hundred miles from York. Even though he was dependent on his Indian guides and hunters Stuart's journey says much for his endurance and tenacity, and his report to Knight made a dramatic story. In order to survive, his group had split into small hunting parties, one of which had encountered Chipewyans and in a bloody skirmish had killed nine of them. Following tracks in the snow, Stuart and Thanadelthur came across the frozen corpses, and all prospects of success seemed at an end. Thanadelthur persuaded Stuart and the rest of the group to remain for ten days inside a rough shelter in the snow while she set off to make contact with her countrymen. On the tenth day she returned with a large band of Chipewyans, and after 'perpetual talking' persuaded them to smoke the pipe of peace with their Cree enemies, and to allow ten of their number to accompany her back to York Fort.

Having heard Stuart's report, Knight turned to the strange Indians. They had knives and ornaments of copper, and told him about a river in their country along whose banks lay lumps of pure copper so heavy that three or four men could not lift them. Stuart had brought back some smaller pieces of the ore, and these Knight sent to London for analysis, but he was more interested in the Chipewyans' report that there was 'a Parcell of Indians as lyes upon the west Seas as has a Yellow Mettle as they make use of as these do Copper.' Day after day his journal entries became longer and more excited as he questioned the newcomers about this metal. A captive woman among them from another tribe assured Knight that 'she has both seen it taken and took it up out of the River her Self as it has washt down out of the Bank it is very Yellow Soft & heavy and that they find Lumps so bigg sometimes that they hammer it betwixt Stones and make dishes of it'. A month later Knight was still interrogating the woman, and there was now an air of desperation in her answers as she tried to convince the Governor, and he tried to convince himself: 'her Eyes had seen it and her hands had felt it that the Mettle was very Yellow & very Soft wch makes Me be fully assur'd it could be nothing else but Gold.' The hills containing the deposits, she insisted, were so near the sea that she had often seen ships out to the west, either Spanish or Japanese vessels, Knight thought. As further encouragement, another Indian added 'white mettle' to the list of minerals to be found in his country, and this Knight immediately assumed must be virgin silver. What language was used to convey all this information is not clear. Long-time Company servants such as Knight and Stuart would have had a fair knowledge of Cree; Thanadelthur had Chipewyan, Cree and possibly some English, and was clearly acting as an intermediary between Knight and her countrymen; but the whole process was fraught with opportunities for misunderstanding on one side and wishful thinking on the other.

One sobering aspect of Stuart's journey was its length and hardship, which threw doubt on the practicality of an overland route to the promised land far to the northwest. 'I know it is

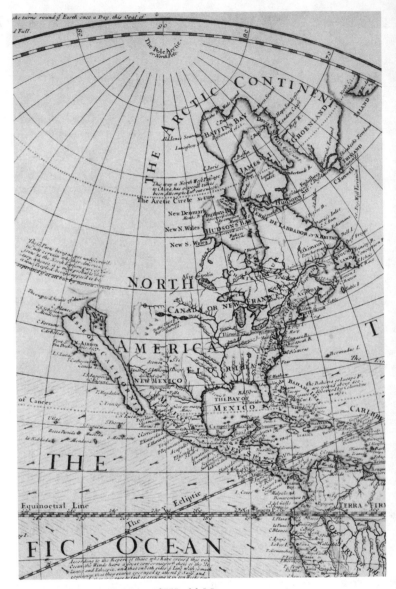

1. JOHN SENEX. Section of World Map, 1725.
British Library

This map by a respected British cartographer shows how little was known in the early eighteenth century of the northwestern parts of the North American continent. California is still represented as an island with only 'The suppos'd Straits of Annian' marked to the north, while nothing is shown west of Hudson Bay.

1500 Miles cross from Sea to Sea,' Knight wrote as he brooded over ways and means of reaching the country of gold and silver. Increasingly, his thoughts turned to the possibility of an approach by sea, and to Thanadelthur's mention soon after her first arrival at York of that large strait to the north where the tide ebbed and flowed and which rarely froze. By now, Knight was contemplating the question that had obsessed navigators and geographers for centuries: was there a Northwest Passage, a strait for sea-going vessels that led from the Atlantic to the Pacific and the rich lands beyond? From his vantage point at York Fort – as far west in the northern interior of the American continent as any European had reached at this time – Knight was gazing into the dark. On the maps the vast area between Hudson Bay and the dimly-known lands of east Asia was marked *incognita* (*Ill.1*). What was sea and what was land was unknown, for on the Pacific coast of America no Spanish ship had sailed higher than latitude 43°N., and Knight had no way of checking the information that the Northern Indian gave him about those distant regions. On the existence or otherwise of a strait their answers varied in a way that drove Knight to distraction. One day it was, 'I could not hear by them that thare is any Straights that parts Asia from America'; the next, 'from there Discourse I begin to think there may be a Passage or Straits that parts America from Asia.'

Even more intriguing than verbal reports were the rough maps that the Northern Indians drew for Knight, who 'did gett them to lay down there Rivers along Shore to the Norward they chalkd 17 Rivers some of them very large'. The seventeenth, he thought, might well be the strait itself, for it led to a bay whose inhabitants wore ornaments made from yellow metal; and each year saw ships out to sea. A copy of one of these maps is still in the archives of the Hudson's Bay Company (*Ill.2*). The mixture of indigenous cartography, Knight's glosses, and later additions makes it difficult to interpret, for it omits the great Arctic peninsulas of Melville and Boothia, and shows the Coppermine River ('Chanchadese' or 'Metal

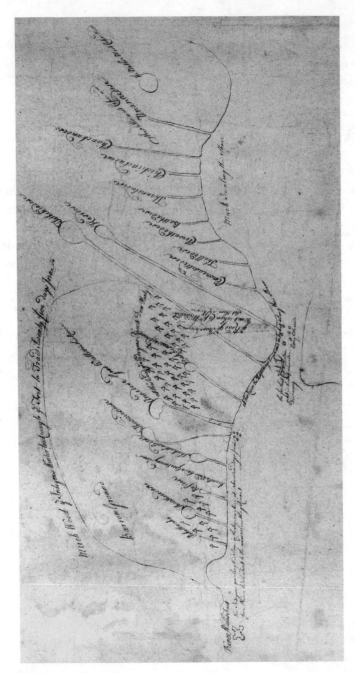

2. 'Northern Indian' map, *c.* 1719
HBC Archives, Provincial Archives of Manitoba (G.1/19) The redrawing of the outlines on this map (opposite) was done by Richard I. Ruggles, and is reproduced here by his kind permission and that of the Manitoba Historical Society.

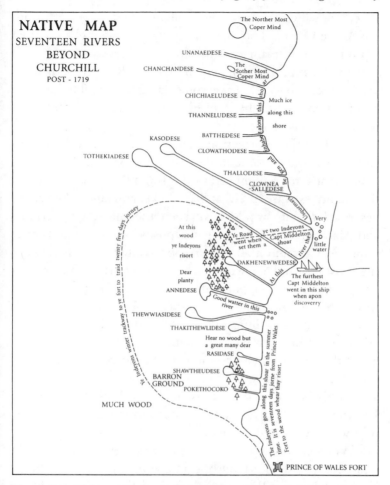

The outlines of this untitled manuscript map are thought to have been drawn by the Northern or Chipewyan Indians who arrived at York Fort from the interior in 1716. James Knight probably added the names and legends, except those referring to Christopher Middleton's discovery voyage of 1741–2 (and 'Prince Wales Fort', the name given to the fort at Churchill after Knight's time). The map has been positioned here with north at the top, to show seventeen rivers running down to the coast of Hudson Bay north of Churchill. The eighth river north from Churchill is shown as the beginning of Eskimo territory, with a legend placed along the coastline stating 'At this River the Usquemays begen and inhabet along this shore.' The two rivers farthest north are shown passing 'The Sother Most Coper Mind' and 'The Norther Most Coper Mind'. The fragment of coastline on the right is the southwestern extremity of Southampton Island, and the channel between it and mainland is Roes Welcome.

River') flowing east into Hudson Bay rather than north into the Arctic Ocean. The map's importance to Knight was that it promised a clear run for ships along the west coast of Hudson Bay to the mines of copper and, hopefully, to the land of yellow metal beyond. Like some latter-day Columbus, the more intently Knight looked westward, the nearer the promised lands seemed to be.

Much of the information from the Native American maps and reports was of value in the right context. The 'sea' of the Chipewyans that Knight assumed was the Pacific was probably the mighty expanse of Great Slave Lake, and among the rivers described to him would have been the Slave, Coppermine and Mackenzie with their rich deposits of copper and other minerals. Certainly the more responsive (and imaginative) of the Northern Indians who reached York Fort in the summer of 1716 were not disappointed with their reception, for Knight was eager to glean any scrap of information about their country, and was willing to pay for it. More than thirty years later one of his men who was with Knight when he interrogated the Indians about the mines of gold remembered how the Governor 'was very earnest in this Discovery, which was always his Topic, and he took all Opportunities of making Presents to the Natives'. Perhaps not surprisingly, Knight was told what he wanted to hear.

Whether the approach was to be by sea or land, Knight was determined to establish a post along the coast north of York at Churchill River, which formed the southern edge of the border between the hunting-grounds of the Chipewyans and their Eskimo (Inuit) enemies. In 1717 Stuart accompanied the party sent to build a post at the mouth of the river which a Danish discovery expedition led by Jens Munk had reached in 1619. Munk's dreadful wintering there had left alive only three survivors, who miraculously managed to sail their ship back across the Atlantic. Almost a hundred years later the skeletons of Munk's men still lay scattered on the ground, but Stuart was ordered to use this ill-omened site as a springboard for another journey inland to bring the Northern Indians down to trade. There was no Thanadelthur to accompany him this time, for after a lingering illness she had died in February despite all Knight's efforts to nurse her back to health. The young Chipewyan woman had 'the Firmest Resolution that ever I see any Body in my Days', Knight wrote. If just fifty of her countrymen possessed her 'devellish spirit', they would drive all other Indians out of the north. Thanadelthur's death was a blow that brought Knight to the edge of despair. His journal entries show that he was still blaming Captain Davis's failure to reach York almost two years earlier for all his misfortunes. They also reveal a degree of mental strain and physical deterioration that boded ill for the future as he railed against that 'blundering Madman whose Obstinacy makes me Allmost Mad when I think of it . . . I cannot Sleep a Nights nor rest a Days it is so continually in my Mind . . . all this brought upon by a Crazy hair braind Sottish fellows Misscarriage . . . it has brought me into Such condition that I am fainting 20 times a day'.

Matters did not improve when Knight reached Churchill in the summer of 1717 to take personal control of affairs at the new post, for it soon became clear that Stuart was in no condition to repeat his inland journey of two years earlier. He was sent back to York where Knight's deputy, Henry Kelsey, reported that he has 'been lunatick 3 or 4 times insomuch that wee have been forct to tie him in his bed', and he died soon after, possibly as a result of his earlier hardships. A last attempt to attract the Northern Indians to the new post to trade was made by a young Company servant, Richard Norton, who with two Northern Indians set off inland and returned to Churchill with a band of their countrymen during the winter of 1717–18, but at great cost to himself. What he told Knight about the country to the north when he returned starving and frozen is not known, but it may have played some part in Knight's new plans. A Company ship-captain who questioned Norton years later about his wanderings in that winter reported that he could remember nothing but 'the danger and terrour he underwent'.

By now Knight was convinced that the discovery must be made by sea, and that he needed to persuade the Company to finance a voyage from England. In the autumn of 1718 he returned home from York Fort on the *Albany*. Its captain was George Berley (or Barlow), and on board as a passenger was a Company sloopmaster, David Vaughan, who that summer had taken the *Success* sloop from Churchill north along the coast of Hudson Bay in an effort to open trade with the Inuit. At one time a ship's carpenter, he had won high praise from Knight – 'you cannot have a soberer or a brisker man' – for bringing the tiny sloop safely back to Churchill through some of the worst sailing conditions that Knight had ever seen. It was a reminder both of Knight's age and his ailments that when he arrived back in England he lay housebound in Limehouse so ill 'by the excessive Cold he got in his Limbs in that Country' that he was unable to attend to business for at least a month. When he was well enough to approach the Company with his plans, he found a distinct lack of enthusiasm. Although the Governor and Committee in London had shown interest in Knight's reports of copper mines – and had seen and handled the samples he had sent home – it clearly regarded his visions of gold and silver with altogether more caution. The Governor of the Company at this time was Sir Bibye Lake, who had trained as a barrister, but then abandoned the law as he accumulated major investments in overseas trade and property. While still a young man, he became Governor in 1712, and proved to be a shrewd and cautious director of the Company's affairs. Shunning all publicity, he slowly consolidated its trade after the battering of the long French wars, and in 1718 was able to declare the Company's first dividend for twenty-eight years. He was not the sort of man to be easily tempted by schemes which carried no guaranteed return.

Negotiations between Knight and the Company were protracted and difficult, and not until 1 May 1719 was agreement reached for an expedition 'to Discover Gold and other Valuable Comodities to the Northward'. Knight would be in overall command of two discovery vessels, the *Albany* of a hundred tons, commanded by her regular captain, George Berley, and the newly-built *Discovery* sloop of forty tons under David Vaughan. Knight had obviously put his homeward passage on the *Albany* to good use in winning the confidence of these two experienced seamen. What evidence there is in the Company's minute books suggests that it fitted out the expedition with reluctance and under some pressure. Knight's contract had ended, and he returned to England as a time-expired servant. He was an independent agent driving a hard bargain, rather than an employee laying a proposal before the Company for acceptance or rejection. To fit out a full-scale discovery expedition in addition to the two regular supply ships sailing to the Bay represented a major expenditure for a Company that kept a tight grip on its finances. Unusually, Knight contributed one-eighth of the cost of the venture, and presumably would have taken an equivalent share of the expected profits. A later witness reported that the Company was opposed to Knight's proposals, but as 'he was *opiniatre*, they durst not disoblige him, lest he should apply elsewhere'. His journals at York Fort had more than once revealed his contempt for stay-at-home Committee members, and it was reported that his only answer to their doubts about his plans was that he knew the route 'as well as to his bedside'. Clearly the imperious veteran, dreaming about a land of straits and rivers where gold lay in great lumps, would be a hard man to dissuade; and a threat to 'apply elsewhere' would be a most effective one, for it raised the spectre of an interloping expedition that might challenge the Company's monopoly. In the heady months of the South Sea Bubble, when investors were rushing to put their money into the most hare-brained speculative schemes, finance for such a venture might not be hard to raise.

The Company's minute and account books tell us much about the preparations for the voyage. A cargo of trading goods (blankets, knives, mirrors and beads) was put on board, together with 3500 bricks and large quantities of lime, building materials that indicated an intention to winter somewhere west of Hudson Bay. The discovery ships carried provisions for only nine months, but the large amount of salt and other preservatives on board indicates that Knight was confident of finding fresh meat for his crews. To judge by the total wages paid, the *Albany* carried a crew of about seventeen, and the *Discovery* ten. In addition ten 'landmen passengers' were on board. From the nature of Knight's quest these were probably miners, smiths and the like; and there is some confirmation of this in a newspaper report of the expedition that referred to 'artificers' being taken. Berley and Vaughan were placed under Knight's orders in all matters except the actual handling of the vessels, but since Knight was sailing with Berley in the *Albany* an outline of the intended explorations had to be supplied to Vaughan in case his sloop lost company. Knight's instructions to Vaughan were notably unspecific. If separated, Vaughan was to get into latitude 64°N. and then head north 'to find out the Straits of Anian'.

Rarely can a navigator have been given shorter and less helpful sailing orders. The Strait of Anian was a will-o'-the-wisp of northern geography, first appearing on maps in the mid-sixteenth century as a narrow strait separating Asia and America, roughly in the position of today's Bering Strait. By the time of Knight's voyage it had wandered south on the maps, and was sometimes shown running inland just north of California. Knight's habit of naming the route he was seeking the Strait of Anian rather than the Northwest Passage, the more usual term used by English explorers, suggests that he was familiar with the Dutch and French maps of the period, and that he was hoping to find a sea-route farther south than that sought by his English predecessors. In France at this time there was speculation about the existence of a 'Mer de l'Ouest' or Sea of the West, whose waters were thought to cover much of western North America. Rivers ran down to its shores from the eastern half of the continent, promising a way to the Pacific for the French explorers and traders pushing west across the continent. The father of this concept was the most celebrated of all French geographers of the period, Guillaume Delisle. Although his maps sketching the great inland sea were kept from the public eye, legal disputes between him and other cartographers led to rumours of the new sea circulating in France and the Low Countries at the time of Knight's stay in Utrecht in 1710. Only two years earlier one of Delisle's rivals, J.B.Nolin, had issued maps and a globe which marked a (rather small) Sea of the West and showed a lengthy Strait of Anian running diagonally across the continent from north of California to Hudson Bay. (*Ill.3*). Knight would almost certainly have been aware of these or similar maps, with their promise that once through an opening on the far coast of Hudson Bay ships could sail steadily southwest into warmer regions. He would have also have remembered the reassuring descriptions given by his Northern Indian informants at York in 1716 that 'there is very little Ice in them [Western] Seas in the Winter and that great Wood does grow all along the Westland Country and that shows there is an open Sea.'

The Company's minute book referred to the expedition's destination in slightly more detail (and with a touch of scepticism) when it noted that Knight's ships were sailing 'to A Discovery of a NW Passage beyond Sir Tho' Buttons which is supposed to Lye to the northwards of 64 degrees'. Sir Thomas Button had commanded an expedition to Hudson Bay in 1612–13, and his name had been given to an imprecise geographical location on the west coast of the Bay. Farther north, in about latitude 64°N., was a stretch of water known as Roe's Welcome or, less reassuringly, as Ne Ultra (No Further). Some charts showed this as a large opening, others as a closed bay. The

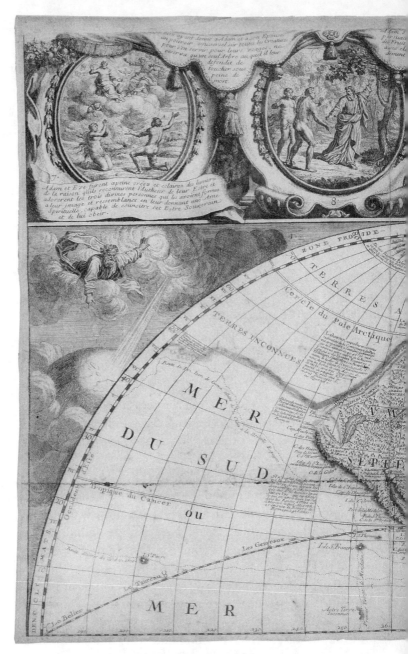

3. J. B. NOLIN. Section from his 'Globe Terrestre', 1708.
British Library

LE GLOBE
REPRESENTÉ EN DEUX
Dre
Sur la Projection de M.ᵉ de la Hyre
sur plusieurs Routiers et Memoir er des
le tout rectifié et calculé selon
et D
GR.
A M.ᵉ L'ABBÉ BIG
D'ETAT

last explorer to reach this region, Luke Foxe in 1631, wrote that this stretch of coastline was 'where the passage I hope doth lye'. Encouraged by both European and Indian maps showing openings and rivers along the west coast of Hudson Bay, Knight intended to sail to Roe's Welcome to find the strait that he was confident led to the Pacific. If he died on the voyage, Berley and Vaughan were to follow the instructions that he would leave in writing for finding the gold and copper mines.

One remaining clause of the Company's instructions has a curious ring to it. The expedition was not to call at any of the Company posts nor to sail south of latitude 64°N. in the Bay unless in such 'Utmost Extreamity' that the safety of the ships and their crews was at stake. At first sight this seems to justify the assertions of later critics of the Company about its hostility to Knight and his project; but from the Company's point of view the effort to keep a distance between the discovery expedition and its Bayside forts had its own logic. Henry Kelsey, Knight's former deputy who had succeeded him at York Fort as Governor in the Bay, had already complained that the 'Discoverers' had brought accusations of illicit trading against him in London during the winter of 1718–19 in an attempt to have him dismissed from the Company's service. As a young man Kelsey had made a spectacular if ill-defined inland journey southwest from York Fort in the early 1690s which took him to the Canadian prairies, where he became the first European to see the buffalo and the grizzly bear. His subsequent career had been less dramatic, but he was the only Company officer in the Bay who in terms of experience and achievement could stand comparison with Knight. His note to a colleague that Knight was 'afraid of being out done' suggests a rivalry between the two men over possible expansion to the north. Certainly, Kelsey was incensed at Knight's 'false aspersions' against him, and complained that 'It is a great Dolor to be represented so Odiously to Our Masters.' With relations between the old and the new Governor strained, it was not surprising that the Company should try to prevent any contact between them. An arrival by the discovery ships at York, perhaps to winter after failing to find a strait along the coast to the north, could lead to serious problems. There was the danger of an open clash between Knight and Kelsey, while the resources of the fort, and especially its carefully-allocated food supplies, would be strained to the utmost by the arrival of the ships' crews. The Company's decision that Knight must keep north of latitude 64°N., and that his expedition should be self-contained, is understandable, although it is now clear that this lack of liaison played its part in the disaster that followed.

Over the years the Hudson's Bay Company had developed into a tight-knit, secretive trading organisation, reluctant to reveal details of even its normal commercial activities; but it was impossible to keep total secrecy about the preparations for Knight's expedition. The crews and miners on the two ships, the suppliers and wharfingers, all would have some inkling of what was afoot. And one London newspaper picked up the rumours. The day after the *Albany* and *Discovery* sailed from Gravesend on 5 June 1719 the *Saturday's Post* reported that Knight had left 'for the North Pole, in order to make a Discovery of a Gold Mine in Terra Borealis'. In an unwitting but altogether appropriate juxtaposition of text the same issue carried a satirical political poem on the 'Strange magick Power of Gold'. The four Company ships that left Gravesend together would have had orders to keep company until they had negotiated the ice-strewn waters of Hudson Strait. When the little fleet reached Hudson Bay the two supply ships turned southwest on their final run to the posts (we know that one of them reached its destination on 17 August), while the *Albany* and *Discovery* held their course for the far side of the Bay. At this point they vanished from European view, and their fate became one of the most baffling mysteries of northern exploration.

The first reports about Knight's ships came from York, where Henry Kelsey was busy putting into effect his own plans for northern expansion. Like Knight, he had heard reports of a copper mine to the north, and he considered that a search by sea for the mine might be linked with the opening of trade with the Eskimos who lived along the northwest coast of the Bay, and with the establishment of a black whale fishery. Kelsey himself had taken two small sloops north along the coast in the summer of 1719, but he was back at York before Knight's ships would have entered Hudson Bay. It was the slooping voyage of 1720 north from York that brought back the first news of Knight's ships, although without any indication that they might have been in difficulties. Kelsey, although he had not sailed on the sloop that year, reported in his letter to the Company in London that 'the Goldfinders' had wintered on the coast to the north and had spoiled the sloop's trade with the Eskimos. He gave no indication of what the sloop's crew had seen or heard to make them think that Knight's ships had wintered. In 1721 Kelsey commanded the sloops in person, and returned with a report that was as brief as it was startling. Contrary winds had stopped him sailing far enough north to 'where the albany sloop was lost we seeing things belonging to those vessels.' On the nature of these objects, and whether they were floating in the water, thrown up on shore, or in the possession of the Eskimos, Kelsey was silent. What in retrospect seems unforgivable about Kelsey's failure to pursue any search for survivors is that he was back at Churchill by 16 August, with several weeks of the navigable season left.

The northern voyage of 1722 revealed more substantial evidence about the disaster. A new sloop, the *Whalebone*, was employed on the voyage under the command of John Scroggs, whose orders were to sail from Churchill along the coast as far as latitude 66°N. in search of the rumoured copper mine. There is no evidence, at least in his written orders, that Scroggs was given any instructions by Kelsey to investigate the loss of Knight's ships. The sloop left Churchill with a crew of ten,

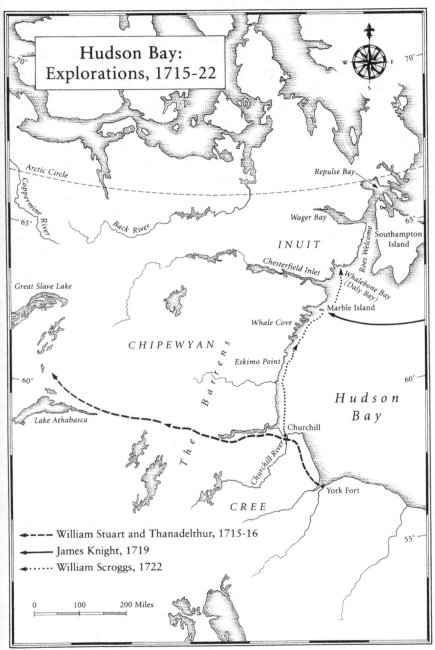

Hudson Bay: Explorations, 1715-22

70°

70°

Arctic Circle

Coppermine River

65°

Back River

Great Slave Lake

Repulse Bay

Wager Bay

INUIT

Chesterfield Inlet

Roes Welcome

Southampton Island

65°

Whalebone Bay (Daly Bay)

Marble Island

Whale Cove

CHIPEWYAN

The Barrens

Eskimo Point

60°

Great Slave Lake

Lake Athabasca

60°

Hudson Bay

Churchill

Churchill River

York Fort

CREE

─ ─ ─ William Stuart and Thanadelthur, 1715-16

──── James Knight, 1719

····· William Scroggs, 1722

55°

0   100   200 Miles

two Northern Indians, and Richard Norton. For reasons known only to himself, Scroggs refused to take on board Christopher Middleton, second mate on one of the Company ships, the *Hannah*. Middleton was an experienced navigator who had long been interested in the possibility of a Northwest Passage, and had left the *Hannah* to winter at Churchill with the specific intention of sailing north on the *Whalebone* the following summer. There is an echo of Knight's earlier inquiries in this new search for mineral wealth, for the two Northern Indians taken on the voyage had not only described the location on the coast of a rich copper mine, but had marked it on a map drawn with charcoal on deerskin. The sloop sailed north, trading with Inuit on the way, until in latitude 62° 48'N. part of a ship's foremast was picked out of the water near a ghostly-looking island that in 1631 Luke Foxe had described as being 'all of a white Marble'. He had named it Brook Cobham, but during the eighteenth century it became known as Marble Island. Despite this disconcerting find Scroggs made no attempt to search the area, and kept north until he reached latitude 64°56'N. Here the tides were strong, and when Norton went ashore with the two Chipewyans he reported 'an open sea' to the west. Scroggs refused to investigate and decided to return to Churchill. He was, a later report alleged, 'a timerous Person and in no Way fond of the Expedition', while many of the sloop's crew were anxious to be back at Churchill in time to take passage home in the Company supply ship.

On the return voyage Scroggs sent a boat ashore at Marble Island where the crew found part of a cabin lining, a medicine chest, ice-poles, and a length of mast among the Eskimos. One account described coming across an Eskimo encampment where there were 'several Yards split into Tent-poles, and tents covered with Sails, and a Copper Pot'. Scroggs assumed that the lost vessel or vessels, which could only be Knight's, had been wrecked among the shoals and rocks off the mainland to the west of the island. He was convinced that there were no survivors, and on his return to Churchill reported to the factor, Richard Staunton, that he had been where the *Albany* and *Discovery* had been wrecked, and that 'Every Man was Killed by the Eskemoes'. When Staunton recorded this in his journal he added his own comment, 'I am heartily Sorry for their hard fortune.' This was the only expression of regret in the Company records, and this seeming indifference allowed later critics to assert that 'some of the Company said upon this occasion that they did not value the loss of the ship and sloop as long as they were rid of those troublesome men.' In London the Committee, even before receiving Scroggs's news, had closed the expedition's account book, merely noting that Knight's ships had been 'castaway to the Northward'. In marked contrast to the Admiralty's prolonged search operations that followed the loss of Sir John Franklin's naval expedition in the Arctic in the next century, the Company made no effort to seek further information about the location or cause of the disaster. Outside Company circles there seems to have been no knowledge of the loss of the two ships and their crews, and soon there were few senior officers left in the Bay who had any knowledge of the events surrounding the lost expedition. Kelsey was retired by the Company in 1722. No reason was given, but his health may have been poor, for he died two years later. Scroggs was ordered home in 1723, and was refused any further command with the Company. Whether by chance or not, the leading participants in the events surrounding Knight's expedition disappeared from the scene without delay. Only among Knight's immediate family did it seem that hope lingered that survivors might still emerge from the mists and ice, for his will was not proved until September 1724, more than five years after he sailed on his final voyage.

After Scroggs returned to Churchill with his disturbing news, the reluctance of Company servants in Hudson Bay to venture far from the posts hardened into a dread of the unknown coast to the north where two ships and their crews had vanished. This attitude was matched in London by the disinclination of the Company to fit out further costly discovery expeditions, and when twenty years later further evidence came to light about the fate of Knight's ships it came from non-Company sources. In August 1742 William Moor, master of the naval vessel *Discovery*, was off Marble Island, and noted in his log that a boat's crew he sent ashore had found 'a great Deal of the Wreck of Captain Barlows Ship and Sloop'. If the men were describing the actual wrecks, rather than just pieces of wood, this is the first reported sighting of the hulks of Knight's ships, but Moor made no attempt to investigate further. Although over the years more pieces of wreckage were picked up on the shores of Marble Island by the crews of occasional passing vessels, it was not until 1767 that a further, dramatic discovery was made.

By the 1760s a harbour on the southwest coast of Marble Island was in use as the summer base for the Company's attempts to establish a whale fishery. Instead of relying on the Inuit to supply whalebone and whale oil, the Company now fitted out one or two sloops each year as whaling vessels. In July 1767 the *Success* and *Churchill* sloops arrived at Marble Island, where their crews set up temporary camp in their usual harbour. The sequence of events that followed is described in the sloops' journals. On 22 July boats from the *Success*, after an unsuccessful chase during which several whales were sighted but none killed, began to search for driftwood thrown up on the island's beaches. While doing so they came across a previously unnoticed harbour near the eastern tip of the island that could only be entered when high tide covered the rocky bar at its mouth. To their amazement the whalers saw that ships had been there, and they took back to the sloop a smith's anvil, cannon and shot. The next day the sloop's master, Joseph Stevens, visited the harbour to see the site for himself. He soon came across the ruins of a large building with stone-and-sod foundations, measuring forty-seven feet by twenty-nine, with roofless walls about five foot high. It seemed to have been constructed on a wooden framework, though the wood had been removed, and only holes showed where the posts had stood. In a treeless landscape where the most prominent objects on the skyline were *inuksuit* or rock stacks, this abandoned building was a puzzling and eerie sight. Scattered on the ground nearby were hundreds of bricks, items of clothing and other debris. A huge mound of coal stood near the entrance, and elsewhere there were piles of wood chips that seemed to have been left over from a carpenter's work on ship's timbers. There were also pieces from a ship's upper works and the shanks of three anchors.

Ten days later Stevens visited the harbour again, this time with Magnus Johnston, master of the *Churchill* sloop. The ground was dug over to try to find any papers left by the crews, but all that the spades turned up was a human skull, the first sign of tragedy, but whether the skull was 'Native or Christian' Stevens was unable to say. More information came from the Inuit interpreters on the sloops. When shown the site, they told Johnston 'that they heard their Country people say that there Was some of the English men Surviv'd the first winter – but wither they was Starv'd with Could or hunger or Destroy'd by the Natives is a thing I cannot find out As yet'. The desolate spot held a morbid fascination for the crews, and Samuel Hearne, the mate of the *Churchill*, took men to examine it. They returned with the news that they had discovered 'A great Number of graves', and dug one of them up, finding in it 'only the Bons of a Stout man who without Doubt is one of the Unhappey Sufferars'. In driving rain, and with lightning flickering over a scene of gothic horror, the diggers found other skeletons on rising ground some little distance from the ruins. No hint was given that the whalers realised that they had stumbled on the graveyard of the Knight expedition, but on a further visit to the harbour the next year a ship's figurehead was found and sent to England. Hearne later added to the information in the sloops' logs. He saw the hulks of the two discovery ships lying in five fathoms of water, and when the figurehead and other items from the site reached England, they were identified as being from the *Albany* and *Discovery*.

In 1769 the whalers returned again to Marble Island, and Hearne heard from an elderly Inuk what purported to be a description of the last days of the survivors. By their second summer (1721) only five were still alive, but in poor condition, and they died one by one on an island where, Hearne wrote, 'neither stick nor stone was to be seen'.

> Two survived many days after the rest, and frequently went to the top of an adjacent rock, and earnestly looked to the South and East, as if in expectation of some vessels coming to their relief. After continuing there a considerable time together, and nothing appearing in sight, they sat down close together, and wept bitterly. At length one of the two died, and the other's strength was so far exhausted, that he fell down and died also, in attempting to dig a grave for his companion.

To add credibility to the old man's recollection, Hearne added that 'the sculls and other large bones of those two men are now lying above-ground close to the house', though he seems to have made no attempt either to retrieve or bury the remains. If true, this account of a few starving men from the ships lingering until 1721 adds to the pathos of their fate, for that summer Kelsey's sloop was near Marble Island. He even sighted 'things' from the ships but with the wind against him made no attempt to search for survivors. Recent searches on Marble Island suggest, however, that the story told to Hearne was not the whole story, perhaps not even part of the story.

The first serious investigations of the harbour to try to determine the fate of the Knight expedition took place in 1970 and

1971. A group led by Ralph Smith found the foundations of a large building about 500 feet from the shore and retrieved various items from the site: nails, fragments of wine bottles and window-glass, pieces of earthenware, a button and a slate pencil. In the centre of the enclosure a brick and mortar platform had probably supported the iron galley stove from one of the ships. A poignant moment came with the discovery some distance from the building of the rusted remains of a portable stove in a rocky niche which commanded a view of the harbour and the sea beyond. Lumps of coal were still scattered around, and it did not take a great leap of the imagination to identify this as the lookout point described by Hearne's Inuit informant where the remaining survivors had spent their last days looking in vain for a ship's sails. In the harbour the sunken hull of what was assumed to be the *Albany* was located. Taking into account the isostatic lift of the last two centuries (which has reduced the harbour to a shallow lagoon) the investigators concluded that even at high tide the entrance across the bar would have been no more than seven or eight feet in 1719. Had Knight been misled, they wondered, by Luke Foxe's observation in 1631 that on the east coast of the island 'there is a Cove or Harbour, made by small islands, that a ship may ride in safety, for all weathers, and have two fathomes at low water'? If so, then the larger *Albany* might well have been badly damaged trying to enter the harbour. This would account for the remains of ship's timbers still lying on the ground in the 1760s, although the bricks and coal on the site (which would almost certainly have been carried on the *Albany* rather than the tiny *Discovery*) indicated that the vessel had not sunk immediately. By this interpretation, Knight's crews would have been trapped on Marble Island, with both vessels either wrecked or unable to get across the bar until scurvy, starvation and exposure brought a slow and agonising death.

More recent investigations during four seasons of land and underwater exploration between 1989 and 1992 have thrown

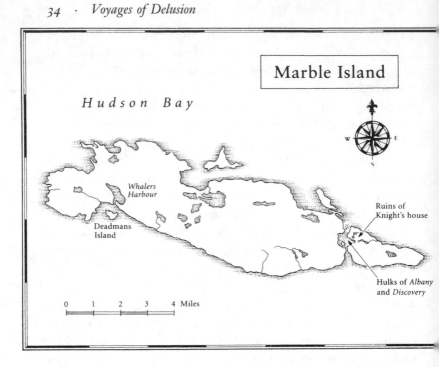

doubt on almost every part of both this and earlier theories about what happened to Knight and his men. Much has been found at that ominous site, and a sounder interpretation of many aspects of the expedition is now possible; but the central issue of what happened to the forty men of the expedition remains as much a puzzle as ever. In July 1989 a team led by anthropologist Owen Beattie arrived on the island to begin work. Their first task was to find and excavate the graves described by Samuel Hearne and Joseph Stevens, so that they could subject to forensic examination such human remains as were found. If, as the records seemed to indicate, Knight's men had died slowly over a period of months, perhaps years, then one would expect to find a graveyard near the ruined house where the dead were interred. If Hearne's Inuit informants were right, three out of the five last survivors were given some sort of rough burial, and only the last two found no grave.

Even allowing for disturbance by animals, the elements and later human visitors, the site was expected to contain the remains of many of Knight's men. The reality was that after two seasons of intensive searching, Beattie's team, scouring wider and wider areas around the house foundations, found only one small human vertebra and three teeth that could reasonably be linked to the lost expedition. The lead content of the vertebra suggested that it came from a Caucasoid individual, while the teeth (possibly dislodged from the skull that was dug up in 1767) were tobacco-stained. It does not seem possible that up to forty men had died in or near the building, and left only these four tiny fragments. The most plausible explanation is that although the bones found among the ruins in 1767 may have been those of the last of Knight's men, the 'great Number of graves' reported at that time were Inuit. The Beattie investigators found several Inuit burial grounds near the harbour, including one with between a hundred and two hundred graves. Recent critical scrutiny of Hearne's writings suggests that his report of the pathetic remains of the last two survivors still lying above ground should be treated with caution. The story was not published until nearly thirty years later, in Hearne's account of his subsequent explorations and adventures with the Company; and at least one other episode in the book – the spearing of an Inuk girl at the Coppermine River – was highly coloured and dramatised by Hearne or his ghost writer.

In contrast to the meagre haul of human remains found on the site, five thousand other items were excavated there, ranging from minute fragments of leather and fabric to coins, a pair of brass dividers, a chess piece, the lid of a china teapot, and almost a hundred buttons. Among other significant objects were more than six hundred animal bones or fragments found in a food preparation pit inside the enclosure, some with knife or saw marks. Two-thirds of these bones came from local wildlife – caribou, geese and seals among them – proof that the men on the island had been successful in hunting for fresh meat. The remaining one-third came either from stock fish or from domesticated animals such as pigs and sheep that had obviously been carried on the discovery vessels. The more that was found – and not found – on the site, the more difficult did it become to accept the story of the gradual death by starvation as told by Hearne and others.

In 1991 the search switched from land to water, and the hull of the *Albany* was soon located. What was immediately recognised as significant was that the ship was lying with its bow pointing towards the entrance of the cove, indicating that it had not been driven across the bar ripping its bottom out as it did so, but had made harbour, been brought about, and then moored. This finding was consistent with Stevens' report on 23 July 1767 that there were hawsers lying on the ground, some of them chafed by ice – proof that at least one of the vessels had been moored, not wrecked. In 1992, after a difficult search, the hull of the smaller *Discovery* was found. Unlike the *Albany* its bow faced the shore, suggesting that the vessels were originally moored alongside each other; bow to stern and stern to bow. Hampered by poor visibility and worsening weather conditions, the divers proceeded more by feel than by sight, but found that on the *Albany* much of the deck and other timbers had been removed, and that one of the *Discovery*'s masts had been cut off.

These recent investigations enable us to make a reasonably good guess as to what happened to Knight and his men during the first part of their stay on Marble Island. Once through Hudson Strait, the *Albany* and *Discovery* headed for the west coast of Hudson Bay in about latitude 64°N., which they would probably have reached in mid-August 1719. They would have spent the remaining ice-free weeks searching for an opening to the west. When no strait was found Knight decided to find a suitable place to winter from which he would resume the search the following spring. It would have been open to him to sail a few days south to the Company posts at Churchill or York, but it seems that rather than plead 'Utmost Extreamity' and seek help from his rival Kelsey, Knight took the fateful decision to winter at Marble Island. He was unlikely to leave this late in the season, for two years earlier he had seen the skeletons of Munk's crew still lying on the ground at Churchill River, and he pointed out to the London Committee that the Danish captain 'had lost about one hundred men by his not having time to build, winter setting in so soon upon him'. The choice, so disastrous in the end, of the harbour at Marble Island indicates that Knight had with him a copy of Luke Foxe's journal with his description of the harbour with its two fathoms of water even at low tide. At some time during September 1719 Knight's two ships crossed the bar into the harbour and were moored. There they would soon be frozen in, for winter came early on that exposed coast. In 1631 the explorer Captain Thomas James had wintered at the 'Bottom of the Bay', ten degrees farther south than Marble Island, but by mid-November he wrote: 'When we stood on the shore and looked towards the ship, she looked like a piece of ice that had been carved into the form of a ship. She was packed solidly in frozen snow, while her bow and both sides were sheathed in ice.' A later drawing made of the ice-shrouded American whaling ships that regularly wintered at the whalers' harbour on the southwest side of Marble Island in the nineteenth century gives some impression of how Knight's ships must have appeared during the winter of 1719–20 (*Ill.4*).

On arrival in the harbour the ships would have been quickly unloaded. The frame of the house, bricks and other building materials, coal, provisions, stores and personal belongings were taken on shore, the house built, and the crews settled to the rigours of a northern winter. What conditions were like in this frozen and isolated spot is difficult to imagine, though the recovery from the site of such items as the chess piece and tea-pot lid hints at some attempt to reproduce home comforts. During those months, as the evidence of the food pits shows, the men hunted and fished. This supply of fresh meat and fish, together with the provisions brought on the

4. Winter at Marble Island.

This drawing by Heinrich Klutschak in his *Als Eskimo under den Eskimos* (1881) shows American whalers wintering at Marble Island during the winter of 1878–9.

ships, should have been more than enough in terms of protein supply for the winter, though whether it was adequate in terms of vitamins to ward off scurvy is another matter. Knight's winters in Hudson Bay would have taught him how important it was to keep the men active and to spend the daylight hours outdoors. What is not known is how many of those wintering at Marble Island had the warm fur clothing that was standard issue for the garrisons at the Company posts; without this a man who ventured away from shelter and warmth would die. The journal kept at Churchill several hundred miles to the south that year describes an exceptionally hard winter, and records the death of a Company servant who had strayed away from the post, his eyes and teeth clamped shut with cold, his body bloated and stiff. But in the absence of evidence to the contrary – and especially of human remains – the assumption must be that when spring came most of Knight's men on Marble Island were alive. What happened to them then is as much a mystery as ever.

Knight's intentions are not in doubt. He would have been eager to cut the ships clear of the ice, carry out what repairs were necessary, and sail once more in search of the Strait of Anian and the mines of gold. For whatever reason, the ships never left the tiny harbour. Despite the evidence that one of them at least had been properly moored, it is possible that the bottom of their hulls had been so damaged in crossing the bar the previous autumn that they could not be made seaworthy. Alternatively, they may have been frozen in so solidly that all the efforts of the crews, perhaps diminished in numbers and weakened by scurvy, could not free them. If there had been deaths, Knight's would probably have been among them. It was not that he was unused to the hardships of northern conditions. At York Factory in the winter of 1714–15 he complained that his quarters were worse than a cow-shed: 'I have never been able to see my hand in it since I have been here without a candle, it is so black and dark, cold and wet withal, nothing to make it better but heaping up earth about it to make it warm.' In the building on Marble Island the evidence of the stove and of the piles of coal shows that there was at least heat and light. Even so, Knight's age and uncertain health make it difficult to believe that he survived the winter.

At some point in the spring or early summer, a decision must have been taken to leave the island – no other explanation fits the lack of human remains from the expedition anywhere near the wintering site. And the great pile of coal outside the building again seems to rule against the crews spending a second winter there. The obvious course for them would be to use the ships' boats to make the voyage to Churchill, about three hundred miles to the south. The question is whether the boats were large and sound enough to take perhaps up to forty men on a voyage along a treacherous coast, encumbered with loose ice, and notorious for its tidal rips and swirling currents.

The piles of wood chips noticed by later visitors to the harbour indicate that there may have been some attempt to build a boat, or perhaps to lengthen an existing one. Apart from any ships' carpenters who were still alive, Thomas Vaughan had begun his service with the Company as a carpenter and shipwright, as indeed had Knight. Whatever the truth, no boats were found at the site, though this is not to say that their remains may not lie underwater.

The probability that Knight's men used a boat or boats to leave the island is strengthened by a tantalising fragment of documentary evidence that has only recently come to light, though its interpretation is far from certain. On 13 June 1725 Richard Norton, by now factor at Churchill, entered in his journal that more than a hundred Northern Indians arrived at the post in a distressed condition. They had been attacked by 'Southern Indians' (Crees), who had killed many of them and their families. But they also told Norton that 'ye Usquemoys [Eskimos] had been to warr with them & had Murdered Severall of them also they found the Albiny friggott where She was Lost Likewise one of the boats & Severall Utensills belonging their unto . . .' The crucial question here is whether the 'they' who found the *Albany* and its boat were the Northern Indians or the Eskimos. There are problems either way. It is inconceivable that the Chipewyans had travelled so far from their hunting grounds that they had reached the mainland coast opposite Marble Island, crossed to the island, and then worked their way to its far end where Knight's ships lay – for this was deep in Eskimo territory. On the other hand, although the Eskimos for their part would have known the location of Knight's ships, it is hardly likely that they exchanged information about the lost expedition with their traditional Indian enemies. Not only was there a language barrier, but the relationship between the two groups was one of war, and of killings on sight.

There remains a further possibility. Clearly, Norton's journal entry is not an unadorned translation of what the Chipewyans told him; it has at least one gloss where he adds the name of the *Albany*. And it must be remembered that there is no evidence that Norton at this time knew that the hulks of Knight's ships were at Marble Island, although he had been with Scroggs on his northern voyage in 1722. Scroggs had found fittings and other relics among the Inuit on the island, but both on its outward and return voyage the *Whalebone* seems to have passed between the mainland and the western end of the island. The assumption at the time and for many years was that Knight's ships had been wrecked – not trapped – and that the site of the disaster was on the dangerous mainland coast immediately west of Marble Island. It was there that Scroggs had found part of a ship's mast floating in the water on his outward voyage. There is no reason to believe that Norton was thinking in terms of Marble Island at all when he wrote his journal entry in June 1725. If we look at the news brought in by the Northern Indians through his eyes, he would have known that the border zone between them and their Inuit foes lay not far north of Churchill. The Inuit did not usually venture south of Eskimo Point in latitude 61°N., and the Chipewyans coming down to the coast from the interior made for Churchill in latitude 59°N. But there were exceptions. When Norton set off from Churchill on his journey with two Chipewyan companions in 1717, they first headed north along the coast, although it is not known how far they went before turning inland. In 1725, Norton's Chipewyan informants must have been farther north than usual to have encountered Inuit in strength, and the most likely spot for the clash between the two groups would have been on the coast near Eskimo Point. They could not have found the wreck of the *Albany* there, for it lay in its land-locked island harbour more than a hundred miles to the north. However, if Norton's mention of 'the Albiny friggott where She was Lost' was his attempt to explain where he thought the Northern Indians came across the ship's boat and other items, then his entry becomes a garbled reference to a location on the mainland coast. Whether or not this is so, the discovery of a ship's boat somewhere north of Churchill supports the theory that the survivors from Knight's crews at Marble Island took to one or more of the boats in an attempt to reach safety. We are of course no nearer to knowing what happened to those men, and the brevity of Norton's report is frustrating. Sloops no longer went north along the coast from Churchill to trade or explore, so there was no opportunity for further investigation; and when Norton wrote his annual letter home to the London Committee later that summer he did not think the Chipewyans' discovery worth mentioning.

If for whatever reason boats were not used for the escape attempt, then for most of the year Knight's men could have crossed on the ice the dozen miles from the western end of Marble Island to the mainland. American whaling crews who wintered on the island in the nineteenth century often did this. Difficult though it could be, it was not the crossing that presented the problem, but the hazards of the journey that would follow. Knight's men were almost certainly not equipped for the long trek to Churchill. They would not have snowshoes for winter conditions, nor footwear adequate for the slush and water of the summer months. Without sleds or dogs, they would have to carry provisions and weapons on their backs. Finally, they would have to face the possibility of attack by the Inuit.

Marble Island was Inuit country, as the number of graves there testified, but the role of the Inuit in the fate of the Knight expedition is a continuing puzzle. At every turn there is conflicting evidence. In 1722 John Scroggs reported to the factor at Churchill that 'Every Man was Killed by the Eskemoes.' He based this on two pieces of evidence, neither conclusive, from his voyage that year in the *Whalebone*. First, various relics from Knight's ships were seen in an Inuit encampment, but Scroggs does not seem to have considered the possibility that these might have been found by the Inuit rather than taken by force. Secondly, Scroggs was reported to have seen 'one of the Eskemaux having a large Scar on his Cheek, like a

Cut with a Cutlash [cutlass], and at that Time a green Wound'. Against this, is the lack of evidence found in the recent investigations of the site of the violent encounter that Scroggs' account implies. A spent musket ball and two Inuit implements among the foundations of the building may or may not have any significance in this respect. For the Hudson's Bay Company men at the time and later, it was only too credible that the discovery crews had been wiped out by Inuit. Few had any direct experience of these people of the north, and their main impression of them would have come from their inveterate enemies, the Northern Indians. In his York journals Knight showed considerable apprehension about the Inuit, although he knew them only by repute: 'savage and brutelike and will drink blood and eat raw flesh and fish . . . very numerous and a bloodthirsty people'. As the Company began regular slooping voyages along the west coast of Hudson Bay to open trade with the Inuit, the sloopmasters were routinely warned to keep careful guard in case of attack; and in 1753 a Company sloop commanded by James Walker only narrowly escaped seizure by hundreds of Inuit at Whale Cove (on the mainland coast south of Marble Island).

In an attempt to improve relations Moses Norton, Richard's son, and chief factor at Churchill in the 1760s, arranged for young Inuks to be brought to the fort and trained as interpreters. When two youths arrived at Churchill in 1765 Moses Norton questioned them about events during his father's time. Two years before the macabre discovery by the sloops' crews of the ruins and graves on Marble Island, Norton heard details of the fate of Knight's expedition from the Inuit youths, who repeated what their elders had told them. It made a harrowing story. The ships had been wrecked getting into harbour, and although the crews got ashore and built huts, none survived the first winter despite trading fresh meat and whale blubber from the Inuit on the island. According to the two boys, Marble Island had become a place of dread for Eskimos, 'as they call it ye Dead Mans Island by so many

Englishmen Perishing on it'. This was the first Inuit version of the fate of Knight's expedition, and although the account given to Hearne four years later by his elderly informant differed in detail (claiming, for example, that some of Knight's men had survived two winters) it too stressed that the Englishmen had died of hunger and disease, and this despite the Inuit supplying them with food. Inuit oral evidence is to be treated with respect, as shown by its recollections in the mid-nineteenth century of the fate of Franklin's expedition; and, more remarkably, that of Frobisher's expeditions to Baffin Island in the 1570s. Almost three hundred years later, the American explorer, Charles Francis Hall, in his search for Franklin relics, heard evidence from local Inuit about Frobisher's visits to their area. The problem with the Inuit testimony of the 1760s about Knight's expedition – the gradual death from starvation despite Inuit assistance – is the lack of graves and human remains to support it with physical proof of dead Englishmen on Marble Island.

Two other tiny and unsubstantiated pieces of evidence give a final twist to the story. One comes from Francis Smith, who while in the service of the Hudson's Bay Company made six slooping voyages north along the coast from Churchill between 1738 and 1744. While trading with the Inuit at Whale Cove, he recollected, 'they used to show him a young Lad, and call him *English Mane*, alluding to his being an *English* Man, whose Age was seemingly suitable to the Time of these Peoples Misfortune, the Lad appeared as of a mixed Breed, which makes it probable that one or more of the People might get Ashore and live sometime amongst the *Eskemaux*, after the Accident'. Then, in August 1747 the crews of the discovery vessels *Dobbs Galley* and *California* in Wager Bay on the northwest coast of Hudson Bay were struck by the unusual appearance of two men who seemed to be slaves of the Eskimos. The English sailors were not allowed to get close to the two men, but the one seen most clearly, though dressed as an Eskimo, 'yet appeared manifestly from his Complexion, which was much fairer, and from his being utterly unacquainted with the management of a Canoe, to be of another Nation, and that he was brought by them to see us'. The men were probably Chipewyan captives, rather than long-lived survivors from Knight's expedition or their descendants, but the ships' crews were intrigued enough to attempt to purchase one or both men from the Inuit. These efforts failed, and the strangers were not seen again.

All that is certain about the fate of the Knight expedition is that its ships reached Marble Island and that the crews wintered there. On these two facts eighteenth-century Company men, Inuit testimony, and modern investigators agree. All else remains a mystery: where and how the men died; how long they survived; the part played by the Inuit. Further underwater archaeology on the wrecks might provide further clues, especially to the possible damage done to the ships on entering the harbour. As of now, it must be said that despite the detailed scrutiny of evidence, old and new, Marble Island is not giving up its secrets easily. 'Dead Mans Island' remains the site of one of the most poignant of all Arctic tragedies, of men trapped and dying within easy reach of rescue. James Knight was both the instigator of the project and its nemesis, for the obsessive driving force that he showed in mounting the expedition also ensured that when the discovery ships disappeared there was no great anxiety to mount a rescue attempt. For a man who left voluminous journals and correspondence books behind him, it is a final irony that despite all the excavations, all the inspection of cavities and cairns near those silent ruins on Marble Island, not one scrap of writing has ever been found to explain what happened to Knight and his men.

2

A Passage to California

'What great Advantages might be made by having a passage to California in three or four Months & so down to
the Western Coast of America into the South Sea . . .'

ARTHUR DOBBS, Memorial on the Northwest
Passage, 1731

TWELVE YEARS AFTER James Knight and his two vessels
sailed into oblivion the possibility of a Northwest Passage
was raised again, this time more publicly. In 1731 Arthur
Dobbs, a newly-elected Irish MP in his early forties, drafted
a seventy-page 'Memorial' in which he argued that a navigable
passage almost certainly existed, and that unless British
explorers found it they would be anticipated by the French.
At this time Dobbs was best known for his writings on Irish
trade, but in 1730 he was introduced to the prime minister,
Sir Robert Walpole, as one intent on making 'our colonies in
America of more advantage than they have hitherto been'.
Soon after completing his manuscript Dobbs sent copies to
men of rank and influence, including Walpole; Frederick,
Prince of Wales; and the Viceroy of Ireland, the Duke of
Dorset. It was the opening shot in a campaign by Dobbs to
find the Northwest Passage that was to last almost twenty
years.

The opening sentence of the Memorial was a half-apology
to its readers: 'You may be Surpriz'd that I should at this time
endeavour to revive an attempt to discover the Northwest
Passage, which has in a manner been exploded since the Year

1631.' This was evidence of how little public knowledge there was of Knight's expedition, for Dobbs clearly assumed that there had been no voyages to find the Northwest Passage since those of Luke Foxe and Thomas James a hundred years earlier. The first part of the Memorial was devoted to an examination of the published accounts of Arctic voyages in which Dobbs painstakingly eliminated those regions where he thought there was no possibility of a passage. At the end of this exercise he was left with the area in the northwest of Hudson Bay known as Roe's Welcome or Ne Ultra where he thought 'the presumptions are strong for a Passage'. Unknown to Dobbs, he was echoing the sentiments of James Knight, though the reasoning of the two men was quite different. Whereas Knight had been greatly influenced by the reports and maps of the Chipewyan Indians, Dobbs based his optimistic conclusions on the height and direction of the tides in Hudson Bay. His arguments based on the tidal observations of earlier explorers were technical and convoluted, but behind the detail lay a simple presumption. If the only entrance to Hudson Bay was from the Atlantic through Hudson Strait, then the farther ships sailed into the Bay and away from the ocean the lower would be the tides. Midway across Hudson Bay the tide rose only six foot; yet when Luke Foxe in 1631 was near the Bay's west coast in latitude 64°10'N. he had observed a neap tide of eighteen feet, which (Dobbs calculated) would rise to twenty-four feet at spring tide. This anomaly could only be explained, the Memorial continued, 'if we suppose a Western Ocean flowing in at a Streight near Ne Ultra into the Bay'. (Confusingly, the Pacific was often referred to not only by its older name of the South Sea but also as the Western Ocean.) Further hopeful signs of a passage came from the sightings of black whales near the west coast of Hudson Bay, for Dobbs could find no reports of whales passing through Hudson Strait into the Bay, and so assumed that they had come from the Pacific.

Dobbs's reliance on tidal observations to indicate the existence of a passage followed well-established precedents. The

5. WILLIAM HOARE. Portrait of Arthur Dobbs, 1755.

By kind permission of Sir Richard Dobbs

account of Henry Hudson's last voyage in 1610 noted that when his ship ran aground as it entered Hudson Bay 'a great flood came from the West and set them on floate: an argument of an open passage from the South Sea'. Accordingly, Thomas Button on his follow-up voyage carried instructions to look for the flood tide, for 'you maie be sure the passage is that waie'. Despite the fact that Foxe's journal was not nearly as emphatic about the eighteen-foot tide as Dobbs claimed, there is no doubt that Foxe thought that if there were a passage, it would be at Ne Ultra. He believed, as did Dobbs, that the passage would be a short one, and not obstructed by ice, because the tide ran so high that the Pacific Ocean could not be far distant. Well-versed though he was in the theory of tides, Dobbs never overcame his lack of direct knowledge of Hudson Bay, where the tidal rips and ice-choked channels of its west coast made reliable observations of the height and direction of the tides a difficult business. Nor did he have a seaman's experience which would have warned him about the difficulty of gauging tides and currents from the deck of a ship, or from hurried boat trips ashore.

Whether the illustrious personages who received a copy of the Memorial from Dobbs made a close study of his tidal arguments is doubtful. Its latter sections would have carried more appeal, as Dobbs set out the advantages that the discovery of a passage would bring Britain in terms of easy access to the South Sea. No longer would ships have to endure the hazardous passage around Cape Horn, or the long track by way of the Cape of Good Hope. In wartime a short northern route would enable Royal Navy ships or privateers to descend unheralded on Spanish shipping and possessions in the South Sea. During peace, the passage would allow merchants from Britain to carry their goods to the west coast of North America where the maps still marked the imaginary countries of Cibola and Quivira that had lured Spanish explorers north from Mexico two hundred years earlier. In the great ocean beyond a whole array of dimly-known lands loomed – Japan, where the cannon of British men-of-war could force an exclusive commercial treaty, the huge landmass of Yedso which was thought to stretch across the North Pacific, and the rich markets of China. To Dobbs these countries promised outlets of huge potential for the sale of British woollens and other manufactures. The appeal to anti-Spanish sentiments, the expectation of exclusive privileges, and the hope of finding new markets, all had a familiar ring: since Tudor times they appeared on the standard list of objectives advanced by generations of projectors. Only a few years earlier such lists had become commonplace again at the time of the South Sea Bubble, when no scheme had seemed too hare-brained for the credulous investors of 1719–20. But the disillusionment that followed the bursting of the Bubble had brought a new caution to merchants and backers alike. In the steady middle years of Walpole's long term of office, extravagant projects and farflung enterprises were out of favour. As Daniel Defoe lamented in 1730, the nation seemed to have turned its back on overseas ventures as though 'there was neither Room in the World nor Inclination in our People to look any farther.'

Dobbs was now to experience this lack of enthusiasm in person. His original intention was to persuade the South Sea Company to divert a couple of its whalers from Davis Strait to Hudson Bay, where they could test the tides at Ne Ultra. When Dobbs found that the Company was not engaged in whaling, he turned to the chartered company that held exclusive trading rights over the area of the proposed search, the Hudson's Bay Company. It was the beginning of a tangled relationship that was to bring fame and notoriety to Dobbs and near-disaster to the Company. His first mention of the Hudson's Bay Company came in the Memorial when he explained how the Company's annual supply ships might find time to make a detour to Ne Ultra on their outward passage, discover whether there was a Northwest Passage there, and then continue their voyage to the Bay posts before returning home. Even Dobbs in later years must have looked back at that proposal – so casual in its understatement of the difficulties and dangers – with embarrassment. If for whatever reason the Hudson's Bay Company could not oblige, then the Admiralty might fit out an expedition at 'Trifling Expense' to make the discovery.

Visits to London from 1731 onwards demonstrated to

Dobbs the gap between plan and execution. He made useful
contacts with ministers and merchants, but however courteous
their response to his exhortations that the Northwest Passage
was there for the finding, they showed no enthusiasm for com-
mitting either public or private funds towards the cost of an
expedition. In 1733 Dobbs met Samuel Jones, Deputy Governor of the Hudson's Bay Company, and for the first time
heard about the Knight expedition and its disappearance. The
news of this unfortunate venture only a few years earlier must
have jolted Dobbs. Although he pointed out that the fact that
Knight's ships seem to have been wrecked had no bearing on
whether or not there was a passage, their fate was an indication
that the discovery he was pursuing was not altogether straightforward. Certainly, the revelations about the expedition did
not make an auspicious beginning to his dealings with the
Hudson's Bay Company. It was Dobbs's first encounter with
the cautious men who ran the Company's affairs, and it evidently gave him food for thought. By their very nature monopolistic companies were wedded to secrecy as a defence against
the twin threat of foreign rivals and domestic interlopers. The
Governor of the Hudson's Bay Company at this time was still
Sir Bibye Lake, whose length of office from 1712 to 1743 was
to earn him the title of 'the perpetual Governor'. Under his
tight rule the Company pursued a policy of secrecy with
obsessive intent. Details of the hazardous passage through
Hudson Strait, the harbours and anchorages in the Bay, and
the trade in furs with the Indians, were all kept from outsiders.
Instructions from the Company's London Committee insisted
that 'no person send any Intelligence to, or carry on any Correspondence, relating to the Company's affairs, with any Person
whatsoever'. Committee members themselves were warned
against letting copies of the charter out of their possession.
The Company's shares never came on the open market, and
none of the names of the thirty or so shareholders was public
knowledge. In a standard guide of this period to the City of
London, Bibye Lake's name appeared, but only in his capacity

as a director of the Royal African Company; there was no mention that he was Governor of the Hudson's Bay Company.

Determined as the Company was to keep its affairs out of sight and, hopefully, out of mind, it met its match in Dobbs. On a visit to England in 1735 he obtained permission from the Board of Trade to inspect the royal charter granted to the Hudson's Bay Company in 1670. Dobbs was taken aback at the extent of the Company's privileges as he read that the charter granted to the Company 'the whole Trade and Commerce of all those Seas, Streights, and Bays, Rivers, Lakes, Creeks, and Sounds, in whatsoever Latitude they shall be, that lie within the Entrance of Hudson's Streights'. This drainage basin, known as Rupert's Land, stretched thousands of miles west across the northern prairies as far as the eastern slopes of the (as yet unknown) Rocky Mountains. In his Memorial, Dobbs had described in glowing terms the advantages which the discovery of a Northwest Passage would bring to British merchants; he now realised that the benefits might well be confined to the directors of the Hudson's Bay Company and its handful of unknown shareholders. And for the first time he had some inkling of the discrepancy between the colossal size of the Company's grant, and the limited scale of its operations.

On the same visit Dobbs managed to obtain an interview with Sir Bibye Lake, and argued that as the Company alone stood to benefit from the discovery of a passage, it should undertake the search. Like his deputy Samuel Jones two years earlier, the Governor was unforthcoming. Once more Dobbs heard about the Knight expedition, its cost, and its disappearance, but he insisted that it would only be necessary to send one or two sloops north from Churchill to Ne Ultra to test the tides and to sail fifty or sixty leagues into any opening to the west. In the end Lake conceded that the Company would probably be willing to bear the small cost involved. He warned that the resources needed for the great stone fortress that was replacing the wooden buildings at Churchill, and the danger of a French war, might delay the sending of an expedition, but that summer he told Richard Norton, now chief factor at Churchill, to be ready to sail north the next year. To his cousin, Judge Michael Ward, Dobbs wrote in triumph, 'I have got the Hudsons bay Company to undertake once more the Northwest Passage.'

Dobbs's exultation was premature, for a comparison of his letters to Lake with those from the Company's London Committee to Norton, reveals very different priorities. In his letter Dobbs laid down in detail the instructions to be given the sloops: the taking of soundings and bearings; the measuring of the tides; the surveying of the coast – all to be carefully recorded in the masters' journals. Finally, 'if they find an open Sea to the Westward, after they pass 65° and the Land should fall away to Westward, and the Tide of Flood meets them . . . then the Passage is gained'. It would be enough for the sloops to sail a couple of hundred miles into the strait, and then to return with news of the discovery. The actual instructions given by the Company to Norton bore only a faint resemblance to Dobbs's recommendations. During the winter of 1735–6 members of the Company's London Committee had been studying journals of earlier expeditions along the west coast, and had questioned one of the men who had been with Scroggs on the *Whalebone* in 1722. They would also have talked with Richard Norton, who was in England on leave, about his experiences on the *Whalebone*. While still in London he was promised a gratuity for undertaking 'Voyages and Expeditions to the Nor'ward', and in May he received his instructions. When he reached Churchill later that summer he was to send two sloops north to Roe's Welcome to open a trade with the Eskimos in whale-oil, whalebone, seals and other marine products. The next year (1737) the sloops were to return to the same area, resume trade, and also search for minerals, until they were joined by the annual supply ship from England. Ship and sloops should then sail farther north, noting the tides, 'and endeavour to make what Discoveries you can'. Of the Northwest Passage there was no specific mention.

While the Hudson's Bay Company was searching its records for information about the coast north of Churchill, Dobbs was making his own enquiries. No one had a better knowledge of the waters of the Bay than the Company's ship-captains, and Dobbs decided to approach one of them, Christopher Middleton, and seek his views on the possibility of a passage. Dobbs knew nothing of Middleton's longstanding interest in the Northwest Passage, or of his wintering at Churchill in 1721–22 with the hope of sailing north on discovery with Scroggs the next summer. He had come across Middleton's name only because the captain's observations on the variation of the magnetic needle in Hudson Bay had been published in the *Philosophical Transactions* of the Royal Society in the same issue in which an article by Dobbs on the 'Aurora Borealis' appeared. It was a coincidence that was to have fateful consequences. Since joining the Company in 1721 Middleton had risen rapidly in its service, and in 1734 was given command of its newest and largest vessel, the 170-ton *Seahorse*. Three years later he achieved a distinction unusual for a sea-captain when in recognition of the several papers he had written, and his advanced navigational knowledge, he was elected a Fellow of the Royal Society. When he met Dobbs, he showed an immediate interest in his proposals for discovery, and agreed – unknown to the Company – to seek further information at the Bay posts about the possible existence of a passage. In doing so, Middleton put his position in the Company's service in jeopardy. For the moment, however, the chance encounter between Dobbs and Middleton seemed to both men to promise fulfilment of their shared enthusiasm for the discovery of the Northwest Passage.

In the event, there was no northern voyage at all from Churchill in 1736. The Company ship carrying Norton and his instructions from London arrived late at Churchill, and the post's sloops were needed to unload cargo. Nothing could have demonstrated more effectively the uncertainties afflicting expeditions closely connected with the routine operations of the Company. Apart from time constraints, another handicap was the lack of enthusiasm at Churchill for exploration. Norton, in his youth one of the more venturesome of the Company servants, showed little liking for the northern expedition, despite the promised bonus. He maintained that the most northerly harbour he knew was Whale Cove in latitude 62°15'N., well to the south of the Welcome, and it was there that Norton arranged for the sloops to await the ship from England in 1737. With the position for the rendezvous now fixed two hundred miles south of the area where Dobbs had hoped the search for the passage would begin, the prospects for the next year did not look hopeful. It is possible that the thought of Knight's lost ships still lay heavily on the minds of those concerned with the expedition at Churchill, and explains the reluctance to venture north of Whale Cove. A note in the post's records indicate that the voyage was regarded as something out of the ordinary, calling for exceptional qualities of diligence, for one man was sent home, 'a Sailor Entertain'd for the Northern Expedition, being discontented, and we apprehend may prove A Seditious troublesome fellow Especially on such an Occasion'.

Despite such precautions the 1737 expedition was a fiasco. The sloops edged their way north to Whale Cove, but there one of the sloopmasters died, and the vessels returned to Churchill. Nor did the Company ship, commanded by William Coats, make the rendezvous. There was nothing surprising about this, for Coats was ordered 'on no account whatsoever' to endanger his ship or to risk losing his voyage to Churchill and home again – and nor did he. The fact that the previous year his ship had foundered in less than twenty minutes among the clashing ice-floes of Hudson Strait would no doubt have made him doubly reluctant to venture away from his regular route. Norton expressed his feelings on the matter when he wrote home that autumn. The sloops had found a perilous coast, unnavigable rivers, and little trade. The London Committee nevertheless ordered Norton to continue sending a sloop north along the coast each summer, but only as far as Whale Cove, and for trading purposes only. No mention was made of tidal observations or discoveries. The venture was now wholly commercial, and the sloopmaster and crew were to share ten per cent of the profits.

Dobbs first received news of the 1737 expedition from Middleton, who had been at Churchill when the sloops returned. Writing in confidence to Dobbs, he said that they had sailed only as far north as Whale Cove and had made no new discoveries. Although they had sighted black whales, the highest tide they observed was only two fathoms, with the flood coming from the north. Dobbs was disappointed that the sloops had not reached the area of the Welcome, but their slim pickings were enough to convince him that a passage existed; all that was needed was 'a Person of Judgment and Capacity' to find it. The venture, he now thought, should be government-sponsored, and he told Middleton that he intended to approach Sir Charles Wager, First Lord of the Admiralty, and perhaps even Walpole himself, whose patronage had recently brought Dobbs the post of Surveyor-General of Ireland. First, he wrote again to Lake, and without revealing that he had already managed to obtain details of the 1737 expedition asked for a report on its findings, and whether he could see its journals. Lake's answer was misleading from beginning to end. The sloops, he told Dobbs, had left 'very early in the Spring' (in fact, on 4 July) and despite being manned by 'the ablest Hands' could find not 'the least Appearance of a Passage', although they had remained at sea until 22 August. The attempt had been made only because of Dobbs's 'pressing Importunity', and had been accompanied 'with the utmost Danger of our Vessels and Mens Lives'. Lake made no mention of tidal observations or journals, nor – crucially – of how far north the sloops had sailed. In reply Dobbs accused Lake and the Hudson's Bay Company of having no interest in finding the Northwest Passage, and finished his letter with the threat that he intended to approach those 'who I believe will undertake it cheerfully, as they are convinced it will be a national benefit'. In this he was encouraged by Middleton who made it clear that he would be interested in commanding a discovery expedition, but advised Dobbs that it should be supported by the government, and be prepared to face two winters in Hudson Bay. As far as his present employers were concerned, he was afraid that the set policy of the Hudson's Bay Company was 'to prevent rather than forward new Discoveries'.

In his efforts to attract official interest, Dobbs found more sympathy than firm support. A letter to Wager at the Admiralty asking whether he would fit out a naval expedition for northern waters brought a disappointing reply. In words that echoed those of Daniel Defoe a few years earlier, the First Lord told Dobbs that as far as enthusiasm for overseas discoveries was concerned, 'a Spirit of that Kind seems to have been asleep for many years'. Although he personally was convinced by Dobbs's arguments in his Memorial, only Lord Granard among his acquaintances showed any interest in the possibility of a Northwest Passage. With relations with Spain deteriorating, Wager held little hope of a naval expedition since, as he put it, 'Parliament may think, especially at this Time, that we ought not to play with the Money they give us, for other and particular Services.' In conclusion, he could only suggest that a private expedition should make the attempt, and if successful might be allowed to take up the new trade that would result. Given the existence of the Hudson's Bay Company's charter, with its monopoly of trading rights, this hardly seemed a practical way forward. On his visits to London, Dobbs had met several influential merchants, but they could not be expected to invest in the kind of expedition he had in mind, for as he himself was beginning to realise, the restrictive charter of the Hudson's Bay Company would make it difficult for outsiders to exploit the discovery. Only when the search for a passage became linked with an attack on the trading monopoly of the Company could Dobbs expect support from merchants for his ventures.

The day after Middleton returned from his yearly voyage to the Bay in October 1739 war was declared against Spain. He warned Dobbs that this probably put an end to any prospect of a discovery voyage, and instead he asked Dobbs to help him get a commission in the Navy. Middleton had served on privateers in the the War of the Spanish Succession, and had a good knowledge of the European and American theatres of operations. The timing was especially frustrating, since that summer he had discussed in detail with Richard Norton at Churchill exactly what had happened on Scroggs's voyage of 1722. Norton had observed a huge five-fathom tide near latitude 65°N. in the Welcome, and remembered that when he went ashore he saw the land opening to the southwest, evidence of 'a clear Passage'. Moreover, in June 1739 six canoes of strange Indians appeared at Churchill for the first time, and told Norton that they frequently traded with Europeans on the west coast of North America. Dobbs lost no time in sending this information to Wager, and tried to turn the onset of war to the advantage of his project. If a Northwest Passage were discovered in 1740, he pointed out, then the next year a naval squadron could be sent through it to pillage the coasts and shipping of Spanish America from California to Panama. Unknown to Dobbs, such a venture was being contemplated by the government at this very time, and although the route was more conventional the motives behind Commodore George Anson's forthcoming voyage were the same as those advanced by Dobbs. Commanding a squadron of six warships Anson was to sail round Cape Horn into the Pacific and there disrupt Spanish shipping and trade, encourage rebellion among the Spanish colonists from Chile northwards, and intercept the great Manila galleon off the coast of California.

With the Admiralty committed to sending fleets to the West Indies, as well as a squadron to go round the world with Anson, Wager's reluctance to hazard men and ships on a minor expedition to Hudson Bay is understandable, but he met Middleton almost weekly during the winter of 1739–40. On one occasion the First Lord and the ship-captain spent time studying a chart of Hudson Bay and had 'a good deal of Discourse' about a possible voyage. And at last there seemed firm evidence for a passage to add to the speculative opinions of Dobbs's Memorial, for Middleton had sent abstracts of Scroggs's journal to both Dobbs and Wager. As yet, the Company had no suspicion of Middleton's dealings with Dobbs, for it had asked him to inspect the journal in order to have his opinion on the possibility of a passage. Clearly, it sensed that Dobbs and his schemes were not going to disappear from view. Now, for the first time, the crucial journal entries of Scroggs's exploration of the Welcome in July 1722 found their way outside the Company's London office. Dobbs and Wager could read about the charcoal maps drawn by the Northern Indians on board the *Whalebone*, the tide surging down the Welcome as the sloop lay anchored in latitude 64°56'N., the sightings of whales, and the boat crew's report of an open sea to the west. All this, Dobbs told Wager, 'almost amount to a determination of there being an easy Passage free from Ice'.

Wager as usual was encouraging and supportive – but no more than that. The matter must be referred to Walpole, he told Middleton; but the great man was always busy with affairs of state. Middleton found himself kicking his heels for hours at a time in antechambers and corridors waiting for the chance to speak to the prime minister. His moment came in February 1740, but the result was mortifying. Middleton reported to Dobbs in Dublin: 'Yesterday I had the Honour to speak to Sir Robert Walpole for the first Time at his Levee; and he answered me with some Earnestness, repeating it twice or thrice, that the Affair was not his Business, and that I must apply myself to Sir Charles Wager.' The First Lord, on hearing this later the same day, shook his head and said that time was passing fast. The dilemma, as Middleton explained to Dobbs, was that Walpole was too preoccupied to give his attention to the matter, while Wager would do nothing without the prime minister's consent. Wager, who had made his reputation as a brave fighting admiral before becoming a respected head of the Admiralty, was now in his mid-seventies, and in the twilight of his career (he died in 1743). During these months Dobbs was in Dublin, busy with his official and parliamentary duties, and his role in the affair was confined to letter-writing. As one approach failed, so another was tried. 'I'm afraid lest France should get the Scent, and anticipate our Discovery', was his refrain for early 1740. Middleton, meanwhile, still in the service of the Hudson's Bay Company, busied himself with preparations for his annual voyage to the Bay. 'Your presence here would much facilitate the Affair', he told Dobbs with some irritation. On 1 May he wrote again shortly before sailing, making arrangements to see Dobbs in November, but then added a postscript that changed the entire outlook. Middleton had just seen Wager, who told him that he had mentioned the expedition to the King (George II), 'and his Majesty seemed to approve it very well, and said that the Expence was such a Trifle, that it should not be obstructed on that Account'. Wager at last had the higher authority without which he had been reluctant to act. With royal patronage, however casually bestowed, this obstacle had been overcome. The way was clear the following year for the first-ever naval expedition to sail in search of the Northwest Passage.

Early in 1741 Dobbs came to London to jog Wager's memory about the projected voyage, and in mid-February he was able to report that the First Lord had promised to remind both Walpole and the King about 'the northwest trial'. Middleton cautiously insured himself against a breakdown in arrangements by keeping all mention of the venture from the Hudson's Bay Company. Throughout January and February he and the other two Company ship-captains, William Coats and George Spurrell, were preparing their ships for their annual voyage to the Bay posts. Then, on 5 March, Middleton received his long-awaited commission as captain in the Royal Navy, and four days later the Board of Admiralty formally approved the fitting out of the *Furnace* sloop for a discovery expedition to the north commanded by 'Mr Christopher Middleton . . . who is very well acquainted with those Seas'. The same day Middleton resigned his position with the Company, whose affairs were thrown into confusion by his late withdrawal, and decided that it had no option but to cancel that year's voyage by the *Hudson's Bay*, the ship Middleton was to have commanded. It is to the credit of the Company that when a few weeks later it agreed to award a gratuity of twenty guineas to its captains for the unusual hazards of the 1740 voyage, Middleton received this sum as well as Coats and Spurrell.

Middleton's appointment was unusual, but then the expedition itself lay well outside the Admiralty's usual sphere of activity. As Wager's doubts about Dobbs's initial proposals had shown, the Admiralty had not yet come to accept that seaborne exploration was one of its regular responsibilities. In 1698 it had sent the *Paramore* to the south Atlantic under the command of Edmond Halley, the celebrated astronomer and mathematician, to test his geomagnetical theories. Halley was granted a commission in the Navy, but had difficulty controlling his crew, and after the voyage his lieutenant was court-martialled. The next year the *Roebuck* sailed for Australian waters on discovery under the command of the former buccaneer, William Dampier, who was given a commission as captain in the Navy. He too had problems with his lieutenant, like Halley's a regular naval officer, and for part of the voyage he slept on deck, pistol at his side, for fear of mutiny. On his return Dampier was court-martialled, fined all his pay for the voyage, and dismissed the service. These were not reassuring precedents, but Middleton seemed in a different category from either Halley, a civilian with no experience of command at sea, or Dampier, who if his lieutenant was to be believed, remained at heart an 'old pyrateing dog'. By contrast Middleton was a seaman of long experience, employed on a regular basis by a company with a royal charter, and had sailed regularly to Hudson Bay on one of the most difficult of all regular trading voyages. In addition, he was a navigator of acknowledged

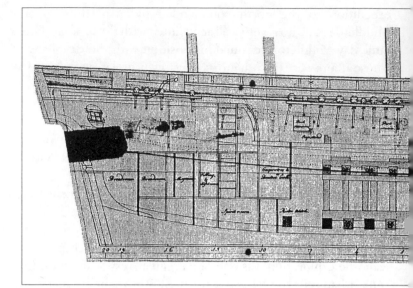

6. Plan of the *Furnace*, 1741.
National Maritime Museum (Hull Plan 6857)

This plan reveals in grey lines and shading the vessel as built at Rotherhithe in 1740 (with beds installed to take two mortars), and in black lines the alterations requested by Middleton in 1741. These included a change from two-masted ketch rig to three-masted ship rig, the adding of an upper deck, and the replacement of the windlass by the more efficient capstan for taking up the anchor. 'For want of time', not all these changes were made.

skills who had been elected a Fellow of the prestigious Royal Society.

For Middleton the two months after his appointment passed in a flurry of activity as he settled his accounts with the Company he had served for twenty years, and supervised the preparation of his new command, the *Furnace*, for the voyage ahead. The 265-ton *Furnace* was one of four bomb-vessels built at Rotherhithe in the summer of 1740. Her fiery name, like that

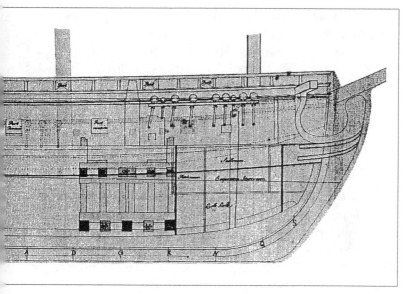

of the *Blast*, *Lightning*, *Terror*, was a traditional one for bomb vessels, whose primary role was to help land forces in siege operations. This class normally carried a massive 13-inch mortar forward (weighing more than four tons), and a 10-inch mortar aft. In September 1740 the *Furnace*, together with two of her sister vessels, was converted to a sloop, and launched the next month. Since December she had been engaged under Lieut. John Rankin in the press-service on the east coast of England. With stout timbers designed to withstand the battering recoil of heavy mortars, the *Furnace* appeared well suited to the dangers of navigation among the ice of northern waters. Bomb vessels, however, were not built for long voyages, and with only four-months' provisions on board her scuppers would be under water, while her deep waist was a serious weakness in heavy seas. To improve both her seaworthiness and her storage capacity, Middleton asked the Navy Board to carry out extensive alterations, including the adding of another deck. A plan of the *Furnace* from these months shows the alterations requested by Middleton (*Ill.6*).

The Board had no experience of fitting out ships for Arctic ventures, and it left much in Middleton's hands. It responded readily to his requests for special equipment and provisions for the voyage. These included extra boats for work among the ice, and a twenty-five foot launch to be left in frame until needed. Further recognition of the arduous nature of the forthcoming voyage came with the Board's approval of additional allowances of sugar, butter, brandy and molasses. The amount of alcohol Middleton thought essential for a crew of sixty seems colossal – eight tons of strong beer and four hundred gallons of brandy for six months – but as he explained, the allowance on the regular voyages to Hudson Bay was 'a Quart of Brandy and a proportion of Sugar once a Week to every 4 Men, but generally of a Saturday Night, and in very bad Weather, and among the Ice, which will be the greater part of the Voyage, a Dram 3 or 4 times a Day to each Man'.

The Admiralty also tried to meet in full Middleton's list of requirements for navigational instruments. This amounted to a cross-section of the most advanced instruments of the day, and reflected his skills in navigation and astronomy. The instruments taken included an azimuth compass of 'the new sort' which would measure magnetic variation, and could also be used to take bearings to celestial objects or to known landmarks such as headlands. In 1738 Middleton had been part of a group of navigators that demonstrated an improved azimuth compass to the Royal Society. Another instrument on his list was a Smith's quadrant. Designed by Caleb Smith, this was a short-lived rival to the 'improved' quadrant that the celebrated John Hadley had developed in 1734 and which soon became standard issue to ships. It did not use double reflection as Hadley's did, but had a prism on the fixed arm. Middleton again had been among those who had tested 'Mr Smiths New Sea-Quadrant' at sea. Middleton also had with him an Elton's quadrant, whose two spirit levels provided an artificial horizon when the actual horizon was obscured. The most interesting entry on the list was a request for a two-foot reflecting telescope and a fifteen-foot refracting telescope 'for Jupiter's Satellites'. Before the development of the chronometer, observation of the satellites of Jupiter was one way of determining longitude, though so complex were the mathematical calculations involved that very few sea officers could use this method.

At the end of April the Admiralty bought a new 150-ton collier, *The Three Brothers*, as a consort vessel, and renamed her *Discovery*. It was the forerunner of those more famous converted colliers *Endeavour* and *Resolution* that a generation later would sail to the Pacific with Captain Cook. Like them it had the advantages for a discovery vessel of strength, shallow draught and considerable storage capacity. The collier had been acquired after consultation with Middleton, who also persuaded the Admiralty to appoint his cousin William Moor as her master. Moor had served for years with Middleton on the Company ships, first as a boy and then as second mate. On Middleton's last two voyages to the Bay, Moor had been chief mate. Bound by family ties and by years of shipboard service together, Middleton and Moor promised strong and experienced leadership for the expedition. Another Hudson's Bay man was Robert Wilson, who was appointed second lieutenant of the *Furnace* (John Rankin, who had commanded the vessel since her launch, remained as first lieutenant, and time was to show some disturbing similarities between his role and that of the regular naval lieutenants who had given Halley and Dampier such trouble). Despite Middleton's pledge to the Admiralty to get 'as many Men as possible that have already been the Voyage' – presumably those who had originally been engaged to sail with him on the *Hudson's Bay* that year – he managed in the end to obtain the services of only three or four who had served on the Company ships. Outside this handful of experienced men, there appears to have been little enthusiasm for the voyage among the petty officers and tradesmen allocated to the discovery vessels. Two carpenters reported on board, but quickly left on hearing their destination. Nor did the surgeon appointed to the *Furnace* make the voyage. Instead,

Edward Thompson (a Company man who was to have sailed on the *Hudson's Bay* with Middleton) was appointed surgeon to the *Furnace*, 'notwithstanding his Qualification is only for a Surgeon's Mate'; another surgeon's mate was made surgeon of the *Discovery*, and both were excused their examinations.

Such appointments reflected the acute manpower shortage of the wartime navy which made Middleton's task of getting together the rest of his crew a difficult and frustrating one. When the *Furnace* went into dry dock in mid-March for her refit, there were forty pressed men on board, the results of Rankin's activities off the east coast. His journal for the previous month shows that some had been seized from colliers, and these for the most part would be hardened sailors, but it also refers to 'pressing ashore'. While the *Furnace* was in dry dock, these men were kept under lock and key on board a depot ship in case they tried to escape, but on Middleton's first sight of them he sent six ashore to sick quarters at Woolwich. Even this was not enough to weed out the infirm, for two days later Middleton received a letter from the Admiralty complaining that of the men sent to the depot ship three were 'very sick, and that most of the others look ailing, having scarce any clothes'. When they returned to the *Furnace*, the order continued, they were to be supplied with clothes from the slops chest. These normally consisted of baggy trousers and checked shirts, and perhaps waistcoats and woollen stockings, all charged against the men's wages. There was no mention of warmer clothing for the voyage ahead, such as that supplied to the Hudson's Bay men. Apart from these scarecrows, Middleton had to take what he could get by way of a press warrant, and at a time when the London newspapers reported that press gangs were in the streets examining anyone 'who has the Appearance of a Seaman', few of the men he picked up could have been suitable for the voyage ahead. If he was not encumbered with disabled pensioners as Anson's ships were, many of his men were in poor shape even before the ships left England. Dobbs had hoped that the expedition would get away on 10 May, but two weeks later the *Furnace* was still waiting for most of her crew, while on the *Discovery* Moor had to borrow ten hands from another ship to take her down river to join the *Furnace*.

To add to Middleton's difficulties, the Hudson's Bay Company showed an understandable reluctance to assist an expedition that 'might affect their Property and be Prejudicial to the Company in their Trade'. This was the warning Sir Bibye Lake gave shareholders at an extraordinary meeting held on 9 April. It was the first for twenty-one years to be called outside the normal annual meeting in November, evidence enough of the Company's concern. Lake requested, and was given, a free hand to deal with the threat implied by the Middleton expedition. Not spelt out at the meeting, but implicit in everything that was said, was the worry that Middleton, with his twenty years of service, might betray the secrets of the Company's trade. The Company did all in its power to limit the potential damage. Dobbs claimed that it enticed back into its service at least one seaman who had intended to sail on the *Furnace*. There was also a tug-of-war over Charles, a young Inuit boy, who had been captured by Cree Indians in 1736, and then bought from them by Company servants. Since 1738 the boy had been in Middleton's care, and probably acted as interpreter for him when his ship traded with the Inuit of Hudson Strait. After Middleton's resignation Charles was handed over to the Company, much to Dobbs's regret, for he 'would have made a good Interpreter at ne ultra'.

The Company's anxiety that the expedition might harm its trade led to increasingly heated exchanges of letters with government ministers. Its only response to an Admiralty request that it should give Middleton orders for the Bay posts to supply him with whatever stores and provisions he needed was a grudging order to its factor at Churchill that he might provide assistance, should Middleton 'be brought into real Distress, and Danger of his Life, or Loss of his Ship'. In explanation the Company pointed out that its supply ships had already left for Hudson Bay, carrying only enough provisions for the garrisons at the posts. This was reasonable enough, but a later letter from the Company revealed an almost neurotic anxiety about the expedition. If it wintered at one of the Bay posts its presence would lead to 'the Destruction of their Trade and Factories, and will occasion the Natives to go and Trade with the French'. The letter therefore asked that Middleton be prohibited from sailing into the southern parts of Hudson Bay, interfering with the Company's trade, or wintering at any of its posts unless in gravest danger. The Hudson's Bay Company was, in effect, trying to persuade the Admiralty to apply the same restrictions to Middleton's ships that it had clamped on the Knight expedition twenty-two years before. It was showing all the cautiousness of a monopoly that had remained in undisturbed possession of Hudson Bay since the ending of war with France in 1713. If a Northwest Passage was discovered, the Company feared that it could do little to prevent ships using it from trading in Hudson Bay, and that its charter might prove only a frail barrier against such activities.

Dobbs had already obtained a copy of the charter from the Board of Trade, and was taking advice to assess its validity. A weakness in the Company's legal position was that the charter of 1670 was a royal grant, and although in 1690 it was confirmed by Parliament, this was for seven years only, and the Company's attempt to renew this confirmation failed. From 1698 it was precariously dependent on royal prerogative, as Dobbs was quick to sense. From his earliest writings, Dobbs had shown himself an advocate of free trade, and already he saw in the Hudson's Bay Company an enemy to his principles and to the interests of the nation, an organisation closed to outside influences and inefficient in its own operations. Not only principle was involved; Dobbs was not averse to lining his own pocket. Shortly before the ships sailed, Samuel Smith, Dobbs's agent and attorney in London, shipped two bales of trading goods on board. Although the amount of goods taken was not great – a couple of bales was a sample rather than a cargo – Dobbs and Smith deluded themselves that their exchange for furs would bring a 2000% profit.

For Middleton these were anxious weeks. His wife had just died, he himself was not well, and his ships were still short of men. Above all, he needed to force from the Company an order allowing him to winter at one of its posts. He knew that the short navigable season in Hudson Bay meant there would be little possibility of returning to England that year. Either he would get through the passage to the warmer Pacific coast of North America, or he must winter in the Bay; and the fate of Munk's crew at Churchill River in 1619 warned of the dangers of wintering in an unprepared location. Only at one of the Company's posts could he find shelter from the severity of the Bay winter, and he stressed to the Admiralty the necessity of getting a promise of assistance from Lake and the London Committee. In Wager he found a sympathetic listener. The First Lord of the Admiralty had made it clear years earlier that he was no great lover of chartered companies, and in letters to the Duke of Newcastle, the influential Secretary of State for the Southern Department, and to the Regency Council (which took the King's place when he was – as now – in Hanover) he attacked the Company's attitude. He wrote, in terms ominous for the Company, that its response was 'very unbecoming a Company who subsists by his Majesty's favour, having only an old Charter which no doubt they have made several Breaches in'. To the Regency Council, Wager complained that while on the one hand the Company showed 'little regard' for the safety of the naval vessels involved, on the other it expected the Navy to protect its ships. To the Hudson's Bay Company the Admiralty pointed out that Middleton was being sent, not on a trading venture, but on a discovery voyage. (Of the bales of goods on board the ships there was no mention – and probably no knowledge.) The conditions it tried to apply to Middleton's expedition, the Admiralty's letter concluded angrily, were harder than 'the practice of any civilized Nation towards the Subjects of another'. Beaten down by the heavy artillery of ministerial disapproval the Hudson's Bay Company surrendered, and gave Middleton a brief order for the post factors, who were to give him the best assistance in their power. It was terse and ungracious, but it was enough.

While still engaged in these skirmishes with his former employers, Middleton received his sailing orders from the Admiralty, though the drafting of them seems to have been left to Dobbs. Certainly they have a familiar ring. Once Middleton reached the Bay he was to sail across it to the west coast and the area of Ne Ultra (Roe's Welcome). There he was to search for the strong flood tide that Scroggs's crew had observed coming from the north in latitude 65°N. Somewhere in that vicinity 'a Strait or an open sea' to the west should be found. No other locations were suggested for exploration – an important point given the criticism levelled at Middleton after his return – and after these brief directions for finding the passage, the instructions turned to the more exciting prospect that awaited Middleton once he had reached the west coast of North America. The possibilities were endless. He might meet 'populous Nations' and negotiate treaties with them. Alternatively, he could look for an offshore island suitable for a settlement. In the warm climes he was expected to reach, Middleton should sow seeds with an eye to the future. In inhabited regions he was to take possession with the consent of the local people; in uninhabited regions this was to be done 'by setting up proper Inscriptions, as first Discoverers and Possessors'. A reference to a fictitious voyage by the buccaneer John Coxton in the 1680s directed Middleton to the good harbour and civilised nation that Coxton was supposed to have found on the west coast of America in latitude 42°N. Finally, the orders noted that Commodore Anson, who had left England for the South Sea with a squadron of ships the previous September, should be on the Californian coast lying in wait for the Manila treasure galleon, and that Middleton might join forces with him. If, on the other hand, Middleton encountered warships from Japan or other countries he should return, so that 'Ships of sufficient Force may be sent out next Season, to begin a Trade, or make a Settlement.'

The contrast between the limitless ambitions of Middleton's instructions and his meagre resources could not have been greater. At the beginning of June, five weeks after the Hudson's Bay Company ships had set sail for the Bay, Middleton's two ships were still at the Nore, the naval anchorage off the southern shore of the Thames estuary. There forty-three men were received from the depot ship, although several were exchanged by Middleton, 'being very ordinary'. By now Middleton was only five short of his complement of men (the overall complement of the *Furnace* was sixty, and of the *Discovery* thirty), but he still needed petty officers. These he hoped to pick up as he sailed north along the east coast of England. As the ships prepared for sailing most of the crews were paid up to 14 March, and the volunteers were given an advance of two-months wages. The number of these was small, probably only the handful tempted by Middleton to leave the Company's service, together with John Lanrick, 'a young gentleman' recommended by Dobbs, and James Smith, the 16-year-old son of Dobbs's London agent Samuel Smith. In health and temperament, Middleton's men were very different from the picked volunteers who sailed on the Arctic naval expeditions of the next century, and many were in poor shape even before the ships left home waters.

3

The Controversial Voyage of Christopher Middleton

'This gave us Great Joy and Hopes of it being the Extream Part of America, and thereupon named it Cape Hope. We work'd up round it thro' much Stragling Ice all night. In the Morning when the Sun clear'd away the Haze, to our great Disappmt. we Saw the Land all round . . . Then our Hopes of a Passage that way was all over.'

CAPTAIN CHRISTOPHER MIDDLETON,
Journal of the *Furnace*, 6 August 1742

'All Nature cries aloud there is a Passage, and we are sure there is one from Hudson's Bay to Japan. Send a Letter directed to Messrs. Brook and Cobham, who are Gentlemen that have been the Voyage, and cannot bear so glorious an Attempt should die under the Hands of mercenary Wretches.'

'Brook and Cobham' to Arthur Dobbs,
21 January 1743

EARLY IN THE MORNING OF 8 JUNE 1741 the *Furnace* and *Discovery* weighed anchor at the Nore, and stood northward along the low-lying Essex coast. No ceremony marked the occasion, and the vessels' departure on the first naval expedition to seek the Northwest Passage was noticed only in a few muddled newspaper items. One reported that the expedition was sailing to discover the Northeast Passage; another that it was bound for Russia.

Of more concern to Middleton was that he was sailing a

month later than planned, and that he was still short of his full complement of men. After a week the ships reached Sunderland (not far from Middleton's birthplace of Billingham), where the captain had taken advantage of his local contacts to arrange for a number of men to be taken on. The *Furnace*'s lieutenant, John Rankin, and her master, Robert Wilson, went ashore, but came back with the frustrating news that twenty men who had been waiting for the ships had left when they failed to arrive. They brought on board only a mate and a single seaman. Also at Sunderland the men bought boots and warm clothes with the wages they had received at the Nore. In itself this was a sign that the Navy Board had not supplied clothing that was adequate for an Arctic wintering. Impatient to make up lost time, and faced with contrary winds, Middleton ignored his orders to join a convoy at Leith. Instead, he sailed straight for the Orkneys, where at Stromness (the traditional last port of call and watering place of the Hudson's Bay Company ships) he took on board water. As night came, Rankin, who was in charge, paid workers on shore to keep filling the casks rather than use crew members who might slip away under cover of darkness. On 27 June the two vessels got under way and sailed west into the open sea.

The voyage across the Atlantic was stormy but uneventful, and on 25 July *Furnace* and *Discovery* entered Hudson Strait. Apart from some large icebergs, the strait was unusually clear of ice – probably because the ships had reached it a month or so later than the time when the Company ships normally made their passage. In early summer, William Moor on the *Discovery* noted, they would expect to find the Strait 'Choak'd with Heavy Ice from Side to Side'. Despite fog, the ships got through the Strait in only five days, and by 31 July they were off the southern tip of Coats Island, about halfway across Hudson Bay. Here, Middleton summoned a council consisting of himself, Moor, Rankin and Wilson. Although the ships were within a couple of days sail of Roe's Welcome, the council decided not to begin the search that year, but to make for the

Company post at Churchill River to winter. At first sight this seems a remarkably half-hearted decision. The small Company sloops were often on the west coast of the Bay, though well to the south of the Welcome, until the third week of August. A whole set of reasons was advanced at the council for the decision: the lateness of the season; delays from fog and ice; the length of time it would take at Churchill to secure the ships and provisions, and to arrange accommodation for the crews. Wintering in safety at Churchill would ensure that when the ice broke up the following spring the expedition would have a full season to attempt the search.

If unheroic, the decision was sensible, especially given the rawness of the crews. Working a ship among ice was arduous and specialist work, as Middleton and his handful of sailors from the Company's service well knew. The experienced Company captain, William Coats, wrote about the perils of ice navigation with all the intensity of one who had seen his ship crushed by ice in Hudson Strait. The problem, he wrote, was the shortness of the navigable season even in the more open waters of Hudson Bay. By the middle of September gales and snow were warnings that winter had arrived: 'The severe frosts are such that you cannot work a ship; possibly as the frost prevails the winds decrease, but to what purpose? When blocks are locks, and ropes are bolts, and sails can neither be taken in nor left out, is surely the last extremity; the new ice near the shores and rivers, and the wash of the sea, stick to your ship and ropes like bird-lime, cand in your sails like pitch, and so all operations by water ceases.'

As it was, hampered by fog and loose ice, the ships took a week to cross the southwest reaches of the Bay to Churchill, their guns firing almost hourly as they tried to keep company in poor visibility. On 8 August, in weather so calm that the ships had to be towed by their boats towards shore, the great stone fortress at Churchill loomed through the mist. Middleton was making a familiar landfall, but in an unfamiliar vessel. *Furnace* and *Discovery* were the first non-Company ships to enter Hudson Bay since the French had left almost thirty years earlier, and their sighting from the fort at daybreak caused consternation. Robert Pilgrim was in temporary command while awaiting the arrival from York Fort of the new factor, James Isham, and the orders that he had received from the Company a few weeks earlier instructed him not to allow any ship to approach the fort without displaying the agreed signals since the war with Spain still continued and war with France was a possibility. Pilgrim called all his men to the ramparts where the cannon were loaded in preparation for 'a vigorous Defence'. When a boat from one of the ships came within range, Pilgrim ordered a warning shot to be fired. On this the boat ran up a white flag, pulled in to shore, and landed an officer. This was not, as might have been expected, Middleton, who would have been known to many of the fort's garrison, having last been at Churchill only two years earlier, but Lieutenant Rankin. As a captain in the Royal Navy, however recent, Middleton knew it was not consonant with his newly-acquired rank to row ashore with letters of introduction. When he reached the fort Rankin showed Pilgrim the letter that Middleton had obtained from the Company ordering its factors to give him 'the best Assistance in your Power'. At noon the two navy vessels sailed past the fort, saluted it with nine guns, and moored in the nearby harbour.

The great mass of Fort Prince of Wales was a bizarre sight in the Canadian sub-Arctic (*Ill.*7). With stone ramparts stretching more than three hundred feet on all four sides, crowned with parapets cut for heavy cannon, it had all the appearance of a fortress bodily lifted from Flanders or some other European theatre of war. It had nothing in common with the modest stockades of the normal fur-trading post. The reasons for its construction are still not altogether clear. It was far too elaborate a structure for defence against possible Native attack – of which in any case there had never been an instance at Churchill. Its position on the low, treeless headland which commanded the entrance to Churchill harbour but was

7. Prince of Wales Fort, Churchill, 1777. From Samuel Hearne, *A Journey to the Northern Ocean* (1795).
HBC Archives, Provincial Archives of Manitoba

exposed to the worst of wind and weather, showed that it was primarily intended as a defence against seaborne assault by the ships of a European foe. The original wooden post (known from this time on as the Old Factory), which James Knight had built in 1717, was about five miles up river, in a more sheltered location, and easier of access for the Indian trade. One oddity about the new fortress was that Churchill's normal garrison of forty or so men was not remotely adequate to man the heavy cannon that were gradually being shipped out from England (there were eighteen in position at the time of Middleton's visit). The most likely explanation for the fort's construction is that it was visualised as a fortified base where in time of war the Company ships and sloops could shelter, and their crews help man the fort's cannon. All that one can say to this is that when, eventually, the fort was attacked – by the French squadron of La Pérouse in 1782 – it surrendered without firing a shot. Its construction had begun in 1731, and followed plans drawn up by Middleton, who had also surveyed the harbour. It proved a costly business in terms of men, materials and time. The factor, Richard Norton, and garrison had at last moved into the new fort in August 1740, though work was by no means finished, and in a sense never would be. Given the size of the structure, and the temperature extremes of its location, constant repairs were needed. Norton had been in charge of building operations from the beginning, though he had no qualifications for the task except enthusiasm and energy. Under his direction year by year the work proceeded. A lime kiln was built, a quarry opened, masons and labourers arrived from England, together with horses and cattle for dragging the heavy stones. When Norton returned to England and retirement in 1741 he painted a reassuring picture of progress: of ramparts ten foot high, with parapets another five foot on top, and board-walks erected for the forty-eight cannon that would one day be in position. Inside the great walls was an underground powder magazine, together with living quarters for the garrison, complete with kitchen, smithy and the like. Time was to show how misleading this description was. Walls collapsed, the recoil after practice firings hurled cannon backwards off the narrow boardwalk, the magazine let in the damp – the list of complaints by Norton's successors was endless, and finally in the 1750s much of the fort was rebuilt under the direction of Ferdinand Jacobs.

Middleton was less interested in the new fortress than in the Old Factory, for this was where he hoped his crews would winter. Certainly he could not expect to find room for the hundred men and officers from his two vessels in the normal accommodation at any of the Company posts. His first enquiry, even before landing, was what sort of condition the Old Factory was in, and he was shocked to be told that it had been demolished. Norton's post journal for the previous year records as many as eighteen men busy 'ripping up the old Factory'. There was nothing surprising about this, for the abandoned buildings contained bricks, timber, nails, all of which could be used in the new fort. Middleton's worst fears were confirmed when, on his first trip ashore, he visited the Old Factory and found it 'nothing but a Heap of Rubbish'. He immediately set carpenters to work on it, but given lack of time and materials they would be able to build only makeshift accommodation to shelter the crews from the harsh winter conditions that lay ahead. This was not Middleton's only worry. Just as important as finding winter quarters for the crew was the necessity of laying up the ships before they were damaged by the ice carried by the swirling tides of the open harbour. There was one obvious spot, Sloop Cove, the usual wintering place of the Company sloops, named Winter Cove on the chart of Churchill River drawn by John Wigate, clerk of the *Furnace* (*Ill. 8*). But a cove able to shelter the Company's sloops with their six-foot draught would not necessarily accommodate the two discovery ships. Middleton's measurements showed the extent of the problem. The height of water in the cove he estimated to be seven

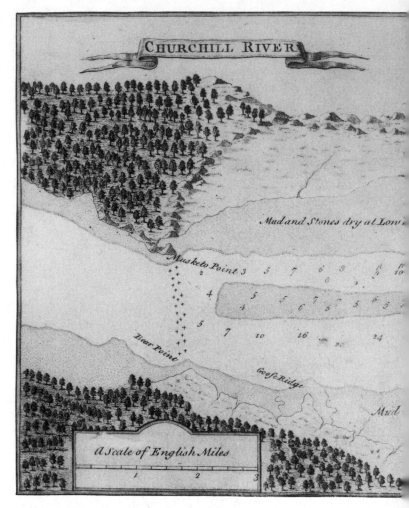

8. JOHN WIGATE. 'Churchill River' [March 1742], 1746.
British Library

The main locations of Middleton's wintering are clearly marked: the 'New Fort', where the officers and a few of the men were accommodated; 'Winter Cove' (more usually known as Sloop Cove), where the *Furnace* and *Discovery* were docked; and the 'Old Factory', where most of the men wintered.

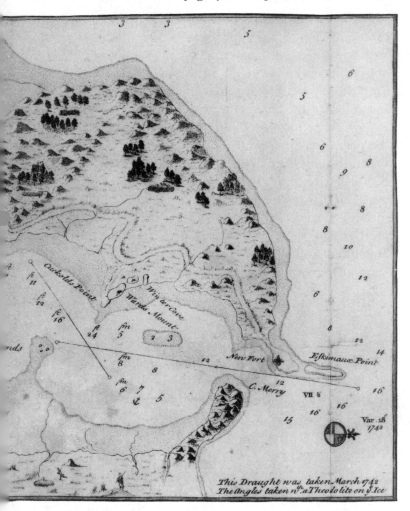

or eight feet at spring (high) tide; the *Furnace* drew eleven foot of water. To make a dock in the cove where the ships could winter, Middleton's crews had to dig down four feet or more. In temperate climes this would not be a huge task for a couple of dozen men, but the ground at Churchill was subject to permafrost, a little-recognised phenomenon at this time. Middleton's journal entries for the first two days of work showed what lay ahead. 'We find it very Difficult digging the Ground being all froze when we get 6 Inches below the Surface, and meet with many Rocks and large Stones, which we are Oblidg'd to blow up . . . Most of our Men employ'd with Spades & Pickaxes, but Have not been able to dig above 4 Inches below the Surface in two Days.'

One hopeful aspect of a generally depressing situation was the help received from the Company men once the tension that surrounded the first few hours of the ships' arrival subsided. The fort's yawl helped the crews to unload the discovery ships, and its horse team then hauled stores and provisions from the open beach to the shelter of the fort. On 16 August the *Churchill* sloop arrived from York Factory, carrying on board the fort's new chief factor, James Isham. Still only in his mid-twenties, Isham had impressed the Company as 'a very Sober, honest, & Diligent, young man', and had been in command at York for the last four years. By chance – unlucky chance he no doubt would have said – Isham was to be a key personality in the story of both the discovery expeditions to Hudson Bay in the 1740s. He and Middleton would have met at least once, during the stay of Middleton's ship *Hudson's Bay* at York in 1737. Despite the difference in age, the two men had much in common, for Isham shared Middleton's sense of scientific curiosity, and during his four years at Churchill was to keep a volume of 'Observations' on the natural history, Native peoples, and trade of the area that was the first to be written down by any Company servant. It was perhaps a sign of Middleton's increased realisation of his dependence on whoever was in charge at Churchill that as the sloop came in sight there was no standing on dignity as he went out to greet the new factor.

Isham continued and extended the policy of assistance that Pilgrim had initiated. Two days after his arrival he went with Middleton to the Old Factory to see the situation for himself, and to discuss arrangements for the winter. There was particular concern since Middleton had been told that the previous year 'most' of the garrison had suffered from scurvy. Norton's post journal for that winter does not bear this out, but certainly some men were ill, and one died, of unspecified complaints. As a sailor, Middleton knew enough about scurvy to appreciate the value of fresh provisions. At Churchill fresh meat in the shape of geese, ducks, ptarmigan and caribou could only be obtained with the help of those expert hunters the Home Indians. These Crees had given up their traditional way of life inland to settle around the posts where they were employed in hunting and fishing, and they were vital contributors to the domestic economy of all the Bayside posts. At Churchill they went twice a year to a spot upriver where they shot thousands of geese in the spring and fall hunts, and also ptarmigan. During the winter they retreated farther inland to trap marten, whose fine fur was much prized, and also rabbits and hares for food. They served as messengers between the posts, and sometimes hauled goods or supplies from one post to another by sledge. The women living with their children in a huddle of tents outside the stockaded posts (and sometimes, against Company orders, inside) prepared skins, made snow-shoes for the winter, and carried out other tasks. There might be as many as 150 or 200 Home Indians living near a post, most of them regarded by the garrison as a degenerate remnant dependent on the bounty of the English, and willing to do anything for brandy. Isham had a better sense of the relationship when he wrote that they could 'not do without the assistance of the English, any more than the English without them'. By the time Middleton's ships made their unexpected appearance at Churchill, most of the Home Indians had left the vicinity of the fort to winter inland, and all that Isham could do was to send a message to York Fort asking the factor there to send some of his local Indians across to Churchill to hunt during the winter.

It was evidence of another of Middleton's worries, the lack of adequate clothing for his men, that Isham also asked his counterpart at York whether he could spare any beaver coats for the discovery crews. As far as Middleton, his officers and ten of his crew were concerned, Isham offered them accommodation in the new fort, where a large building inside the ramparts, one hundred foot long and thirty feet wide, was divided into three sections. In the middle was the warehouse where the trading goods and furs were kept, and at either end were living quarters. Isham also sent the fort's bricklayer to the Old Factory to help repair the stoves there, while in return one of the carpenters from the *Furnace* helped to put a new keel on the Company's sloop. For the Company's garrison and the discovery crews a policy of mutual co-operation was the only one that made sense. Once winter arrived, both groups would be almost totally cut off from the outside world; their only contact with other Englishmen would be letters to and from York when Indians could be found to make the overland journey of 130 miles between the two posts. Even for the hardened winterers in the Company's service the approaching months of cold and darkness were ones to be endured, a time when they would need all the survival techniques they and their predecessors had acquired to get through the long winter months. For Middleton's inexperienced crews the approach of winter must have been a time of apprehension and dread, and no doubt the Company men were not averse to telling them of the tough times ahead. The policy of co-operation did not meet the approval of the London Committee when a year later it read in Isham's journal that the fort's team of horses had helped to bring the supplies for Middleton's men up from the beach. From the comfort of the Company's London headquarters in Fenchurch Street, one committee man scrawled in the margin against this entry: 'Why did not the Capt. make the sailors draw or carry this & other things?' It was the same petty-minded attitude that James Knight had criticised years before when he wrote to the London Committee that if some of them had spent a winter in Hudson Bay 'they would Sett a Little more value upon Mens Lives.'

Meanwhile, the back-breaking work at Sloop Cove continued. The next spring tide was on the last day of August, and Middleton had twenty men digging and blasting each day. Others were repairing the Old Factory, continuing with the unloading of the ships, and digging a deep pit in the inner yard of the fort where the strong beer could be stored for the winter. At Sloop Cove there was no snow yet, but storms of wind and rain hampered the operations. Even within the confines of the harbour the sea was rough enough to sink the boats moored astern of the ships, and they had to be hoisted onto the tackles. Topmasts were lowered, spars, yards and rigging, cannon, and all except the lower tiers of ballast were taken out of the ships. Still the *Furnace* drew eleven foot of water aft and ten foot forward even though she carried only a few cables, three anchors and just enough ballast to keep her manoeuvrable. On 30 August she was brought into shallow water near the entrance of the cove, and the rest of her ballast was taken out. Her draught was now down to just under ten feet forward and aft, but the next day's high tide carried her only to the entrance of the cove, where she grounded, with a heavy list, losing part of her protective false keel as she did so. The *Discovery* just got in, but the whole length of the *Furnace* still lay outside the dock. The next day, 1 September, the first snow fell. The deeper the men dug, the more frozen they found the ground – 'near as Hard as portland Stone, & Scarce to be enter'd with Pickaxes'. Since the dock was now awash, the work of drilling and blasting to remove the stones could only be done if the water was baled out. With the men numbed and frozen this was almost the worst of their tasks. After six days one huge rock still resisted all efforts to remove it. In a final effort to get the ship farther in the anchors were embedded ashore above the high-water mark, and with the help of the capstan the heavy bomb-vessel inched forward, but at a cost. As the men ran round with the bars of the capstan Middleton was trapped against the side of the companionway and knocked senseless. When he recovered he continued to be 'in great Pain & Difficulty of breathing'. On 13 September, a month after work began, Middleton decided that the *Furnace*, now without her false keel, was far enough in, and he secured her with six cables. As he warned, high tides the following spring would be lower than the autumn highs, and there was always the danger that the ships would be trapped. Unknowingly, Middleton was perhaps near an explanation of what had happened to Knight's ships twenty years before.

With the ships reasonably secure, Middleton put his crews to the task of finding and cutting wood for winter fuel. Much of this had to be obtained upriver, for the trees at Churchill were few and stunted. Boats from the ships and the fort were used to tow down rafts of timber for firewood. Normally, part of a garrison's summer task would be getting in wood for the long winter months, and once again Middleton's crews started at a disadvantage. Isham's 'Observations' described how the wood rafted down the river each summer was heaped near the fort in two huge piles, each twenty foot high, and 160 yards round – and this was enough for only one winter's firing. September 20th was a day of bad news all round. Search parties found no sign of the *Discovery*'s cutter, which had drifted out into the river and was never seen again. The Home Indian sent to York Factory by Isham more than a month earlier to request help in the form of hunters and beaver coats returned with the news that he had been unable to cross the Nelson River. Isham meanwhile had discovered that Richard Norton, his predecessor as chief factor, had supplied the hunting Indians at Churchill with unusually lavish quantities of ammunition, so there was little chance that they would appear again at the fort that winter. This was the more worrying because the fort had run short of snow-shoes, six or even eight feet long, and essential for winter travel. Intricately laced with thongs of caribou skin 'like what may be observed in the frame of a racket', they were normally made by the Cree women. Isham noted that his men had only fifteen pairs between them.

The Navy men presumably had none at all, though Isham put two Indian families to work making some. Finally, the weather had turned so cold that the carpenter temporarily lost his sight. These were the central years of the Little Ice Age, and a week later the temperature at Churchill had dropped to the level of the great frost in England two years earlier, when the Thames froze so hard that fairs and houses were built on the ice. But at Churchill it was still only late September. By the beginning of October the river was frozen up to two miles from the shore, though a channel remained open in the middle of the estuary. Within a few days even that had disappeared, and men were crossing the Churchill River, eight miles wide at this point, on the ice.

With winter setting in, Middleton was determined to make the most of the anniversary of the King's coronation on 11 October. Cannon were hauled off the ships at Sloop Cove, and at noon a twenty-eight gun salute was fired on the shoreline in the presence of the ships' companies. The officers drank to the King's health and to the success of British arms, though not with total success, since 'the Wine, with which the Officers drank the aforesaid Healths, and which was good Port wine, froze in the Glass as soon as Pour'd out of the Bottle'. With drums beating and colours flying, the men marched to the new fort where they paraded in the snow-covered square, fired several volleys, and again drank toasts. That evening Navy and Company men, joined by the Home Indians, celebrated the occasion with thirty gallons of brandy. Not surprisingly, the day concluded, Middleton remarked in his journal, 'with all possible Demonstrations of Joy'. It was perhaps a sign of the difference in outlook between naval captain and company factor that Isham's journal contained no mention of any of this. Instead, it had a rather sombre entry to the effect that an Indian messenger who at last had managed to get through to York Factory returned with the news that the factor there had no beaver clothing to spare, and could not send any Indians to hunt at Churchill until the following spring. At this, the crews from the Old Factory reported to the fort to obtain what winter clothing could be spared: cloth for stockings, caps and mittens, and a coarse blanket to wear over their normal dress (there was no mention of the beaver coats, mittens and headgear that the Company men regarded as essential). Middleton concluded his entry on an acerbic note, 'These things they were oblidg'd to take up of the Factory here, as we were not Provided.'

One reassuring note was that the ships were safe, locked fast into their shallow docks by ice that stretched away a mile or more into the distance. But already Middleton was worrying about what might happen in the spring, when the ice broke up, and great slabs would be tossed around on the tide. He and the other officers could only cross the two miles to Sloop Cove on snow shoes, for the snow was now ten to twelve feet deep. At the fort Middleton's men and the garrison were constantly employed clearing the yard of snow. Further cele-brations cheered the men; for the King's Birthday on 30 October, and Gun Powder Treason (or Guy Fawkes Day) on 5 November, each concluding with thirty gallons of brandy. The cold was now so severe that at night when the stoves went out, wine and strong beer froze. And outside, even full-strength brandy froze solid overnight. Middleton's attempt to measure the refraction of the sun's altitude with his Elton's quadrant failed when the instrument's twin spirit levels froze. A man could not walk more than forty yards without frost-bite searing those parts of the skin not covered by a double layer of clothing. The fort's Home Indians shot a fair number of ptarmigan during November, trapped the occasional hare, and caught a few fish. By 11 December fifteen hundred partridges had been brought in, and these were served out to the men at the rate of two a day; but even if distributed evenly among the crews, this amounted only to seven or eight-days' rations. From the journal entries it seems that much of the fresh meat went to the sick, and for most of the men salt pork or beef would have remained the standard diet. Middleton described how a hole was cut in the ice of the river (by now five or six feet thick) to freshen the salt meat. As he explained, dipping a chunk of meat in the water made it 'pliable and soft, though before its Immersion it was hard frozen'.

On 24 December came the first reference to scurvy, with Middleton's note that two or three men at the Old Factory were afflicted with it, and had been even before landing. His only remedy was spruce beer (a long-standing antiscorbutic), and brandy, which was quite the reverse. Long known as 'the plague of the sea', scurvy was a mystery to the medical profession. Its causes were unknown and its treatment a matter of guesswork. At the same time as Middleton's men were showing initial signs of scurvy, Anson's crews in the Pacific were dying in their hundreds from the disease and the journal-keepers on his ships dwelt in harrowing detail on its spread. Among its symptoms were large spots and ulcers appearing over the whole body, swollen legs, putrid gums and rotting flesh. But there seemed almost as many different symptoms as there were sufferers: 'Some lost their Senses, some had their Sinews contracted in such a Manner as to draw their Limbs close up to their Thyghs, and some rotted away.' Physical degeneration was often accompanied by depression and lethargy. Only after Anson's voyage, and partly as a result of its appalling losses, did the naval surgeon James Lind carry out research that provided evidence of the antiscorbutic properties of lemon juice. Not until the discovery of the existence of vitamins in the early twentieth century was scurvy properly diagnosed as resulting from a vitamin C deficiency. Greens, milk and citrus fruit all contain vitamin C in varying degrees; but none of these was available to Middleton's crews. A preponderance of salt meat in their diet, and the consumption of spirits, were supplementary factors in the onset of the disease. There is little doubt but that a second winter in these Arctic conditions would have seen the death or disabling from scurvy of most of the expedition's men.

The liberal provision of alcohol for the Christmas and

New Year festivities brought other problems. Isham complained that three of his men got drunk on navy spirits, and they were put in irons after one endangered his life by falling asleep at the river's edge and another abused Isham's deputy. It took an application of navy-style discipline by Isham, with punishments ranging from twelve to twenty lashes carried out in front of the rest of the garrison, to restore the situation. Despite the occasional irritants of the relationship between navy crews and company garrison, within the confines of the fort Isham and Middleton seemed to have shared each other's interests and each other's company. It was during this winter that Isham began writing his 'Observations on Hudsons Bay', though they were not sent to England until 1745. There is no doubt that Isham found Middleton a more congenial companion than his normal wintering colleagues at Churchill. There is a revealing preface to his 'Observations' in which he explained: 'Being in a Disconsolate part of the world, where there is Little conversation or Divertisment to be had ... I have in cold Days and Long winter Nights, amusd. my self with the following Observations.' Middleton, as well as keeping his official daily journal, was also making observations of a more scientific kind. These were sent home on the Company ship, read before the Royal Society within two weeks of Middleton's return in October 1742, and printed in the Society's *Philosophical Transactions* under the title of 'Captain Middleton's Account of the Extraordinary Degrees and Surprizing Effects of Cold in Hudson's-Bay, North America'.

At a time when Arctic exploration was in its infancy, and those whalers and traders who had first-hand experience of northern waters and northern lands rarely recorded their experiences, both sets of observations were unusual. Isham's remained unpublished until 1949, but Middleton's would have been read in those scientific and literary circles that subscribed to the *Philosophical Transactions*, and they were also reprinted in at least one of the popular collections of voyages and travels of the period. Isham accompanied Middleton on several of his excursions to take astronomical observations, and included some of the captain's data in his own volume. Among Middleton's observations were those of longitude, latitude and declination of the magnetic needle at Churchill, together with some remarks on methods of observing altitudes of the sun and stars with the help of a quadrant. Observations that required exposure of instruments for more than a few minutes – eclipses of the satellites of Jupiter and the sun's refraction – proved impossible as metal and lenses iced over, and spirits froze. Where Middleton's and Isham's observations turned to more general conditions at Churchill they have several identical passages, although who copied whom is impossible to say. Isham had the greater local knowledge, Middleton the more accomplished writing style.

One such passage described the efforts to keep warm inside the living quarters of the fort. The stone walls were two foot thick, with small windows whose wooden shutters were kept closed eighteen hours a day. The interior was heated by four brick wood-burning stoves, so large that each consumed a cartload of fuel a day. Once the wood was well alight the tops of the stoves' chimneys were shut. This kept the heat in the rooms but also left them full of smoke that 'makes our heads ake'. Several times a day 24-pound cannon balls were heated red-hot and hung in the window embrasures. But when the stoves died down at night the inside walls of the house became coated with a thick layer of ice that had to be cut away with axes each morning. Beer, wine and ink froze solid, and Middleton's own watch (made by George Graham, a leading instrument-maker) continued to keep good time only because he carried it in his pocket by day, and kept it with him in bed at night. Some idea of the conditions within the posts during the winter comes from an apology by Richard Staunton, factor at Moose Factory at this time, to the London Committee for the state of the journal he was sending home: 'I do not at all doubt but your honours will pardon the dirtiness of it, for I have with many times written with hands as black as a chimney sweeper, and clothes as greasy as a butcher.'

Men could venture outside only if dressed in several layers of clothing. First came a flannel shirt, double-lined waistcoat, caribou skin breeches, two pairs of thick worsted stockings reaching to the crotch, and three pairs of socks. Over these, the Company men wore a full-length beaver coat, caribou-skin boots, elbow-length lined beaver mittens, a flannel cap and face-mask, topped by a large beaver head-covering that came down to the shoulders. Isham allowed himself a wry comment on the ungainly appearance of his men as they set forth – 'a bag upon the back, with a tin pott and hatchet by the side, with a Beard as Long as Captain Teache's, and a face as black as any Chimnly Sweepers – and this is the figure we make appearing more Like Beasts then men.' Even for men swathed in warm clothing, frost-bite was always a danger. Middleton noted the importance of what today would be called the wind-chill factor when he stressed the effect of a combination of wind and low temperatures. 'Some of the men that stir abroad, if any Wind blows from the northward, are dreadfully frozen; some have their Arms, Hands, and Face blister'd and frozen in a terrible manner, the Skin coming off soon after they enter a warm House, and some have lost their Toes.' The dilemma for men disabled in this way was that a long period of inactivity was likely to lead to scurvy. 'I find nothing will prevent that Distemper from being mortal', Middleton wrote, 'but Exercise and stirring abroad.'

The daily journals kept by Middleton, William Moor and John Rankin tell only part of the story of the wintering, and probably not the worst part. All three were accommodated at the fort, and the eighty-eight men at the Old Factory were left without any senior officer in charge. Middleton's next recorded visit to them after his August reconnaissance with Isham was not until 18 January, and in as far as anyone seems to have been in charge there it was Shaw, the inexperienced surgeon of the *Discovery*. No description exists of the con-

ditions at the Old Factory, but they must have been grim in
the extreme despite the post's more sheltered location. Even
before its abandonment and destruction, the original post
had been intended for a regular garrison of only about forty
men, although extra quarters had been added in the 1730s
for the masons and labourers sent out to work on the great
stone fortress. How effective the repair work had been in
the autumn remains open to doubt, and certainly the building's interior would have had neither the essential fittings
nor the personal possessions that made life endurable for
the Company's men. They were more often away from the
post than in it, for the secret of their relatively good health
during the winter months was that they pursued an active if
arduous life outdoors. They built log huts or skin tents in the
woods, and spent the days in wooding, hunting and fishing. As
a later factor observed, 'we endeavour to imitate the customs of
the natives who are inured to the climate'. Most of the navy
men had neither the willingness nor the aptitude to follow
suit. Their instinctive reaction to the extreme cold would have
been to remain indoors, as near the stoves as possible, and
look to brandy for comfort – there are several references in
Middleton's journal to sledges carrying casks of brandy being
dispatched to the Old Factory. Without exercise or fresh food,
crammed together in overcrowded and insanitary conditions,
the men were vulnerable to disease and above all to scurvy.
Middleton was aware of the dangers of the situation as repeated
entries in his journal show. In the depth of winter, he pointed
out, 'we can hardly look abroad without freezing our Faces,
Hands or Feet, and then lying in for Cure brings on the Scurvy,
and whoever takes to his Bed hardly ever gets abroad again,
but falls into a Looseness which generally carries him off in 8
or 10 days'. The crews, few of whom had any experience of
northern conditions, needed forceful leadership, and above all
leadership by example, if they were to survive; but since the
officers were living at the New Fort the men at the Old Factory
were left to their own devices. Though the two sites were only

five miles apart, the distance was impossible to cover except on snow-shoes. And the fact that intervening higher ground meant that neither set of buildings was visible from the other must also have had a depressing impact on the forgotten men, as they no doubt saw themselves, at the Old Factory.

By mid-January the situation at the Old Factory was so serious that Middleton, belatedly, sent the *Furnace*'s surgeon, Edward Thompson, there. It was Thompson's first recorded visit to the Old Factory, though his three years at the Company's post at Moose River would have given him more knowledge than most of winter conditions. The surgeon returned after four days with six sick men on a sledge; two others had to be left behind because they were too ill to be moved. When Middleton visited the Old Factory, he encouraged the men to go out to collect wood, shoot ptarmigan, and cut holes in the river ice for freshening their salt meat, but there were never enough snow-shoes to go round. By late January the condition of the men was deteriorating fast. Eight or ten were suffering from frost-bite, and another half-dozen were down with scurvy. On his next visit to the Old Factory Thompson had to amputate the toes of those worst affected by frost-bite. It hardly improved matters that Middleton himself was now struck down with what he called 'country distemper' (probably pleurisy) – 'a violent Pain in my breast . . . continued 24 hours in much Pain & Agony, sweating all the time, & great Difficulty of breathing . . . fainted twice'. When he was back on his feet Middleton was greeted with the sight of the Company's men, fit and healthy, coming into the fort for supplies and then returning to their log-tents.

By the beginning of February there were still four men at the Old Factory, ill with scurvy, and a dozen at the fort incapacitated with scurvy, frost-bite or pleurisy. By 11 February only fifteen men at the Old Factory were fit enough to venture outside (out of a total number of about eighty). The fact that some were out and about suggests that a reasonable amount of warm winter clothing had been supplied from the

Company warehouse, though almost certainly it would have been shared on a rotation basis. More sick men were dragged by sledge to the fort, and more deaths occurred, all from scurvy. A near-lethal allocation of alcohol was still being distributed: a daily allowance, half of spruce beer, half of brandy, and in addition sugar and a bottle of brandy once a week to every four men so that they could make punch. As the temperature began to rise (though it was still cold enough to freeze the spirit in Middleton's theodolite), attention turned to the ships, frozen tight in their winter quarters. The carpenters followed the example of the Company men and put up a log-tent at Sloop Cove so that they could live near their work. A meeting of Middleton's council of officers had decided that the alterations to the *Furnace* that had been approved by the Navy Board the previous year should be completed. The most important of these was to fit a false deck over the main deck to bring it level with the quarter deck; this, it was hoped, would prevent heavy seas coming inboard during rough weather. As late as the end of March heavy snowfalls covered everything with a deep layer of fresh snow, and drifts which had been piled up by the wind reached the top of the fort's parapets. Fires were lit on board both ships in an attempt to thaw them out, for the ice was several inches thick even below decks.

By 5 April most of *Furnace*'s crew were back on board, but not surprisingly found the ship 'very Cold'. Now a start could be made at cutting both vessels clear of the ice, so that they could be floated off on the spring tides. How formidable a task this would be was shown by Middleton's journal entry of 7 April in which he noted that the ice in Sloop Cove was ten-foot thick, with another thirteen feet of snow on top. The *Furnace* was covered with ice and snow up to her quarterdeck rails, and 'appears more like a lump of Ice than a Ship'. Middleton himself was still living at the fort, and day-to-day operations at Sloop Cove were supervised by Lieutenant Rankin. While the carpenters worked at constructing the new deck, most of the men were hacking away at the ice around the ships' sides. They were partly sheltered from the driving snow by a sail hung across the bow, but even so could not work in the freezing conditions without spells in front of the fire every hour or so. The smith was kept busy mending damaged pickaxes and shovels, while the cooper repaired casks that would help to float the vessels. That moment seemed a long way off as a succession of high tides flowing around the ships failed to budge them. As the ice from around the vessels was slowly cut away, so the more difficult task of clearing it from beneath the hulls had to be faced. Middleton explained the process: 'Our People continue cutting the Ice under her Bulge [bilge], being oblig'd to lie upon a Board lay'd upon the Ice and Water, and to reach under the Bulge as far as they are able. She's fast froze to the Ground; the Men almost numb'd with the Cold.'

During the winter and well into the spring the co-operation between Middleton and Isham continued. At the beginning of April the *Furnace*'s blacksmith was mending utensils for the fort, while Isham sent Indians to the Old Factory to kill ptarmigan for those of Middleton's men still left there. A Company servant had spent the whole winter twenty-five miles upriver fishing with net and hook under the ice to catch fish for the discovery crews. But now relations between captain and factor began to fray. As the season approached when the inland Indians would come down to the fort with their furs, so Isham became nervous about possible interference with them. Probably at the factor's request, Middleton read an order to his crews forbidding them to trade with the Indians. There were, however, other causes of tension. For Middleton, with his crews weakened by death and sickness, the healthy men of the fort's garrison were tempting replacements. On 19 April John Armount threw in his lot with Middleton and the discovery expedition. He was, Middleton claimed, 'a good Sailor'. Whether this was so or not, he was also one of the three trouble-makers who at Christmas had been flogged by Isham for drunken and violent behaviour. According to Isham, Middleton was trying to lure others from the Company's service, but could get none 'in their right Senses to comply'. This was not to be wondered at as the back-breaking work of cutting the ships free continued – 'late and early' each day, as Middleton put it.

Throughout May all hands were employed in cutting ice from underneath the *Furnace*, often lying full-length to do so; embedding anchors in the frozen ground on each side of the ship to get some purchase; lashing sixty empty casks under the hull. All the efforts to move the heavy hulk of the *Furnace* resulted only in bent anchors, parted cables and shattered blocks. The ship had heeled over to starboard when she had been pulled and pushed into the shallow dock the previous autumn, and her starboard bilge was still frozen to the ground. Even with poleaxes the men had not reached the seven or eight strakes of the hull closest to the keel to cut the ship free. No amount of tugging, levering or cajoling would move the ship; it was, once more, a matter of slow chipping and cutting away of ice that in the deep shadow of the ship's hull would never thaw. And it was work that could only be done when the tide was out. The situation was the more frustrating in that in the distance the ice in mid-river was beginning to break up, although in early June the river banks were still frozen hard. The first goose had been sighted (and shot) on 28 April as the great flights began to pass overhead on their way north, and by the end of May the Indians employed by Middleton about twenty miles upriver had killed five thousand. The men had fresh goose every day, and vast amounts were salted in cask for the voyage ahead. Although there was now fresh meat in plenty, men were still dying from scurvy – one on 24 May, another on 31 May. Almost totally lacking from the diet of the crews were fresh greens. The Company posts farther south had their little gardens to provide vegetables and herbs, but at Churchill the short growing season usually defeated all attempts, though

there are occasional references to dandelions, lettuce and tur-
nips being grown. Middleton recorded the last snow on 12
May, more than eight months after he had recorded the first
snow flurries of winter on 1 September 1741 – and there were
still hard frosts to come.

To compensate for the deaths among his crews, Middleton
continued his efforts to attract men from the Company's service, and finally managed to enlist five for the voyage. Whatever strain this put on relations between him and Isham, in
other ways Middleton was punctilious in protecting the Company's trade – something that would be held against him later.
On 2 June Isham's deputy, Ferdinand Jacobs, was sent on
board the two ships to check that no clandestine trade had
taken place; and this could only have been arranged with
Middleton's consent. An entry in Rankin's journal indicates
that Jacobs, or another Company man, was stationed on board
the ships for the rest of their stay at Churchill.

It was 10 June before the *Furnace* finally inched backwards
out of the dock as the high tide surged in, and another three
days before she floated clear into the river to join the *Discovery*.
It had taken more than ten weeks to cut the ships free, and
the cost had to be reckoned in terms of damage to anchors,
hawsers and other essential parts of the ship's gear, and above
all in terms of the drain on the men's health and vigour. The
awful toil at Sloop Cove had come at the end of a winter
during which ten men had died of scurvy, two more had died
of other causes, and many others were enfeebled or had toes
and fingers amputated after frost-bite. There was some truth
in Dobbs's later accusation: 'It was wintering there that broke
the Spirits of the Men. They had a . . . most miserable slavish
Life.' Today Sloop Cove has all but disappeared as a result of
isostatic lift in Hudson Bay. There is no longer any sign of a
saltwater cove, or of the docks blasted out with such effort
for Middleton's ships – only a summer meadow with a small
freshwater pond, out of reach of even the highest tides. But
the site is immediately recognizable, for the mooring rings

9. Inscription on the rocks at Sloop Cove, Churchill, the wintering place
of the *Furnace* and *Discovery*, 1741–2.
Photograph Provincial Archives of Manitoba.

used by the Company sloops in the eighteenth century are
still there, set into the rock face at the back of the meadow.
And, even more evocative, high on the same rocks are carved
the names of the *Furnace* and the *Discovery*, and the date
'1741' (*Ill.9*).

With the ships at last afloat, all was hustle and bustle as
they were prepared for sea. Topmasts had to be set up, spars
and yards heaved up and rigged, cannon and ballast lifted on
board. Casks of gunpowder and provisions were brought
from the fort with the help of the Company's team of
horses and two sloops. The beer buried for the winter in
the fort's yard was dug out and 'was found hard Froze to a

Lump of Ice in Shape like the Cask'. Huge amounts of geese were brought downriver from the Indian encampment, salted into casks, and taken on board. As the temperature rose, so the insects appeared, an ever-present torment for men who had no protection of mesh or repellent. Insects are rarely mentioned in the post journals, but in his 'Observations' Isham more than made up for the silent stoicism of his colleagues as he described how the swarms of sand flies were so dense that a man could not see his way, while if he was foolish enough to open his mouth he was liable to be choked. But these, he thought, were minor pests compared with the mosquitoes, whose bites could make a man's head swell to the size of a barrel. A bushel of mosquitoes might be swept off a hunter as he emerged from the woods, and they had to be shovelled off the ground before a door could be opened. Years of experience had taught the Company servants to keep inside at certain times – after rain and at dusk – but the discovery crews, mostly novices in the ways of the north, must have suffered grievously from the insects as they worked to get the ships ready.

By now the river was busy with the canoes of the Indians coming down from the interior to trade their furs at the fort – thirty canoes on one day, and fifty on another. Isham was more than ever alert to the possibility of illicit trade between the ships' crews and the canoes. There was contact but no evidence of trade, and the bales of goods put on board the *Furnace* in the Thames by Dobbs's agent remained in the hold. Middleton arranged for two of the Northern or Chipewyan Indians who had come down to trade (Claydiddy and Clayhulla) and for one Home Indian (Pissquatanu) to accompany him on the first part of the voyage along the west coast of Hudson Bay. His understanding was that the first two knew the country as far north as Roe's Welcome, while the Cree spoke both some English and the language of the Northern Indians, and so would be 'of great service to the Main Design'. Middleton agreed with Isham that once he had finished with the Indians' services he would put them ashore within reasonable travelling distance of Churchill.

On 1 July 1742 the two vessels weighed anchor and headed north out of the harbour. Letters by Middleton to Sir Charles Wager and to the Admiralty were left with Isham to send to England on the Company ship later that year. They were carried by Captain Spurrell on the *Sea Horse*, together with the factor's own report of the year to the London Committee of the Hudson's Bay Company. Isham made it clear that he had followed the Committee's instructions carried by Middleton that Company factors should give the discovery expedition the best assistance in their power. This included, he pointed out, allowing the crews to use the Old Factory for shelter, helping with the loading and unloading of the ships, supplying provisions and above all 'wearing Aparel for the men which they Stood greatly in need of'. Everything had been carefully itemised and costed at Bay prices – the total came to £146-3-6. Isham also acknowledged the help given by Middleton, and in particular by his armourer. The fort's armourer had died the previous October, and Middleton's had taken over the essential work of repairing the muskets of the Indians who came down to Churchill. In other ways, Isham complained, the captain 'did not show himself to be a Well wisher to Your Honrs Interest'. His men had cut up the cover of the lime kiln at the Old Factory for firewood, and done other damage. Middleton had threatened Isham when the factor stopped him taking one of the fort's Home Indians on board to flog him. Most irritating of all, with the aid of 'Liquor, fine words and Preferments', he had persuaded five of the Company servants to join his ship. Since the fort garrisons were finely balanced in terms of the ratio between men and jobs, and the economy-conscious London Committee made little allowance in its manning arrangements for possible casualties, this loss of men presented Isham with a serious problem. It was little wonder that he finished his letter home on a plaintive note. 'The Captn etc. has been a Very Troublesome Guess [sic], I Humbly

Desire if any Ships Come again to winter, Your Honrs will please to send a More fuller Order in What manner to Act.'

From Churchill the discovery ships sailed north along the west coast of Hudson Bay until on 9 July, four hundred miles north of Churchill, the west and east shores of Roe's Welcome came into sight. Middleton was taking soundings and measuring the tides, but William Moor admitted that the *Discovery* was so thinly manned that he could not follow suit. Here a field of ice blocked their way, and the ships sailed east across the entrance of the Welcome in an attempt to find clear water. Conditions became increasingly hazardous, and large ice floes hammered against the hulls of the ships as they were pushed by high winds and tides dangerously near the shore of South-ampton Island. When the wind dropped the ships warped and grappled their way from one ice floe to another until they had gained some sea room. Then, under topsails, using ice poles to fend off the floes, at times being towed out of trouble by their boats, they worked their way across the Welcome until a headland was sighted on its western shore in latitude 65°10'N. The ships were now farther north than Scroggs had reached in 1722, and as far as they knew farther north than any other European vessel in these waters. Middleton marked the occasion by naming the headland Cape Dobbs, 'after my worthy friend'. Behind the cape lay an inlet, and the usual council of officers decided that the ships should try to find shelter there. The ice, they pointed out, stretched thirty miles to windward, and was pushing the ships towards the shore. On 13 July, the ships were towed inside the inlet and anchored in a small bay on its northeast shore. They were not a moment too soon, for large ice floes poured in from the Welcome, fouling and cutting cables, damaging anchors and smashing ice poles. Middleton named the providential inlet, strait or

10. CHRISTOPHER MIDDLETON. Section of manuscript chart of his explorations, 1742.
Admiralty Library, Taunton (Vv2, Vol I, p.1)

This chart was the basis of Middleton's engraved 'Chart of Hudson's Bay and Straits', 1743. Repulse Bay at the top of the chart is shown though not named. An important feature of the chart are its arrows indicating the direction of the tides. The arrows show the west coast of Hudson Bay affected by two tidal flows: one coming west from Hudson Strait, the other passing through Frozen Strait and then down Roes Welcome. See also maps on pp.120–1.

river (all three terms were used in the journals) after Sir Charles Wager. He had taken care to name his first two discoveries after his two most important patrons (*Ill. 10*).

As the ships anchored Inuit came on board, but they had little to trade, and for the crews their presence was a disturbing one. When Lieutenant Rankin was sent in one of the ship's boats with nine men and the three Indians to investigate the inlet, Middleton made sure that they were well armed. He named the anchorage Savage Sound. The high sides of the inlet were without tree or bush, but Middleton spotted some scurvy grass and sorrel which his shore party brought back for the sick. As he explained, 'Many of the Men are very ill with their old Distemper, the Scurvy. Those that were on their Recovery when we left Churchill are relaps'd, so that near Half of them are unserviceable.' Those that were fit were issued with ice poles to push away the ice that clattered up and down the inlet with the tides. After four days Middleton found a small cove farther up the sound where the ships could lie clear of the worst of the ice. Rankin returned with disappointing news; the flood tide came from the south (that is from the entrance of the inlet), and none of his three Indians recognised the country. To add to Middleton's problems, great chunks of ice continued to drive into the inlet, soon endangering the vessels even in their sheltered cove. On another boat excursion Rankin managed to get seventy-five miles up the inlet before turning back when he came across three islands in mid-channel and 'saw a Fall or a Fresh to the west Side of them'. A boat trip by Rankin in the other direction to see if the mouth of the inlet was clearing of ice put his crew in great danger as huge pieces of ice tumbled over each other on the flood tide. 'Our boat must have been smashed into a thousand pieces,' Rankin reported, had he not been able to steer it into a bight in a large field of ice.

When Middleton received the lieutenant's report on 27 July he pointed out that with ice driving up and down the inlet, and still packing the Welcome, there was no question of leaving the ships' anchorage; but he added in words that summed up his predicament, 'I hope there is no Time lost by our being in Safety here.' Acutely aware of the limited season for navigation in Hudson Bay, Middleton would have remembered that only four days later than this the previous year he and his council had decided not to proceed on exploration because of the lateness of the season. The sighting of several black whales farther up the inlet revived hopes of a passage or strait nearby, and Rankin together with the master Robert Wilson was sent on yet another boat expedition to check the tides along the shores of the inlet, and in particular to see if there was any opening through which the whales might have come other than the one the ships had entered from the Welcome. Middleton seems not to have been optimistic, and it was with a feeling of resignation that he added, 'This we may do as there is no going out untill the ice is clear in the River & Welcome.'

Since no imminent departure was likely, some of those suffering from scurvy were rowed to an island five miles from the anchorage where there was plenty of scurvy grass (so called because of its antiscorbutic properties) and sorrel. They were left there with tents and provisions, but otherwise without any medical attention. After four days Rankin and Wilson returned with a rather inconclusive report. At their farthest point up the inlet they had gone ashore and from high land once more saw islands to the west and on their far side 'a great Run or Fall of Water'. They sighted black whales, and thought that there was 'a great Probability' of another entrance into the inlet, although they had not found it. In his journal Middleton added two details not included in the report submitted by Rankin and Wilson. At their farthest point west in the inlet the tide flowed only six feet (compared with ten to fifteen feet at the entrance), and water taken up in a bottle there tasted 'barely brackish'. With these depressing observations, and with the ice beginning to clear, there was no point in staying longer in the inlet.

On 4 August the ships cleared the inlet, and turned north along the west coast of the Welcome. For three days they tacked backwards and forwards among loose ice, slowly getting farther north. The tide seemed to be coming from the east by north, and as the Welcome narrowed the tidal surge was so strong that the ships could hardly steer. The ships were now coasting along a low, shingly beach on the east side of the Welcome that reminded Middleton of Dungeness in Kent, but on 6 August they crossed over towards the western shore where a 'fair Cape or Head-land' came into view in the late afternoon sun, with a clear horizon beyond. Here, on the very edge of the Arctic Circle, it seemed to the jubilant crews that the entrance to the passage had been found. In 'Great Joy and Hopes', Middleton named the headland Cape Hope, for it seemed to mark the northernmost tip of the continent. The next morning quickly brought disillusionment, for as the haze cleared the land could be seen closing in on all sides, and 'our Hopes of a Passage that way was all over'. Middleton named the stretch of water Repulse Bay, and followed it to within a few miles of its shoreline where the water shallowed and the tide died away altogether.

Amid the disappointment on board the ships one puzzle remained. Where did the flood tide come from that had whirled the ships about as they headed up the Welcome towards Cape Hope? On 8 August Middleton went ashore with several of his men on an island (White Island) at the northeastern end of the Welcome. They were an odd group in composition – George Axx the gunner, John Hodgson the carpenter, John Wigate the clerk, and one of the Indians. They were picked because they were among the few fit men left on the *Furnace*, and an arduous climb lay ahead. Middleton and his little group scrambled fifteen miles over the high ground of the island until they could look down on the other side where Foxe Channel and Foxe Basin stretched away to the east. They were near the point where in 1615 the ship of William Baffin and Robert Bylot had been forced back, 'thick pestred with ice' after sailing along the northeast shores of Southampton Island. To the north loomed the great mass of Melville Peninsula, while almost at their feet was a channel, full of small islands, about twelve miles across at its narrowest point. The flood tide came running through, but under the ice; for the channel was still frozen from side to side. It could only be named, Middleton decided, Frozen Strait, for even if the old ice broke up in the next few weeks it would be followed so soon by the next winter's new ice that it would never offer a practical navigation for ships.

The council called when Middleton returned was a lugubrious affair. The priority, its members decided, 'was to make the best of our way out of this cold, dangerous and narrow Strait'. As a rider – and a face-saver – it was also decided that on the return down the Welcome they should investigate the 'large Openings, broken Lands and Islands, with strong Tides' that had been seen but not examined along its west coast during the outward voyage. Up to a point this was done, but only from on board ship. Middleton claimed in his journal that the coast from Cape Hope to Brook Cobham (Marble Island) was all mainland, and that he had now seen the bottom of a deep bay in latitude 64°N. spotted on the voyage north. If this was Daly Bay this may well have been so, but he had certainly not noticed the entrance to Chesterfield Inlet that lay slightly to the south. The ships did not drop anchor until they reached Marble Island, where Rankin was sent ashore to test the tides and get water. Unrecorded by Middleton, William Moor on the *Discovery* also sent a boat ashore for water, and its crew returned with the news that they had found 'a great Deal of the Wreck of Captain Barlows Ship and Sloop'. Whatever the men had seen, there was no further investigation; if anything the grim relics would have been a reminder of the dangers of entrapment in an Arctic winter. After a few more inconclusive tidal observations the ships set sail. First, the two Northern Indians were left on the island, with a boat, guns and ammunition, tools and provisions. As guides they had been a disappointment, but they had performed good service for the expedition in hunting caribou, especially during the enforced stay in the Wager, and according to Moor the crews heaped gifts upon them as they rowed ashore. The Cree Indian, 'the linguist', was too far from his own country to be left at Marble Island. Since, according to Middleton, he wanted to see England, he was entered on the ship's books. Middleton concluded his journal entry for 15 August: 'I find I can do no more to the Purpose I am order'd upon, and my Men are Most of them very Much distemper'd, so that by Consultation we find the best Method to bear away for England.' Almost eleven months of wintering at Churchill had been endured to make possible six weeks of exploration. In his journal on the *Discovery* Moor tersely summed up the results of the expedition, 'there is no Passage into the other Ocean between Churchill and the Latitd.67°N.'

The voyage home was mercifully swift. The ships reached the Atlantic exit of Hudson Strait on 26 August, and anchored at Stromness in the Orkneys on 16 September. Because of sickness among the crews, it took another three weeks for the discovery ships to reach the Thames. In letters to Thomas Corbett, Secretary to the Admiralty, Middleton gave vent to his feelings about his crews, as well as paying tribute to his officers and, by inference, to himself.

> No Ship was ever pester'd with such a Set of Rogues, most of them having deserv'd hanging before they entered with me, and not three Seamen among the whole Number of private Men, so that had it not been for the Officers, who, every one of them, work'd like common Men, I should have found no little difficulty to get the Ships to England ... of those Men whom I carry'd out with me, not one third of them were Seamen, that 14 of the very best died in the Country where I winter'd, that it was a small Miracle to preserve the Vessels afterwards upon my Voyage, and bring them safe home, having at that Time not above two Men that could go to the Helm,

above one half being afflicted with the Scurvy in a miserable Manner.

Middleton was accustomed to the volunteer crews of the Company ships, and his strictures on the crew of the *Furnace* were probably too harsh, and sharpened by disappointment. Several of them rallied to his defence when his conduct of the expedition was questioned; but he was right in claiming that for the most part they were not fitted in health or disposition for so demanding a voyage. In the end, it was the Admiralty that must carry much of the responsibility for the low quality and inadequate clothing of Middleton's crews, although it must be said that similar crews were being sent to sea in this wartime period into even more dangerous situations. And Middleton had not proved an ideal commander in the trying conditions of the wintering at Churchill. There is an unedifying contrast between the close attention he paid to his astronomical observations and his apparent reluctance to visit his sick and dying men at the Old Factory just a few miles away. Under the circumstances Middleton's explorations were of high standard. His chart of the expedition's explorations, published in 1743, was the first attempt at an accurate survey of the west coast of Hudson Bay, and was a striking advance on the rough charts of the region produced by earlier voyagers. It included all the main features of the area except – unfortunately for Middleton – Chesterfield Inlet. His surveys seemed to have closed the last significant gap along the western shores of Hudson Bay. As John Lanrick, one of the 'young gentlemen' on the expedition, wrote from the Orkneys, 'There was no such Thing as a Passage into the Western Ocean, as was expected.'

When Middleton's ships reached the Thames in October 1742 Arthur Dobbs was in Ireland, where he had received

Middleton's letters from Churchill and from the Orkneys. His first reaction to Middleton's report of his explorations was one of shared disappointment. 'All the fine Hopes' raised by the observations of Foxe and Scroggs had vanished, he conceded. However, a lingering curiosity about the timing of the tidal flows in the Welcome, and the question of the route followed by the whales sighted there, prompted further queries to Middleton, and Dobbs was clearly not prepared to accept defeat until he had seen the captain's journal and charts. His immediate attention was given to a more alluring prospect that he had been mulling over during the expedition's absence with the aid of copies of Company journals and other documents that Middleton had sent him before the discovery ships sailed. This was 'to open the Trade to the Bay by dissolving the Company'. With the Company's monopoly removed, more enterprising traders would push inland up the rivers that flowed into Hudson Bay until they reached the headwaters of rivers that ran into the Pacific. This would mount a challenge to the French, and push British interests across a huge and previously unknown swathe of the North American continent.

Middleton answered Dobbs's queries as best he could. He countered Dobbs's reliance on an absolute theory of tides by pointing out that 'no Rule can be fixed, where Tides flow into deep Bays, obstructed by Islands or Counter Tides', and he was unmoved by Dobbs's appeal to join in his new project. He would continue to supply Dobbs with any information that was useful to him about the Hudson Bay area, but made it clear that he hoped 'never to venture myself that way again'. He had more pressing matters to occupy his time, for Sir Charles Wager was no longer at the Admiralty and Middleton was without a patron or a command. His observations on the 'Surprizing Effects of Cold' had been read to the Royal Society on 28 October, and had brought him the award of the Society's Copley Gold Medal. This was a fine honour, but did nothing to compensate for the financial loss he had suffered by exchanging employment by the Hudson's Bay Company for His Majesty's service. If he had stayed with the Company, he told Dobbs, he would have earned £1400 (this was a surprisingly large sum which must have included bonuses and other perquisites, and perhaps some imaginative accounting). As a captain in the Navy he had received a mere £160, and suffered damage to his health.

Unperturbed by this, Dobbs wrote again to Middleton in mid-December 1742 once again asking for his support in opening up the interior of Hudson Bay to British traders. Middleton responded by patiently pointing out the fundamental flaws in his scheme. The difficulty lay in a combination of topographical and human characteristics. The rivers draining into Hudson Bay, unlike the great waterways of the St Lawrence and other river systems that the French were following farther south, were so shallow and obstructed that they could float only two-man canoes, and even these had to be portaged much of the time. Less than half a dozen servants at the Company posts were capable of handling canoes, and there was no equivalent among them of the enterprising French *coureurs de bois* who were pushing far into the interior. Rather, the massive stone fortress at Churchill exemplified the static mentality of British trading operations in the Canadian north. This letter was, in professional terms, Middleton's death warrant, for it dashed to the ground Dobbs's visionary plans of canoe routes from the shores of Hudson Bay that would take British traders, if not to the Pacific, at least to within easy reach of the great ocean.

Before Dobbs received this discouraging reply, he had studied Middleton's journal, which he had received in December, and wrote to him on 22 January with surprising news: 'You have made a much greater Progress in the Discovery of the Passage, than you imagined when there ... I really think that you have prov'd the Passage, tho' you were not at once able to perfect it ... I think I may congratulate you upon your having found the so-much-wish'd for Passage.' Quite simply, the Wager was not a river but a strait, and if

Middleton had continued farther up he would have met the
flood tide rushing in from the western ocean in the same way
that ships entering the Strait of Magellan from the Atlantic
met the tide from the Pacific when they were halfway through.
Middleton's entrance into the Wager was narrow and choked
with ice, whereas if he had made a proper search of the 'broken
lands' farther south he would have found a larger and easier
entrance. It was a weary and irritated Middleton who tried
to respond to this suggestion, breathtaking in its patronising
implication that Dobbs from his desk in Dublin could discern
straits and channels in Hudson Bay that had somehow escaped
Middleton's notice. He could not persuade the Hudson's Bay
Company to pay the wages due to the men at Churchill who
had joined the *Furnace*; it also owed him money, he grumbled;
and all in all he was beset with 'many other Things which
have been very fatiguing'.

Within a few days Dobbs's claim that Middleton had
unknowingly discovered the Northwest Passage turned into
something more ominous when he asserted that he had
received from London a warning letter. Dated 21 January
1743, it was written in an inflated and elaborate style.

> SIR,
> This Script is only to open your Eyes, which have been
> sealed or closed with too much (we can't say Cunning)
> Artifice, so that they have not been able to discover our
> Discoverer's Pranks.
>
> All Nature cries aloud there is a Passage, and we are sure
> there is one from Hudson's Bay to Japan. Send a Letter
> directed to Messrs. Brook and Cobham, who are Gentle-
> men that have been the Voyage, and cannot bear so glori-
> ous an Attempt should die under the Hands of mercenary
> Wretches, and they will give you such pungent Reasons
> as perhaps will awake all your Industry. They desire it
> may be kept secret as long as they shall think fit. They
> are willing to venture their Lives, their Fortunes, their

All, in another Attempt; and they are no inconsiderable
Persons, but such as have had it much at Heart ever since
they saw the Rapidity of the Tides in the Welcome. The
frozen Streights is all Chimera, and every Thing you have
ever read or seen concerning that Part of our Voyage. We
shall send you some unanswerable Queries.

Direct for us at the Chapter Coffee House, St Paul's
Church-yard.

A second letter accused Middleton of deliberately concealing
the existence of a passage through the Wager, and of first
ignoring the advice of the Indians he had with him, and then
of sacrificing them. Its postscript added, 'Direct for us as
before. Fox was an honest man.'

If Dobbs's version of events is to be believed, in his effort
to discover the truth he went to London in the early spring
to meet the mysterious 'Brook and Cobham' (pseudonyms
taken from Foxe's name for the island in Hudson Bay later
known as Marble Island). They were revealed as Edward
Thompson, surgeon of the *Furnace*, and John Wigate the clerk,
who Dobbs said convinced him that Middleton had falsified
his journal and chart. It was perhaps of some significance in
this sorry business that Middleton and Wigate had clearly
quarrelled, for the Admiralty records show that as late as July
1743 Wigate had received no pay for the voyage because
Middleton refused to sign the necessary certificate. It was a
remarkable coincidence that three months after the return of
the expedition, Dobbs in Ireland and two members of Middleton's crew in London were simultaneously seized with doubts
about its explorations. It would have come as no surprise to
Middleton to learn in April that there was a 'close Design'
against him by Dobbs, Thompson and Wigate, joined by Lieutenant John Rankin. This last was a serious defection. Not
only was Rankin an officer, whose testimony would carry more
weight than that of the surgeon and the clerk, but only a few
weeks earlier Middleton had come to Rankin's defence after

hearing that no less a personage than the First Lord of the Admiralty, the Earl of Winchilsea, suspected the lieutenant of being drunk in his presence. For a junior officer Rankin seems to have moved in high circles, for his explanation of any unsteadiness was that he had been dining with the Duke of Portland, a Whig grandee of the period (though his main claim to fame was that he was considered 'the handsomest man in England'). In return for Middleton's support, Rankin wrote Middleton on 12 February an effusive if mis-spelt note that is still among the Admiralty records, thanking him for 'giving me a good Carrectir', and adding, 'I shall for Ever Think My Self bound to pray for your good Health, and Prosperity, If ever it should be in my pour to serve you by Night or Day.' That same month Rankin was posted to a ship under the command of Captain George Gosling who later wrote to Middleton that Rankin had assured him that everything possible had been done towards making the discovery, but that there was no Northwest Passage.

The Admiralty responded with unusual promptness to Dobbs's expressions of concern. His acquaintanceship with Winchilsea may have helped, although his main supporter on the Board of Admiralty seems to have been John Cockburn, one of the Lords Commissioners from 1742 to 1744. On 2 May, Dobbs appeared before the Board of Admiralty, and presented it with a formidable list of queries or 'Objections' about the voyage. Four members of the expedition – Rankin, Wilson, Thompson and Wigate – were then called in turn before the Board, were read the queries, and asked to give their replies in writing. Later in the month the Admiralty warned Middleton that it considered the affair to be 'of a very serious Nature', and demanded that he give 'a very particular and clear Answer to the several Points of Misconduct, with which you are charged'. Middleton's response took the form of a 150-page manuscript delivered to the Admiralty in July 1743, and published by him later in the year as part of his *Vindication*. It marked the beginning of a two-year pamphlet war which filled twelve hundred pages of eight books published between 1743 and 1745.

Long before the end, the charges and counter-charges had become confused and repetitive as the exchanges developed their own momentum, generating much heat but little light. In the best traditions of pamphlet warfare, as the subject-matter of the publications became thinner so their titles lengthened. In 1744 Dobbs published his *Remarks upon Capt. Middleton's Defence: wherein His Conduct during the late Voyage For discovering a Passage from Hudson's Bay to the South-Sea is impartially Examin'd; His Neglect and Omissions in that Affair fully Prov'd; The Falsities and Evasions in his Defence Expos'd; The Errors of his Charts laid open, and His Accounts of Currents, Streights, and Rivers, Confuted; Whereby it will appear, with the highest Probability, That there is such a Passage as he went in search of*. Not to be outdone, Middleton replied with an awesome counter-blast of his own: *A Rejoinder to Mr. Dobbs's Reply to Captain Middleton; In which is expos'd, Both his Jesuitical Prevarications, Evasions, Falsities, and false Reasoning; his avoiding taking Notice of Facts, formerly deducted and charged upon him as Inventions of him or his Witnesses; the Character of the latter, and the present Views of the former, which give rise to the present Dispute. In a Word, An unparalleled Disingenuity, and (and to make use of a Verodobbsical Flowering of Rhetoric) a Glaring Impudence, are set in a fair Light*. Although *Remarks, Replies* and *Rejoinders* tumbled off the presses in quick succession, it is unlikely that the Board of Admiralty paid further attention to them once Middleton had dealt with Dobbs's original charges in his *Vindication*. It was at this time that the first survivors from the ill-fated *Wager* of Anson's squadron straggled back to England with desperate stories of shipwreck, murder and mutiny. Among them was John Bulkeley, gunner of the *Wager* and one of the ringleaders in the disorder that followed the vessel's loss. He sent his journal of events to the Earl of Winchilsea at the Admiralty, only to have it returned on the grounds that it was 'too large ever to be perused'.

A few nuggets of information can be prised out of the later pamphlets, but the main points of dispute are clear to see in the accusations levelled at Middleton in 1743 and in his replies. Dobbs attacked Middleton on grounds both of incompetence and dishonesty. The captain, he claimed, had misinterpreted tidal observations, not realised the significance of the sightings of whales on the west coast of Hudson Bay, failed to follow the Wager to its end, and neglected to examine the broken coast between Cape Dobbs and Brook Cobham. Some of this might be attributed to Middleton's ineptitude, but he had also invented an imaginary Frozen Strait to explain the tidal flows in the Welcome, falsified reports and journals, and not only ignored the advice of the Northern Indians on board but deliberately landed them on a desolate island in the territory of their Eskimo enemies in an effort to silence them. Thompson's attempt to build up a vocabulary of Northern Indian words had been brought to an abrupt end when Middleton confiscated his papers, and threatened to cut off his ears if he was found talking to the Indians again. He had exaggerated the ill health of the crew in order to find an excuse for returning home early, and had kept his officers in the dark about his intentions, threatening to 'cane the Lieutenant, broomstick the Master, and lash all the others'. This behaviour, Dobbs concluded, could only be explained by Middleton's continuing links with the Hudson's Bay Company, which had offered him £5,000 either to abandon the voyage or to search for a Northwest Passage elsewhere.

This last accusation reveals the real point of the campaign against Middleton, hinted at in Dobbs's letter of 22 January in which he told Middleton that if it was agreed that a passage might yet be found, this would be 'a great Inducement to open the Trade to the Bay'. The Northwest Passage had become part of a wider scheme to abolish the monopoly of the Hudson's Bay Company and expand trade well beyond the Bay. Middleton's refusal to accept that a navigable passage existed led directly to the attack on him, for in seeking official and mercantile support for his new plans Dobbs would be faced with considerable scepticism after the failure of the recent expedition to find a passage in the place he had confidently predicted. To shift the blame to Middleton and the Company would clear his own reputation, and open the way for a second expedition to the Bay, this time under a commander less scrupulous of the Company's interests than Middleton.

Dobbs's case was supported by four main witnesses: Thompson and Wigate, Rankin and William Moor. This last defection was a demoralising blow to Middleton, for he had not only taken Moor into the Company's service, but had brought him up 'as my Child, from the Age of 12 or 14'. The four men repeated their charges in published statements, in affidavits, and in evidence given before committees of enquiry; yet unless we accept the authenticity of the pseudonymous letters there is no evidence that any of them held these critical opinions on the handling of the expedition before Dobbs's arrival in London in the spring of 1743. The letters from 'Brook and Cobham' need one further mention before they disappear into deserved obscurity. The first was dated 21 January 1743, and gave Dobbs 'the first Hint of the Captain's Roguery', yet he made no mention of it in his correspondence with the Admiralty later that spring. Middleton was almost certainly right when he referred to the letter as 'a Shaft out of Mr. Dobbs's own Quiver' – a fraudulent invention by his opponent. Rankin's journal, which mysteriously disappeared when Middleton wanted to borrow it during the controversy, confirms the captain's account of the voyage. Moor's log, sparse though it is, contains no hint of disagreement with the handling of the expedition, and in letters to Middleton in April and May 1743 he was scornful of the insistence of Thompson, Wigate and Rankin that there was a passage. Rankin with his 'Cock-and-Bull Story' was 'an Old Woman', while he could only think that 'the Doctor and Wygate ... intend to make what Disturbance they can imagine'. When the deplorable Moor next expressed an opinion on the voyage, it was Rankin's earlier 'Cock-and-Bull Story' about a passage that he solemnly repeated.

George Axx, gunner on the *Furnace*, became a key witness because he had been one of the shore party that on 8 August 1742 had climbed the high ground on White Island and had looked down on the Frozen Strait. In April 1743 Axx was said to have written to Wigate denying the existence of such a strait and enclosing a rough chart that showed the northern end of the Welcome as land-locked. If this were so, then the tide flowing down the Welcome must come through some other channel to the west, probably from the Pacific. Dobbs printed both the letter and the chart, but Middleton retaliated by publishing a denial of authorship by Axx, and in *Forgery Detected* included a sketch of the Frozen Strait drawn by John Hodgson, carpenter of the *Furnace*. Although he was also a member of the shore party of 8 August, it is doubtful whether Hodgson managed this without prompting by his former captain. It is little wonder that the forthright William Coats described the pamphlet exchanges between Middleton and Dobbs as producing only 'an abundance of rubbage and impertinence'.

The rival charts published by Middleton and Wigate are the best guides to the differing interpretations of the discoveries. Middleton's was based on the manuscript chart (*Ill. 10*) he delivered to the Admiralty after his return, and published in 1743. It shows an unbroken coastline north from Churchill, the Wager as a river, and to the north the tide flowing through Frozen Strait down the west coast of the Bay. Wigate published his rival version in 1746. Much of it was based on Middleton's chart, but with some significant differences. It shows the Wager as a strait open to the southwest, has no opening to the north where Middleton placed Frozen Strait, and indicates the tide flowing east and northeast out of the Wager and the other inlets. Wigate added names to two of these inlets, presumably to give them added verisimilitude. 'Lovegrove's Opening' was named after a crew member of the Company's sloop at Churchill that had traded with the Inuit at Whale Cove. On one of these voyages, Lovegrove was supposed to have told Middleton's men at Churchill, he went ashore and 'saw an open Sea Westward of it'. A little farther north 'Rankin's Inlet' was allegedly sighted by the lieutenant on 12 August 1742 when he was on Marble Island. There was, he stated later, a strong tide flowing out of the inlet, but Middleton refused him leave to investigate it.

On all but one of these disputed points Middleton was correct. The discovery expedition of Moor and Smith in 1747 found the Wager to be a closed inlet, while in 1821 Captain William Edward Parry of the Royal Navy took his ships *Fury* and *Hecla* to the Frozen Strait and Repulse Bay almost eighty years after Middleton had turned back there. Coming into Frozen Strait from the east, along Foxe Channel, Parry was able to get his ships through to Repulse Bay, but he found no difficulty in believing that at the time of Middleton's visit the strait was thick with ice. He added that 'our subsequent experience has not left the smallest doubt of Repulse Bay and the northern part of the Welcome being filled by a rapid tide flowing into it from the eastward through Frozen Strait'. Any lingering doubt about the reality of Middleton's Frozen Strait was dispelled by the fate of the next naval expedition to reach the area, Captain George Back in the *Terror* in 1836. His instructions were to follow Parry's route through Frozen Strait and into Repulse Bay, but as he worked his way through Foxe Channel in late August he encountered 'an apparently solid sea of ice', in parts eighteen feet high. By September the *Terror* was frozen in near Cape Comfort at the eastern entrance of Frozen Strait. Held by the ice as 'in the grasp of a giant', Back wrote, 'the ship creaked as it were in agony', and was saved only by being lifted by floes two feet out of the water and onto the main ice-field. It was the following summer before the *Terror* struggled clear of the ice and in a shattered condition made its way back to England.

Middleton's one error was to keep alive hopes of a passage

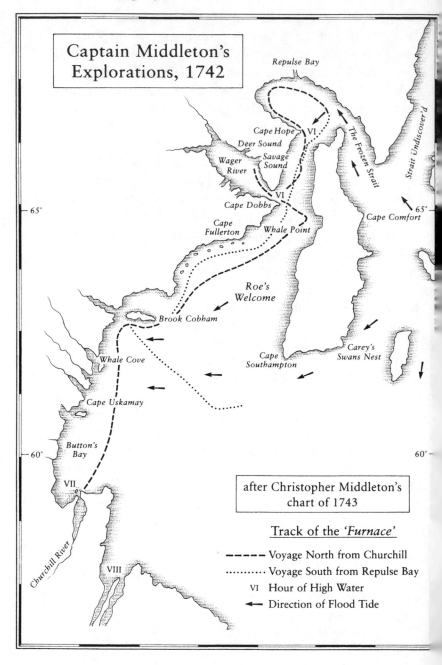

Captain Middleton's
Explorations, 1742

Repulse Bay

Cape Hope VI
Deer Sound
Savage
Wager Sound
River VI
Cape Dobbs
Cape Whale Point
Fullerton

The Frozen Strait

Strait Undiscover'd

—65°   65°—
Cape Comfort

Roe's
Welcome

Brook Cobham

Whale Cove

Cape Uskamay

Cape
Southampton

Carey's
Swans Nest

Button's
Bay
—60°   60°—
VII

Churchill River

VIII

after Christopher Middleton's
chart of 1743

Track of the '*Furnace*'

— — — — Voyage North from Churchill
·············· Voyage South from Repulse Bay
VI Hour of High Water
◄— Direction of Flood Tide

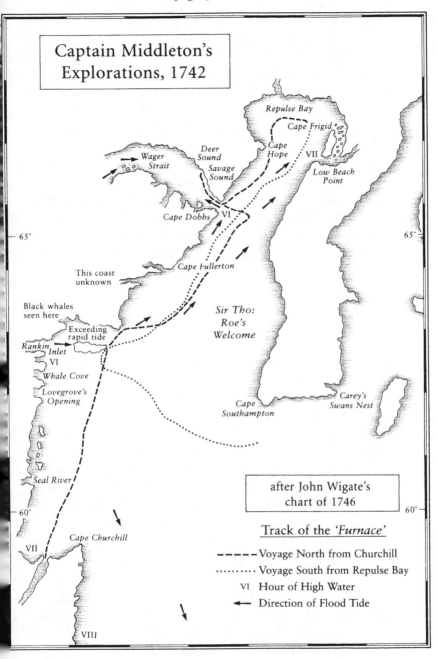

Captain Middleton's
Explorations, 1742

Repulse Bay

Cape Frigid

Deer
Sound
Savage
Sound

Cape
Hope

VII

Low Beach
Point

Wager
Strait

65°

65°

Cape Dobbs

VI

This coast
unknown

Cape Fullerton

Black whales
seen here

Sir Tho:
Roe's
Welcome

Exceeding
rapid tide

Rankin Inlet

VI

Whale Cove

Lovegrove's
Opening

Carey's
Swans Nest

Cape
Southampton

Seal River

after John Wigate's
chart of 1746

60°

60°

Cape Churchill

Track of the *'Furnace'*

VII

- - - - - Voyage North from Churchill

·········· Voyage South from Repulse Bay

VI   Hour of High Water

←   Direction of Flood Tide

VIII

through Hudson Bay. Despite his assertions to the contrary, on his return leg he had not sailed near enough the coast of Hudson Bay south of the Wager to have made a close examination, and so had missed the entrance of Chesterfield Inlet near latitude 64°N. His lapse, if such it was (Middleton's instructions ordered him to look for a passage *north* of latitude 65°N.) was understandable, and he expressed his feelings on a landlubber's criticism with some asperity. 'Could the very knowing Mr.Dobbs imagine that the Ship was to coast a shore, where Land is as high as that over Torbay or above Plymouth, in the manner Boats do, at half a Mile Distance, especially with a Wind, most part of the time, two or more Points on the Shore, and a Tender which was a bad Sailer?' With his crews discouraged and sickly, Middleton had made only a perfunctory examination of the broken coast between Cape Dobbs and Brook Cobham. After the disappointments of the Wager and Repulse Bay, the main desire of all concerned was to finish the work of discovery and return to England. There is no reason to doubt Robert Wilson's description of the crew's reaction: when the 'poor scorbutic Creatures heard it was agreed to return from the Frozen Strait, they were overjoy'd, and ready to leap out of their Skins, as the Saying is'.

The testimony of the three main witnesses produced by Dobbs, together with several petty officers and crew members who also gave evidence against Middleton, was wrong on almost all counts. The most likely explanation of their willingness to swear false statements is that they were rewarded for them. Money was not necessarily involved. Middleton maintained that the hostile witnesses were promised posts of one kind or another, and it is significant that William Moor commanded Dobbs's privately-financed expedition to Hudson Bay in 1746. It is a sign of the unscrupulous way in which the campaign against Middleton was conducted that Moor, in a letter written to Dobbs and intended for publication, insisted 'I have no future Views of a Command,' although Dobbs had already told Judge Ward that Moor would command the proposed private expedition to Hudson Bay, as he was 'very sober and carefull and will also be an Adventurer [investor] himself'. Thompson, perhaps the most virulent of the witnesses against Middleton, sailed on the same expedition as surgeon and member of the Council. Rankin, on the other hand, played no part in Dobbs's plans, perhaps because his evidence before the Admiralty enquiry in the summer of 1743 had in the end been far from helpful to Dobbs. It was a crucial part of the case against Middleton that when he sent Rankin and Wilson on their last boat trip in the Wager on 27 July 1742 he instructed them to go no farther than Deer Sound. Middleton claimed that this was a mistake by his clerk (Wigate) in writing out the orders, and that as the boat was pulling away he told Rankin to go as far as he could without delaying the departure of the ships a few days later. Set against the evidence of the written order signed by Middleton, this would not have appeared a very convincing rebuttal were it not that Rankin acknowledged in his statement to the Admiralty that his captain 'verbally consented that I might run up the River or Strait, as far as I could conveniently do, without retarding the Ships from sailing out of the River'.

Middleton produced no fewer than fifteen witnesses from the discovery crews to resist the attack on his reputation, together with a rather unexpected letter of support from James Isham who referred to Thompson and Wigate as 'those two base Men'. Robert Wilson, master of the *Furnace*, was his most steadfast ally. It is doubtful if the way in which Middleton obtained some of the affidavits he later printed would bear close examination. Some show a suspicious similarity of wording, while others demonstrate remarkable feats of memory by witnesses on points of detail. None of this alters the fact that a considerable group from the discovery crews was willing to stand by Middleton at a time when he must have seemed to them to be under attack by those in authority. Wilson's recollection of Middleton's helpfulness to members of his crew as he showed them how to take astronomical observations or keep a ship's log fits with what we know about him during his years with the Company, and would have assisted him now. Dobbs accused him of using his influence to procure advancement for his witnesses, but far from helping others Middleton could do little for himself. He was not offered a command after the Admiralty dropped its inquiries in 1743 about his handling of the discovery expedition, even though the country was at war and there was a shortage of capable officers. The drawn-out pamphlet war between Middleton and Dobbs did his cause no good since it continued to link his name with accusations of incompetence and bribery, and in a generally unsuccessful war the Navy had enough bad publicity without employing an officer with a shadow hanging over him.

At the beginning of 1745 Middleton petitioned the Admiralty in an effort to bring the seemingly endless exchanges between himself and Dobbs to an end. He asked that he be put on trial and 'either punished with Infamy, or honourably acquitted'. The Admiralty's response was to ask Dobbs whether he wished to proceed with a private prosecution against Middleton, an invitation which Dobbs declined in a long letter in which he explained that certain key witnesses were abroad, and that in any case he had never intended to bring criminal charges against Middleton at his own expense. On the other hand, if the Admiralty would order a court-martial on Middleton, he would be delighted to give evidence. This prevaricating reply was treated with the contempt that it deserved: on the margin of Dobbs's letter the Secretary to the Admiralty scribbled a laconic 'nothing done upon'. It was now ready to re-employ Middleton, and in June 1745 he was appointed to the *Shark* sloop. It was not much of a command, hardly the 'Ship of Force' for which Middleton had longed, but the captain was in no position to object, and within weeks he was at sea once more.

4

The Maritime Philosopher's Stone

'Whereas the discovering a north west passage through
Hudson's Streights, to the western American ocean, will
be of great benefit and advantage to the trade of this kingdom: and whereas it will be a great encouragement to
adventurers to attempt the same, if a publick reward was
given to such person or persons as shall make a perfect
discovery of the said passage: may it therefore please your
most excellent Majesty that it may be enacted.'

Act of Parliament: CAP.XVII (1745)

THROUGHOUT 1744 AND 1745 Dobbs was busy preparing the ground for a further discovery voyage to Hudson
Bay. Unlike the naval expedition commanded by Middleton,
the new venture was likely to be a private one, whose fitting out
and financing would need all Dobbs's powers of persuasion. In
these terms at least, he was not found lacking. Dobbs's numerous political and mercantile contacts were brought into play
as in March 1744 he petitioned the Privy Council to provide
two ships for a fresh attempt to discover the Northwest Passage, 'which is so near being brought to perfection'. If naval
vessels could not be spared, then Dobbs hoped that an official
reward might be offered to those who would make the discovery at their own expense.

The timing was unfortunate, for a few days before the
petition was referred to the Admiralty the long-expected war
with France broke out and, as Dobbs admitted, 'is likely to
disconcert all my Scheme'. Discussions with the Earl of Winchilsea confirmed the Admiralty's reluctance to become

involved, and Dobbs turned to the alternative possibility of a Parliamentary reward for the discovery of a passage. He hoped that Parliament might set £10,000 as the sum to be offered, and busied himself working out the details, which were revealed to Judge Ward in Dublin. To buy and fit out a ship and a sloop would cost between £2000 and £2400, Dobbs estimated. This amount he proposed to raise with the help of fifteen associates in London and Ireland who would each hold one-sixteenth of a share in the venture. William Moor would command the expedition, and Edward Thompson and John Wigate would also go. If the passage was found, then the crews would be paid double wages, and the officers given a share in the reward. At most the total cost would be £4000, leaving £6000 of the reward to be distributed among the investors, together with any profits from trade on the voyage. In a final burst of optimism, Dobbs concluded that 'it cant be calld a Lottery except from the dangers of the Sea there being almost a Certainty of all the Tickets being Prizes.' At this stage Dobbs was brought back to earth by a double setback. Some of his merchant associates who were prepared to invest in the enterprise warned that it was too late to think of buying and fitting out ships to leave for Hudson Bay that year. The same message came from a meeting that Dobbs had with Walpole's successor as first minister, Henry Pelham. He was well disposed towards the scheme, Dobbs reported, but advised that any application to Parliament should be left until the following year.

If 1744 was in some ways a disappointing year for Dobbs, at least it saw the publication of two books by him. The first was his *Remarks upon Capt. Middleton's Defence*, in which he summed up his case against the captain. The second, in March 1744, was a more far-ranging work. His *Account of the Countries adjoining to Hudson's Bay*, dedicated to the King and distributed by Dobbs 'among all our Grandees', formed an integral part of his design to open the trade of Hudson Bay and its hinterland. He had been working on it during the time that the *Furnace* and *Discovery* had been away, and ironically he owed much of its information to the copies of Company records sent to him by Middleton before sailing on his discovery voyage. Its publication marked the beginning of a campaign against the Hudson's Bay Company and its monopolistic rights, and the Northwest Passage was one of the weapons used in that attack. 'By the unaccountable Behaviour of the Hudson's Bay Company', Dobbs wrote, 'the Government and Parliament have a just and legal Right to lay open the Trade to all the Merchants in Britain.' Much that the Company had kept secret over the years was now revealed. Its charter was printed, and its vast geographical grant was contrasted with the Company's few footholds along the shores of Hudson Bay. Dobbs envisaged not only an expansion of trade but also of settlement, for he accused the Company of representing the climate as much harsher than it actually was. He dismissed Middleton's account of the bleak winter at Churchill with the words, 'I should suppose this more severe than usual, or wrote with a View to serve the Company, by setting it forth in its worst Colours.' For the first time the Company's closely-guarded standard of trade with its Indian suppliers appeared in print, and allowed Dobbs to claim that the Company made a huge 2000% profit. The expansion of French exploration and trade to the south and west of Hudson Bay was described in alarmist terms as Dobbs argued that a change in British policy was long overdue, and that the trade should be thrown open to the enterprise of private merchants.

Dobbs's reading of those French works of the period which described Indian reports of great rivers and straits leading to the western ocean increased his fears that the French would sniff out his own plans for reaching the Pacific, or perhaps anticipate him by discovering a more southerly route to the great ocean. How much Dobbs knew about the activities of the French explorers in Canada at this time is not certain, but his continuing warnings to Walpole, Newcastle and other ministers about the importance of the struggle between Britain and France for the great central plain of North America revealed his fear that the enterprising French would restrict English traders and settlers to the coastal fringes of the continent. In the same year that Dobbs's *Account* was issued, the first general history of French Canada was published in Paris by Father Charlevoix, who had spent many years as a Jesuit missionary in the country. Charlevoix had long been a supporter of the idea that to the west lay a great inland sea (the Mer de l'Ouest first propounded by Guillaume Delisle), connected both to the Pacific and to the Northwest Passage. Jacques Nicolas Bellin, the official French cartographer who supplied the maps for Charlevoix's history, added a memoir in which he estimated that the Pacific lay only three hundred leagues west of Lake Superior. French fur traders or *coureurs de bois* followed the river routes west from the St Lawrence and the Great Lakes in search of the great waters that their Indian informants reported lay just over the western horizon; and by the 1740s the Sieur de la Vérendrye and his explorer-sons had established posts far to the west on Lake Winnipeg and the Lower Saskatchewan River. These lay across the Indian canoe routes down to Hudson Bay, and posed a growing threat to the Company's trade at York and its other Bayside posts. To Dobbs this twin-pronged French effort to dominate the northern fur trade and to find a river-and-lake route to the Pacific threatened all his hopes, and confirmed his belief that the complacent management of the Hudson's Bay Company should be replaced by a more dynamic syndicate.

Dobbs's anxieties about the French challenge were increased by the knowledge he had recently picked up about the wanderings southwest of Hudson Bay of Joseph La France, a much-travelled *coureur de bois*, who had worked his way from the Great Lakes into the Winnipeg basin and then doubled back along the Nelson River to York Factory, where he arrived in 1742. From York he sailed to England on a Company ship, and at Dobbs's instigation was retained by the Admiralty 'on a Prospect of his being of Service in the Discovery of a North-West Passage'. Viewed through Company eyes, the *coureurs de bois* were disreputable but intimidating figures, living off the land, and travelling vast distances with their Indian companions. The French traders were everything, it seemed, that their British counterparts on the shores on Hudson Bay were not. In London La France met Dobbs, and gave him a description of his travels across and along the Indian trade routes leading down to the English posts on the Bay. He followed this with a report of the alleged journey of one of the Home Indians at York Factory with thirty companions all the way across the continent to the Pacific coast, where huge tides rose and fell, and black whales spouted far out to sea. There is no reason to doubt the existence of this Cree informant – there is a later reference in the Company records to him, now 'antient', at York – nor that he might have travelled inland. But as told by La France, or reported by Dobbs, the story of the band's two-year odyssey was sheer fantasy. It included, inevitably, a great strait along a distant coast that 'lay almost East and West; for he said the Sun rose upon his Right-hand, and at Noon it was almost behind him, as he passed the Streight, and always set in the Sea'.

Like many informants, La France was not averse to giving satisfaction for moneys received, and he helped Dobbs to construct a 'New Map of Part of North America' (*Ill. 11*). A merchant, William Bowman, described the rather odd process. He and Dobbs met La France in the dining room of the Golden Fleece in New Bond Street, London, and 'on the floor we chalkt out this map, till he was satisfied it corresponded to the Idea of his Travels'. In the map as it appeared in Dobbs's *Account*, La France's route was set in the wider context of Anglo-French rivalry in North America. The French thrust from the Great Lakes towards the Pacific is shown, though farther south Dobbs introduced those discredited figments of the imagination, the Long River and Lake Tagulauk, which had appeared in Baron de Lahontan's popular but partly-fictitious *New Voyages* at the beginning of the century. La France's river trail from Lake Winnipeg (Ounipique) down to

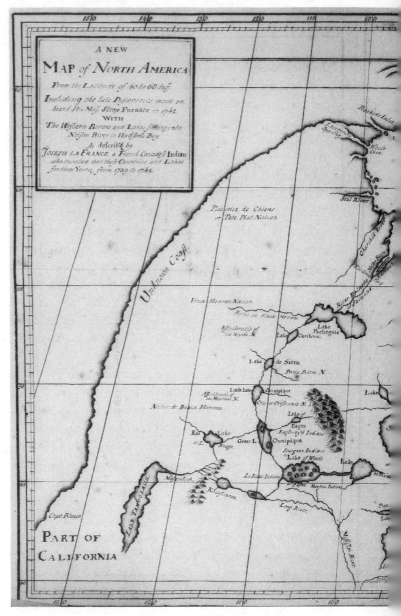

11. ARTHUR DOBBS. 'A New Map of North America'
British Library

The manuscript original of the map engraved for Dobbs's *Account of the Countries adjoining to Hudson's Bay* (1744).

York is marked, although in distorted form. But the most striking feature of the map is the way in which Dobbs shows the Californian coast north of Cape Blanco swinging northeast to connect in some rather indistinct way with openings on the northwest coast of Hudson Bay. With this map before them readers could see at a glance the importance of Dobbs's new discovery expedition to find a passage and of his plans for inland expansion.

Dobbs had more ammunition in his locker, if of lesser calibre. Belief in the existence of a Northwest Passage had long been buttressed by reports of navigators who claimed that they had sailed through the passage. In his original Memorial Dobbs had introduced one of the most intriguing of these reports, the voyage of Juan de Fuca as printed by Samuel Purchas in his collection of voyages of 1625 (see pp.413–16). The account had been passed on to Purchas by the English merchant and promoter Michael Lok, who in the 1570s had been the promoter of Martin Frobisher's voyages to the Arctic. In 1596 Lok met in Venice an old Greek pilot, Apostolos Valerianos, who under his Spanish name of Juan de Fuca had spent forty years in the service of Spain in the West Indies and the South Sea. Fuca related an intriguing story to Lok. In 1592 the Viceroy of New Spain had sent him north from Acapulco with two small vessels to investigate the coast beyond California for signs of the Northwest Passage that the English were known to be seeking. Between latitude 47°N. and 48°N., as the land trended northeast, Fuca discovered a huge inlet. It was thirty or forty leagues wide at its entrance, and its northern shore was marked with 'an exceeding high Pinacle, or spired Rocke, like a piller'. Fuca followed the inlet into a sea with rich countries on its shores. After sailing for more than twenty days he decided that he had now reached 'the North Sea' (Atlantic) and that it was time to return to report his discovery.

It is still uncertain whether Fuca's story, however distorted it may have been in the telling, had any basis in fact. In the

years after the raids of Drake and Cavendish in the South
Sea the Spanish authorities in New Spain were undoubtedly
nervous about the coast to the north, and records show that
a Greek-born pilot had served in Mexico between 1588 and
1594, and that he had met Lok in Italy. The discovery on the
northwest coast of America in the late eighteenth century of
an opening near the latitude of the strait that Fuca claimed to
have entered revived speculation that his account was true,
and for the last two hundred years the Strait of Juan de Fuca
has appeared on the maps straddling the border between the
USA and Canada. It is not impossible that Fuca made a voyage
out of Acapulco, but there is no archival record of a discovery
expedition in 1592, with or without Fuca on board, which
sailed as far north as latitude 48°N. The farthest north that
any Spanish vessel reached in this period was latitude 43°N.,
and that was not until 1603. Nor does Fuca's description of
the strait, and of the countries, 'rich of gold, Silver, Pearle,
and other things', that lay only a few days' sailing beyond
correspond to the reality. Whether the story printed by
Purchas was concocted by Lok, or whether the merchant was
himself beguiled by a hard-luck story by the old pilot, has
never been determined. Dobbs devoted only a page of his
Memorial to the story, and although he commented 'if we may
. . . give Credit to the Account . . . it will absolutely confirm
there being a Passage', he did not place any great emphasis
on it. Observations taken from the journals of known explorers
such as Foxe furnished the main part of his argument, and
clearly he did not feel in need of help from tales of dubious
authenticity.

By the time he published his *Account of Hudson's Bay* in
1744 Dobbs had found another contender for the first discoverer of the Northwest Passage. Included in the book as
'farther Proof' of the passage was the account of an extraordinary voyage said to have been made by a Spanish admiral,
Bartholomew de Fonte, in 1640 (see pp.417–22). Sailing more
than five thousand miles north from Lima, passing the coasts

of Mexico and California, Fonte's ships reached the northwest coast of America. In latitude 53°N. – ten degrees farther north than the Spanish landfall of 1603 – they discovered the entrance of a river which Fonte named Los Reyes, which took them into a network of waterways leading far inland. Sailing eastward through the Sea of Ronquillo, Fonte came across a Boston fur-trading vessel, commanded by one Captain Shapley. The two men exchanged compliments and gifts before Fonte returned to the Pacific coast, which he reached on 5 September. Meanwhile, one of his captains, Pedro de Barnarda, had investigated the regions farther north, and reported that Davis Strait was frozen solid in latitude 80°N. To Dobbs the encounter in mid-continent of the Spanish and New England ships made it 'plain that there is a navigable Passage from Hudson's Bay to California', although the account concluded that 'there was no Passage into the South Sea by that they call the North West Passage'– explicable as a misprint to those who took the matter seriously. By contrast, Dobbs argued that Shapley's ship had entered Hudson Bay and then sailed through an opening on its west coast into Fonte's Sea of Ronquillo.

The account had originally appeared as a letter in an issue of a short-lived periodical, *The Monthly Miscellany or Memoirs for the Curious*, in 1708, at a time when imaginary voyages were all the rage. Four years earlier Jonathan Swift had published *A Tale of a Tub*, in which Lord Peter had discovered and bought 'Terra Australis', while George Psalmanazar, claiming to be a Formosan, had issued his fantastic but well-received *Description of Formosa* in which he invented his own Formosan language. *Robinson Crusoe* and *Gulliver's Travels* were still to come, but there were precursors in plenty. Since William Dampier's *New Voyage Round the World* of 1697 the South Sea had come back into fashion, and it was in this context that the unknown writer composed for publication the Fonte letter. Whatever his expectations they were disappointed, for the account seems to have attracted no interest until its resurrection by Dobbs in 1744.

How Dobbs came across the Fonte account has never been

clear. The inclusion of the letter in his *Account of Hudson's Bay* was the first time that it had appeared in print since 1708, and certainly the first time that it had been given serious attention. Within a few years of its publication by Dobbs it would cause a great stir in France where Joseph Nicolas Delisle addressed the Royal Academy of Sciences in Paris on the subject of the Fonte voyage. According to his colleague, Philippe Buache, a manuscript copy of the letter had been sent to Delisle, then an adviser to the Russian government at St Petersburg, from 'Lord Forbes' in England, who during his years as British ambassador to Russia had known Delisle. Pieces of the jigsaw now fall into place. Baron Forbes, naval officer and diplomat, became 3rd Earl of Granard, an Irish peer, in 1733. Five years later, Sir Charles Wager, then First Lord of the Admiralty, told Dobbs that Granard was one of his few acquaintances who was interested in the Northwest Passage; and in 1746 he became an investor in Dobbs's discovery expedition to Hudson Bay. How and why Granard became interested in the Fonte account is not known, but it seems likely that it was he who supplied Dobbs (as well as Delisle) with copies. This provenance of the account would also explain why Wager took it seriously enough to have enquiries made about Captain Shapley in Boston, where he was informed that a family of that name had lived in the mid-seventeenth century.

At the time of its publication by Dobbs, there was no way of disproving the Fonte account, for the northwest coast of America was still unknown to Europeans. A Russian expedition commanded by Vitus Bering had sailed across the North Pacific from Kamchatka to the Alaskan coast in 1741, but news of this was slow in reaching western Europe. The first, rather muddled account of Bering's voyage was published in England in 1743, but not until 1747 was fuller information available, and even then there was room for differing interpretations of the Russian discoveries. Geographers could combine the real and the imaginary on maps that showed the pinpricks of coast sighted by the Russians in the context of the straits and rivers of the Fonte letter. It took another fifty years and a whole series of voyages to discredit the Fonte account, and meanwhile its description of fertile countries, of straits and rivers stretching from Hudson Bay to the Pacific coast of North America, allowed Dobbs to emphasise the opportunities that awaited British merchants using the Northwest Passage. Above all, it helped him to bring together his two objectives, the discovery of a Northwest Passage and the abolition of the monopoly of the Hudson's Bay Company.

Those few men in England familiar with the Bay region could point to the weaknesses in Dobbs's general exposition. Captain William Coats grumbled in his private journal that 'what Mr. Dobbs has thought fitt to call a description of Hudson's Bay, is so erronius, so superficial, and so trifling, in almost every circumstance'. James Isham condemned parts of the *Account* as no better than 'a Romance', and like Coats insisted that since Dobbs had never been to Hudson Bay he could have no real idea of conditions there. Coats appealed to the 'experience and concurrent testimony' of those who had voyaged to the Bay and lived there; but it was just this testimony that the Company's continuing policy of close secrecy kept from the wider world of trade and politics. When the second edition of John Oldmixon's standard history of *The British Empire in America* was published in 1741, the sole additional entry on the Company since the first edition of 1708 was the rather stale news that its territories had been restored by the Treaty of Utrecht in 1713. On developments since then Oldmixon could say nothing, since despite his 'pressing instance' the Company had not responded to his request for further information. While the observations of Coats, Isham and other Company servants remained unpublished, then the writings of polemicists hostile to the Hudson's Bay Company went unchallenged. It was left to Middleton, embittered and discredited after Dobbs's attack on his reputation, to assert that the search for the Northwest Passage was now a cloak to cover other designs.

Dobbs followed Pelham's advice and delayed further action until early 1745, when a group of his London merchant associates presented a petition to the House of Commons requesting a government reward for the discovery of a Northwest Passage. The 'late discoveries' were cited to show that 'a safe and navigable Passage, free from Ice for some Months in the Year' might be found between the northwest of Hudson Bay and the Pacific. It would be difficult to imagine a more complete misrepresentation of Middleton's explorations. Once through the passage the petitioners entered the expansive world of Dobbs's earlier Memorial, with glowing references to the opening of trade with countries both known and unknown along the coasts of Asia and in the South Sea. The House of Commons was not likely to turn its back on such a prospect, and appointed a Committee of all MP's who were merchants or represented sea ports, to consider the petition. The Committee had powers to send for 'Persons, Papers and Records'. In the event the Hudson's Bay Company produced the records, a rather meagre collection of sloops' journals from Churchill, and Dobbs produced the persons. He asked the Admiralty for leave to summon various members of Middleton's crews before the Committee. They were all, he wrote revealingly, 'Proper Witnesses ... by their confirming the Strong Presumptions of a North West Passage'. Dobbs's main worry was that Middleton himself might be called as a witness. Admiral Edward Vernon, hero of the early Caribbean operations of the war, was now an M.P., and apparently sympathetic to Middleton – as might be expected of a naval officer who had also experienced his share of opprobrium. Whether or not Middleton was called, his evidence was not produced in the Committee's report of late February. The main witnesses were William Moor, John Rankin and Edward Thompson. Of Middleton's supporters among the discovery crews only Robert Wilson, master of the *Furnace*, seems to have appeared before the Committee. In these circumstances it is not surprising that the Committee's report reproduced Dobbs's arguments as faithfully as if he had written it in person. Once again the story was told how witnesses went ashore in the Wager and 'perceived the Streight to tend away to the Southward of the West, as far as they could see'. The report added that the west coast of Hudson Bay, from Churchill to the Wager, appeared to be 'broken land'. No mention was made of the Frozen Strait and Repulse Bay, of Middleton's tidal observations, nor of any other considerations that might have argued against the existence of a passage.

With the Committee's report probably the sole guide to most MPs, the House decided that the discovery of a Northwest Passage would be of 'great Benefit and Advantage to the Trade of this Kingdom'. Accordingly it recommended that a reward should be offered for 'a perfect discovery' of the same. The resultant Act, 'for giving a publick reward to such person or persons, his Majesty's subject or subjects, as shall discover a north west passage through Hudson's Streights, to the western and southern ocean of America', received the royal assent in May 1745. It was a curious piece of legislation. The year before Dobbs had hoped that a reward of £10,000 would be offered, and he based his estimates of cost and profit on that amount. The Act instead offered £20,000. No evidence has been found to explain this putative generosity by an assembly usually circumspect in financial matters. One possible explanation is that £20,000 was the amount offered by the Longitude Act of 1714 for a 'Practicable and Useful' method of determining longitude. If one took a global view of the nation's maritime future, as some MPs certainly did, it could be argued that a discovery of a navigable Northwest Passage combined with a reliable way of finding longitude at sea would allow Britain to dominate the oceans of the world. The Board of Longitude had met for the first time in 1737, and from that time on John Harrison's marine clocks, together with rival methods of ascertaining longitude, were much in the public eye (and in 1749, seven years after Middleton, Harrison was awarded the Copley Gold Medal of the Royal Society).

Apart from the similarity in the awards offered, there were noticeable differences between the two Acts. The Longitude Act made no stipulation as to the nationality of the successful candidate. The Northwest Passage Act limited the award to British subjects – an indication that it was assumed that whichever nation found a navigable passage would gain most from the discovery. The 1714 Act, as befitted its subject matter, was mathematically precise, with different amounts of money offered according to the degree of exactitude achieved by the successful method. The 1745 Act, in contrast, was slipshod in its wording. The award was for 'a perfect Discovery', but this was never defined except in one clause that specified that the ship or ships 'shall find out and sail through any passage by sea between Hudson's Bay and the western and southern ocean of America'. Whether this was to be a continuous voyage, how long it should take, how practical the passage might be for trading vessels – all this was left unsaid. Other clauses had their origins in the circumstances of the Middleton expedition. So it was made clear that all British subjects were required to give 'all aid and assistance' to any discovery expedition; but this was followed by a rider noting that nothing in the Act should 'take away or prejudice any of the estate, rights, or privileges of or belonging to the governor and company of adventurers of England trading into Hudson's Bay'. The next few years would show that this was an almost impossible balance to strike.

On 12 March 1745, the same day that the House of Commons decided to introduce the bill, Dobbs opened subscriptions for the impending voyage, and asked the Admiralty whether the *Furnace* might be hired for the voyage. By the end of the month he had drawn up Articles of Agreement that were to be signed by all subscribers. Two ships were to be fitted out, at a cost not exceeding £10,000. If they discovered the passage, then the reward would be claimed, the ships sold, and the total proceeds shared among the subscribers. A committee of eight, the North West Committee, was set up, with

Samuel Smith as secretary. Smith probably played a more important part in the events of these years than the sources reveal. Onetime secretary and director of the South Sea Company, as Dobbs's agent and attorney in London Smith was responsible for putting into practical effect many of the instructions and suggestions that Dobbs sent him from Ireland. The Articles of Agreement went on to stipulate that after the division of the reward, 'each of the Subscribers shall signify, whether he is willing to be concerned in prosecuting further Discoveries, through the said Passage, and in opening a Commerce with the Natives of the Countries, which may be discovered adjoining, or near, to the said Passage'. The venture was organised on the familiar model of a single joint-stock voyage; and despite Dobbs's optimism, it was a highly speculative undertaking in which hopes of a 100% profit, and a footing in the new trade, had to be set against the risks involved.

The fact that despite the disappointments of Middleton's voyage another was now in preparation might be seen as a tribute to Dobbs's persuasiveness – or perhaps as an indication of the credulity of his associates. John Campbell declared that the Act of 1745 and Dobbs's new expedition were 'the Topic of common Discourse, and of almost universal Expectation'. Curiosity and anticipation, however, were not quite the same as participation, and there was no great rush to invest. The Articles of Agreement envisaged the expedition sailing in May 1745, but apart from the difficulty of finding subscribers at a time when confidence in commercial undertakings was being undermined by the imminent prospect of a Jacobite rising, six weeks proved too short a period to find and fit out ships and crews for an Arctic voyage. The Admiralty made no move to release the *Furnace*, and the venture had to be postponed for a further year. The money advanced was put into East India bonds, and the subscription remained open during the winter. Investors were still slow in coming forward, and although in March 1746 Dobbs told Judge Ward that subscriptions totalling £6,000 had come in, and more would follow, only seventy-two out of the one hundred shares were finally taken up.

The subscribers fell into two main groups. Firstly, there were men prominent in government, whose interest in the expedition appears to have been aroused by personal contact with Dobbs, or by previous participation in overseas ventures. This group included the Earl of Chesterfield, one of the best-known politicians of the day, who became Secretary of State for the Northern Department in October 1746. Before this he had been Lord Lieutenant of Ireland, where he had shared Dobbs's interest in Irish trade and industry. Chesterfield's godson, Solomon Dayrolles, who had accompanied him to Ireland, was a subscriber, as was another of his relatives, Charles Stanhope, onetime Secretary to the Treasury. The Duke of Montagu was a subscriber who should perhaps have known better, for he was rumoured to have lost £40,000 in a failed colonising attempt in the West Indies. The Irish peer, Granard, apart from his long-standing interest in the Northwest Passage, had at one time hoped to challenge French settlements in the Great Lakes region of Canada. Lords Newport and Southwell were two other Irish peers, the former, like Dobbs, a Fellow of the Royal Society. Richard Southwell, Secretary of the Council in Ireland, and Richard Gildart, were, respectively, MPs for the trading cities of Bristol and Liverpool. Other MPs were Daniel Mussendon, who had served with Southwell and Gildart on the Parliamentary Committee set up to examine the petition of the London merchants in 1745, and Lord Conway, who had been Dobbs's ward in Ireland. Sir John Rawden (another FRS), the Archbishop of Tuam, and George Berkeley, the much-travelled Bishop of Cloyne, were on the fringes of this group. Other Irish subscribers were Bernard Ward, son of Judge Ward, Dobbs's brother the Reverend Richard Dobbs, and Justin MacCarty, son of the Earl of Clancarty.

The larger and more coherent group was composed of about thirty London merchants. Several of them were engaged in the African and West Indian trades, and some were associated with Dobbs in his other ventures. Seven of them formed, with Dobbs, the North West Committee. That the preparation of the expedition should be left to the merchants was to be expected. They had experience of overseas ventures, and in the buying of ships, cargoes and provisions. This reliance on the merchant investors followed precedents established in the sixteenth and seventeenth centuries, when the organising committees of many colonial and trading enterprises had been composed of merchants, even though the list of subscribers had often been headed by a group of notables. If the expedition had been successful there is no doubt that many of the merchant investors would have taken up the option offered in the Articles of Agreement, and formed the nucleus of a new trading company to exploit the discovery. As a French agent in London reported to Paris at this time, there was more to the discovery venture than met the eye, and Dobbs's real objective was the replacement of the Hudson's Bay Company by a new company.

This aspect of the forthcoming expedition caused the Hudson's Bay Company to take an even more anxious interest in Dobbs's activities than it had at the time of the Middleton voyage. Once again an extraordinary meeting of shareholders was convened, and as in 1741 this decided to leave the protection of the Company's trade and privileges to the Governor and Committee. In May 1746 letters were sent to the Bay posts giving a detailed description of the two discovery vessels bought by the North West Committee, the *Dobbs Galley* and the *California*. The first, commanded by William Moor, was described as 'a Ship about 220 Tons Square Stern'd a Griffin at the Head before formerly used in the Portugal Trade 10 Guns 38 Men painted yellow and black'. The *California*, American-built, was '120 Tons Square Stern'd a Womans head before carrys 28 Men'. Her commander was Francis Smith, previously master of the *Churchill* sloop. His appointment to the discovery expedition was another blow to the Company, for Smith had made six trading voyages north from Churchill. On the last of these voyages in 1744 he had sailed beyond

Whale Cove as far as the Rankin's Inlet of Middleton's voyage, where Smith suspected Knight's ships had been lost. The ships carried what the Company letters described as 'the Frame of a Factory House', together with a lieutenant and twenty-five soldiers. This last was incorrect, but must have set nerves jangling at the Company's London headquarters. The policy to be followed by the factors was set out in detail. They were not to allow any vessel to approach the forts unless it made the correct signal, and were to oppose 'Discoverers or pretended Discoverers' in all possible ways. There was a danger that any vessels sighted might be French or Spanish, sailing under false colours in the hope that they might be mistaken for a discovery expedition. The factors were to prevent vessels wintering at the Company's posts unless they were in distress, and were prepared to give security not to trade with the Indians nor to entice any servants from the Company's employ. Copies of the 1745 Act had already been sent to the factors, and their attention drawn to the clause protecting the interests of the Company. There were even references to the action to be taken should the expedition attack any of the forts and over-power the garrison. All in all, the factors were put on high alert, and this held for two years since the original assumption was that the discovery ships would sail in 1745. This explains the response of the factor at Moose Factory in June 1746 to a letter from his counterpart at Albany reporting that a wreck had been sighted by the local Indians: 'if there is any Wrack found I hope it is some of our Pretended Discoverers that was come out last fall from England.' This was not quite as vindictive a reaction as might appear, since the alternative would have indicated the loss of a Company vessel. In the event, nothing more was heard of the supposed wreck.

The Company's instructions to its factors not only revealed its fears that the discovery expedition, led by two of its former officers, was in reality an interloping expedition, but show how limited its range of responses was. Its hands were tied by the clause in the 1745 Act that stated that all

British subjects 'shall give the said adventurers all aid and assistance requisite'. For the Company the situation was even more exasperating than at the time of Middleton's voyage, for it was in no doubt as to the wider, commercial motives that lay behind the outfitting of the new expedition. Dobbs's instructions to the two captains do much to justify the fears of the Company that they were confronted by a rival trading organisation. Moor and Smith were to encourage trade with the Eskimos on the west coast of the Bay by giving 'more for their Furrs, &c. than is usually given by the Company' in order to build a relationship for the future. When the captains reached Northern Indian country they were to open up trade, inquire about the location of the copper mine, and perhaps make a 'Treaty of Friendship'. It could have been Knight or Kelsey speaking. Although the instructions make it clear that the work of discovery was not to be delayed or diverted by trading activities, they also reveal how the explorers' activities could lead to the development of commercial contacts which would be bound to damage the Company's trade in the Bay. The order to trade for furs at a more favourable standard than that set by the Company was a hint of things to come.

The navigational instructions given to the captains reflected the views expounded by Dobbs during his criticism of Middleton's handling of the earlier expedition. When the ships reached the west coast of the Bay they were to look for a passage either at Rankin's Inlet or through the Wager. Guided by the tide, they should 'boldly push into the Opening' and keep heading westward. There was little mention of ice, and as in 1741 this part of Dobbs's instructions exuded optimism: 'wherever, upon trying the Tide, you are convinced it flows from the Westward ... you may depend on having an open and large Passage, as the Ocean cannot be far distant'. If the unthinkable happened, and no passage was found, then the expedition was to return to England without wintering in the Bay, so as to prevent unnecessary expense. It was character-istic of the unreality of these sailing orders that they assumed that a thorough examination could be made of the intricate, ice-choked west coast of Hudson Bay in the short navigable season that existed between the ships' passage through Hudson Strait and the latest time for returning home before the Bay froze over. It is more likely that Dobbs never intended the injunction against wintering in the Bay to be taken seriously, and raises the question of whether there were further orders given to the captains in addition to those that were made public.

Once through the passage, and beyond the territories claimed by the Company, the captains would have a free hand to take possession of any uninhabited lands, make treaties with 'civilized fixed Inhabitants', and winter 'in a warm Country' on the Californian coast before making preparations for the return voyage. Here the sailing orders toppled into the realms of fantasy as the captains were instructed on their way back to make 'easy Sail, and observe the whole Coast on the North West of America'. They were to make careful observations of all the rivers, bays and headlands; draw charts and views; note bearings, tides, soundings and magnetic variation; negotiate further alliances with native inhabitants, and conduct trade with them. All this, Dobbs estimated, 'will fully employ the Months of April, May, and June'. In cases of difficulty, a council was to be called, a nine-man body consisting of the captains, first and second mates, the surgeons, and Henry Ellis, a last-minute addition to the expedition who sailed as draughtsman, mineralologist and agent. Decisions would be by majority vote, a practice taken from the buccaneering and privateering voyages of an earlier generation, when captains had neither the authority nor the permanence of their naval counterparts. Although William Moor's length of service at sea and his appointment to the larger discovery vessel pointed to him as the senior commander, this was nowhere specified. The fact that he (together, presumably, with Francis Smith) was required to deposit a bond of £500 for 'the Observation and Performance' of the expedition's instructions, hints at some doubts on the part of Dobbs and the North West Committee about the competence and perhaps integrity of the two captains. We have little information about the crews, and how they were enlisted. Apart from Moor, only Thompson of those who had been on Middleton's voyage is known to have sailed on the new expedition. Wigate and Rankin were noticeable by their absence. One source states that the Admiralty had granted a three-year protection against pressing to all crew members, but there is no confirmation of this in the Admiralty records. 'Extraordinary wages' were paid, and bounties were promised for all on board the two ships if the passage was found and the parliamentary reward paid: £500 for the captains, £200 for the mates and lesser amounts for the rest of the crews.

Sailing on the expedition were two supernumeraries who played important roles in the events that followed, not least because they kept journals that were published after the ships' return. That they also became bitter rivals has to be taken into account when reading their narratives. Henry Ellis was a young man of twenty-five, born in Monaghan, Ireland, who had spent the previous five years at sea, first in the coasting trade and then on voyages to the Mediterranean and the West Indies. He returned to England from Italy only four days before the discovery ships were due to leave, but still thought it worth approaching the organisers in the hope that he might yet find a place on the expedition. To his surprise, not only was his request accepted but he was offered 'a Command'. If this means command of one of the ships, then Ellis's version of events is difficult to believe. William Moor and Francis Smith had been appointed as captains more than a year before, and both had experience of northern waters, which Ellis did not, as he admitted when he explained why he had turned down this particular offer. By his own account he sailed on the *Dobbs* as hydrographer and mineralogist, and as agent for the North West Committee. If this was so, then the latter role again indicates some doubts among the Committee about the reliability of the two captains.

The other published account of the voyage was issued under the pseudonym of 'The Clerk of the *California*', a mysterious and elusive figure. Until recently it has been impossible to determine whether the man behind the pseudonym was Theodore Swaine Drage, or Captain Charles Swaine, a seaman who later commanded two expeditions from Pennsylvania to the Hudson Strait and Labrador area, and in 1768 wrote a book entitled *The Great Probability of a North West Passage: Deduced from Observations on the Letter of Admiral De Fonte.* The most recent evidence suggests that Drage and Swaine were one and the same (see pp.212–14 below), although there is no clue as to the reason for this deliberate confusion of identity. Certainly, the man who sailed on the *California* was known to his captain, Francis Smith, and to the Hudson's Bay men he encountered during the voyage, as Drage (or Dragg). More than twenty years later he wrote to the Earl of Hillsborough recalling how he came to join the discovery expedition. He had been captured by the French while on a voyage from Lisbon to London, then exchanged, and eventually reached England in the company of a friend who had engaged with London merchants to sail with Captain Smith on the *California*. The identity of this friend is not known. The implication is that he also went on the discovery voyage, but there is no reference in any of the surviving records to the sort of independent gentleman implied by Drage. The letter to Hillsborough also made it clear that he intended from the beginning to write an account of the voyage. Narratives of voyages and travels were enjoying renewed popularity. Even before the appearance in 1748 of the best-selling authorised account of Anson's voyage around the world earlier in the decade, there had been five unofficial accounts of the dramatic events on that voyage. With a book in mind, Drage was in a good position to collect and copy documents relating to the voyage, and he later stated that the only important source to which he did not have access was Captain Moor's log. This has vanished, as have most of the papers of the North West

Committee. If the sparse log that Moor kept as captain of the *Discovery* on Middleton's voyage is any guide, the disappearance of his log of the *Dobbs Galley* is perhaps no great loss; but it would have provided some balance to the one manuscript log of the voyage that has survived, that kept by Francis Smith. This is a disappointing record. As a seaman's log it is perfunctory; as a personal relation of a turbulent expedition it is maddeningly uninformative.

During the late spring of 1746 the *Dobbs Galley* and *California* were fitted and strengthened at Deptford, and on 10 May fell downriver to Gravesend. Dobbs followed the custom of the Governor and Committee of the Hudson's Bay Company and went to Gravesend to take his leave of the expedition, which sailed on 20 May. In the months of silence that followed, Dobbs showed his usual optimism that the ships would return 'with success' the following autumn. During their absence he became involved in an acrimonious exchange of opinions with Leonhard Euler, onetime professor at the St Petersburg Academy of Sciences, about the significance of Vitus Bering's Russian explorations. These had a direct bearing on the arguments about the possibility and location of a Northwest Passage, but for the moment Dobbs was prepared to let the results of his discovery expedition settle the issue. 'A few months now, if our ships return safe, will give us a certainty on one side or the other,' he told Euler, before adding, 'I am sanguine enough they have now sailed through and discovered this much wished for Passage.'

Dobbs was not alone in his optimism, and it is a sign of the effectiveness of his campaign that some observers in England considered that the new discovery venture had a good chance of success. Most surprising among these was William Coats, the Hudson's Bay Company captain whose harsh comments on Dobbs's *Account of Hudson's Bay* can absolve him of any partiality towards its author. With his twenty years' experience of navigation in Hudson Bay, Coats' remarks are not to be taken lightly, particularly since they were private reflections and not intended for publication. Coats did not accept Middleton's argument that the strong tide in the Welcome came through Frozen Strait, and concluded that it was 'so notorious a trip in him as will justifie all Dobbs has imputed to him'. Nor did Coats believe that the Wager was a river, as Middleton insisted, and he agreed with Dobbs that the high tides along the west coast of Hudson Bay came from the inlets opposite Marble Island. He clearly believed that there was a passage, and 'that if the company had thought it their interest (and if there were not political reasons to the contrary) that discovery had been determined long before this time'. Elsewhere he referred to the Northwest Passage as 'a scene of treasure and honour', and it may be that Edward Thompson – although not the most reliable of witnesses – was correct when he maintained that Coats had volunteered to lead a Hudson's Bay Company expedition to discover the Northwest Passage, and had been rebuffed.

During the months that the ships were away, a revised edition of Herman Moll's classic reference work, *A Complete System of Geography*, was published. Its editor, Stephen Whatley, once again examined the controversy between Dobbs and Middleton. Like Coats, he rejected Middleton's account of the Frozen Strait, and concluded that the flood tide along the west coast of the Bay came from the Pacific. Whatley's concluding remarks about the discovery ships were further testimony to the optimism with which the expedition was regarded in some quarters: 'there has been no News of them, that we know of; but it is suppos'd they are gone thro' the Passage, and an Account of them is expected by the first homeward bound East-India Ships'.

Finally, there was the revised and expanded edition by Dr John Campbell of John Harris's *Navigantium atque Itinerantium Bibliotheca: or, a Compleat Collection of Voyages and Travels*, a work monumental in size, and passionate in its advocacy of British overseas trade. The most important step towards its expansion would be the discovery of the Northwest

Passage, and in Campbell's estimation Dobbs was 'a Man born to revive the old heroic spirit'. With memories of the rewards and misfortunes of Anson's circumnavigation still fresh – Anson had brought back a huge treasure from the South Sea but had lost five of his six ships on the voyage – Campbell stressed that British naval vessels could sail quickly and unde- tected through a northern passage to Spain's Pacific pos- sessions. No longer would ships be crippled and crews decimated by the terrible passage around Cape Horn. 'We might, very probably, reach, in six Weeks, Countries that we cannot now visit in twelve or fifteen Months; and this by an easy and wholesome Navigation, instead of those dangerous and sickly Voyages, that have hitherto rendered the Passage into the South Seas so infrequent and ingrateful to British Seamen.' Like Dobbs, he pointed to the new areas that would be opened to British merchants by such a route: the unknown coasts north of California; the rich islands thought to lie east of Japan; previously inaccessible regions in the East Indies. Nearer home, Campbell launched himself on one of his more improbable flights of fancy when he envisaged that the stream of ships heading northabout round the British Isles for Hudson Bay and the Northwest Passage would use the Orkney Islands as their base, and transform them into a new Indies.

Campbell's conviction that a passage existed was based on the same arguments about tides that Dobbs had advanced, but it also owed much to the old philosophical concept of 'a bal- ance' in the affairs of man and nature. So, as there was a strait (Magellan's) in the southern hemisphere, so there must be a matching one in the northern. Since the coast of Asia had been shown by the recent Russian discoveries to extend farther northeast than had once been thought, then to balance this disproportionate mass of land, the American continent could not extend as far west as some maintained. To preserve the equilibrium of land and sea, there must be a great expanse of water between Asia and America, just as there was between America and Europe, and any passage through Hudson Bay to the Pacific would therefore be a short one. Such wishful thinking matched that of Dobbs, for both men's interest in the passage was driven by their hopes of finding a route easily navigable for ocean-going ships. The desire for discovery for its own sake played no part in their thinking. For them the Northwest Passage promised an almost magical enlargement of British trade. As Campbell put it, its discovery would be 'a kind of maritime Philosophers Stone'.

5

The Disputatious Voyage of William Moor and Francis Smith

'These orders were quite a Secret to Captain Smith, and every one else, and made it plainly appear that Captain Moor was not to return to his Ship, if he made the Discovery, and that if he was so lucky as to perfect it, would then only come to her for the Conveniency of getting Home, in order to gain the whole Honour and Profit of the Discovery to himself.'

Clerk of the *California*, An Account of a Voyage for the Discovery of a North-West Passage, Vol II (1748), 11 July 1747

THE EXPEDITION WHICH CARRIED so many hopes made an inauspicious start. There is evidence of hurried last-minute preparations in a petition of 2 May 1746 from the North West Committee to the Ordnance Office which requested six cannon, twelve swivel guns and seventy-five muskets. Despite the Committee's eloquence about the benefit to the nation that the discovery of a passage would bring, the Ordnance Office responded that 'it was intended they should be at the whole Risque and Charge themselves'; then unbent sufficiently to recommend that, with the King's permission, the required arms might be lent to the Committee. This permission came on 14 May, although it was probably too late to be effective since the *Dobbs Galley* and *California* had sailed downriver from Deptford the previous day, and during the week that the ships lay at Gravesend there was no mention of cannon being put on board. Further problems arose when the crew of the *California* refused to work, and went ashore without leave because they had not been paid their promised two-months' advance wages. By the time this dispute was settled the convoy in which the discovery vessels were to sail, and which included the four Hudson's Bay Company ships bound for the Bay that year, had already left the Thames estuary.

The *Dobbs Galley* and *California* caught up with the convoy near Yarmouth, but mishaps continued during the passage along the east coast. At Tynemouth the first mate of the *Dobbs Galley* went ashore and failed to return, while Captain Smith tried without success to recruit a carpenter and three or four seamen for the *California*. Storms separated the two ships as they sailed north, and it was 7 June before they were reunited at Stromness in the Orkneys and joined their new escort – none other than Captain Middleton in the *Shark* sloop. He had requested a posting to the Orkneys, whose waters he knew well from the many calls he had made at Stromness as captain of one of the Company ships. He could not have foreseen that one of his duties would be to protect discovery ships whose mission, if successful, would discredit him. Nor could he avoid personal confrontation, for soon after sailing on 12 June the captains of all the ships in convoy were summoned on board the *Shark* for consultation. What passed between him and his former colleagues, and in particular his cousin William Moor, is not recorded in the expedition's records, and Middleton's log of the *Shark* has not survived.

On 17 June, with the convoy almost two hundred miles west of the Orkneys, and clear of the operating zone of enemy privateers, the *Shark* turned back; and the next day the discovery vessels lost sight of the four Hudson's Bay Company ships. On 21 June the expedition nearly came to a premature end when fire broke out in the great cabin of the *Dobbs Galley* and spread to the powder room below. Henry Ellis's narrative describes the panic that gripped most of the crew as they ran aimlessly around the deck. 'It is impossible to express the Confusion and Consternation this Accident occasioned: The dangerous Place the Fire was in, gave every one on Board the greatest Reason to expect, that Moment, or the next at most, was their last. You might hear on this Occasion, all the Varieties of Sea-Eloquence; Cries, Prayers, Curses.' While some of the crew tried to hoist out the boats, others shook out the reefs in the topsails in an attempt to catch up with the *California*, a long distance ahead. While these two contradictory manoeuvres were being attempted, the helmsman realised that he was standing immediately above the fire and as he left the wheel to look after itself the ship was taken aback, with its sails flapping and crashing. Fortunately a few men kept their nerve, and managed to extinguish the fire before it reached the barrels of gunpowder.

Five days later the first ice was sighted, huge floes drifting south from Greenland. The ships stood away south, but as they got closer to Hudson Strait icebergs were sighted, one 'equal in Size and much resembling a large Gothick Church', Drage wrote. On 8 July, Resolution Island at the entrance of the Strait suddenly appeared through the fog, only half a mile distant, and both ships had to be towed clear by their boats as the swell drove them towards the shore. The navigation of the Strait proved a slow and tedious business, though the arrival of Inuit kayaks to trade made a diversion. For Company seamen passing through Hudson Strait there was nothing novel about these encounters; and even where the logs of the ships' captains have survived, they have only brief descriptions of the Inuit. By contrast, Ellis and Drage were keeping journals that they hoped to publish on their return to England, and they realised that full descriptions of the little-known and much-feared 'Eskimaux' would be of interest to their readers. Their observations on the appearance, dress, boats and hunting skills of the Southern Baffin Inuit were the most detailed and accurate published to this time, and have remained of interest.

After the *Dobbs Galley* had fired its cannon to signal the ships' presence off the Upper Savage Islands near the north side of the Strait (the yearly meeting point for the Company ships and the Inuit) more than twenty kayaks appeared. The first kayaks to approach the ships stopped at a musket-shot's distance; their occupants shouted 'chima' or 'chimo' in greeting, and held up whalebone. As the ships' crews returned the salutation, the kayaks came alongside to trade. At no stage did any of the Inuit attempt to come on board. They traded mainly whalebone and seal-skin clothes, in return for iron implements ranging from axes to needles. When his small cargo of whalebone and skins had gone, an Inuk might strip naked to barter the seal-skin clothes he was wearing. As trade progressed, other kayaks came out from the shore, together with three umiaks, each holding up to forty women and children. These were ungainly, oval-shaped craft, called luggage-boats by the Company seamen, for they were used for transporting families together with their provisions and utensils as they moved from one part of the Strait to another. They had no seats, so the women stood, whether they were paddling the boat or were passengers. The kayaks by contrast were long and narrow, eighteen feet in length and only three feet across in the middle. Ellis described how 'their Frames are made of Wood or Whalebone, very slender, and covered with Sealskin-Parchment all over, a Hole in the middle excepted, which has a Rim of Whalebone or Wood round about to prevent the Water coming down off the Deck, and affords only room for one Man to sit in'. With eight-foot double-bladed paddles they could speed through the water at seven or eight miles an hour. They were so delicately balanced that when a paddler left his seat to get at the trading goods stowed at his feet, another kayak had to come alongside to steady him. Clipped to the outside of the hull was fishing tackle and a harpoon. Clothed from head to foot in their waterproof seal-skin outfits, the Inuit seemed welded into their flimsy craft, and were at one with an environment where others would perish.

In 1741 Middleton had negotiated Hudson Strait in five days; in 1746 it took the *Dobbs Galley* and *California* almost a month to get through. On 16 July the ships were threatened by monster ice-floes heaving towards them. To keep out of harm's way, they grappled to a smaller floe, though it was still six acres in size. Grappling would have been an unfamiliar technique to most readers of Ellis and Drage; for although the Davis Strait whalers used it they were no more likely to put pen to paper to describe what was involved than were the Hudson's Bay Company captains. Drage's account of the process suggests that at least some of the discovery ships' crews had experience of ice navigation. He described how men jumped from the deck onto the heaving surface of the ice, and after driving ice-hooks three-foot long into the ice, moored the ship's bow and stern to them until it lay alongside the giant floe 'as quietly and closely as if at a Key-side'. For more than two weeks the crews continued to work the ships through the ice. On one occasion the vessels found themselves perilously near the main icefield, and they crashed helplessly into one floe after another. It was a desperate business trying to fend off the floes with ice poles although they were made of ash, eighteen feet long, and shod with iron. On one occasion heavy ice almost smashed the rudder of the *California*; on another the ships were forced two miles apart. Masthead lookouts could see no break in the ice ahead, and even when leads opened they soon closed again. On 25 July the *Dobbs Galley* narrowly escaped disaster when a huge floe drove alongside, and a projecting tongue of ice slid under the ship and tipped her almost on her beam's end. Every day ropes froze and ice had to be cleared from the ships with handspikes and axes. Not until early August were the ships clear of the strait, only to encounter contrary winds that brought further delays. The captains had set the wrong course after they left the Upper Savage Islands, for although the Company ships were nine days longer in crossing the Atlantic to the entrance of the Strait, they sailed through it with little trouble from ice. By 2 August the *Prince Rupert* was at York Fort while the *Dobbs Galley* and *California* were still struggling to clear the Strait.

Slowly the discovery ships sailed across Hudson Bay until

on 11 August they sighted its west coast. In hazy weather, and with officers on the two ships recording different latitudes, it was by no means certain exactly where the expedition was. Two days later the ghostly white sheen of Marble Island was sighted, and with the ships' position now known, Moor decided to call a council. Its report began with an explanation for the apparent lack of activity. Because of the 'thick Weather, and hard Gales', the expedition had been unable to explore the coast as laid down in the captains' sailing orders. With Marble Island in sight, the council decided that the most sensible course was to send the two longboats ashore to measure the tides. Five years earlier Lieutenant Rankin had landed from the *Furnace* at a cove on the island's southwest coast, and claimed that while there he had observed a high flood tide coming from the west. The boat crews spent two days and nights on Marble Island, but to very little effect. Attempts to measure the tide from the anchored longboat of the *California* produced some perplexing observations that reduced Drage to near-gibberish: 'there must be two Tides here, the one an eastern Tide [and] a different, or Western Tide, under Shore; or perhaps which was more probable, it flowed Tide and half Tide (that is, that the Flood runs still the Way of the Flood, until it be half Ebb on Shore, and the Ebb runs likewise its Course in Continuance until it be half Flood upon the Shore) and we were kept in this Uncertainty.' Attempts to measure the tide from the shore fared little better, for the pole that the seamen stuck in the beach lacked markings. The direction and height of the tides neatly plotted on the maps of Dobbs and his supporters had little relevance when applied to the swirling waters off the fractured western coastline of Hudson Bay. As a result of Dobbs's obsession with tidal flows, much time was spent by the expedition laboriously investigating coastal rips and currents that would have been better employed in surveying the actual shoreline. By now tidal measurements were a distraction rather than a guide to explorers seeking a passage through Hudson Bay.

Soon the point of the landing on Marble Island was half-forgotten as the men, happy to be released from the cramped confines of the ships, roamed about the island, shooting geese, swans and ducks. The cove where Rankin had landed in August 1742 was rediscovered, but was thought to be too shallow to serve as a harbour for the ships, which were still several leagues out to sea. From a high point on the island the mainland was within sight to the west, and at sunset on the first evening what appeared to be a large opening or inlet could be picked out – the Rankin Inlet of Wigate's chart. Another promising sign was the sighting of two black whales, coming from the west it was thought. More ominously, a two-foot piece of oak with trunnel holes, and a stave from a buoy, were found among the drift wood on the beach. Almost certainly, they came from Knight's ships.

These forlorn reminders of the perils of navigation in the region were much in the minds of the council which was summoned when the boats returned to the ships in deteriorating weather. These meetings of the captains, mates, surgeons and agents invariably led to dissension and delay. Instead of one voice there were nine; but Moor, no doubt remembering what had happened to Middleton, stuck to his instructions to call a council 'in all Difficulties where Doubts may arise upon the most prudent Method of proceeding to make out the Discovery'. This particular meeting lasted two days before agreement was reached. A proposal to wait forty-eight hours, and then if the weather improved to investigate Rankin Inlet on the mainland coast, was opposed by Captain Smith and his mate, for they pointed out that it was probably where Knight's ships had been wrecked. The next day the council met again, this time on the *California*, where all agreed to winter in the Bay, and to return the following summer to explore the inlet. It was 17 August, by which time in 1741 Middleton had already been nine days at Churchill. The delay in getting through Hudson Strait meant that it was impossible to carry out any extensive explorations in the 1746 season. It must also have occurred to all except the most committed supporters of Dobbs that even if a Northwest Passage existed between Hudson Bay and the Pacific, there were problems about the practicability of one that could be reached only through the dangerous and ice-choked waters of Hudson Strait, open at best for no more than a few months each year.

At neither meeting was the possibility of returning to England raised, although the captains' sailing orders were specific in their instruction that if no passage was found they were to return 'forthwith ... without Wintering in any part of the Bay'. Orders or no orders, a return to England with an explanation that all had been accomplished was a two-day jaunt on an offshore island might not have been well received by the investors. And very possibly Moor and Smith had their £500 penalty bond in mind. Discussions on the second day of the council meeting seem to have centred on where rather than whether to winter. The Nelson River near York Fort was the choice, not a difficult one. Farther south and more sheltered than Churchill, the climate was not as severe, the ice broke up earlier, and there would be more wood and game. The fact that York Fort was a more important centre of the fur trade than Churchill cut both ways. There would be more Indians to hunt for the expedition; on the other hand, wintering there would intensify Company suspicions that the real objective of the Moor expedition was commercial sabotage.

The ships reached the estuary of the Nelson River on 25 August where they dropped anchor for the first time since leaving the Orkneys. Although Nelson River was recorded in the council minutes as the intended wintering place, the nearby Hayes River, with York Fort on its north bank, seems to have been the preferred choice of the captains; and the next day the ships cautiously steered towards the sandflats that lay off

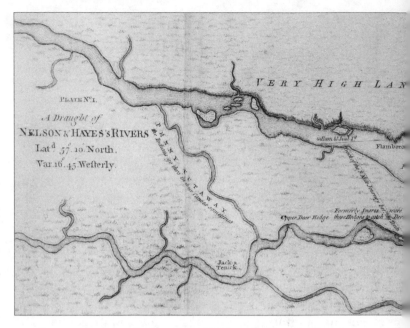

12. JOSEPH ROBSON. 'A Draught of Nelson & Hayes's Rivers', 1752
HBC Archives, Provincial Archives of Manitoba

Robson's sketch sets the scene for the discovery expedition's wintering of
1746–7: the location of York Fort on the peninsula between the Nelson and
Hayes Rivers; the shallows off the point and in the estuary of the Hayes
River; the anchorage at Five Fathom Hole; and Ten Shilling Creek on the
south bank of the Hayes River where the discovery vessels wintered.

the entrance to the Hayes (*Ill. 12*). This navigation was notoriously difficult, even for the Company captains who made the
voyage on a regular basis. Ships could get no nearer to the
factory than Five Fathom Hole, about seven miles away, where
after anchoring they had to send their goods ashore by boat.
Even this spot was hard to find among shifting sand banks and
channels, and it was normally marked by buoys and a beacon.
Both Moor and Smith had been at York during their service
on the Company ships, and they took care to send their pin-
naces and longboats ahead, with the ships following slowly
behind. The *California* reached Five Fathom Hole safely, but

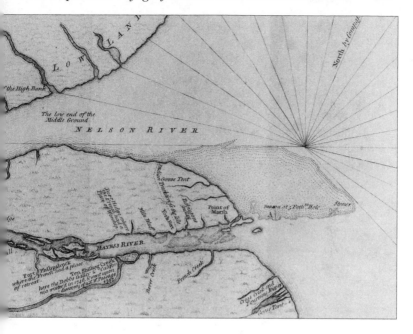

the *Dobbs Galley* with its deeper draught ran aground some way off. At this moment a boat with six armed men that had put off from the factory arrived at the scene. To the horror of the ships' crews the boat's crew took up two marker buoys, and began cutting down the beacon that showed the anchoring place. The *California* sent its first mate in a boat to ask the Company men to stop, but they refused on the grounds that 'It is the Governor's Order, and how did we know but you were French.'

For this episode and many others during the next ten months, we have access to both sides of the story; for the 'Governor' was James Isham, newly arrived from England in the *Prince Rupert* to take command at York, and as always an assiduous recorder of events. There is no doubt that he recognised the *Dobbs Galley* and *California*. He had gone on board the discovery ships in the Thames, and had then sailed in company with them from Yarmouth to the Orkneys and beyond. His explanation that the ships might have been captured by the French would have been more convincing if the boat's crew that he sent to cut down the beacon had not cheerfully closed to within a pistol's shot of the *California* while doing so. Drage maintained that Isham acted in anger, for the Home Indians' first report of strange vessels off the factory described two large ships and two smaller ones in the offing. Fear and hazy weather magnified the *Dobbs Galley* and *California* into men-of-war, and their longboats into bomb vessels. Isham's temper would not have been improved by the realisation that once more he would have to deal with discoverers or, as he put it, with 'pretended discoverers'. At the Orkneys, Isham had supplied the crews of the *Dobbs Galley* and *California* with some tockies (long beaver coats) from the stores on the Company ships so that they might be better equipped for the Arctic conditions that lay ahead. As he wrote in his personal notes, he 'little thought or imagind that those ships wou'd Ever attempt to come to Hays's River to winter their ships and men'. There were two strands to his reasoning. As the next weeks were to show, it was extraordinarily difficult to find a safe wintering berth for the ships in the Hayes River. Secondly, York was more distant than Churchill from the coast where the ships were to search for a passage. As Isham explained to a parliamentary inquiry held three years later to investigate this and other matters concerning the Hudson's Bay Company, 'he had done nothing but what he could answer to his Masters'. If the discovery captains had sent a boat ashore as soon as the factory was sighted, much unpleasantness might have been avoided, but Moor admitted to the same inquiry that at no time had he signalled to the watchers ashore.

The negotiations that followed bordered on the farcical. Isham refused to allow the ships to enter the river unless they carried authority from either the government or the Company. The year before, Dobbs and his associates had taken trouble to make certain that the Act of Parliament offering a reward for the discovery of a passage contained a clause stipulating that subjects of the crown should offer all necessary help to discovery expeditions; but it now transpired that neither Moor nor Smith had a copy of the Act on board. Since he had been in England when the Act was passed, Isham would have known that it also contained a clause specifically protecting the interests of the Company, but he was just as much in the dark as the discovery captains about its precise wording; for although the Company had sent a copy of the Act to York the year before, it could not now be found. Nor could Isham lay his hands on a copy of the Company's instructions that had been sent to factors giving them 'proper and full directions' as to how to act if any discovery vessels appeared. Isham sent a message to his deputy, Samuel Scrimshire, who was at Cross Creek some miles from the fort, asking him if he knew where Thomas White, the outgoing factor, had put his copy of the Act – but to no avail. In the event, neither side was deterred by their mutual ignorance. Francis Smith on the *California* produced the privateer's commission or letters of marque that both ships carried (a customary precaution in wartime), and used that document as the expedition's authority for seeking assistance. Isham in turn sent the captains a letter that claimed that the Act (which he misdated to 1744) laid upon him the 'Duty to hinder any ship or ships from Entering in or near any of the Companys territory in Hudsons Bay'. The Act, of course, said no such thing.

Alarmed by warnings from men at the fort about the dangers of the spring deluge that swept down the Hayes River each year as the ice broke up, Moor and Smith decided to look for a wintering place on the Nelson River, on the other side of the peninsula of land on which York Fort stood. Gillam's Creek on the far bank of the Nelson seemed a possibility, for Smith noted that it would make a good harbour for the ships, and that they would be able to get out to sea earlier the next summer than from the shallow Hayes River. Moor, however, refused to take the *Dobbs Galley* back over the shoals where he had already run aground once, even though Smith offered to go first in his smaller vessel and find a safe channel. By now both ships had moved closer inshore from Five Fathom Hole, and were anchored in Three Fathom Hole. It was proof of the difficulties of these waters that in the previous month the Company ship *Prince Rupert*, commanded by the experienced Captain Spurrell, had twice run aground trying to reach Three Fathom Hole, and had to be unloaded before she could be refloated.

After the two captains investigated creeks on the seaward side of the factory, they turned again to their preferred option – a secure mooring place on the Hayes River above York Fort. It was also their final option, for it was now early September, and a retreat from Hudson Bay and through Hudson Strait would soon be impossible. Isham was still opposed, and again warned of the dangers of a spring deluge as the ice broke up. It was not just a question of humanitarian concern for the safety of the crews; the last thing Isham would want the following summer would be to have seventy or more shipwrecked men on his hands. But the factor's main concern was for his trade. Hayes River was one of the busiest trade routes from the interior to Hudson Bay, and each summer scores of canoes laden with valuable furs came down to York Fort. Ships moored upriver from the fort would be in a position to intercept and divert that trade. Isham had not seen the expedition's instructions to trade for furs at a more favourable rate than the Company's, but he probably guessed at their existence. To meet this concern the council on board the discovery ships had to send Isham a long letter with assurances that 'tis our intent to carry on no illicit traffick'. Hampered by his continuing inability to find either a copy of the Act of Parliament or the Company's accompanying instructions, Isham conceded that he could do no more to stop the expedition wintering above the factory. His firing of a single cannon shot near the boat carrying Moor and Smith upriver past the factory to look for a suitable mooring place was a final, petulant gesture of disapproval.

By 7 September the two captains had found a wintering spot at Ten Shilling Creek, about four miles above the fort and on the opposite bank of the river. Only Henry Ellis seems to have expressed doubts, for he feared that the creek might be too shallow to float the ships out and into the main channel of the Hayes the following summer. Slowly the ships sailed in from the estuary until they were level with the factory, with the *Dobbs Galley* grounding at least once, there to wait for the fall tides before they could get into Ten Shilling Creek. Having been forced to accept the expedition's presence, Isham now did much to help. On the evening that the ships arrived opposite the fort, he sent on board a gift of ten geese, together with lettuce and cress from the small garden that sheltered beneath the factory's southern stockade. He also lent the crews a storehouse for their provisions, and allowed them to dig a pit for the ships' beer. This last was a slow business, as Middleton's men had found at Churchill, for three feet down they encountered 'a frozen Part', the permafrost. It was at this time that Isham was taken aback by the sight of one of the discovery crews. His journal entry for 14 September noted: 'an English woman by appearance came on shore walkd. abt. ½ an hour upon the bank, & went on board again.' This turned out to be Kitty, the wife of Captain Smith, who is not mentioned in any of the expedition's records. She was the first white woman to winter at York, and the first to winter anywhere in Hudson Bay during the eighteenth century. Isham was clearly intrigued by her presence, for a few days later he invited 'Capt.smith & his Lady' to the fort for dinner.

During the months that followed, various members of the discovery crews visited York Fort, and the published accounts of Ellis and Drage gave readers at home their first glimpse of one of the Company's Bayside factories. Situated close to the bank of the Hayes River, it had an outer stockade, inside which were storehouses and workshops; then an inner stockade which ran close to the four bastions of the main building. This timber structure was two storeys high, and was crowned by a

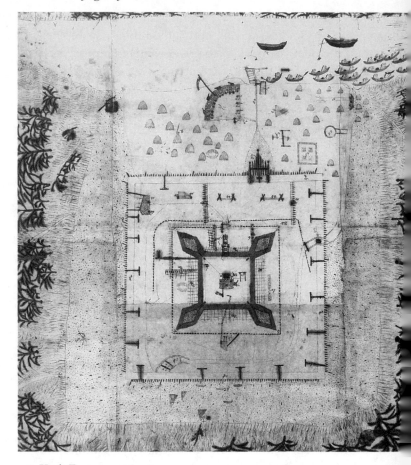

13. York Fort, *c.* 1746
HBC Archives, Provincial Archives of Manitoba (G.2/5)

This plan (south at the top) was almost certainly drawn by James Isham, factor at York. The key to the numbers on the plan is lost, but the main features of the wooden fort with its four bastions on the north bank of the Hayes River are clear. Its outer stockade is pierced by a single gate, and there are outbuildings and wood piles between the outer and inner stockades. Outside the stockade the wood has been cleared to give an open view and field of fire. On the bank a half-moon battery of cannon commands the seaward approach, while upriver a flotilla of Indian canoes is arriving from the interior with their cargoes of furs.

parapet with cannon. The factor had a spacious apartment of four rooms on the first floor of the southeast bastion, facing the river, while the area below was given over to a large day-room and some smaller rooms or 'cabins' for the factor's deputy and the principal tradesmen. A large brick stove heated both floors. Other members of the garrison lived in rooms in the northeast bastion, which also had a large stove, while the remaining two bastions contained store rooms, the trading room and a powder magazine. It was at the trading room that the Indians gathered with their furs during the early summer, although they were forced to remain outside and all trade was conducted 'through the window'. Beyond the outer stockade, the trees and bushes had been cleared to give an open view and a clear field of fire, and on the riverbank a half-moon battery of cannon commanded the estuary. The factory, Drage concluded, 'hath but a mean Appearance on the Outside, but is warm and convenient'. Joseph Robson, who had moved to York after his spell supervising the construction of the stone fortress at Churchill, would have disagreed with this last remark. In summer water seeped through gaps in the logs, in winter the frost penetrated; and he predicted that the fort would not last more than twenty-five or thirty years before it rotted away. Ellis was unimpressed by the fort's defensive qualities, which he thought would be unable to withstand attack by a European enemy. Here at least Isham would have agreed with him: 'If Every man was made of Steel or brass what could we do with a formidable Enemy by Sea, in a wooden house that will make good tuch wood, our barricadoes or outworks a handfull of men may Shove down with their Shoulders.' Long after Isham's lifetime his gloomy forecast was borne out when in August 1782 York followed the example of Churchill two weeks earlier, and without firing a shot surrendered to a French force that came across the peninsula from the Nelson River. Today the site of the York Fort of Isham's day has disappeared beneath the waters of the Hayes River.

The task of getting the *Dobbs Galley* and *California* safely laid up at Ten Shilling Creek revealed some tension between Moor and Smith. On 20 September Smith decided that the tide would be high enough to float the *California* into the creek, only to be told by Moor that he intended to take in the *Dobbs Galley* that same day. The wrangle was settled by a toss of the coin; Moor won, and boats from both ships tugged and pushed the *Dobbs Galley* into the creek. It was four days before conditions were favourable enough for the *California* to get in; but by the early afternoon of the 24ᵗʰ she was moored astern of the *Dobbs Galley*. The creek, Smith noted, was very narrow, with just enough room for the two ships abreast; and a little distance beyond the *Dobbs Galley* it was so full of stones that there was barely enough water for a longboat. Despite changes elsewhere to the banks and channels of the Hayes River, Ten Shilling Creek is still readily identifiable. Now too shallow to take anything much larger than a canoe, the creek's entrance is still about two ships' width across. Later the same afternoon Isham appeared on the scene, ostensibly fishing, but more probably to check on events at Ten Shilling Creek. The discovery ships, he wrote, were 'in a Sad Situation of a place', exposed as they were to flood waters rushing down the creek the following April. Not only Isham had the next spring in mind. Having won the argument with Smith and got his ship in first, on 3 October Moor squeezed the *Dobbs Galley* back out past the *California* so as to be nearer the entrance of the creek. This would ensure that he would be the first to get his ship out in the spring. In terms of personal relations between the two captains the omens were not good either for the wintering or for the resumption of the voyage the next year.

The crews now turned towards the building of winter quarters, which showed that lessons had been learned from Middleton's stay at Churchill five years earlier. Moor and Smith had planned to construct separate quarters for their crews, but the difficulty of finding two sites, and their dependence on Isham for a supply of bricks and mortar for the vital

The Wintering Creek in **Hayes River.**

A View of Montagu House from **Beaver** **Creek**

14. 'The Wintering Creek' and 'Montagu House'. From Henry Ellis, *A Voyage to Hudson's-Bay* (1748).
HBC Archives, Provincial Archives of Manitoba

Top: The discovery vessels moored in Ten Shilling Creek. Their topmasts have been taken down, but the creek has not yet frozen over. The drawing exaggerates the width of the creek and the height of the trees.

Bottom: Montagu House or Winter Hall, with Beaver Creek in the foreground. Outside the two-storied building are three log-tents: the nearest one the cookhouse, the two more distant ones storeplaces.

stove, not to speak of the services of his bricklayer to build it, persuaded them to join forces in erecting a two-storey log house about half a mile from Ten Shilling Creek. It faced Beaver Creek, while stands of trees behind protected the site from the northerly winds. The accounts both of Ellis and Drage have much detail on the building, rather grandly named Montagu House by Moor and Ellis (after the Duke of Montagu, one of the more prestigious subscribers to the expedition), but usually called Winter Hall or Winter House by Smith and Drage. Ellis was responsible for drawing the plan of 'our intended Mansion' (*Ill.14*). It was built of wood felled nearby, and was twenty-eight foot long by eighteen foot wide, with a shallow pitch to its roof. The top storey had a passage running lengthwise down the middle which separated the captains' two large apartments in the front from the smaller rooms for the other officers at the back. The lower storey was divided in half between the ships' companies, with the stove in the middle. Isham's notes show that this must have been a massive affair, for he had provided seven hundred bricks and six hundred half-bricks for its construction. What the expedition would have done without these Company bricks to build the stove, essential not simply for comfort but for survival, is nowhere mentioned. All the officers and some of the men were to move into the house, but forty of the men – more than half the total number of the ships' complements – would live in log-tents, a practice borrowed from the Company.

The first snow of the winter fell on 16 September, and by 9 October, Ten Shilling Creek was frozen over. By the beginning of November the cold was intense, the river had frozen over as far downriver as York Fort, and conditions for those still on board the ships had become unbearable. Great fires were lit, and blankets nailed over hatches and portholes, but temperatures remained well below freezing. The ships' interiors were covered with a thick rind of ice, and liquids froze solid. Francis Smith and several others were afflicted with that same 'country distemper' or pleurisy that had troubled

Middleton at Churchill. 'They were seized with a Shivering, and Sickness at the Stomach, like the Attack of an Ague Fit, and were very faint . . . Pains in their Heads or Backs . . . very low-spirited.' It was time to move out of the ships and into winter quarters ashore, either to the house, which had just been completed, or into the log-tents. As the men went ashore, they put on winter clothes. Again, Isham went beyond the call of duty in supplying the discovery crews with forty-three long beaver coats. Since he had already supplied some to the ships at the Orkneys, most if not all of the seventy-four crew members would have had beaver coats to wear, and they were also able to buy beaver caps and mittens and other items of winter clothing at the fort. The fact that some of the Company men discarded their cumbersome tockies in favour of lighter leather coats was an indication that however severe the conditions seemed to the unseasoned discovery crews, they were not as extreme as at Churchill. Cases of frost-bite and snow-blindness were recorded, but several of these were the result of carelessness. Ellis described how one feckless individual who was carrying an open bottle of brandy from the house to his tent used his finger as a stopper, only to find that his finger had frozen in the neck of the bottle and had to be amputated. Generally, though, the crews were more warmly clothed and living in a more sheltered location than Middleton's unfortunate men had been in their tumbledown quarters at Churchill.

In addition to the three small log-tents near the house which served as a cookhouse and storage places, the crews of the discovery ships each built three log-tents for use as living quarters. The nearest of them was a mile from the house, the farthest six miles away at French Creek. Their locations had been carefully chosen. They were situated near a creek, which provided water and a frozen road for the carriage of provisions by sledge; in a wood, which gave shelter and fuel; and at some distance from each other, so that men did not stray onto the hunting and wooding grounds of other tents. The tents were crude structures, fourteen or sixteen feet long, with a single door and an opening at the ridge-pole to let air in and smoke out. They had no floors, logs served as seats, and the bedding was laid on pine needles. The log-tents were shelters for the night or during bad weather; and their lack of creature comforts reflected the fact that their occupants were expected to be out during the day, hunting and fishing. Moor and the surgeon Edward Thompson would have remembered that the contrast in the level of activity at Churchill during the winter of 1741–2 between Middleton's men, huddled in the Old Factory, and the Company men out and about whenever possible, had done much to account for the difference in health between the two groups.

The domestic economy of a log-tent was described by the clerk of the *California*. Each tent held five or six men and a boy. Two went out shooting partridges and snaring rabbits; two others cut and brought back wood, as well as taking messages to the house and bringing back provisions; another was appointed cook, and with the help of the boy prepared meals, brewed a health-giving if repulsive spruce beer from pine needles, and kept the fire going. To encourage the men to hunt and trap, provisions were supplied for only five days out of seven. Given the shortage of skills and snow-shoes among the crews, it is doubtful whether this model of outdoor existence sketched by Drage was closely followed – though later in the winter he himself lived in one of the log-tents. Moor complained that his crew of forty or more had only three pairs of snow-shoes between them, and it is unlikely that Smith's smaller crew had more. Where the snow had drifted it might be up to fourteen feet deep, and impossible to cross without snow-shoes. There is a passage in Drage's austere account of rigours endured and discipline observed that one suspects might have had more general application than he admitted. Once the hunters and wooders had returned from their day's efforts, he wrote, 'the Tent Door was made up, Dinner got, afterwards a good Fire which made the Tent impenetrable to all Cold; and, as every Man was allowed half a Pint of Brandy a Day with proportionable Sugar, they made Spruce Beer, Flip, most generally, with which they smoaked their Pipes, and about eight o'Clock to Bed'.

As winter set in, so fresh meat became more difficult to find. On 21 November four hunters from the *California*'s log-tents returned with only seven ptarmigan, and the next day they got nothing. In response to a plea from the captains, Isham allowed a few Home Indians to hunt for the discovery crews, but this gesture led to squabbles between Moor and Smith about the distribution of the catch. On 10 December Isham received a letter from Smith complaining that Moor had insisted on taking for his crew the entire week's catch of 105 ptarmigan just brought in by the Indians. Isham feigned surprise that such a dispute should arise between the two groups, 'which I imagingd. to be one family'. In the end he agreed to take personal responsibility for dividing the spoils of the hunt between the crews, but a further six letters were exchanged before the affair of the partridges finally subsided. A further source of friction between Isham and the captains arose from the factor's decision to station Augustine Frost and another man in a tent near Montagu House in order to prevent contact between the discovery crews and the Indians. For Ellis this action was reprehensible behaviour by Isham, an example of 'Cruelty of Christians towards Christians', since it prevented Indians from bringing in fresh meat. In his notes on Ellis's book Isham responded angrily to this and other accusations, and his journal shows that he was punctilious in sending two, sometimes three, Home Indians to shoot ptarmigan for Moor and Smith. The fact was that the unexpected arrival of more than seventy crew members from the discovery ships at York, which had a garrison of only thirty-three men, put a huge strain on the food resources of the area. The men at the fort were so short of meat themselves that Isham applied to the captains for some of their salt beef, promising to repay them with venison in the spring.

In early December a meeting of the ships' council was

held at which it was agreed to lengthen and deck the longboat of the *Dobbs Galley* to give the expedition a small schooner that could go close inshore to investigate promising inlets. The lack of such a craft had restricted survey work around Marble Island in August, when the ships had to stand well out to sea. The longboat was drawn up on the bank of Ten Shilling Creek, and a log-tent built over her so that the carpenters could keep working regardless of weather. Such purposeful activity by a few men was offset by a decline in both the health and discipline of the crews in general. Lack of fresh meat and greens, and an over-generous supply of spirits, resulted in scurvy, 'this foul and fatal Distemper' as Ellis called it in a passage in which he described its horrifying symptoms:

> Our Men when first seized with it, began to droop, to grow heavy, listless, and at length indolent to the last Degree: A Tightness in the Chest, Pains in the Breast, and a great Difficulty in breathing, followed; then ensued livid Spots upon the Thighs, swelled Legs, Contraction of the Limbs, putrid Gums, Teeth loose, a Coagulation of the Blood upon and near the Back Bone, with Countenances bloated and sallow. These Symptoms continually increasing, till at length, Death carried them off, either by a Flux or a Dropsy.

Ellis blamed the outbreak of scurvy on two barrels of brandy broached for the Christmas festivities, but the first signs had already appeared early in December, and one of Moor's crew died of the disease on 20 December. In all, seven men died of scurvy during the winter, and many more were weakened and disabled. The Company men were not affected, and a rather self-righteous Isham agreed with Ellis about the cause of the sickness among the discovery crews: 'Drinking night and Day . . . its no wonder their men was afflicted with the Scurvy.'

With the drinking came violence. Even Ellis, official spokesman for the expedition, referred to 'immoderate drinking' and 'all the Folly and Madness that attend it'. Isham's man, Augustine Frost, peering out from his tent near Montagu House, complained that he expected every hour to be murdered, and picked out the *Dobbs Galley*'s surgeon, Edward Thompson, as the main culprit. Inside the building affairs had reached a deplorable state, though the published accounts of Ellis and Drage have little on this. It is Isham's journal, and his copies of letters exchanged with the discovery crews, that reveal the hidden history of the Moor expedition during its months at York; and they show that the wrangle over the distribution of ptarmigan was the prelude to more serious problems. By Christmas, relations between the officers at Montagu House had deteriorated to such an extent that Moor was guarded by four men with drawn swords, and Smith begged to be allowed to take refuge at York Fort. By the end of the month the ill-feeling between the captains had spread to their henchmen, for Ellis and Drage were at loggerheads. Ellis accused Drage of plotting to murder him, while Drage for his part was so fearful for his safety that he retreated to French Creek and the most distant of the log-tents. By the middle of January, Smith had finally persuaded Isham to allow him to stay at York Fort, where he was soon joined by his wife. How far Kitty Smith was involved in the troubles of the winter is not clear, but there is an unfriendly reference to her in a letter from Moor to Isham demanding that Smith should 'take his Madam also! & not to give me the trouble to remove her'. The two captains were not on speaking or writing terms, and communicated only through Isham. The factor's role as reluctant intermediary brought coals of fire on his head, and this at a time when he was crippled by gout. 'Warm flannel & patience' were the best remedies, Isham told himself, but he was allowed no peace. His hospitality to Smith brought a threatening letter from Moor, a stance quickly abandoned when the senior captain realised that he still needed Isham's help. The effect of all this on the morale of the crews can only be imagined. While Smith was several miles distant at the fort, several of his men were seriously ill, but he refused to return to Montagu House even when his boatswain died. It was left to the first mate of the *California* to conduct the funeral. If Moor was right, sick men from the *California* were lying on the dark, windowless ground-floor of Montagu House, while above their heads their captain's airy and well-lit apartment remained empty.

Isham, it seemed, could do nothing right as far as his unwelcome visitors were concerned. On 20 February Moor and Smith met for the first time in two months, but within days Isham was entangled in an obscure dispute with James Gwyn, surgeon of the *California*, who accused the factor of trying to lure away one of his patients. During March, Francis and Kitty Smith returned to Montagu House; and as spring advanced the crews were able to cut their vessels clear of the ice. Unlike Middleton's experience at Churchill, this proved a relatively painless task. It took less than two weeks to cut the *Dobbs Galley* clear, and only three days to free the *California*. The dreaded spring deluge came on the last day of March, but it proved less a flood than a trickle, only a foot or so high. (The following year it swept down Ten Shilling Creek mast-high, and threatened to engulf the factory.) In the first week of April, Montagu House was dismantled and the crews moved back on board their ships. For Isham it was a worrying time. It would be two months or more before the flotillas of trading canoes from the far interior arrived, but already bands of Home Indians were returning from the woods where they had spent the winter, and some were mingling with the discovery crews and getting alcohol from them. Moor answered Isham's complaints with a grievance of his own, for he had heard that there were caribou upstream. Unless he were provided with venison, he would blockade the river. 'My men shall not Linger tantalus Like, in the midst of 200 Deer Ready Kill'd,' he threatened, before adding a postscript in which he meekly asked Isham whether he could spare some more snow-shoes. Fresh meat was undoubtedly in short supply. In mid-March Isham complained that there were still no ptarmi-

gan to be found, and although the situation improved some-
what in the next few weeks only two thousand seem to have
been shot during the entire spring. Since four birds was the
normal daily ration for a Company servant, Isham was fully
justified in regarding this total as only a trifle among a hundred
men. Nor is there much evidence that the discovery crews
were able to fend for themselves. Smith's journal has a disconsolate entry for 18 March: 'This day the two hands returned
that was up the river fishing but brought neither fish, flesh
nor fowl but themselves.'

As tempers frayed with hunger and sickness, Isham's
attempts to remain aloof from the captains' quarrels – 'being
Very unwilling to Dable too much in muddy water', as he
explained on one occasion – were greeted with outrage by
both sides. A casual reference by Isham to the instructions that
he assumed Moor had been given produced a furious response
that '*Neither you nor C.Smith do or shall* Know what they are.'
As one quarrel petered out, another took its place. In April
Smith tried to involve Isham in an episode in which he claimed
that his cabin-boy, Will, had been bribed by Henry Ellis with
ginger-bread to steal papers from the *California*. It was as
though each captain felt that Isham was his partner in some
great enterprise, in which the factor was not quite pulling his
weight. It would be nearer the mark to suggest that these two
small communities, stranded for the winter on the icebound
banks of the Hayes River, were playing out a black farce; for the
reality was that once again an expedition that was indifferent if
not downright hostile to the interests of the Hudson's Bay
Company, could survive only with help from the servants and
resources of that same Company.

May brought the geese on their northward migration, and
at last there was plenty of fresh meat, while five hundred fish
were caught by the *California*'s crew in a single day. Drage
counted 24 May as the beginning of summer – because the
first mosquitoes appeared then – but all attention was centred
on the 28th, when it was hoped that the spring tides would

float the ships out of Ten Shilling Creek. In preparation, the ships were lightened of all except their essential fittings. On the day both ships began to move slowly out of the creek, but the heavier *Dobbs Galley* grounded at the entrance, and blocked the way. The ship's longboat might have helped at this stage, but its conversion into a schooner had been completed earlier in the month, when it was launched as the *Resolution*. It took four days of effort and bad-tempered exchanges between Moor and Smith before the ships were finally worked out of the creek. Smith's journal shows the difficulties as the *California*'s crew warped, trimmed and further lightened the ship before she floated into the main channel of the river. From Isham's point of view it was unfortunate timing that the ships reached the river opposite the fort at the very moment when the trading canoes of the interior Indians began to arrive. He took what precautions he could. Men were stationed on the river banks near the ships, while others kept watch from the ramparts of the fort. The account of the clerk of the *California* shows that although an attempt was made by some sailors to trade as the canoes passed close by the ship, the Indians refused to open their bales of furs. He added that when the ships returned to England it was a 'heavy accusation' against the captains by some subscribers that they had not carried out any trade. When he was not swatting away the clouds of mosquitoes that made summer harder to endure than winter, Drage was carefully noting the construction of the Indians' birchbark canoes. They were ribbed for strength, covered with a bark cladding no thicker than a coin, light enough to portage around rapids, and easily repairable. It was lack of skill in handling these versatile craft that kept the garrisons of the Company factories pinned to the shores of the Bay, and left the way open to the accusations of Dobbs and his associates that the Hudson's Bay Company 'slept at the edge of a frozen sea'.

The discovery ships sailed from York on 24 June, but not before a final flurry of exchanges had taken place. On the point of sailing, Francis Smith seems to have forgotten the hospitality that Isham had given him for two months, and in the most peremptory terms ordered the factor to supply him with molasses. 'I Require & Demand that you immediately assist me,' his letter ran. It says much for Isham's good nature that having first explained that he had no molasses to spare, he then relented and sent some out to the *California* at Five Fathom Hole. To his superiors in London the factor wrote an account of the events of the winter, together with a weary plea that 'if ships comes upon Discovery's the next Year, that your Honors. will please to send a proper person to assist me, as I think I am not capable of written against, or answering so many Lawyers and others'.

After the bickering of the winter months it was unlikely that Moor and Smith would see eye to eye on the matter of the explorations that lay ahead, and the accounts of Ellis and Drage seem at times to be describing completely separate expeditions. Yet the prospects appeared favourable, for the ships would be in the region where the passage was thought to lie before the end of June. In terms of the navigational season they would have a month's advantage over previous expeditions; but if exploration began early so did disagreements. Four days out from York, the ships had passed Churchill and reached Eskimo Point near latitude 62°N. There Moor announced his intention of exploring the hundred-mile stretch of coast north to Marble Island in his converted longboat. With two months supplies for the ten men on board, the *Resolution* headed off on what was virtually an independent discovery voyage. Moor had hoped that Smith, who had a good knowledge of parts of this coast through his trading voyages for the Company to Whale Cove, would accompany him, but met with no response from his fellow captain. Smith pointed out that Moor's planned survey was not sanctioned either by the instructions of the

North West Committee, or by the decision of the council the previous August that the priority in 1747 should be Rankin Inlet on the coast opposite Marble Island. Smith decided to follow that decision, and like Moor he used his longboat – now strengthened and partly-decked – for a close examination of the coast. Both ships kept well offshore. Since no council was called to consider the various options, Moor's decision went unexplained, though it may have been that he was influenced by the maps issued by Dobbs and Wigate that marked 'Lovegrove's Opening' on the coast he now set off to search. On the *California* Drage interpreted Moor's independent action as proof that he hoped to find the passage in person, and so 'gain the whole Honour and Profit of the Discovery to himself'.

In the event, neither boat expedition was successful. So little of interest did Moor find along the coast that Ellis, who was also in the schooner, devotes more pages of his account to their dealings with the Inuit than to the actual survey. Floating ice hampered the boat, and when Moor discovered a large opening in about latitude 62°50′N. that Ellis named Corbet's Inlet he failed to investigate it fully. Moor maintained that he could see the end of the inlet, but this was contradicted by Ellis, who wrote that the boat had stayed at the entrance and could 'not see any end to it'. Pinning down who went where is hindered by the fact that Moor's log has disappeared, and that Ellis's account of the explorations was written after the voyage in an effort to prove that a passage might yet be found. When Moor returned to the ships he told Smith that he had been among islands and shoals, but that there was 'no Appearance of a Passage to the Wtwards'. Farther north, the longboat of the *California* had no more success as its crew struggled to make sense of the tides near Rankin Inlet. After three days Jeremiah Westall, the second mate in command of the boat, returned with the news that he had found no tide flowing from the west, but that from a vantage point on one of the offshore islands he could see to the west an opening many miles across, with clear water on the far side. Smith sent the longboat back, this time under the first mate, James Holding, to investigate. Accompanied by Drage, Holding climbed the high land behind the mainland coast, only to find that Westall's stretch of water consisted of three lakes, 'which we were then sensible, to our no small Mortification, was our Western Sea'. Smith's offer to let other members of the *California*'s crew go ashore to see the lakes for themselves – clearly a form of insurance in case of future criticism – met with no volunteers, so 'chagreen'd with the Disappointment' were they.

From Marble Island the two ships sailed north towards the Welcome, with the schooner and the *California*'s longboat keeping inshore to make a close examination of the coast. This was the more necessary since Middleton on his dispirited return out of the Welcome five years earlier had sailed well offshore. There was no coordination between Moor and Smith: the boats were not sailing in company, nor on the other hand were they examining different stretches of coast. If Moor gave his boat-crew any written orders they have not survived, while those from Smith to Westall instructed him to report but not explore any inlets he saw. The reason given by Drage for this restriction makes the whole business seem even odder. Captain Smith, he wrote, did not regard Westall as trustworthy enough to be allowed to enter and explore any newly-discovered inlet. After Westall's earlier claim that he had seen a wide opening to the west this lack of faith in him was perhaps not surprising, but it hardly explains why the first mate, Holding, or Smith himself, did not take charge of the search. Neither Drage nor Ellis went on the boats, evidence perhaps that the search was not expected to yield much that would need recording. The rendezvous appointed for the boats to rejoin the ships was Cape Fullerton at the entrance to the Welcome. The ships reached the cape on 17 July, and waited for the boats. After a day or two the captains became first irritated and then alarmed as they beat backwards and forwards in fog and ice between Cape Fullerton and Cape Fry to the north, firing guns and leaving messages on shore to alert the

15. HENRY ELLIS. 'A New Chart of the parts where a North West Passage was sought in the Years 1746 and 1747'.
HBC Archives, Provincial Archives of Manitoba

Shows the broken coastline opposite Marble Island, and farther north Chesterfield Inlet, entered by the expedition's boats in July 1747, but not followed to its end.

lost boats. To add to their bad humour, the tidal flow at Cape Fry was only ten feet, far short of the eighteen feet or more that Foxe was supposed to have observed along the same stretch of coast in 1631.

The schooner and the longboat finally appeared in the early hours of the morning of 23 July, and the reason for the delay was explained. Independently of each other, they had discovered and entered a previously unknown inlet in latitude 63°44'N. In Drage's account it appears as Bowden's Inlet, named after William Bowden, a merchant who had subscribed to the expedition. Rather more grandly, Ellis named it Chesterfield Inlet in honour of a more prominent investor, the Earl of Chesterfield, one of the best-known politicians of the day; and it is this name that has survived. The boats had come across the most important inlet on the west coast of Hudson Bay, more than two hundred miles deep, but unnoticed by previous explorers because its entrance was

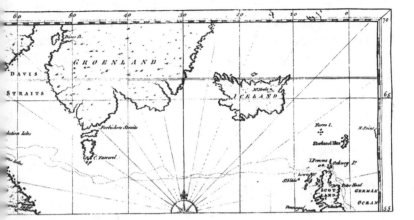

screened by islands (*Ill. 21*). While sailing north a week earlier to the rendezvous at Cape Fullerton, Smith had merely noted it as a bay. Drage related the new discovery to earlier explorations when he suggested that the opening was in fact the Whalebone Bay of Scroggs's journal of 1722, sighted but not explored by Richard Norton on Scroggs's voyage that year. Westall in the longboat was the first to discover the inlet, lying between bold shores seven or eight leagues across. Despite his orders not to explore any openings, he entered the inlet and sailed up it for four days. All the signs were promising: the shores became steeper, the tide continued strong, and the water was deep and salt. Then, after four days, and with the boat about sixty miles up the inlet, the water shoaled and became fresher, and the tide dropped to nine feet. As Westall turned back, he saw the *Dobbs Galley*'s schooner coming up the inlet. Together the boats returned to the ships, where Smith was furious at what he saw as Westall's escapade. The ships had been exposed to dangerous sea conditions off Cape Fullerton for more than a week, at a time when they should have entered the Welcome. Even more frustrating was the fact that Westall, having disobeyed orders, had then not followed the inlet to its end. As Smith pointed out, his discovery was inconclusive, for all that could be reported was that 'there was an Inlet in such a certain Latitude'. And a challenge by one of the longboat's crew to Westall's report that the water was fresh at the turning-back point was an uncomfortable reminder of the disputes over Middleton's explorations. Smith's immediate reaction was that they should return to the inlet, and follow it as far as they could go, but after discussion with Moor he agreed that they should first explore the Wager. All the tidal observations made by the two captains during the days of waiting off Cape Fullerton indicated that the main tide in the Welcome came down from the north, from the direction of the Wager. That the Wager was the entrance to the Northwest Passage was a cardinal point of belief for Dobbs, and both Moor and Smith must have felt under pressure to confirm this. If further time was spent investigating the new inlet, and it proved to be yet another dead end, it might then be too late to sail north to the Wager, which Middleton's voyage had shown was often choked with ice.

Because of thick, hazy weather and a difference of opinion between Moor and Smith over their latitude, the expedition did not reach the Wager until 29 July. As the ships came up to its entrance they were swept in by a violent tidal flow, with pieces of ice crashing all around. 'The Water raged, foamed, boiled and whirled about as if it had been a great Torrent', Ellis wrote. The *California* spun round four or five times before its crew could regain control, and it took three hours before the ships reached quieter waters farther up the inlet. Eventually they found an anchorage about forty miles higher up than Savage Sound (where Middleton's ships had found refuge in 1742), and there a council decided that the boats should take a month's provisions and explore the Wager 'to determine whether it is a Passage to the Western Ocean of America, or not'. The boats this time were commanded by Moor and Smith in person. Thompson and Ellis were with Moor in the schooner, and Drage accompanied Smith in the *California*'s longboat. At the last moment Smith decided to leave his first mate, James Holding, in command of the *California* while the boats were away, since the second mate, Jeremiah Westall, who was originally left in charge, had made it clear that he would not wait beyond late August for the boats' return.

The boats sailed up the gloomy, rocky inlet until a hundred and fifty miles from the entrance it narrowed to three miles across, and as darkness fell 'a very loud unaccountable Noise, resembling the Sound of a vast Cataract, or prodigious Fall of Water', was heard ahead. The next day the source of the noise was revealed as a tidal wave of water crashing through a gap in the rocks that in places was no more than sixty yards across. This was the reversing fall between the Wager and Ford Lake, where the tide was surged in from the Wager at a frightening sixteen knots, and the boats had to wait for half-tide when water levels were the same on each side of the falls. Although their optimism was considerably dampened by this obstacle, once past the falls the crews could see clear water for some leagues ahead. Two days later they came to shoal water. At daybreak on 4 August 'we went ashore', Ellis wrote, and saw that 'our hitherto imagined Strait ended in two small unnavigable rivers'. In his account Drage doubted whether there was enough water even for a canoe. An additional disappointment was the failure of an Inuit group encountered at this spot to show any knowledge either of a sea to the west or a copper mine to the north. Ellis chalked out a rough map for them to study, but to no avail – 'they seemed not in the least to understand me'.

The council meeting held when the boats got back to the ships on 7 August was a depressed affair, and neither captain seemed prepared to give a lead. Thompson thought that there might be some openings on the north shore of the Wager worth investigating, while Ellis wanted to head out into the Welcome and explore Repulse Bay. Only Thompson's proposal was accepted, and he and Ellis set off in the *Resolution* for the north shore. After five days they returned with a familiar story of distant openings that turned into closed bays as they were approached. It was at this point in his account

Douglas Harbour

The Fall in the Upper part of Wager Bay

16. 'Douglas Harbour' and 'The Fall in the Upper Part of Wager Bay'.
From Henry Ellis, *A Voyage to Hudson's-Bay* (1748).
HBC Archives, Provincial Archives of Manitoba

Top: The discovery vessels anchored at Douglas Harbour, on the north shore
of the Wager.

Bottom: The reversing fall between the Wager and Ford Lake. The *Resolution*
schooner, its small jolly boat and the longboat (half-hidden) of the *California*
are shown waiting for half-tide, when the water level on each side of the fall
would be the same.

that Ellis claimed that whatever the attitude of members of the council might be, many of the seamen retained their enthusiasm, 'discoursing over all the Points that were of greatest Consequence to the Success of our Voyage; such as the Nature of Tides, the Indications that might be drawn from them, and the Circumstances requisite to be observed about them; the Figure of the Globe, the Disposition of Land and Water, the Advantages that would arise to Great-Britain, from a Discovery of the North West Passage, and such like'. One 'honest Seaman, whose sole Delight was a delicious Dram', swore that 'Now had I rather find the NORTH WEST PASSAGE than HALF an ANCHOR of BRANDY.' Subsequent events indicate a rather different picture. At the council meeting that followed the schooner's return, Ellis once more argued for a northward diversion to Repulse Bay, but again this was rejected. 'There were some who began to be tired of so much Labour and Hardship', and only wanted an end to the voyage, Ellis wrote grimly. Instead, it was decided to investigate the tides in the Welcome and at the southern tip of Coats Island. There was no mention of the deep inlet to the south which had been discovered by Westall, although when the decision had been taken in late July to head for the Wager it was on the understanding that if no passage was found there then the ships would go back to the newly-discovered inlet and follow it farther inland. Drage at least was under no illusion about the meaning of the 14 August decision as he described how quickly the crews got the vessels ready for sea, 'the sick looking on it to be in their Way Home'.

The councils, with their majority votes, almost guaranteed compromise and indecision. The captains were often at loggerheads, Smith was distrustful of his second mate, and Moor must have been nervously aware of Ellis's watchful presence. In this situation the fainthearts usually won the day. Some useful surveying work had been done, thanks to the sensible decision to use boats rather than the ships in close coastal work. The accounts and charts of Ellis and Drage have much new detail on the west coast of Hudson Bay, and Chesterfield Inlet was a major discovery; but their disagreement on the names of some of the more important features of that coast was a recipe for future confusion. Rankin's Inlet, Chesterfield's Inlet and Cape Montagu in Ellis's account appear as Douglas's Bay, Bowden's Inlet and Cape Smith in Drage's narrative. The different names are indicative of the overlapping, disjointed nature of much of the exploration, marked by rivalry rather than by collaboration.

As the *California* sailed out of the Wager most of the crew were so ill that Captain Smith had to take the helm, while the mate went aloft to reef the sails. Only Ellis seems to have kept his enthusiasm for discovery. As the ships sailed down the Welcome he went ashore in a small boat on its eastern shore to test the tide. After finding that it flowed from the north, as Middleton had always maintained, the boat's crew had a desperate thirty-mile return through heavy seas before they got back to the ship. At the council meeting that was held after Ellis's return, an unnamed officer of the *Dobbs Galley* refused to go ashore with the boat again, and he was supported by the petty officers and men. Faced with this threat of mutiny, and with Moor's report that one-third of his crew were too weak to come on deck, the council decided to make for home. The passage through Hudson Strait was stormy and cold, and more of the crews went down with scurvy. The only reassurance was the sight of two well-manned Hudson's Bay Company ships in the Strait, and as far as possible the discovery ships kept company with them for the rest of the voyage. When the ships arrived at the Orkneys, Moor reported that three men had died on the Atlantic crossing, while Smith had to borrow an officer and some hands from a man-at-war to help navigate the *California*. The discovery ships finally reached the Thames in the middle of October, their enfeebled crews in little better condition than Middleton's had been five years earlier, and their captains with a gloomy report to make to the expectant Dobbs and the North West Committee.

6

A Parliamentary Inquiry and
its Aftermath

*'And the Person who had promoted this Discovery . . . hopes
it won't be taken amiss of him, that after so many years
Trouble and Attendance, at a great Expence to his Private
Fortune, and Loss to his Family; that he should hereafter
retire and leave the Prosecution of the Discovery of the
Passage and Extension of the British Trade to some more
happy Adventurer.'*

[ARTHUR DOBBS], *A Short Narrative and
Justification* (1749)

AFTER THE RETURN OF THE *Dobbs Galley* and *California*
in October 1747 the crews were paid off, except for
Moor and Smith, whose conduct was still being investigated
by the North West Committee the following February. No
record remains of the Committee's findings, but the opportunity to blame the two quarrelsome captains for the failure of
the voyage was too good to miss. Arthur Dobbs later claimed
that Moor and Smith had been appointed only because no
other seamen with knowledge of the Hudson Bay navigation
were available, and that he and the Committee had been
'defeated in their Expectations, by the Timidity, ill Conduct,
or bad Inclinations' of the captains and some of the other
officers. The expedition itself had cost £1500 more than had
been raised by subscription, and Samuel Smith wrote to the
original investors appealing to them to make up the deficit.
The incentive he offered was the likely success of a petition

that the North West Committee had just presented to the Privy Council. Supported by merchants from London, Bristol, Liverpool and Cardiff, this asked the Crown for a charter to run for a fixed period, during which both the subscribers to the 1746 expedition and the new merchant investors would have the same rights in all lands they discovered as the Hudson's Bay Company had in its settlements. Dobbs once more used his contacts in the political world to gain support for the new scheme. He wrote to Judge Ward in December 1747 listing those he had seen: the Duke of Dorset, Lord President of Council; the Earl of Chesterfield, Secretary of State for the Northern Department; Lords Anson and Vere Beauclerk at the Admiralty; and Andrew Stone, the influential secretary to the Duke of Newcastle, Secretary of State for the Southern Department. All of these, Dobbs added, 'think well of my project, and wish it Success'.

What had been implicit in Dobbs's earlier campaign was now brought into the open; the search for the Northwest Passage was subsumed into an attempt to gain a commercial charter. 'The Prayer of our Petition,' Smith wrote to the investors, 'is founded upon the great Expense the Subscribers have been at in the late Attempt, the Probability of a passage, and the great loss the publick sustains by the not settling; and inlarging the trade of that Vast Continent.' In effect, the proposed new company would replace the Hudson's Bay Company in all except a few locations, for as one of the Company's directors pointed out, the provision that it would be allowed to keep its existing settlements amounted in Dobbs's definition to little more than a concession that the Company could have 'a House and Garden' at each of the Bayside sites. The Privy Council referred the petition to the Attorney-General and Solicitor-General (the Law Officers of the Crown) for an opinion, and whereas the Company argued that Dobbs and his merchant associates were using the Northwest Passage as a pretext for attacking its charter, they in turn stated that the expedition of Moor and Smith had gone some way towards discovering the passage. Despite the flimsiness of this claim, most published comment supported Dobbs and the North West Committee, and was hostile towards the Hudson's Bay Company. The first report of the expedition's misfortunes to appear in the London press – published anonymously but almost certainly written by the surgeon, Edward Thompson – castigated the Company, whose profits 'are what no body, but the persons concerned can conceive'. Politicians, merchants and journalists could only take their facts where they found them, and Dobbs and his supporters monopolised the printed word. The effect of anti-Company publicity can be seen in the writings of John Campbell. Unlike many commentators, he was not inclined to censure monopolistic companies wholesale, but the Hudson's Bay Company he condemned for its policy of secrecy, for encouraging the belief that Hudson Bay was 'the most forlorn and dreadful Part of the Universe', and for its failure to find the Northwest Passage.

It was in this context that Henry Ellis's account of the voyage, published in August 1748, played its part. The first indication that there would be a book of the expedition came with a newspaper advertisement at the end of January 1748 announcing the forthcoming publication of an account by a member of the discovery crews, identified only as the clerk of the *California*. A few days later another advertisement promised 'A Genuine and Authentic Relation' of the voyage by Henry Ellis. The ill-feeling between Drage and Ellis, so evident during the wintering at York, now spilled over into authorial rivalry. In the race to publish, Drage managed to get out his first volume in May 1748, but this was concerned only with the outward voyage and the first months at York. His more important second volume, which dealt with the explorations of the 1747 season, did not appear until February 1749. Ellis's account of the expedition was briefer than Drage's, but it attracted more publicity and attention. It was reprinted the next year in a pirated edition at Dublin, and translated into French and Dutch. Written in his capacity as agent for the

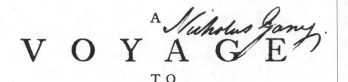

A
V O Y A G E
T O
H U D S O N's-B A Y,
BY THE
Dobbs Galley and *California*,

In the Years 1746 and 1747,

For Diſcovering a

NORTH WEST PASSAGE;

WITH

An accurate Survey of the Coaſt, and a ſhort
Natural Hiſtory of the Country.

TOGETHER WITH

A fair View of the Facts and Arguments from
which the future finding of ſuch a Paſſage is
rendered probable.

By *H E N R Y   E L L I S*, Gent.

Agent for the Proprietors in the ſaid Expedition.

To which is prefixed,

An Hiſtorical Account of the Attempts hitherto made
for the finding a Paſſage that Way to the *Eaſt-Indies*.

Illuſtrated with proper Cuts, and a new and correct Chart
of *Hudſon's-Bay*, with the Countries adjacent.

L O N D O N:
Printed for H. WHITRIDGE, at the *Royal Exchange*.
M.DCC.XLVIII.

17. Title-page of Henry Ellis, *A Voyage to Hudson's-Bay* (1748).
HBC Archives, Provincial Archives of Manitoba.

This copy was in the possession of Nicholas Garry, Deputy Governor of
the Hudson's Bay Company from 1822 to 1835.

North West Committee, Ellis's book was in effect the official narrative, and anticipated Drage's second volume by six months. In other ways, too, Ellis seemed to hold all the advantages. He was granted an audience with Frederick, Prince of Wales, and allowed to dedicate the book to him, referring to 'the gracious Audience you were pleased to allow me, soon after my Return from this Voyage; the many judicious Questions you were pleased to ask, and the generous Care you expressed, for the happy Progress of this Design'. Other important patrons were Lord Halifax, soon to become President of the Board of Trade, and Lord Barrington, one of the Lords Commissioners of the Admiralty. A further mark of respectability came in 1750 when Ellis was elected Fellow of the Royal Society on the grounds of his 'uncommon zeal for the making of discoveries and promoting Natural History, Geography and Navigation'.

For Drage, who had taken care to preserve full records of the expedition, the favourable reception given to Ellis's slipshod book was infuriating. He took revenge in the second volume of his own account where he portrayed Ellis as Moor's partner in a conspiracy to make the discovery in secret, so wrecking the expedition's chances of success. Drage's critical opinion of the rival book would have been supported by Isham, who was outraged at Ellis's version of events during the wintering at York which he thought was 'neither consistant with truth, Justice, nor honour'. Isham thought slightly better of Drage as a witness, though his comment that he was 'more perticular as to truth' than Ellis was damning with the faintest of faint praise. Isham's comments never saw the light of day, and Drage's could be dismissed as those of a jealous rival. In 1748 Ellis's book was the only account of the explorations available, and its viewpoint was that of an apologist for the North West Committee. In its pages on the wintering at York the Company was shown in the worst possible light, while the explorations of the summer of 1747, Ellis explained, 'tho' they did not absolutely show where the Passage lay, yet seem to have firmly established the Certainty, that such a Passage there is'. There was more on this in the last section of the book, characteristically entitled, 'The great Probability of a Passage ... notwithstanding the same was not actually discovered in the Last Expedition'. In words that echoed those of Dobbs, Ellis maintained that the only explanation for the high tides on the west coast of Hudson Bay was a short connecting strait with the Pacific. He ignored suggestions that Hudson Bay might be connected to Baffin Bay, as he did Middleton's evidence that the flood-tide flowing through Frozen Strait was responsible for the unusually high tides in the Bay. Instead he pointed to two places where the entrance of the passage might lie: Chesterfield Inlet and Middleton's Repulse Bay. The first had not been followed to its end; while a strait opening out of Repulse Bay would explain the tide flowing southward down the Welcome. To readers who might be baffled by the technicalities of tidal flows, Ellis offered an explanation in homely language. They should think of Hudson Bay in terms of a labyrinth, he wrote, whose entrance was through Hudson Strait. The problem was to find the way out on the far side, helped by the fact that 'the Tide is a Kind of Clue, which seems to lead us by the Hand through all the Windings and Turnings of this Labyrinth, and if studiously and steadily followed must certainly lead us out'. In conclusion, Ellis stressed the danger that other nations might discover the passage, for the Russians were known to be sending expeditions towards the northwest coast of America. All in all, Ellis argued, 'another Expedition, properly conducted, cannot fail of producing an absolute Certainty whether there is such a Passage or not'.

In the same month that Ellis's book was published, the opinion of the Attorney-General and Solicitor-General on the petition of the North West Committee brought a sense of reality to the scene. The Law Officers opposed any new grant that would result in two companies holding charters to trade in the same region, and they showed some scepticism about the Northwest Passage. They acknowledged that its discovery would be useful, 'if it ever be made', but would not concede that the financial loss incurred because of an unsuccessful attempt to find it gave the North West Committee any right to recompense in the form of a charter. In effect they accepted the argument laid before them by the Hudson's Bay Company that the North West Committee 'complain of the Company's having a charter, yet apply for one to take away the Company's lands and property . . . complain of the Company's privileges, and require the same . . . complain the Company refuse strangers to take away their trade, yet demand an exclusive trade themselves'. The acceptance by the Privy Council in December 1748 of the Law Officers' recommendation came as a further blow to Dobbs, whose hopes of ministerial backing were now shown to be illusory. Not for the first time, he had mistaken polite acknowledgements of interest for promises of active support. After consulting the Duke of Argyle, Walpole's old adviser in Scotland, Dobbs had already decided to lay the whole matter before Parliament, and in March 1749 a Committee of the House of Commons was appointed to investigate conditions and trade in Hudson Bay. Outside Parliament, agitation against the Company developed in a way that bore the familiar hallmarks of a well-organised campaign, and during April and May twenty-eight petitions reached the Commons from the ports and manufacturing towns praying that the trade of Hudson Bay should be thrown open. It was part of a series of co-ordinated attacks on several of the chartered companies led by Liverpool and Bristol merchants, with substantial support from London and the other trading towns.

As the petitions arrived, the Parliamentary Committee was busy questioning witnesses, twenty-two in all. Of these fifteen were former servants of the Company, six were merchants, and the remaining one was Dobbs. Most of the merchants were associated with the move to open the Bay trade, and their evidence was predictably optimistic about the prospects of expansion. Of the ex-servants of the Company summoned before the Committee many were hostile to their old employers. The first called, Joseph Robson, had been dismissed by the Company two years earlier. Others had left the Company's service to sail on the two Northwest Passage expeditions; yet others had been in the Bay many years before, and had little useful to tell the Committee. The one-sided nature of the evidence stemmed partly from the decision of the Company not to produce any witnesses before the Committee, though it reserved the right to be heard before the House of Commons at a later stage. Among the witnesses who did appear, Dobbs must have been sorely disappointed by his interrogation. He was given no opportunity to expand on his favourite subjects of the Northwest Passage and the restrictive practices of the Hudson's Bay Company, but was questioned only about the authenticity of the narrative of the itinerant French-Canadian trader, Joseph la France, that he had printed five years earlier in his *Account of Hudson's Bay*. Other witnesses were asked about a wider range of subjects, and these included the possibility of a Northwest Passage. William Moor's evidence was as inconclusive as his explorations. He still thought that there was a passage, but admitted that it was farther north than he had expected, and he did not know whether it was navigable. John Carruthers, who more than thirty years earlier had been with Governor Knight at Churchill, was more doubtful still. He concluded that it was 'the general Opinion of Sea-faring Men that there is no such Passage', and even if one existed he would rather sail into the Pacific round Cape Horn than face the hazards of its icy waters. Edward Thompson conceded that the Wager was a closed bay, but still clung to the hope that the flow of the tides, the sighting of black whales, and Indian reports of a great sea to the west, showed that there was a passage. Probably of more interest to the Committee than these rather tired arguments was Thompson's recollection of the exploration of Chesterfield Inlet in August 1747. He had been one of the crew of the schooner *Resolution* which had followed Westall's longboat into the inlet. At the point where the schooner turned back, they were sounding fifty fathoms with the lead, there was a strong tide, and the water was so salt that it 'candied' on the men's boots. It was a sign of the one-sided selection of witnesses, that neither Jeremiah Westall nor any other member of the crew of the longboat was summoned, even though they had sailed fifteen miles farther up the inlet than Thompson.

For Dobbs the most depressing statements on the subject of the Northwest Passage came from his merchant allies. It was they who posed the real threat to the Hudson's Bay Company; for they had supplied much of the capital for the 1746 voyage, and would be largely responsible for financing any future voyages to Hudson Bay. Both John Hanbury of London, who had been an investor in the 1746 enterprise, and John Hardman of Liverpool, who was the main organiser of the petitions flooding into Parliament at this time, made the same point. The failure of two expeditions had discouraged attempts to find a passage, and the only realistic course was to leave its discovery to a time when the opening of Hudson Bay to all merchants would lead to a natural increase in trade and population. Others echoed the same theme, for there was a growing realisation that the difficulties that the two discovery expeditions had encountered considerably diminished the commercial attractiveness of a passage, even if one were found. Not only would ships have to be strengthened, and captains engaged who were experienced in ice-navigation, but since the Atlantic end of the passage was blocked by ice for three-quarters of the year it could be used only during a restricted season. Even with careful timing, there would always be the possibility that ships coming through the passage from the west would arrive at Hudson Strait too late to pass into the Atlantic, and would be trapped in the Bay for the winter. A safe use of the passage was hardly possible unless the Bay posts could be used as wintering places; and this meant that they had to be in the hands of those organising the trade through the passage. The merchants were adopting the only practical approach when they insisted that abolition of the Company's monopoly must precede any further discovery voyages.

For its part, the Company made strenuous efforts to convince the Parliamentary Committee that it had taken seriously its responsibility to find a passage, and if it was trying to make much out of little, it could at least claim that it was not as lethargic as its opponents claimed. As the Company's solicitor, Joshua Sharpe, pointed out in his *Case of the Hudson's-Bay Company*, if the Company vessels had not found a passage, then neither had the non-Company expeditions. Sharpe's pamphlet was one of a half-dozen publications issued in the spring of 1749, and these included the second and weightier volume of Drage's account. The clerk of the *California* had little time for Ellis's speculations about Chesterfield Inlet. Rather than the entrance of the Northwest Passage, Drage preferred to regard it simply as 'an Inlet, the End of which has not been determined'. It was the more striking, then, and a sign of things to come, that he took seriously the farrago of nonsense that was the Fonte letter printed by Dobbs a few years earlier. Many of the obvious problems with distances and locations he put down to printer's errors, and his analysis of the account was accompanied by the first printed chart to show the supposed discoveries of Admiral de Fonte (*Ill.18*). On this the opening on the northwest coast of America through which Fonte's ships passed into a network of interior waterways was identified as the fabled Strait of Anian that had appeared on maps since the mid-sixteenth century. In his accompanying text, Drage asserted that the location of the southern shore of Fonte's entrance was the same as that of the southern shore of the Strait of Anian, in latitude 51°N., longitude 147°47'W. Although he did not give the source for this surprisingly exact location, it came from Pascoe Thomas, schoolmaster on Anson's *Centurion* during the voyage round the world, who published an account of the voyage in 1745. At the end of his book Thomas appended a list that had been captured from the Spaniards of the latitudes and longitudes of various places

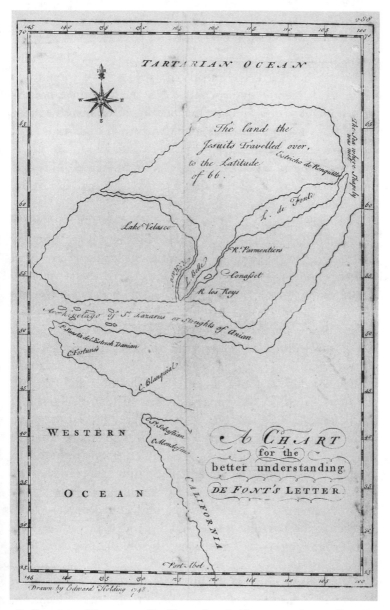

The land the
Jesuits Travelled over,
to the Latitude
of 66.

Estrecho de Ronquillo

The Sea where Shapely now met

TARTARIAN OCEAN

W E
S

L. de Fonte

Lake Velasco

R. Parmentiers

L. Belle

Conasset

R. los Reys

Archipelago of St. Lazarus or Streights of Anian

Po Puerta del Estrech Damian

C. Fortuno

C. Blanquial

WESTERN

P. S. Sebastian

C. Mendofino

*A Chart
for the
better understanding
DE FONT'S LETTER.*

OCEAN

CALIFORNIA

Port Abel.

Drawn by Edward Holding 1748.

18. EDWARD HOLDING. 'A Chart for the better understanding De
Font's Letter', 1749.
British Library

This sketch, published in Vol. II of the Clerk of the *California's Account of a
Voyage for the Discovery of a North-West Passage* was the first published chart
to depict Admiral de Fonte's voyage of 1640. The waterways through which
Fonte's ships passed are shown, but there is no effort to set these simple
outlines in the more general context of North American geography.

in the South Sea. The farthest north of these was 'The Point of Suestra del Estrech Danian' in latitude 51°N. longitude 147°47'w. A sceptic might wonder why the longitude, notoriously difficult to determine in this period, rather than the more straightforward latitude, was given with such exactitude. For the more credulous, this information, contained in an otherwise mundane table of observations, strengthened the long-standing suspicion in Britain that the Spaniards had discovered the Strait of Anian but had kept it secret.

As well as the books of Drage and Ellis, several pamphlets were published at this time on the Hudson's Bay Company and the Northwest Passage. Two of them seem to have been written (anonymously) by Dobbs. One offered *Reasons to shew, that there is a great Probability of a Navigable Passage*. Despite the optimism of the title, the pamphlet indicated how weak the arguments for the existence of a passage had now become. The last expedition had shown that the Wager was a bay, not a great strait leading to the western ocean; tidal observations were inconclusive if not downright unhelpful; and reliance was now placed on the fantasy voyages of Juan de Fuca and Bartholomew de Fonte. The writer conjured up a situation in which Fuca in 1592 and Fonte in 1640 both reached Hudson Bay, probably through Chesterfield Inlet. Even the unfortunate James Knight was brought back into the picture. The small amount of wreckage from his expedition and the lack of survivors pointed to the fact that only one ship had been wrecked in the Bay, and it followed that the other had reached, and perhaps negotiated, the passage before disappearing from view.

A surviving copy of Dobbs's second pamphlet, *A Short State of the Countries and Trade of North America. Claimed by the Hudson's Bay Company*, has handwritten annotations by an unnamed director of the Company. The contrast between the ambitious, extravagant proposals of Dobbs and the cautious policies of the Company is nowhere better illustrated than in those pages where the Company director's derisory comments accompany Dobbs's assertions. In a way familiar to those who had read his earlier books, Dobbs accused the Company of failing to expand the trade of the Bay region, so leaving the way open for the French. It had made little effort to find the Northwest Passage despite the advantages which such a discovery would bring. Once through the passage and into the north Pacific, then gold, silver and precious stones would lie within the grasp of British merchants, Dobbs claimed; agreed, scribbled his annotator, and 'when the Sky falls a great Number of Larks may be catched'. The argument was being conducted at two different levels. Dobbs and his associates were proposing vast, expansive schemes, filling in the blank spaces on their small-scale maps of North America with an easy confidence, and predicting a tenfold increase in trade 'in a very short Time'. The Company was thinking in practical terms, of the possible rather than the ideal, and with emphasis on the difficulties rather the opportunities of the Bay trade.

The pamphlet revealed a change of tactics by Dobbs. He no longer advocated another full-scale expedition to find the passage, but agreed with the merchants of the North West Committee that trade must precede discovery. Rumours had persisted throughout 1748 that a new voyage was being prepared, but if there was such a plan it was soon abandoned. The *Dobbs Galley* and *California* had been sold early that year, and Drage later recollected that 'The Adventurers differing among themselves on settling their accounts, all designs for a future Expedition were dropped.' It was at this time that an enthusiastic cleric wrote a long poem urging Dobbs to lead in person an expedition to find the Northwest Passage:

> Dauntless proceed, charg'd with a Kingdom's Fate!
> Go, crown'd with Blessings of this native Land;
> While shouting Thousands wait thee to the Strand.

There would have been others, beginning with Captain Middleton, who would have supported this plea for the great promoter to experience the hazards of the icy waters of

Hudson Bay in person, but Dobbs resisted the temptation. Instead, he announced his retirement from the struggle in favour of 'some more happy Adventurer'. Although this withdrawal was not quite as complete as his public statement implied, it confirmed that there had been a change of priorities by those campaigning for an opening of the Hudson Bay trade. Of the twenty-eight petitions on this subject presented to Parliament in the spring of 1749, only five mentioned the Northwest Passage. The final petition was from the Company itself, and it too reflected changing attitudes as it pleaded that it should not be condemned because its Governor and Committee had 'not persisted to waste their Capital in looking for a Passage, which they have no reason to think exists'.

This forthright approach makes the reasoning behind one of the Company's publications at this time quite incomprehensible. In March 1749 it placed an order with the cartographer and engraver, R.W.Seale, for two hundred copies of a map of North America that he had engraved the previous year at the Company's request. Several copies of this 'Map of North America with Hudson's Bay and Straights' (*Ill.19*) are still in the archives of the Hudson's Bay Company, where they rub shoulders with less imaginative productions. It is a handsome affair, with decorative versions of the Royal Arms and the Company's coat of arms in its upper corners, but its most striking feature is the number of gratuitous errors that it contains. Although most of North America west of the Great Lakes remained unknown to Europeans, maps were available in England and France which showed with a reasonable degree of accuracy the most important geographical features of the eastern half of the continent. On Seale's map many of these were grotesquely misplaced and distorted, but the oddest features of the map lie farther west, where Fonte's discoveries jostle against imaginary lands of huge extent. Whether Seale drew as well as engraved this curious piece of speculative geography cannot be established with certainty. The Company's financial ledgers refer to sums being paid to Seale, first for engraving, and then for printing, but they do not indicate whether he drew the map as well. Since there is no entry in the records of money being paid to another cartographer for designing the map, the logical inference is that Seale or a member of his staff was responsible. By this time Seale was much in demand both as a cartographer and an engraver, and during his lifetime drew and engraved hundreds of maps for periodicals, histories and collections of travels. He had assisted in the engraving of Henry Popple's celebrated 'Map of the British Empire in America' in 1733, and ten years later engraved Middleton's chart of his explorations in Hudson Bay.

That the Hudson's Bay Company could find good use for a map of its territories at this critical moment in its history is not surprising. In March 1748 Joshua Sharpe was asked to compose his *Case of the Hudson's-Bay Company* for distribution to MPs, and during the same month Seale ran off two hundred copies of his map. It seems likely that the map was intended to accompany Sharpe's pamphlet, perhaps with the boundaries claimed by the Company against the French marked in colour (as they are on two of the surviving copies of the map). But what is almost beyond belief is that the Company, shrewd and businesslike, allowed this particular map to be issued in its name. It was at once inaccurate and speculative, an example of the imaginary geography strenuously criticised by the Company in these years. It could well have been drawn by Dobbs to accompany his *Short State of the Countries and Trade of North America*, where he had enthused about the existence of 'rich, civilized Nations, near or upon the Coast of the Western Ocean'. One can only surmise that no Company director saw the map until Seale delivered his two hundred copies, and if this was so then it is probable that any intention of circulating it was quietly dropped. The discrepancy between the title of

19. EDWARD SEALE. 'A Map of North America with Hudson's Bay and Straights', 1748.
HBC Archives, Provincial Archives of Manitoba (G.4/20a)

Drawn in 1748, and engraved in 1749, this map stands with Holding's 'Chart for the better understanding De Font's Letter' as the earliest representation of Northwest America based on Fonte's supposed discoveries. California as an island and the Strait of Anian can be found on the other maps of the period, but the outline of the Pacific coast north from Anian to Lancaster Sound (inexplicably displaced west from Baffin Bay) owed nothing to other

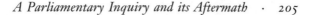

cartographers. Instead, it relied on Fonte's narrative, marking his track, and showing his place names, although it made no attempt to show a system of inland seas and straits as later maps were to do. Even more striking are the great mass of 'De Gama's Land' and 'Compaignes Land', stretching for thousands of miles across the North Pacific, and farther west the island of 'Jedso'. These lands, where precious metals were reported to be so common that even domestic utensils were made of gold and silver, had emerged from a jumble of reports about Portuguese, Spanish and Dutch voyages east of Japan.

the map and the actual area shown on it adds weight to the supposition that the cartographer had been given the title on the assumption that he would produce a standard map of North America for the Company's use; and that during the rush of business that accompanied the Dobbs crisis the Company had not approved, or even seen, the drawing on which the engraving was based. It is perhaps of significance that when in 1750 the Board of Trade asked the Hudson's Bay Company for a map of its territories, it responded, not with a copy of the Seale map, but with one drawn for it that year by a different cartographer.

With or without Seale's bizarre map in front of it, in May 1749 the House of Commons spent several days considering the report of its Committee. In general the attention of the House moved away from the points of detail that had occupied much of the time of the investigating Committee, and centred on the issues of national policy raised by the controversy. In particular it needed to consider whether the Hudson's Bay Company was an effective rival to the French in North America, and whether it should not make more effort to open up the interior. Here the Company was vulnerable, but its opponents had weakened their case by loud exaggeration. In reply to repeated questions the Company's servants doggedly insisted that cost, difficulties of terrain and transportation problems, ruled out any large-scale movement inland. The future was to show that expansion into the interior was not quite the fearsome prospect imagined by the old hands at the Bay posts, but in 1749 it was they and not the Company critics who spoke with the voice of experience. A motion before the House that the Company's monopoly should be subject to legal scrutiny was defeated by more than two to one. Ministers may have been concerned as they heard evidence suggesting that the Company lacked energy in exploiting its vast grant, but they had no guarantee that either of the alternatives proposed at this time – the establishment of a rival company, or the opening of the trade to individual merchants – would have produced a firmer bulwark against the French. A newspaper report seems to have reflected the view of most MPs when it commented that 'as it appeared to be impossible to preserve this trade without forts and settlements on the coast of Hudson's Bay, and as such forts and settlements must be supported either by exclusive companies, or at the publick expense, the affair was dropt'.

With this verdict, the search for a Northwest Passage through Hudson Bay by privately-financed expeditions was to all intents and purposes over. It is significant that in 1750 the final pamphlet of this period on the passage, written by Henry Ellis, suggested that the search might switch to the Pacific coast of North America. There, he pointed out, 'the Weather is milder, and the Seas clearer of Ice', and discovery ships would not have to cope with the 'Difficulties and Obstructions' put in their way by the Hudson's Bay Company. Ellis himself seems to have been involved in discussions with the Admiralty in December 1749 about a possible naval expedition to find the Pacific entrance of the passage. Reports in the *London Evening Post* described meetings between Ellis and the Board of Admiralty, and in particular Lord Anson, about a new discovery voyage. Ellis, they reported, was to command an expedition of three naval sloops 'to the back of America, where, as the Sea is open and the Weather mild, he would have better Opportunities of coasting, and passing from thence into our Northern Seas'. There is no note of such meetings in the Admiralty records, and it is most unlikely that Ellis would have been offered a commission, but it is not out of the question that some sort of northern expedition was under consideration with Ellis as its agent. Certainly, both the French and Spanish governments took the reports seriously, and exchanged opinions on how best to resist British incursions into the Pacific that might come either round Cape Horn, or through a northern passage. In the end, negotiations with the East India Company, which held monopoly rights over much of the region the naval vessels would sail through if they reached the North Pacific or the Eastern Seas, seem to have delayed agreement on the venture until the approach of war with France turned the minds of ministers and officials to more urgent matters. It would be more than ten years before the Admiralty again gave its attention to the Northwest Passage.

The leading participants in the search for a passage in the 1740s experienced very different fortunes. That fine seaman Christopher Middleton found little joy in his service in the navy after his appointment in 1745 to the *Shark* sloop, for she was 'very Old, much Worne & almost unfit for the Service'. When two army officers came on board there was no room to stow their chests; they were left on deck, with Middleton's, and were under water much of the time. In 1747 he was involved in a heated quarrel with the owner of a vessel in his convoy, and was then accused by a member of his crew of fraud, forgery and assault. The investigating officer found that the first two charges were without foundation, but that Middleton had struck his boatswain. He had questioned other officers about Middleton, and concluded, 'I fear by their accounts he is passionate, which I have given him a Caution of.' When these incidents are added to the controversy that followed his earlier discovery expedition, it is not surprising that with the coming of peace in 1748 he joined hundreds of other naval officers on the half-pay list. In the winter of 1751–52 Middleton wrote two letters to the the Hudson's Bay Company shortly after its dismissal of Captain William Coats for illegal trading; but if he was seeking reinstatement in the Company's service ten years after his abrupt resignation he was disappointed. He remained on the Navy's half-pay list, receiving 4s. a day, until his death in February 1770.

About the circumstances of Middleton's last years there is some uncertainty. The *Monthly Review* for 1784 has a melancholy report to the effect that he had died 'in the utmost penury and distress', having sold his Copley Medal, and having seen all four of his children die before him, 'some of them, at least, in a more wretched situation than himself'. The evidence of Middleton's will throws doubt on this. Drawn up in December 1769, only a few weeks before his death, it refers to a daughter Judith by his first marriage, his second wife Jane (originally his servant according to local sources), who was to receive £40, and two girls and a boy by his second marriage. The Copley medal was bequeathed to his son, and his books, instruments and a unspecified sum in South Sea annuities were left to him and his two sisters jointly. The values seem small, but the will indicated that although Middleton may have lived in straitened circumstances during his enforced retirement he did not die a pauper. Even so, his skills as a navigator and hydrographer make the story of his wasted career after 1742 a sad one. His survey of the northwest coast of Hudson Bay was a major advance on what had gone before, and except for its omission of Chesterfield Inlet was to stand the test of time well. Several of the names on the modern map of Hudson Bay come from Middleton's chart of 1743 – Cape Dobbs, Wager Bay, Repulse Bay and Frozen Strait – but his own name took long to appear. It was in October 1982 that the name Cape Middleton was given (by the Canadian Committee on Geographical Names) to the northernmost point of White Island in Hudson Bay, appropriately enough overlooking the Frozen Strait that had been the subject of so much dispute in his lifetime.

Also placed on the half-pay list in 1748 was John Rankin, Middleton's lieutenant on the *Furnace*. Rankin's part in the explorations of 1742 was marked by his name appearing on the contemporary maps of Hudson Bay. 'Rankin's Inlet', opposite Marble Island, first appears on Dobbs's 1744 'New Map of North America', and was to survive. The modern maps of the region still show Rankin Inlet, the name an ill-deserved memorial to a worthless officer whose mendacity helped to wreck the career of his former captain. Of those who sailed on both discovery expeditions to Hudson Bay, William Moor and Edward Thompson gave evidence to the inquiries of 1748 and 1749, but then disappear from view. Francis Smith achieved a moment of prominence when the clerk of the *California* in his account of the expedition gave the name Cape Smith to the northern entrance of the Wager, but this has not survived, nor has any trace of him after 1748.

James Isham, in some ways the unsung hero of the two discovery expeditions to Hudson Bay, saw out his remaining years in the service of the Company at York Fort until his death there in April 1761 at the age of forty-five. Because of crippling bouts of gout, Isham could travel little himself, but in the 1750s he set in motion a series of inland journeys by Company servants at York. Most notable of these ventures was by Anthony Henday, who in 1754–55 accompanied Cree and Assiniboine groups across the northern prairies, possibly to within sight of the Rocky Mountains. The new policy was a sign that the Company had realised that as the French thrust even deeper into the interior its servants could no longer, as Isham had put it, 'sitt quiet and unconcern'd' at their Bayside posts. His 'Observations' on the inhabitants, natural history and trade of Hudson Bay set a precedent that others followed, notably his protégé at York, Andrew Graham, parts of whose later 'Observations' found their way into print in the *Philosophical Transactions* of the Royal Society. Like many Company servants in the Bay, Isham led a double life in family terms. He married a young English woman in 1748, and had one daughter by her, but he also had a son (who entered the Company's service) by a Cree woman at York Fort. It was characteristic of the man that right up to his death his thoughts were with the Company. His successor, Graham, recorded in the York journal, 'the day before he Expired he Gave me a Strict order to transact the Company's Business'. As the news of his death spread to the other Company factories, Humphrey Marten wrote from the new post on the Severn River recently established by Isham that he was 'my beloved Friend and I may truly say Father . . . a Man who was the Idol of the Indians'.

The two main publicists for the Northwest Passage enterprise, Arthur Dobbs and Henry Ellis, both prospered. Dobbs was appointed Governor of North Carolina in 1752, and took up his post two years later. In North Carolina, as in other colonies, these were difficult years, with the French war and opposition to many aspects of British rule dominating the political scene. Given Dobbs's impatient, at times overbearing, personality it is not surprising that his governorship was a turbulent one. Of his associates from the days of the campaign against the Hudson's Bay Company, Dobbs remained especially close to Samuel Smith, and although he failed to get him appointed as agent in London for the colony, Smith remained Dobbs's personal agent. Nor was the Northwest Passage forgotten. For Dobbs it still existed, awaiting explorers of 'Resolution, Capacity, and Integrity'. Near the end of his life in 1763, he responded to news of Britain's conquest of Canada from the French with the comment, 'I have nothing to wish for but the opening of the Trade to Hudson Bay and discovery of the passage to the Western American Ocean, which I have labour'd to obtain these thirty Years, and then I should die in Peace.' In his last official letter home before his death in March 1765 at the age of seventy-five he still hoped that Britain would 'discover and have an open Trade to the western American Ocean'. Dobbs's attack on the reputations of those who opposed him on the question of the Northwest Passage was cynical and unscrupulous – as Middleton had found to his cost – but there can be no doubt that to the end of his life Dobbs was obsessed by the belief that a passage existed.

Henry Ellis, only twenty-six when he returned from his voyage to Hudson Bay, had a long and varied career ahead of him. He became captain of a slaver in the African trade; was later appointed Governor of Georgia, and then of Nova Scotia; and was adviser to ministers on American affairs during the reign of George III. His retirement was spent in Italy, where he died in 1806. As a Fellow of the Royal Society with practical experience of the sea, he may have been involved in the discussions between the Council of the Society and the Admiralty in the 1770s about ice conditions in northern waters, and on the prospect of sending expeditions to the Pacific to find the Northwest Passage. As late as 1789 he was writing to a friend expressing belief in the existence of a passage. Unlike Dobbs, Ellis had seen at first hand the difficulties in trying to relate speculative theories about the passage to a seaman's task in harsh weather conditions on an icebound coast; but like Dobbs, he seems to have retained his belief in a passage to the end.

Ellis's rival on the 1746–47 discovery expedition, the clerk of the *California*, presents a baffling problem of double identity. There is no doubt that on the voyage he was known as Drage, the 'Mr Dragg' of Isham's journal. Theodorus Drage was born in about 1712, and little is known about his early life except that his first wife died in 1740, and was buried in York Minster after a funeral procession so lavish that it was recorded in the local histories. As we have seen, he joined the 1746 discovery expedition as the clerk of the *California* on release from a French prison, and his account of the voyage was written under that pseudonym. After the publication of the second volume in 1749 Theodorus Drage vanished from view for ten years. In 1750 a Captain Charles Swaine appeared on the scene in the American colonies and, claiming to be the clerk of the *California*, set about gathering support in Pennsylvania and other colonies for a voyage to Hudson Bay to find the Northwest Passage. Among his sponsors was Benjamin Franklin, who in February 1753 wrote from Philadelphia to a New York friend that 'I have procured a subscription here of £1300 to fit out a vessel in search of a North-West Passage; she sails in a few days, and is called the Argo, commanded by Mr.Swaine, who was in the last Expedition in the California, Author of a Journal of that Voyage in two Volumes.' The *Argo*, a sixty-ton schooner with a crew of fifteen, sailed on 4 March and reached the entrance of Hudson Strait before the end of June. All attempts by Swaine to get through the Strait failed, even though he tried to follow the vessels of that year's Hudson's Bay Company convoy through the ice. Forced back, Swaine explored the coast of Labrador, where there were reports of a strait between latitude 55°N. and 56°N. that led into an interior sea and possibly through to Hudson Bay. No such opening was found, but the next year Swaine and the *Argo* returned to the same stretch of coast with a mineralogist, John Patten, on board. While ashore prospecting for minerals, Patten and two other crew members were killed by Inuit, and the *Argo* returned without making any further attempt to reach Hudson Bay. The instructions for the two voyages of the *Argo* have never been found, and despite the evidence of Franklin's letter it is by no means certain whether they were genuine discovery ventures or interloping attempts to exploit the fur trade of Hudson Bay.

The failure of the voyages seems to have done Swaine's reputation no harm, and after serving as a commissary to General Braddock's army in 1754 during the opening stages of the frontier hostilities against the French, he held a number of public offices in Pennsylvania, and also engaged in the Indian trade. On 27 October 1758 Charles Swaine married Hannah Boyte in Philadelphia. Exactly a year later, on 27 October 1759, the register of the same church records that on that day Hannah Boyte married 'Charles Swaine Drage'. For the first time the names of Drage and Swaine come together, and as they do so the mystery deepens. It now seems clear that the date of the second entry in the church register, which was inserted later, was a clerical error, and that Hannah Boyte married only once, on 27 October 1758. For the next half-dozen years there are numerous references to both Drage and Swaine, often in the same context. For example, between 1762 and 1764 both men – or the one man with two names – served with Colonel Bouquet at Fort Pitt on the Pennsylvanian frontier. It is now that a composite figure emerges, with a variety of names, selected it seems at random: Charles Swaine,

Charles Swaine Drage, Theodorus Swaine, Theodorus Swaine Drage. But from about 1765 the name Charles Swaine falls from sight. The change is marked in 1768 with the publication of a book, written anonymously, *The Great Probability of a North West Passage: Deduced from Observations on the Letter of Admiral De Fonte*. One copy exists with a covering letter from its author to the Earl of Hillsborough, signed 'Theodorus Swaine Drage', but including as an appendix to the book part of his journal for the 1753 voyage to the Labrador coast. For the first time the clerk of the *California* admitted to being the captain of the *Argo*, and claimed that after the coming of peace in 1748 he left England for the American colonies 'solely with the purpose of making this Discovery' of the Northwest Passage.

In a final twist to a bizarre story, Drage was ordained an Anglican clergyman in 1769, and served as such in the Carolinas. He died in November 1774 in Camden, South Carolina, where he was remembered as 'a very fine Old Gentleman'. His possessions were sent to his widow, who called herself Hannah Swaine Drage, in Philadelphia. Among them was '1 box of sundry loose papers Manuscripts, etc'. Those papers might explain much, but they have not been traced, and no explanation can be offered for the mystery of the man with different identities. All that one can say is that, like Dobbs and Ellis, the clerk of the *California* seems to have believed in the existence of a Northwest Passage until the end of his life.

7

The Edge of a Frozen Sea

*'I left the print of my feet in blood almost at every step
I took.'*
Journal of Samuel Hearne, 25 July 1771

A S THE REVERBERATIONS of the attacks of Dobbs and
his associates died away, the Hudson's Bay Company
faced a future in which it could no longer rely on obscurity
for protection. The new facts of life were soon brought home
to it. In his *Brief Essay with regard to Trade*, the economist
Josiah Tucker angrily criticised the Company's 'escape' at the
hands of the Parliamentary Committee, and considered its
monopoly designed 'to enrich a few rapacious Directors'. In
private Tucker was even more scathing, and urged the government to buy out the Company It was a line followed by many
commentators of the period. Then in 1752 appeared the first
book based on personal experience of the Company's employ,
Joseph Robson's *Account of Six Years Residence in Hudson's-Bay*.
This 'honest and just' book, as one reviewer described it, had
much on the oppressive behaviour by Company factors in the
Bay, on the defects in the construction of the great stone
fortress at Churchill, and on the Company's trading practices.
In one cutting remark it summed up the case of the critics:
'The Company have for eighty years slept at the edge of a
frozen sea; they have shown no curiosity to penetrate farther
themselves, and have exerted all their art and power to crush
that spirit in others.'

There is no reason to doubt the accuracy of Robson's

criticism of the building techniques used at Churchill, but elsewhere his remarks need to be regarded with caution. He had been dismissed the Company's service in 1747 as 'a man who had constantly neglected his duty', and had appeared as a hostile witness before the Parliamentary Committee two years later. Moreover, it is now clear that much of his book was secretly written by Dobbs, who intended it to 'further expose the management of the Company'. The great projector's retirement from the fray, it seems, was more apparent than real. In Hudson Bay, James Isham read Robson's book and commented, 'Good Lord deliver Us from such Falsity's.' Despite the amount of first-hand evidence the Company could call upon from its servants in the Bay, it made no attempt to answer its detractors. The documents wrung from it during the Parliamentary investigation of 1749, and the printed *Case of the Hudson's Bay Company* of the same year, remained its only public contribution to knowledge in England of the Bay region and its trade. Isham's notes on Ellis's book, where he corrected statement after statement, and his caustic verdict on Robson's *Account*, remained unpublished, as did his more general 'Observations' on Hudson Bay. The journals, letters and charts from the Bayside factories reached the Company's offices in Fenchurch Street, but got no farther. In terms of public opinion the Company lost its case by default, and it owed its survival more to government nervousness that its closure might encourage the French in Canada than to any positive enthusiasm for its conduct of affairs.

In Hudson Bay itself the situation was different, for in the 1750s the Company showed a new energy in exploiting its territories. As well as the inland ventures of Anthony Henday and others from York there were fresh attempts to investigate commercial possibilities along the east and west coasts of the Bay. At Churchill, still the farthest north of the Company's posts, slooping voyages again headed north along the coast to trade with the Inuit, and through these voyages the question of the Northwest Passage once more came to the fore. A company that during the onslaughts on it during the 1740s had strenuously denied the existence either of a passage or of rich mineral deposits to the north now found itself gradually drawn into a search for both. What remained unchanged was that this search was carried on away from the public gaze. The Company neither sought nor gained credit for its new burst of exploring activity until long after the event. Its attitude remained that of the director in 1748 who responded to Dobbs's complaint that the Company never published any of its journals or charts with the laconic comment, 'It would have been imprudent.'

The new series of slooping voyages north from Churchill began in 1750 under the command of James Walker. It is a measure of his inadequacy as a seaman that his instructions are more interesting than his voyages. From the beginning it is clear that the Company, however brave a face it presented to outside criticism, had become more sensitive about allegations that it had little knowledge of the vast region granted to it by the Crown. At Churchill the factor Joseph Isbister passed on orders to Walker from the London Committee instructing him to trade with the Eskimos at Whale Cove, and then to sail north as far as possible, observing tides and making charts of the coast. In 1752 Isbister added to these general instructions a more specific directive. Walker was to search in latitude 64°N. for a large inlet called Kish-Stack-Ewen ('Swiftly Flowing Waters') by the Northern or Chipewyan Indians. This was roughly the latitude of Chesterfield Inlet, and the Company men soon identified the inlet of Indian report with the opening discovered but not fully explored by the Moor and Smith expedition in 1747.

Walker remained unmoved by his instructions, and failed to reach latitude 64°N. on any of his five voyages. Isbister was not inclined to blame him on this account, informing the London Committee 'no great discovery will Ever be made on that Coast if no more than one Vessel is sent'. It was not without reason that sloop-masters were reluctant to venture too far north. Shipwreck in those lonely waters would almost certainly lead to the death of the crew, and even a minor mishap to a lone sloop might prove fatal if it stopped the vessel from returning south before the ice closed in. Walker carried his safety-first policy to extremes. In one year he was back at Churchill by 22 July – weeks before earlier expeditions had even reached the west coast of the Bay. The fact was that provision of a consort vessel would have reduced many of the risks associated with northern navigation. The dangers of the coast were shown by the *Churchill* sloop's voyage in 1755 under the command of a new and energetic master, John Bean. He reached latitude 64°N. and headed inshore, where his tiny vessel was twice almost blown onto the rocks by gales. Undeterred, Bean spent a week exploring the coastline, but both this year and the next he was searching too far north. The entrance of Chesterfield Inlet lies between latitude 63°28'N. and 63°40'N., whereas Bean was sixty or seventy miles farther north in the vicinity of today's Daly Bay. Unknown to him as he traced the complicated shoreline of what he despairingly called 'the Labyrinth', he was following the track of John Scroggs and Richard Norton in the *Whalebone* sloop more than thirty years earlier. And on board the *Churchill* was the young Moses Norton, Richard's son, who would soon play a prominent part in exploration to the north. After two years Bean gave up the search, convinced that there was 'some mistake in the Discoverers of this fly away River for if there was such a River it Resembells old Brazill viz not to be seen but by some chimerical persons'. The slooping voyages from Churchill continued, but they were for trade, not exploration.

The next and more important phase of the search for the elusive inlet on the west coast of Hudson Bay began when Moses Norton went on leave to England in 1760. With him he took a map drawn on deerskin to show the London Committee (*Ill.20*). Sketched by Norton from information given to him by Northern Indians, the map covers the country north and northwest of Churchill from the Kish-Stack-Ewen to the

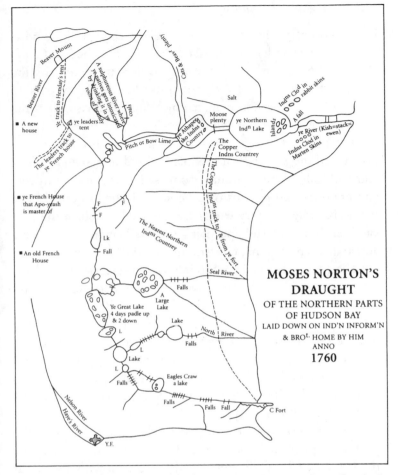

Within the map:

Beaver Mount

Beaver River

Casks & Bear plenty

A sulphureous River which yr natives gets inoxicated by drinking it in rounds of Bandy

ye track to Henday's tent

A new house

ye leaders tent

The leaders track to ye French house

Pitch or Bow Lime

Salt

Moose plenty

Indns Clod in rabbit skins

ye Northern Ind^n Lake

Islands

A fall

ye River (Kish=stack= ewen)

Indns Clod in Marten Skins

A Athapescow Indns Country

The Copper Indns Countrey

ye French House that Apo-yeash is master of

F F

F

An old French House

Lk

Fall

The Nearest Northern Indns Countrey

The Copper Indns track to & from ye fort

Seal River

Falls

A Large Lake

Ye Great Lake 4 days padle up & 2 down

L

L

Lake

L

Falls

Lake

North River

Falls

Eagles Craw a lake

Falls

Falls

Falls

Fall

C Fort

Nelson River

Hayes River

Y.F.

MOSES NORTON'S DRAUGHT
OF THE NORTHERN PARTS
OF HUDSON BAY
LAID DOWN ON IND'N INFORM'N
& BRO$^t.$ HOME BY HIM
ANNO
1760

20. MOSES NORTON. 'Drt of the Northern Parts of Hudsons Bay laid d wn on Indn. Information'. 1760.

The redrawing of the outlines on this original parchment map (HBC Archives, Provincial Archives of Manitoba: G 2/8) was done by Richard I. Ruggles, and is reproduced here by his kind permission and by that of the Manitoba Historical Society.

The map, which is oriented roughly north-south, has as its right-hand boundary the west coast of Hudson Bay, with Churchill shown near the bottom ('C Fort'). At the top of the map Kish-Stack-Ewen appears as a wide river connecting with a series of interior lakes and rivers flowing down from the Athabaska region. The top left-hand section of the map shows Anthony Henday's route and French 'houses' or trading posts on the Lower Saskatchewan. The east-west distances are compressed on this map, and its alignments are often incorrect; but for Norton it held out promise of a new route into the interior where beaver, marten and moose, and deposits of coal, pitch and salt would be found.

interior country where Anthony Henday's route and the posts of the French traders are marked. Norton returned to Churchill in 1761 as deputy factor with orders to search for the river, and a promise of a £40 gratuity for doing so, only to find that he had been anticipated by William Christopher, the new master of the *Churchill* sloop.

On his first voyage north that summer Christopher had discovered the entrance of the inlet behind its screen of islets, and had sailed up it a hundred miles. It was wide and deep, and unobstructed by falls or cataracts. Although he had been forced back by contrary winds, he intended to return the next summer. In their letter approving this the London Committee added that it hoped that Christopher would determine whether the Kish-Stack-Ewen 'be a Streight or passage, or not'. Christopher's journal for his first voyage is missing, but his later journals and letters indicate that he was well aware that the opening he had found was the Chesterfield Inlet of the 1747 discoverers, claimed by some to be the entrance of the North-west Passage. His use of the alternative name of Bowden's Inlet (given by Francis Smith) suggests that he had Drage's book to hand as he headed north. The expedition of 1762 was well-organised and purposeful. Norton accompanied Christopher, and as well as the sloop they had a cutter, the *Strivewell*. The sailing instructions given to Christopher and Norton by the factor at Churchill, Ferdinand Jacobs, show that this was a discovery venture, for they were to head north to the inlet without making the usual stop to trade at Whale Cove.

The sloop and cutter sailed from Churchill on 13 July, and their departure was marked by a touch of ceremony that again demonstrated that this was regarded as something more than a routine trading voyage, for the crew saluted the fort with seven guns and three cheers. Thick ice along the coast slowed progress, and it took two weeks to reach the inlet. On 3 August they reached Christopher's farthest point of the previous year, and then found the tide decreasing as they sailed on. The country was regular, with grass, herbs and small flowers, and Norton landed at intervals to search, unsuccessfully, for minerals. Caribou and ptarmigan were seen, but none of the fur-bearing animals marked on the Chipewyan map. On 5 August the sloop was towed by the cutter into a wide expanse of water which was named Baker's Lake. The water was fresh, and there was no tide. The two boats sailed west along the southern shore of the lake until on 9 August Christopher and Norton landed on a small island and from it saw the land closed to the west. They named their landing place Despair Island, but in order to leave no room for doubt Norton took the cutter and closely examined the lake's western shore. The only opening he found was a rivulet which shallowed to two feet after four or five miles and then petered out in falls and dry ridges. After following the inlet two hundred and thirty miles into the interior the search had ended in frustration and disappointment. Not only was Kish-Stack-Ewen or Chesterfield Inlet not the entrance to the passage; there was no sign of the woods, furs and minerals of the Indian reports and maps. 'Thus Ends Mr.Bowdens Inlet, and of a late Authors Probability of a NW Passage,' Christopher entered in his journal.

The London Committee received Christopher's report that there was 'no Passage through this River or Inlet into the South Sea' with equanimity. To Norton it expressed its satisfaction that the little expedition had returned safely, and reassured him that though the inlet had 'proved to be of no Consequence or Benefit, either to the Nation or the Company yet we commend your Diligence in so effectually fixing that point'. Here lay the nub of the matter. In 1763 Joseph Robson published a book, *The British Mars*, in which he once more berated the Company for its failure to search for the Northwest Passage and the copper mines. He came up with a scheme for finding the passage that outdid all others in absurdity: the stationing of five small leather boats in different parts of Hudson Bay which would simultaneously observe the time, strength and direction of the tide. Ludicrous though Robson's

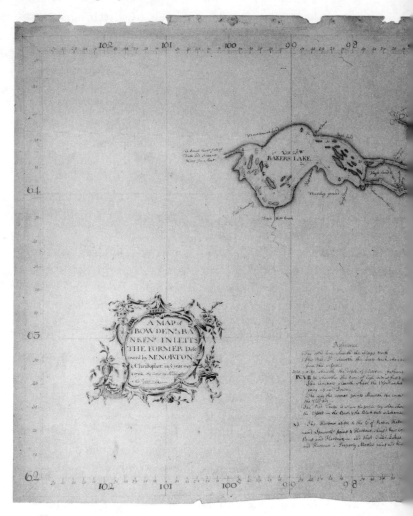

21. [SAMUEL HEARNE?]. 'A Map of Bowdens and Rankens Inletts'. *c.* 1765.
HBC Archives, Provincial Archives of Manitoba (G.2/9)

This chart, possibly drawn by Samuel Hearne, shows the results of the slooping voyages along the west coast of Hudson Bay between 1761 and 1764. 'Bowdens Inlett' is Chesterfield Inlet, shown here ending in Baker Lake. The longitudes have errors of between 1° and 2°, and its latitudes (more important in this context) much smaller errors of about 10'.

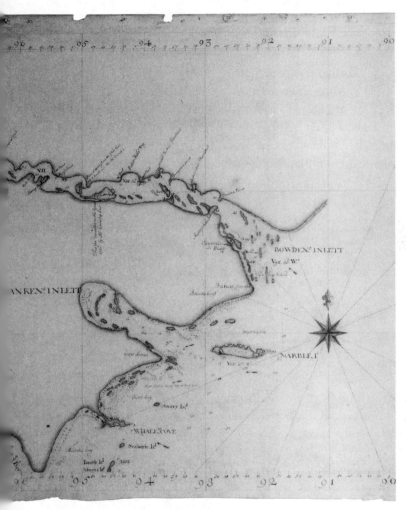

plan was, it reminded the Company that if there was a new attack on its charter, and it was once more accused of failing to search for a passage, it must be able to provide evidence to the contrary. So it approved Christopher's suggestion that he should investigate the coast south of Chesterfield Inlet, and this he did in 1763, followed by Magnus Johnston in 1764. Once more Rankin Inlet was probed, and 'all other Places that we shall think there is any Hopes', but to no avail. Norton wrote to the London Committee, 'I am Certain and Shure that there is no Pasage into ye Western Ocan in this Hudsons Bay.' Unlike the perfunctory coastal explorations carried out by Company sloop-masters in the 1720s and 1730s, the surveys by Christopher, Norton and Johnston were thorough and well-planned. Their results were recorded on a chart that brought together their explorations, marking the tracks of the sloop, anchoring and landing places, depths, time of high water and tidal flows (*Ill.21*). Although Christopher used a Hadley quadrant, an Elton quadrant and a theodolite in making his surveys, the chart did not reach later standards of accuracy; but it brought clarity to a stretch of coastline where inexpert and overlapping surveys had left confusion and ambiguity. And it left no room for a Northwest Passage.

Moses Norton received his £40 gratuity from the Company, but did not abandon his intention of finding the rivers, minerals and furs to the northwest that his Indian informants described. Rather, he changed the approach from the sea to the land, taking advantage of the skills and endurance of the Chipewyans. It was an adaptation of James Knight's original scheme that had sent William Stuart and Richard Norton inland accompanied by Native guides. The failure of those attempts to find minerals or a strait had convinced Knight that he should try an approach by sea; now Norton was attempting the reverse. Since the reports of the country to the north were coming from the Chipewyans, it seemed logical to follow their tracks inland. As early as 1762 Norton had sent two Northern Indian 'captains' to investigate further, and after five years Idotliaze and Mattonabee returned in 1767 with much to report. Far to the north, in 'Esquemay' country and well beyond Kish-Stack-Ewen, the two Chipewyans had reached another river. There were three copper mines near its mouth, and woods and fur-bearing animals along its banks. They had made a deer-skin map of their travels from which Norton copied the outline, added names and annotations, and took the result to England the next year (*Ill.22*). In January 1769 it was laid before the London Committee as Norton explained his new plans for expansion to the north.

The map, which has achieved almost iconic status, is of importance in several ways: firstly and most immediately, as a spur to new ventures by the Company; secondly, as an indication of the extent of Chipewyan knowledge, both direct and indirect, of a vast region of the Canadian North; and finally, as an example of the difference of approach between Native American and European mapping conventions. This last has caused much confusion among scholars – including the present writer – who could not account for what seemed to be the fundamental errors of the map. It shows a coastline running approximately south to north from Churchill to the Coppermine River, roughly halfway along Canada's Arctic coast. As with the Native American maps used by James Knight forty years earlier, there is no sign of the right-angle bend to the west at Melville Peninsula. So the 'Copper Mine River' at the top of the map, with three mines marked near its mouth, is marked flowing east to a coast shown running in a more or less straight line from Churchill, instead of running north from the interior into the Arctic Ocean at Coronation Gulf. If, to the modern eye, this is the most puzzling feature of the map, there are other problems, not least the proliferation of rivers and inlets north of Bowdens or Chesterfield Inlet. The large lake marked with an 'X' is Great Slave Lake, shown with a 'River Kis-ca-che-wan' at its northwest corner which according to one of Norton's accompanying notes flowed into the Pacific (The river is in fact the Mackenzie, running north towards the Arctic Ocean.)

An analysis and realignment of the map by the anthropologist June Helm has added greatly to our understanding of it.

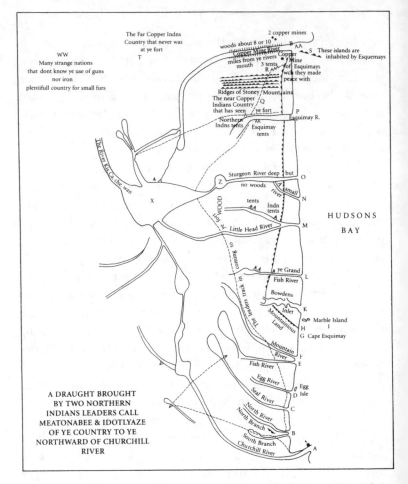

22. MOSES NORTON. 'Captain Mea'to'na'bee & I'dot'ly'a'zees, Draught'. 1767–68.
The redrawing of the outlines on this map (HBC Archives, Provincial Archives of Manitoba: G 2/27) was done by Richard I. Ruggles, and is reproduced here by his kind permission and that of the Manitoba Historical Society.

This is a copy on paper by Norton of the deer-skin map brought in to Churchill by the Northern Indian leaders, Mattonabee and Idotliaze, in 1767. It represented Chipewyan knowledge of a vast swathe of the interior as far west as Great Slave Lake and as far north as the Coppermine River. June Helm has demonstrated that by tilting and reorientating the map, its main features begin to fall into place. The process can best be visualised by imagining the coastline of the map bending back 90° on a hinge at about the halfway point, so that 'Sturgeon River' becomes the modern Back River, flowing north into the Arctic Ocean, as does the Coppermine River farther west.

She points out that whereas a non-Native viewer of the map instinctively starts with the familiar – Churchill, Marble Island, the west coast of Hudson Bay – and then moves inland, the Chipewyans of Norton's day would begin at Great Slave Lake, 'the hub of the map' with its network of river systems, and work outwards. The mental map of the Native peoples who criss-crossed this region was of lakes and streams, for these formed their system of markers and signposts, and the farther in distance from Great Slave Lake the outlines drawn by Idotliaze and Mattonabee were, the more distortion was there of scale and direction. And since the Chipewyans had no knowledge of the region stretching north from Wager Bay, the massive peninsulas of Boothia and Melville do not feature at all. The map is essentially one of interior drainage systems; but one further aspect of the map was to become significant when it was rediscovered twenty years later. It showed no trace of the Repulse Bay which Middleton had asserted blocked the way to the north, and implied a clear run for a ship from Churchill along the west coast of the Bay to the Coppermine River and the Arctic Ocean.

Norton had already whetted the Company's appetite for mineral discoveries by sending to London in advance a lump of copper brought to Churchill by Idotliaze and Mattonabee; and he returned to Churchill in the summer of 1769 with the Committee's authorisation to send Samuel Hearne, mate of one of the sloops at the fort, on an overland journey far to the north. The reason why Hearne was selected is not explained in the Company records, but given the small size of the garrison

---

Other problems with the map may be explained by possible additions by Moses Norton before he took it to England. He seems to have inserted Bowdens (Chesterfield) Inlet without realising that Mattonabee and Idotliaze had already marked it on the map farther north, where it is named 'Little Head River'. It is a sign of different priorities that their representation emphasised the twin drainage systems of the modern Thelon and Dubawnt rivers running into Chesterfield Inlet, rather than its seaward opening that Norton had entered in 1762 in the *Churchill* sloop with such a sense of excitement.

at Churchill he was not a surprising choice. At twenty-five Hearne was in the prime of life, good on snowshoes, and with enough service at sea to give him some competence in surveying. He had been in the Navy during the Seven Years War, and was appointed mate of the *Churchill* sloop in 1766. On his new venture he was ordered to look for the mines of copper that lay near 'the Far Off Metal River', and in general to report on that region's potential in terms of minerals and furs. These instructions were much as Norton had anticipated, but they were followed by an unexpected extra directive from the London Committee. 'Another material point', his instructions added, was to investigate 'whether there is a Passage through this Continent where its pointed out in the Draught of the American Traveller'. Only a few years after the slooping voyages of Christopher and Norton seemed to have closed once and for all the question of a Northwest Passage through Hudson Bay, it had come to life once more.

Even more than other episodes in the story of the eighteenth-century quest for a passage, the supposed discovery of 'the American Traveller' is shrouded in obscurity. In March and April 1769 London newspapers printed enquiries from a merchant in Philadelphia about the publication of the journal of a seaman who was reported to have sailed through Hudson Bay to the Pacific. More details followed. The seaman had been in the service of the Hudson's Bay Company when his ship passed through an opening at Repulse Bay, and into a strait that led to the polar sea. He had recently told his story to a government minister in London, and had promised to publish his narrative together with a chart. The fact that this had not appeared made the original Philadelphia correspondent wonder whether 'the two great monopolizing companies' (the Hudson's Bay Company and, presumably, the East India Company) had 'tied his hands up with a golden chain'. Within a month or two the promised book had appeared, *The American Traveller*, written by 'an Old and experienced Trader'. A manuscript copy of this work which was sent to the Earl of Dartmouth, a leading politician, established that the author was Alexander Cluny (or Clunie), a former servant of the Hudson's Bay Company. Part of the book was devoted to a Dobbs-like advocacy of colonies in the Hudson Bay region. One advantage of such settlements would be the discovery of the Northwest Passage, which the accompanying map showed running westward from Repulse Bay into the polar sea (*Ill.24*). This was precisely as the merchant in Philadelphia had forecast, and indeed it seems likely that this well-informed but distant correspondent was fictitious, and that the newspaper entries were a 'puff' designed to publicise the forthcoming book. It did not include any account of a voyage through the passage, and on the map the passage was indicated by dotted lines and a hesitant inscription to the effect that 'Here is supposed to be the North West Passage.' At the far end of the strait, however, capes were shown bearing the names of two regular Company captains of the mid-eighteenth century, Spurrell and Fowler. These features suggested that the Company had discovered the passage in the course of secret explorations in the far north of the Bay.

Men who knew Cluny were able to point out how preposterous his claims were. At York Fort, Andrew Graham claimed that Cluny was a wharfinger who had spent only one winter in Hudson Bay (in 1744), and had no opportunity to sail north from the Company posts. Cluny himself was questioned soon after the publication of the book about the authenticity of his map, and told his interrogator (almost certainly Daines Barrington, a Fellow of the Royal Society of whom we shall hear more) that in 1746 he had been shipwrecked in latitude 79½°N., and that he had sailed in a Greenland whaler in an ice-free sea as far north as latitude 82½°. The ship had turned back only because of the lack of a consort vessel. Cluny's claims in his letter to the Earl of Dartmouth bordered on the incredible. While in Hudson Bay in 1744, accompanied by five men on snowshoes and a dog-sledge, he had travelled several thousands of miles westward 'into the wilderness, many parts of which were never before trodden by European feet'.

23. Frontispiece to Alexander Cluny's book, *The American Traveller* (1768), showing men on snowshoes, accompanied by a dog-sledge, in a frozen landscape.
British Library

The frontispiece of his book supported this fantasy with a drawing of the indomitable little party (*Ill.23*). For the Hudson's Bay Company the most damaging part of Cluny's various stories was the implication that some at least of the discoveries he described had been made while he was in the Company's service, and that they were being kept secret.

The Company's swift reaction to Cluny's claims was evidence of its new sensitivity to accusations that it was indifferent to exploration, but Hearne's expedition was not initially a response to *The American Traveller*. It was the logical corollary

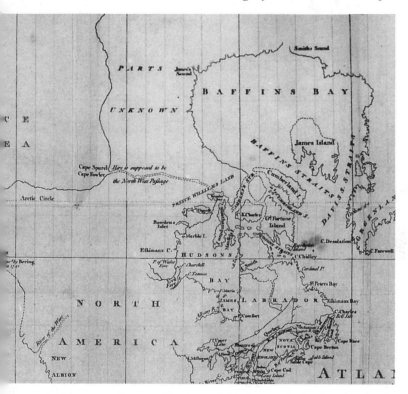

24. ALEXANDER CLUNY. Section of 'A Map of North and South America' from his *American Traveller* (1768).

of the coasting voyages to find the copper mines to the north, although it was to have a much wider significance than those limited operations by sea. After two false starts Hearne carried out his task in 1770–72 by journeying with a band of Chipewyan men, women and children led by Mattonabee, who had reached the river of copper a few years earlier. Like William Stuart in 1715–16, Hearne travelled on foot across the Barrens of the northern tundra, 'scarcely any thing but one solid mass of rock and stones, in general a total want of soil'. But unlike Stuart, Hearne kept a journal, which was to become a classic account of northern travel. Some indication of winter conditions was given in his entry, almost offhand in its wording, for 21 November 1770: 'Between seven and eight in the evening my dog, a valuable brute, was frozen to death; so that his sledge, which was a very heavy one, I was obliged to haul.' The weeks of December 1770 were particularly hard: 'For the last three days had not tasted a morsel of any thing, except a pipe of tobacco and a drink of snow water; and as we walked daily from morning till night, and were all heavily laden, our strength began to fail. I must confess that I never spent so dull a Christmas.' As the spring thaws came, travelling became even more back-breaking, for the sledges were abandoned, and Hearne had to carry his possessions on his back through knee-deep slush and water. What with 'the quadrant and its stand, a trunk containing books, papers, &c., a land-compass, and a large bag containing all my wearing apparel; also a hatchet, knives, files &c.', his load weighed more than sixty pounds.

After six months the party at last reached the Coppermine River in July 1771, but for Hearne it proved a sad disappointment. The river was shallow and unnavigable, while the reputed mines of copper dwindled to 'a jumble of rocks and gravel'. It took four hours of searching before Hearne and his companions found a lump of copper impressive enough at four pounds weight to make it worth bringing back. From this spot Hearne followed the river downstream until it became tidal and he sighted the polar sea. Whether he got quite as far as the shoreline is open to doubt, although he viewed the distant prospect 'with the aid of a good pocket telescope. The ice was not then broke up, but was melted away for about three quarters of a mile from the main shore.' Hearne was the first European to reach the northern coast of the American continent, although he placed the mouth of the river in latitude 71°54'N., almost four degrees or two hundred miles too far north. This error was a reminder that many of the Company explorers of this period were handicapped by deficiencies in surveying skills and by inadequate instruments. Extraordinary though it seems after the hardships endured and the distances covered, Hearne did not wait for clear weather to take an observation with his heavy Elton's quadrant at the mouth of the Coppermine River, and instead estimated his latitude by a seaman's dead reckoning. He was disillusioned by the failure to find anything of commercial value after the hardships of his journey, and sickened by the massacre by his Chipewyan companions of an unsuspecting Inuit group at a spot a few miles from the river's mouth that Hearne named Bloody Fall. No other European would see the mouth of the Coppermine River until John Franklin's small group reached it in 1821 after a journey even more terrible than Hearne's, for eleven of the party of twenty died, two shot by their fellows.

The band's return track opened up further new areas to Hearne's gaze as Mattonabee turned southwest to Great Slave Lake in search of beaver and moose. The group finally returned to Churchill in June 1772 after a circuitous journey of almost nineteen months, during which there were times, Hearne wrote, when 'I left the print of my feet in blood almost at every step I took.' His map showed the vast extent of country he had travelled – its extremities marked by the Company fort at Churchill, the mouth of the Coppermine River, and Great Slave Lake (*Ill. 25*). Whatever the commercial disappointments of Hearne's journey, its geographical implications were profound. As Hearne pointed out, the American continent was clearly wider than many had supposed, for even when he was at his farthest point inland from Churchill his Chipewyan companions reported that there were other tribes to the west, 'and they knew no end to the land in that direction'. Hearne's gruelling journey eliminated the possibility that a passage for shipping might be found through the American continent, for he had crossed its northeastern shoulder from Hudson Bay to the polar sea without finding a salt-water strait or even any sizeable river. Yet his explorations, at first sight so damaging to hopes of finding a navigable Northwest Passage, were soon linked to those of Russian vessels thousands of miles to the west, and brought hopes that there might be an possible

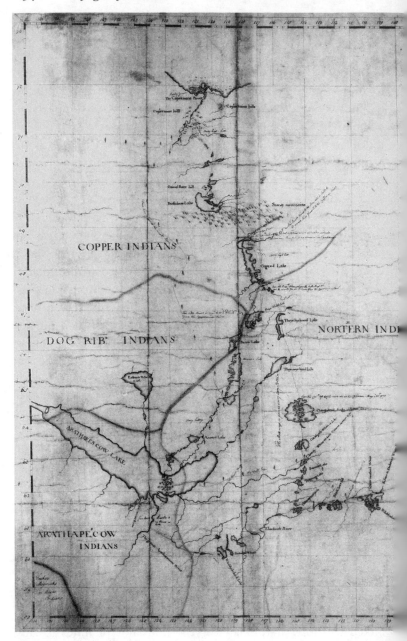

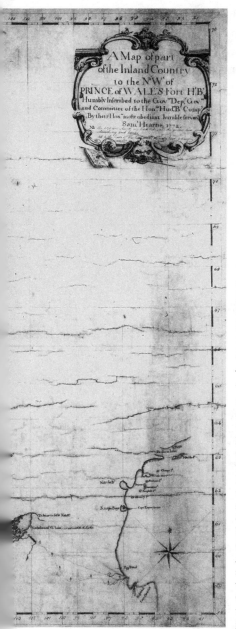

25. SAMUEL HEARNE. 'A
Map of part of the Inland
Country to the N^h W^t of
Prince of Wales's Fort'.
1772.
*HBC Archives, Provincial
Archives of Manitoba (G.2/10)*

This manuscript map shows
the great extent of country
covered by Hearne and the
Chipewyan band on their overland trek from Churchill
(bottom right-hand corner of
the map) to the Coppermine
River (top). A dotted line
traces Hearne's outward route;
a solid one his return track to
Churchill farther to the west
by way of Great Slave Lake
('Arathapes Cow Lake').
Although Hearne's account
and maps were not published
until 1795, the Hudson's Bay
Company made them available
to the Admiralty and cartographers.

ice-free route for ships through that sea which Hearne had glimpsed from the mouth of the Coppermine River. A new generation of hopeful projectors replaced Dobbs and his associates, and within four years of Hearne's return to Churchill the greatest navigator of the age sailed from England for the Pacific, to search once more for the Northwest Passage.

II

The Pacific Approach

'If I were to go upon this Discovery, I would go first into the South-Seas, *bend my course from thence along to* California, *and that way seek a Passage back.'*

WILLIAM DAMPIER, *A New Voyage Round the World* (1697)

8

Maps, Hoaxes and Projects

'The nearest way to the East-Indies is to be found only on our maps and globes.'

[G.F.MÜLLER], *A Letter from a Russian Sea-Officer* (1754)

A T THE BEGINNING of the eighteenth century the lands and waters of the north Pacific were for Europeans among the least-known areas of the inhabited globe. This remote region presented baffling problems to geographers, not least the relationship of Asia and America. Whether the two continents were connected by a land-bridge, or separated by water – and, if the latter, by ocean or by a narrow strait – was uncertain. French explorers pushing west along the rivers and lakes of North America could throw no light on the puzzle, for they had not got far beyond the line of the Mississippi. On the Pacific coast the Spaniards from their Mexican ports had by the early seventeenth century carried out sketchy surveys of the coast only as far as Cape Blanco near latitude 43°N., where in 1603 Martín de Aguilar reported that he saw the mouth of a large river, after which the coast trended northeast. This sighting helped to revive the notion that California might be an island, lying just south of the Strait of Anian, and speculative maps soon began to show this proximity of island and strait, with the mainland coast beyond turning towards Hudson Bay (*Ill. 1*).

In the world of reality, Cape Blanco marked the southernmost point of the longest unexplored coastline in the world.

Across the waters of the north Pacific the next known point of land was the Asian peninsula of Kamchatka. What lay between was unknown. In *Gulliver's Travels* Jonathan Swift could place Brobdingnag in that space without fear of contradiction. Elsewhere cartographers showed the Strait of Anian, Fuca's inlet and Aguilar's river, and the hazy outlines of Yedso, Company Land and Gama Land, on evidence little stronger than that for Gulliver's land of giants. Because of this lack of information, the search for a Northwest Passage through Hudson Bay was a blind one. The Pacific might be only a short distance away, as Dobbs claimed, or several thousands of miles to the west. As the outline of the Pacific coast of northwest America was slowly revealed during the course of the century, so theories regarding a possible passage, and the very direction of the quest, changed.

On the opposite brinks of this great void in Europe's knowledge stood two peninsulas, California and Kamchatka, five thousand miles apart, the one hot and arid, the other snow-covered and fogbound for much of the year. The physical contrast was indication enough of the immensity of the task attempted in the eighteenth century, which took the form of a giant, if hesitant, pincer movement. The Russians in the far north, and the Spaniards from their ports in Mexico, slowly groped their way towards each other, although the final link across the gap that still lay between them was to be forged by an English navigator, James Cook. Just as Lower or *Baja* California was in the early eighteenth century the farthest extremity of the vast Spanish land empire, only at this time being shown by the land journeys of Father Kino to be a peninsula rather than an island, so Kamchatka was the most distant outpost of a Russian empire that stretched from the Baltic to Siberia. The Russians had reached the southern tip of Kamchatka in 1706, but what lay beyond was uncertain. In 1648 a Siberian Cossack, Semen Deshnev, had sailed round the eastern extremity of Siberia (Cape Dezhneva) in a flimsy boat, but knowledge of his exploit was fragmentary. Tsar Peter I (the Great) was unable to give convincing answers when questioned about the extent of the Asian continent during his visits to western European capitals in 1716 and 1717; and in 1725, shortly before his death, he appointed Vitus Bering, a Danish seaman in the Russian navy, to command an expedition east from Kamchatka to throw more light on the matter. In recent years Russian and other scholars have argued intensively but inconclusively about the precise reasons for Bering's first voyage, usually known as the First Kamchatka Expedition. At least three motives have been put forward: the discovery of the relationship between Asia and America; the tracing of the Asian coast north of Kamchatka; and exploration of the lands rumoured to have been found in the seventeenth century in the ocean southeast of Kamchatka.

After a colossal trek from the Russian capital of St Petersburg on the Baltic across the land-mass of the Asian continent, Bering and his party reached the east coast of Kamchatka. There he built a small vessel, the *St Gabriel*, and in the summer of 1728 sailed north through the strait dividing Asia and America that now bears his name. Bering then turned back, without sighting the opposite (American) shore, so leaving the way open for different interpretations of his discovery. Four years later Mikhail Gvozdev sighted the American shore while on a voyage in Bering's old ship, but he referred to it merely as *bolshaya zemlya* (big land). News of Bering's important yet inconclusive voyage reached western Europe in a surprisingly short time. In London the *Historical Register* for 1730 printed a short account of the voyage which noted that it had increased the chances of finding a north*east* passage, along the top of Asia. Bering's own account, accompanied by a map, was printed in J.B.du Halde's history of China, published in Paris in 1735, and it soon became widely known (*Ill.26*). The map

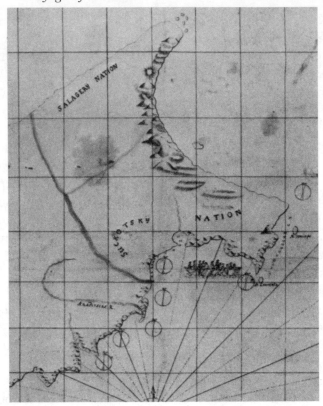

26. Bering's voyage of 1728.

Lefthand map. Sections of a German copy, dated 1729, of a map drawn by Petr Chaplin, midshipman on Bering's voyage of 1728. Although the eastern extremity of Asia is clearly shown, there is no hint of land across the water to the east. BL K. Top. 114.43(1).

Righthand map. The first published version of the map was printed, together with an account of Bering's voyage, in Vol IV of J.B. du Halde, *Description géographique de la Chine*, Paris, 1735.

showed the eastern tip of Asia as an unnamed cape close to the right-hand margin of the page, and so avoided any commitment to the existence of land across the water to the east. Even so, it considerably reduced the possibility of a northern land-bridge between Asia and America. In the same way that the *Historical Register*'s account had pointed out that Bering's

voyage left the way open for a northeast passage around Asia, geographers more interested in the northwest passage around or through America could take satisfaction from the reports of the track of the *St Gabriel*.

In 1731 Bering was entrusted with a second, more ambitious project. The Second Kamchatka or Great Northern Expedition was in effect a whole series of ventures involving surveys along the rivers and coasts of Siberia and voyages south through the Kuril Islands towards Japan. The main expedition under Bering was to build two brigs at Okhotsk, sail them to Kamchatka, and then head southeast in search of the mysterious lands which Dutch navigators claimed to have sighted in the previous century. For ten years the Danish fleet-captain and a small army of associates, scientists and officials laboured at their task, struggling against difficulties of distance and climate, financial stringency and local apathy. From St Petersburg to the Sea of Okhotsk was almost nine thousand miles, and everything that could not be obtained locally – from shipbuilding materials to weapons and ammunition – had to be carried by sledge or packhorse. So laborious was the route that at one time serious consideration was given to the possibility of supplying the expedition at Okhotsk by ships sailing round the world by way of Cape Horn. The French astronomer Joseph Nicolas Delisle (younger brother of the better-known Guillaume), who had been at the St Petersburg Academy of Sciences since 1726, produced at the Russian government's request a map and a memoir that greatly influenced Bering's track on his second expedition. Like Dobbs, whose memorial on the Northwest Passage was being circulated in Britain at this time, Delisle was convinced that there were large countries in the northern seas between Asia and America. How they related to the Strait of Anian he was not sure, but he could 'not help feeling that somewhere between Asia and America there must be an important strait, whatever its character may be'.

Following Delisle's advice, Bering in the *St Peter* and Alexsei Chirikov in the *St Paul* left Avacha Bay on the east coast of Kamchatka in the spring of 1741. They headed southeast towards latitude 45°N., where Company Land and Gama Land were thought to lie, but in searching for these imaginary lands the two ships became separated, and much of the effectiveness of the expedition was lost. One of Bering's officers, the Swede Sven Waxell, was fiercely critical of the plan drawn up by Delisle and his colleagues at the St Petersburg Academy, who 'obtained all their knowledge from visions . . . it would only be reasonable were such unknown lands first to be explored before they are trumpeted abroad as being the coasts of Yezo or de Gama . . . my blood still boils whenever I think of the scandalous deception of which we were the victims'.

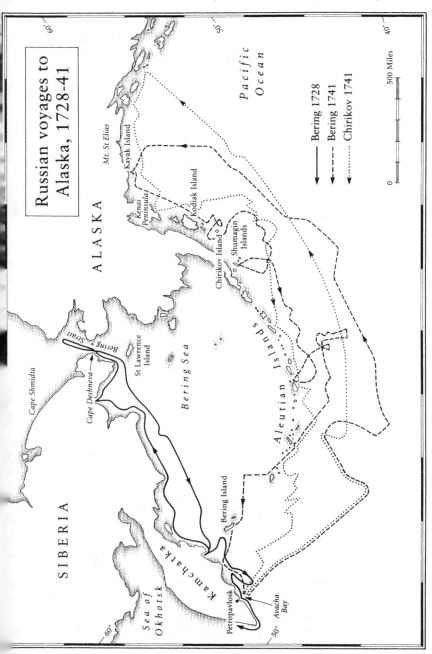

Russian voyages to Alaska, 1728-41

Bering 1728
Bering 1741
Chirikov 1741

500 Miles

0

Pacific Ocean

ALASKA

Mt. St Elias

Kayak Island

Kenai Peninsula

Kodiak Island

Chirikov Island

Shumagin Islands

Aleutian Islands

Bering Strait

Cape Shmidta

Cape Deshneva

St Lawrence Island

Bering Sea

SIBERIA

Sea of Okhotsk

Kamchatka

Bering Island

Petropavlosk

Avacha Bay

60°

50°

40°

60°

50°

Chirikov sailed northeast after losing company with Bering until he sighted the American coast in latitude 55° 21'N. (near present-day Sitka in Alaska), but soon after lost both his boats with their crews. Unable to land, Chirikov turned for home, and after a difficult voyage through the Aleutian chain of islands reached Kamchatka. Bering held a more northerly course than Chirikov, and his first sight of land was the towering peak of Mount St Elias. He anchored at Kayak Island, but his crew landed there only long enough to take on water, a decision which brought from Georg Wilhelm Steller, his German naturalist, the despairing comment that ten years of preparation had resulted in only ten hours of exploration. The *St Peter*, with its crew stricken with scurvy, sailed back through the Shumagin and Aleutian Islands, but was wrecked on a small island near Kamchatka where Bering and many of his crew died. Bering's lingering death on an open beach in December 1741 was, in Steller's words, miserable and pitiful, as the commander lay half-buried in the loose earth, refusing all help. The survivors, led by Waxell and Steller, reached Avacha Bay the following summer.

The American landfalls of Bering's second voyage represented one of the defining moments in world geography, although this was clearer in retrospect than at the time. The journals show that expedition members were convinced that they had landed in America, and for Steller in particular, even a shore excursion of a few hours was enough to reveal a land of great promise:

> America is of a noticeably better character than the most extreme northeast part of Asia, although the land toward the sea, whether viewed close up or from afar, everywhere consists of amazingly high mountain ranges, most of whose peaks are covered with perpetual snow. Yet these mountains, compared with those of Asia, have a much better nature and character . . . [they] are firm, covered above their rock mantle not with moss but with good soil; therefore up to the highest peaks, they are densely overgrown with the most beautiful trees . . . here at 60

degrees latitude the very beach itself is right from the waterline studded with the most beautiful forests.

Nevertheless, the expedition had not proved that the land sighted was the American continent, and that it was part of the 'big land' sighted by Gvosdev across Bering's strait in 1732. Doubts about the significance of the expedition's explorations were increased by the failure of the Russian authorities to publish any proper account of the voyage until 1758. As Waxell complained, 'there has been no one willing to take the trouble to tell the world anything of what the expedition actually achieved or of its conclusion'.

A report of Bering's voyage was printed in London newspapers in October 1743, but its information was hopelessly garbled. The account's major error was its insistence that Bering, when shipwrecked near Kamchatka, had only just set out on his voyage, though Chirikov 'had been more lucky, and had even discover'd the Coast of America'. Making do with shreds of evidence, interested parties put forward their own interpretations of Bering's voyage, and in London these were printed in the Royal Society's *Philosophical Transactions*, and then given much wider circulation in the pages of the *Gentleman's Magazine*. In these exchanges, the German scholar Leonhard Euler, onetime professor at the St Petersburg Academy of Sciences, took a very different line from those fervent advocates of a Northwest Passage, Arthur Dobbs and John Campbell. Euler maintained that if the coast sighted by Bering ran all the way south to California, then the only possible passage would be far to the north in a frozen sea. Dobbs and Campbell, predictably, pointed out that the short stretches of coast glimpsed by Bering and Chirikov left ample room for straits and passages. Campbell's own view of Bering's second voyage was that just as Columbus, sent to find the Indies, believed that the islands he discovered were part of them, so Bering, with orders directing him towards America, wrongly assumed that the land he saw was continental rather than insular. It was in Russia's interests, Campbell suspected, to promote 'a Belief of the running out of the two great Continents, till they almost meet each other', for this would discourage northern explorations by Britain or other European powers that might infringe on Russia's new sphere of interest east of Siberia.

There was considerable uncertainty, then, about the precise nature of the discoveries made on both of Bering's voyages. This confusion was now increased by the dramatic intervention of two French scholars, Joseph Nicolas Delisle and Philippe Buache. In 1747 Delisle returned to France after more than twenty years at the St Petersburg Academy, and unknown to the Russian government took with him maps and manuscripts relating to the recent discoveries. This information he shared with Philippe Buache, his uncle by marriage, who could claim to be the leading geographer in France through his appointments as *premier géographe du roi* and *géographe adjoint* to the prestigious Academy of Sciences in Paris. The Academy had been founded by Louis XIV in 1666, and geography and cartography were among its major interests. On 8 April 1750 Delisle read before it a paper on Bering's voyages, and accompanied it with a manuscript map constructed by Buache. As far as the Russian explorations were concerned, Delisle had disappointingly little new to say, although he asserted that Bering had given him important information about his first voyage which the seaman had omitted from his journal – that when he reached the eastern tip of Siberia in August 1728 he had every indication of land across the water. As far as the second voyage was concerned, Delisle repeated the fiction that Bering's ship was wrecked soon after leaving Kamchatka, and he devoted most of his attention to the voyage of Chirikov in the *St Paul*, on which his half-brother Louis de la Croyère was serving. He described the track of Chirikov's ship across the north Pacific, the loss of its boats off the American coast, and the return voyage, on which Louis died.

Little of this was new to European geographers, but what followed was, in the words of one French scholar, 'une bombe', for Delisle produced, as if from a conjurer's hat, the Fonte letter of 1708 and linked it with the Russian discoveries. He claimed that a manuscript copy of the letter had been sent to him at St Petersburg from England in 1739, and that he found considerable conformity between it and the more recent Russian findings. Buache's accompanying map showed a northwest America sliced by straits and rivers, where the coastal stretches sighted by the Russian ships were interspersed with Fonte's discoveries (*Ill.27*). Farther south the openings found by Fuca in 1592 and by Aguilar in 1603 led straight into a gigantic 'Mer de l'Ouest', a North American Mediterranean which stretched across much of today's western United States and Canada. The map and Delisle's 'Explication' brought together, in a mixture of the scholarly and the sensational, the individual strands of French speculation about the geography of western North America that had begun with Guillaume Delisle. The celebrated geographer had died in 1726, and never showed his Mer de l'Ouest on a printed map because, as he once explained to Louis XIV, he did not want foreigners to know of its existence. But his manuscript maps and memoirs survived, and included information gathered by French missionaries and fur traders in the late seventeenth century about great rivers and seas to the west of the Great Lakes. Joseph Nicolas Delisle and Philippe Buache had no inhibitions about printing either Guillaume's speculations or their own, and in June 1752 the publication of Delisle's memoir and Buache's map launched a radically new interpretation of the geography of western America in a hubbub of publicity and controversy.

Within months the two French scholars had fallen out, in a way revealed by Bradock Mead, a British geographer who wrote under the *nom de plume* of John Green. He had already translated into English du Halde's history of China, which contained the account and map of Bering's first voyage, and in the 1740s had compiled a monumental four-volume edition of voyages and travels. In 1753 Thomas Jefferys, a leading engraver and publisher of maps, published Green's 'New Chart of North and South America', together with a volume of *Remarks*. Green considered the Fuca and Fonte accounts to be 'palpable forgeries', and maintained that the publicity surrounding the Fonte letter and its report of transcontinental waterways was intended to divert the British from seeking the Northwest Passage in its most likely location. According to Green, this was along the northern coastline of North America, or across the Pole, and then into the Pacific by way of the strait that Bering had reached on his first voyage. He criticised the attempts by Arthur Dobbs and the clerk of the *California* to explain the Fonte letter, but reserved his most severe censure for the map published under Buache's name in June 1752. Much of the influence of the speculative maps based on the accounts of Fuca and Fonte stemmed from the fact that they were published by French cartographers, for Paris in the eighteenth century was the centre of geographical science just as Amsterdam had been in the previous century. The great names of European geography in this period were mostly French: members of the Delisle and Vaugondy families, together with other cartographers of international renown such as Jean Baptiste Bourguignon d'Anville and Jean Nicolas Bellin. Philippe Buache, attached to the Delisle clan by marriage, always made much of his relationship with his father-in-law – 'beau-père Guillaume Delisle' – but he was in his own right a scholar of acknowledged learning and originality. His writings on the physical structure of the globe, and in particular the relationship between mountain chains and ocean basins, were well-known and highly regarded. In London the editor of the widely-read *Gentleman's Magazine* published translations of three essays by 'the celebrated M. Buache' within a few years.

In his *Remarks*, John Green freely admitted the superiority of French cartographers – 'The French have long engrossed the Care of Geography to themselves, and it must be confessed have brought it to greater perfection than any Nation in Europe' – and he was astonished that Delisle and Buache should adopt a narrative as patently spurious as the Fonte account. Above all, Green was staggered by the fact that the two geographers, having apparently accepted the Fonte letter as genuine, had not in fact followed it. Buache's map of June 1752 showed, without explanation, the entrance of Río los Reyes in latitude 63°N. rather than in latitude 53°N. as stated in the text of the Fonte letter (which had been printed, in French translation, in Delisle's memoir). Since the river marked the beginning of Fonte's inland discoveries, it followed that all subsequent features on the map were also placed ten degrees farther north than the 1708 account implied. So the Strait of Ronquillo that Fonte sailed through to meet Captain Shapley's Boston ship near an 'Indian town' was shown ending near Baffin Bay in latitude 72°N. rather than near Hudson Bay. In that latitude, well north of the Arctic Circle, Green pointed out, it was unlikely that there would be a ship, trade or Indian towns!

In a postscript of December 1752 Green added some information which explains the appearance that September in Paris of a second map of the Fonte discoveries (*Ill.28*), this time published under Delisle's name, and designed by Jean Nicolas Bellin, the geographer in charge of the government's Dépôt des Cartes, Plans et Journeaux in Paris. The most striking difference between this new map and Buache's June production was that Río los Reyes was placed once more in latitude 53°N., as stated in the Fonte letter. With Fonte's route through the rivers and lakes of the interior of the continent now pushed hundreds of miles to the south, the Strait of Ronquillo was shown opening into Hudson Bay near the Wager. Green revealed that Delisle had sent the Royal Society of London a copy of his map, accompanied with a note explaining that the ten-degree error in the June map was the result of Buache failing to follow the instructions given to him by Delisle. In 1753 Delisle issued an atlas of maps based on the Fonte discoveries, while Buache responded to his colleague's condescending statement that he had been unable to obey orders by

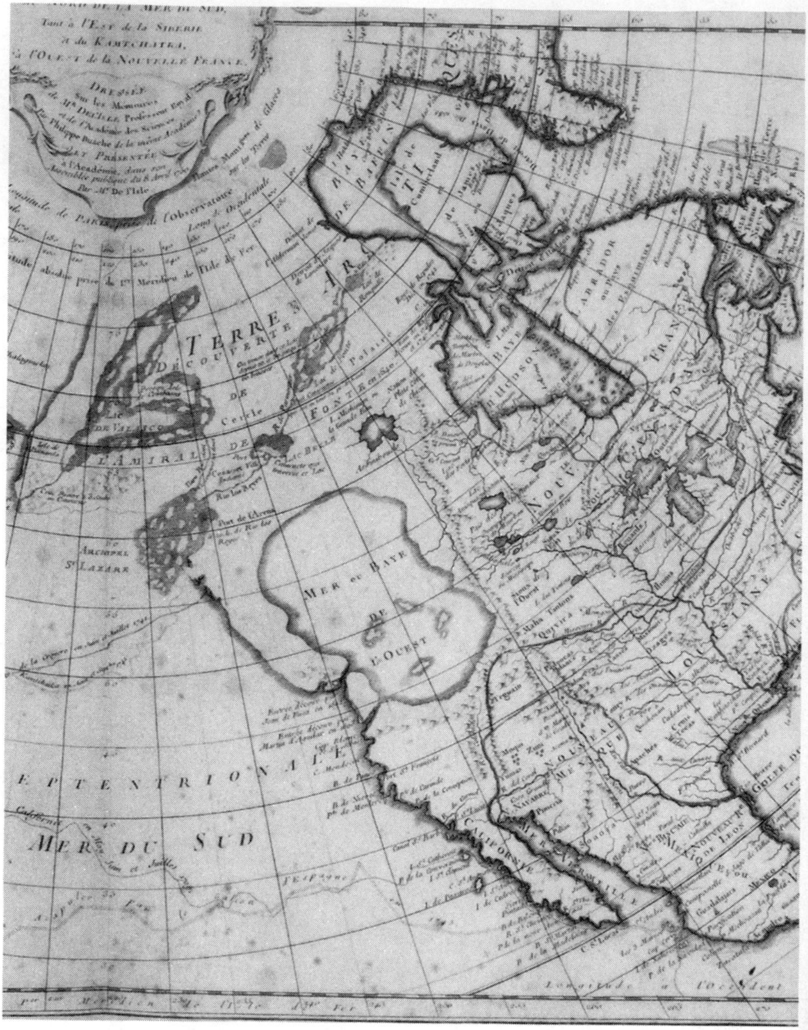

27. PHILIPPE BUACHE. Carte des Nouvelles Découvertes au Nord de la Mer du Sud'. June 1752.
British Library

Buache's map was the first of the French speculative maps showing the supposed discoveries of Admiral de Fonte, as well as a huge Mer de l'Ouest, drawn here with the entrances thought to have been discovered by Juan de Fuca in 1592 and Martin d'Aguilar in 1603. Although this map was constructed in collaboration with J. N. Delisle, whose memoir of 1750 included a French translation of the Fonte letter of 1708, Fonte's Río los Reyes is shown in latitude 63°N., rather than in 53°N. as stated in Fonte's supposed account. As a result of this shift, Fonte's subsequent discoveries were pushed north to the latitude of Baffin Bay.

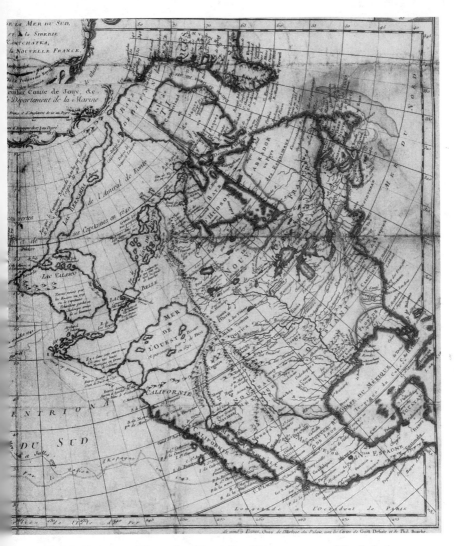

28. J. N. Delisle. 'Carte des Nouvelles Découvertes au Nord de la Mer du Sud'. September 1752.
British Library

Three months after the publication of Buache's map, Delisle issued his own interpretation of Fonte's discoveries. With the Río los Reyes now restored to latitude 53°N., Fonte's explorations are shown taking him, via Lac Belle and Lac de Fonte, to Lac de Ronquillo (near where he met Shapley in his Boston ship). The west coast of Hudson Bay is now only a short distance away. There were to be numerous variants of this map, but it stands as a prototype of those subsequent maps whose outlines of northwest America were influenced by Fonte's account.

publishing in the same year a handsome volume of eleven maps and 150 pages of text, *Considerations Géographiques et Physiques sur les Nouvelles Découvertes au Nord de la Grande Mer*. On the new maps Río los Reyes was again shown in latitude 63°N., and Buache insisted that this was a deliberate departure from the normal interpretation of the Fonte letter. His explanation for the discrepancy is not easy to accept. He claimed to have first seen the Fonte account in 1748, when he was shown a manuscript copy of the letter that had been sent to Delisle in Russia. According to Buache, the wording of the manuscript copy was different from the more familiar printed version of 1708, which stated that Fonte 'sail'd to the River los Reyes in 53 Degrees of N.Latitude' (see p.418 below). By contrast – or so Buache asserted – Fonte had sighted the northwest coast in latitude 53°N., and *then* sailed 456 leagues north along the coast to Río los Reyes. Following this, Buache placed the entrance of the river in latitude 63°N. We know that the copy of the Fonte letter that Delisle received at St Petersburg had been sent to him by Lord Forbes, formerly British ambassador in Russia, who also probably drew Dobbs's attention to the account. What seems beyond the bounds of credibility is that Forbes made deliberate alterations in the text of the printed letter, or that the significant difference between printed and manuscript versions alleged by Buache were copyists' errors.

At every stage, Buache was intent on stressing his own priority in the field of Fonte-style maps. So when in 1749 the clerk of the *California* published what is generally accepted as the first such map (*Ill.18*) in the second volume of his account of the discovery voyage to Hudson Bay of Moor and Smith, Buache responded by claiming that his own map of the Fonte discoveries, although it did not see the light of day until 1750 and was not published until 1752, was actually drawn in 1748. In the third section of the volume, Buache subjected the clerk's map to a hostile and dismissive scrutiny. His own general map of northwest America published in his *Considerations* of 1753 shows considerable differences from his map of the previous

June. The Mer de l'Ouest is smaller, and has a suggested connection with the Fonte waterways to the north. These in turn point more openly to Hudson Bay and Baffin Bay than in the first map. It would be pointless to look for consistency in Buache: his work at this time seems to have been driven by a mixture of political aims, scholarly curiosity and publicity seeking. The Delisle/Buache maps at one level were intended to spur on French overland attempts in North America to reach the Pacific before the British, but the approach of the Seven Years War stifled such ambitions. Ironically, rather than encouraging French western expansion the systems of Delisle and Buache did much to reignite fading British interest in the possibility of a Northwest Passage. At another level, Buache's work was an example of speculative geography at its most complex and fantastic. Accounts of voyages, some genuine, some apocryphal; reports and rumours, French, English, Spanish, Russian, Native American, Chinese (Fou-Sang was thought to have reached northwest America in the fifth century) – all were welded by Buache into a fanciful structure of the geography of northwest America that was to survive, though not without damage, for almost half a century.

For his part, Delisle was soon to retreat to the quieter havens of astronomy, but we have a revealing glimpse of him in the memoirs of Charles de Brosses, the scholar who in 1756 published an influential collection of Pacific voyages. In 1754 he met Delisle, who was eager to be put in charge of the maps in the forthcoming publication. There advanced into the room, De Brosses recalled, a large, ruddy-faced man. 'He said to me, "Monsieur, I come from Kamtschatka, I know Siberia by heart, my name is Delisle, brother of the great Guillaume. I bring you my writings and my maps. Whatever you might say to me, the Northwest Passage is real, Admiral de la Fuente is no less real and did not lie in one word."' This melodramatic self-introduction failed to have the desired effect on De Brosses, who had already written a paper in which he condemned the Fonte account as apocryphal; and he decided to entrust his maps to Didier Robert de Vaugondy, *géographe ordinaire du roi*.

The thesis on the Fonte discoveries split the world of French geographical scholarship. There were cartographers of repute – Jean Janvier, Louis Denis, R.J.Julien – who were attracted by the plausibility or novelty of the Delisle/Buache system, and produced maps along the same general lines. By contrast, two of the best-known French geographers outside the Delisle family circle threw their weight against the new interpretation. In May 1753 Vaugondy presented the Academy of Sciences with his 'Observations Critiques' on the Fonte discoveries. Here he stressed the internal inconsistencies in the letter of 1708, the prodigious distances Fonte and his officers were supposed to have covered in a few months, and the puzzle as to why neither the Spanish in 1640 nor the English in 1708 had responded to the supposed discoveries made on the admiral's extraordinary voyage. Two years later he dismissed the Fonte account out of hand as 'une pure fiction', and his map of North America in his *Atlas Universel* of 1757 marked nothing on the Pacific coast north of Aguilar's supposed opening. Buache, who had already been embroiled in a pamphlet war with Vaugondy over the Fonte discoveries, reacted furiously to the publication of Vaugondy's great atlas, arguing that its size and comprehensiveness would damage the market for the works of cartographers such as himself. Of other cartographers involved in the debate, Jean Nicolas Bellin was in a good position to judge the reliability of the Delisle/Buache maps, since his post as custodian of plans and journals gave him full access to the reports and maps of La Vérendrye and other French overland explorers in North America. As befitted his official status, he preferred to leave a region blank on the map rather than fill it with doubtful detail. He was sceptical of the reality of the Mer de l'Ouest, the Strait of Anian and the Fonte account, and favoured the traditional French piecemeal approach to the Pacific along the rivers west of the Great Lakes. Bellin accepted the Russian discoveries, but observed that it was still far from certain whether the land reached by Bering's ships was part of the American continent or islands. Although Bellin sometimes included the Mer de l'Ouest, and the coastal openings of Fuca and Fonte on his maps, they were drawn with dotted lines – the cartographer's equivalent of a question mark.

In England the controversy was followed with interest. Within a month of the publication of Buache's first Fonte map in June 1752, information about it appeared in London newspapers. It was, the report concluded, 'a Performance, certainly of as great importance as any which Geography had for a long Time afforded, both by the vast Extent of Seas and Lands it exhibits, and the Insight for a shorter Cut to the East Indies'. The letters of Peter Collinson, London merchant, Fellow of the Royal Society, and correspondent of Benjamin Franklin, provide further evidence of interest outside France in the Delisle/Buache maps. At the beginning of 1753 Collinson wrote to Franklin in Philadephia, who was at that time organising the voyage of Charles Swaine from that port to Hudson Bay, and described a recent map that he had seen. Clearly one of those constructed by Delisle or Buache, it revealed 'a River from about Hudsons bay Derived from a Great Island lake full of islands and another river falling from that lake into the Eastern [sic] Ocean above California'. Advertisements in the newspapers show that London sellers of maps and prints made a point of having the latest foreign, and especially French, maps in stock. Whether or not the two nations were at war made little difference to the flow of French maps across the Channel, since many of them were imported by way of Amsterdam. To some cartographers, and to the map-buying public, a blank space on a map was an admission of failure. The islands, rivers, straits, even continents, which were shown in unexplored regions might in the end prove to be non-existent, but for the moment they made the map attractive in appearance, and controversial in content. Speculative maps also had a more serious function, as Robert de Vaugondy explained.

Where precise information was lacking, then he might construct a map which showed alternative possibilities, a visualisation of various hypotheses for scholars and others to contemplate. So Bellin had constructed maps for Delisle showing the Fonte discoveries, but in his own maps he had been more cautious. Vaugondy was a *géographe de cabinet*, what the English would later call, in a not altogether friendly way, an armchair geographer. In the preface to his *Atlas Universel* of 1757 Vaugondy explained how such a geographer approached his task. He 'gathers, without leaving his study, all the details he can acquire, combines and compares them with authentic relations and determines them with the help of astronomical observations'. This was a counsel of perfection, and in the 1770s Vaugondy was to construct maps showing those decidedly unauthentic Fonte discoveries which he had treated so roughly when they were first published by Buache and Delisle.

John Green's 'New Chart' and accompanying *Remarks* were followed by further publications in 1754. A handy little volume was issued containing the text of the Fonte letter; a translation of Delisle's *Explication*, together with a simplified version of his map of September 1752; *A Letter from a Russian Sea-Officer*, first published in French in 1753; and finally *Observations on the Russian Discoveries* by Arthur Dobbs. Of most interest was the pseudonymous *Letter*, for this represented the first Russian response to Delisle's original memoir. It was written by Gerhard Friedrich Müller, the scholarly Secretary of the St Petersburg Academy of Sciences, who was commissioned by the President of the Academy to expose Delisle's 'evil representations' about the second Bering expedition, and so his pamphlet was published in French, German and English. Although neither Russian nor a sea officer, Müller had been closely connected with the expedition, and had also acted as an interpreter between Bering and Delisle after the Dane's return from his first voyage. He stressed that on his second voyage Bering had completed his explorations before being shipwrecked, and that like Chirikov he had sighted the Ameri-

can coast. In his piece, Dobbs admitted that there were inconsistencies in the Fonte letter, but refused to reject it out of
hand, and claimed to have discovered more information about
some of its personalities. Not only had a Shapley family lived
in Boston, as he had asserted in his 1744 *Account of Hudson's
Bay*, but also a shipowner named Gibbon; and, to cap it all, a
Fonte or Fuente had once served Spain in the South Sea.
Dobbs then repeated his earlier interpretation of the recent
Russian discoveries. Still clinging to his belief that Indians who
lived not far from Hudson Bay had been at the western ocean,
he thought it impossible that the American coast stretched
northwest from California almost as far as the tip of Asia. The
stretches of coast sighted by the Russians, he thought, were
'islands, some of which may be very large, interspersed in that
north-western ocean'. Characteristically, he considered that
the placing of the Strait of Ronquillo on the Buache maps
ten degrees farther north than the Fonte letter stated was
an unscrupulous attempt by the French to discourage further
British searches for a passage through Hudson Bay.

The publication in the *Gentleman's Magazine* of one of
Delisle's controversial maps, together with a long summary of
the dispute between the various geographers, ensured that the
Russian discoveries, and the new outlines of northwest America
based on the Fonte account, were well-known in Britain. What
was lacking in the debate was any authoritative account from
Russia of Bering's voyages (Müller's *Letter* had been a hasty
response to Delisle, written in a month), and any corroboration
or denial from Spain of the Fonte voyage. Not until the late
1750s did such contributions appear, and their impact was not
as clear-cut as might be imagined. Müller was immersed in the
formidable task of writing a multi-volume account of Russian
exploration, and it was 1758 before he was able to publish, in
his third volume, a narrative of the First and Second Kamchatka Expeditions. This was translated from the German into
English in 1761 (with an improved second edition in 1764),
and into French in 1766. Müller's *Voyages from Asia to America*,

29. G. F. MÜLLER. 'Nouvelles Carte des Découvertes faites par des Vaisseaux Russiens'. 1758.

Müller's map, issued under the auspices of the St Petersburg Academy of Sciences, represents the official Russian view of the discoveries made by

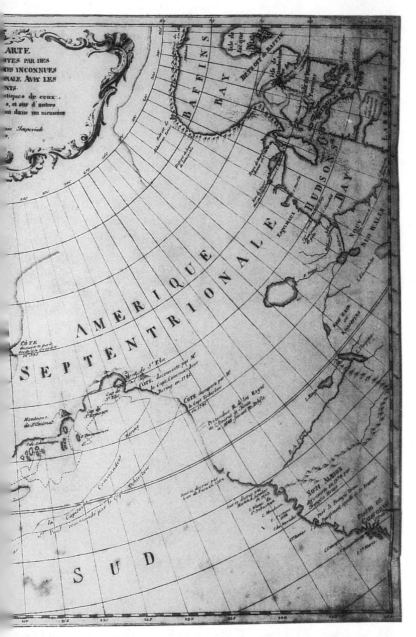

Bering's two expeditions. Bering's track to the eastern tip of Siberia in 1728 is traced, with Gvosdev's landfall four years later on the American shoreline, also shown. Farther south there are the tracks of Bering and Chirikov in 1741, with dotted lines joining their scattered landfalls along the Alaskan coast.

as the English edition was called, became the standard account of the 'Bering phase' of Russian expeditions in the north Pacific. Müller admitted that Bering on his first voyage had not brought back the conclusive information expected, but he insisted that his explorations in 1728, and Gvosdev's four years later, had shown that 'there is a real separation between the two parts of the world, Asia, and America; that it consists only in a narrow straight'. His account of the second expedition described the explorations of both Bering and Chirikov, as well as those of the subordinate expeditions connected with the project. He pointed out that the Russian explorations had diminished the chances of finding a Northwest Passage through Hudson Bay since they seemed to show that beyond California the coast curved away far to the northwest. The Delisle/Buache system of inland seas and straits Müller rejected, adding that 'it is always much better to omit whatever is uncertain, and leave a void space, till future discoveries shall ascertain the affair in dispute'.

Müller's own map of the Russian discoveries, first printed in 1754, was published in his book in 1758 (*Ill.29*). For the first time, Bering's track across the Pacific, and his landfalls, were shown alongside those of Chirikov. The map illustrated the official Russian view that the land first sighted by Bering and Chirikov was part of the North American mainland, as was much of the coastline glimpsed on their desperate return voyages. This assumption resulted in the turtle-head shape of the Alaskan peninsula of Müller's map, which if accurate would hinder efforts to sail through either a Northwest or a Northeast Passage. Offshore the Shumagin and Aleutian island groups were shown, but in the wide expanses of the North Pacific a whole range of imaginary lands such as Yedso were eliminated. Müller warned against placing too much trust in the accuracy of his map – 'My work herein has been no more than to connect together, according to probability, by points, the coasts that had been seen in various places.' Nor does he seem to have seen all the charts made by individual officers on the *St Peter* and *St Paul*, many of which were to remain unpublished until the twentieth century. Yet his map remained for fifteen years the standard representation of the region, and many preferred Müller's tentative outlines to the beguiling but fanciful maps of the Delisle/Buache school.

The scholars of one nation seemed to hold aloof from the debate on the Fonte letter. To the geographers of Europe, accustomed to the silence of the Spanish government about its overseas ventures, there was nothing unusual about the fact that no investigator in Spain, whose archives might be expected to reveal the reality or otherwise of the Fonte voyage, had come forward to pronounce on the admiral's exploits. To many the refusal of the Spaniards to comment on the letter of 1708 was confirmation of its authenticity. When sceptics pointed to internal discrepancies in the account, others claimed that these were errors by the printer or translator. Benjamin Franklin's verdict was typical of many. He believed that the Fonte letter was genuine, although 'an abridgement and a translation, and bad in both respects; if a fiction it is plainly not an English one, but it has none of the features of fiction'. It was one of the most striking aspects of the Fonte fantasy that in 1757 clear evidence came from Spain that the letter was a fake – the hoax that some had always supposed it to be – and yet, through a publisher's or editor's act that could hardly have been accidental, this testimony was concealed.

In 1757 a three-volume history of California, *Noticia de la California*, was published in Madrid, and was soon recognised as one of the most informative works on the Spanish colonial empire. Ostensibly the work of Padre Miguel Venegas, the book was largely written by another Jesuit, Padre Andrés Marcos Burriel. Two appendices in the third volume of the work dealt with the question of the Northwest Passage. Appendix VI contained an account of English voyages in search of a passage, and a critical examination of Henry Ellis's writings on the subject. Appendix VII was of even more interest in that most of its 150 pages were taken up with a detailed scrutiny of the Fonte account, and the system of speculative geography attributed to Delisle and Buache. Burriel printed the Fonte letter, and proceeded to show the discrepancies between it and the Buache map published in 1752. However, this was not the most important part of his investigation; John Green and Robert de Vaugondy had done much the same a few years earlier. The most significant part of Burriel's work lay in his scrutiny of the voyage itself, and in his efforts to find mention of it in the Spanish records. Since 1750 Burriel had been working on a commission established to report on the archives of Spain, and this gave him an excellent opportunity to investigate the authenticity of the Fonte account. He listed those places where mention of the admiral and his voyage might be expected: the naval records at Madrid and Cadiz; the Archives of the Indies in Seville; contemporary accounts and maps. But after as thorough a search as time allowed Burriel had found nothing, not a single reference.

He then turned to the narrative of the voyage itself. The letter began with the statement that news of an expedition from Boston in 1639 led to Fonte receiving orders from Spain to sail north from Lima. If this was true, Burriel pointed out, it meant that information came from New England to Spain (presumably by way of London), a decision was taken in Madrid, orders for an expedition sent to Mexico, and thence to Lima, and ships fitted out – all within a year, since Fonte sailed early in April 1640. Furthermore, Burriel asked, was it likely that the Spanish government, faced with rebellion in Portugal, Catalonia and Naples, and harassed by Dutch and French attacks on its shipping, would order four ships of war to be sent into unknown regions to investigate a vague report about a Boston expedition? The pace of the explorations of Fonte's squadron surpassed even the speed with which the expedition had been prepared. On 22 June Fonte, when at the entrance of Río los Reyes in latitude 53°N., ordered Captain Barnarda to explore northward. Five days later Barnarda wrote to Fonte that he was at the Sea of Tartary in latitude 61°N.;

and this letter reached the admiral, far inland at Lake Belle, before 1 July! Burriel gently inquired whether it had been sent by land or water, or perhaps by air. He next turned to the two Jesuits mentioned by Fonte, who during their mission had been as far north as latitude 66°N., and had stayed two years at the Indian town of Conosset. He pointed out that the activities of the Jesuits were strictly supervised, and that a mission could not be set up without a licence; yet nowhere in the records of the Society of Jesus could he find any trace of this extraordinary mission many hundreds of miles north of any Spanish settlement.

Even more surprising, considered Burriel, was Fonte's reaction when, having sailed six thousand miles from Lima with four warships to prevent Boston seamen discovering the Northwest Passage, he finally encountered the New England vessel commanded by Captain Shapley. Instead of seizing ship and crew, Fonte gave Shapley a thousand pieces of eight and a diamond ring, and twenty pieces of eight to each member of the crew. After this improbable act of generosity Fonte returned to his ships at Conosset, where he received more news of the wandering Barnarda. In a letter dated 11 August the captain informed him that there was no communication between the Pacific and Davis Strait, and that one of his sailors had reached the head of the strait in latitude 80°N. In another message Barnarda told Fonte that he himself had sailed as far as latitude 79°N. where he found the land covered with ice, but that now, 29 August, he awaited the admiral at Río los Reyes. These exploits Burriel could only compare with those of the Argonauts. Burriel listed other points that aroused suspicion: the extraordinary linguistic ability of Fonte's interpreter, who was able to understand Indians in remote parts of the continent, and the speed and fidelity with which Indians carried letters for the Spaniards over vast distances. He discussed the hardships and perils normally experienced by discovery ships, and contrasted them with the smooth progress of the Fonte expedition. All these considerations, wrote

Burriel, pointed to one conclusion: the Fonte letter was a forgery.

Although other commentators had challenged the authenticity of the Fonte letter, none had worked with Burriel's advantages of access to Spanish archives. He showed that the account was indisputably false, that it was unworthy of consideration by serious geographers. His painstaking research should have ended speculation about whether the letter was genuine, but when an English edition of the book, *A Natural and Civil History of California*, was published in London in 1759, appendices VI and VII were not included. No indication was given of this omission, which was the only major departure from the original, and one that was followed by a French and a Dutch edition of the work, both translated from the English. Reasons of space and economy would not appear to explain the excision of the two appendices, particularly when the long-standing British interest in the Northwest Passage is remembered. Suspicion about the motives for the omission is increased by a reading of the anonymous editor's preface to the expurgated English version, in which he stressed the importance of current theories about the region north of California. He referred to the different opinions held by geographers as to whether there was a strait, an open sea, or a land bridge, between Asia and America in the far north, and then wrote: 'this is far from being a matter of idle speculation . . . as the subjects of a maritime power we have the greatest concern in it, since every discovery of this kind must affect our navigation and commerce.' Secure in the knowledge that his readers would not be aware of Burriel's demolition of the Fonte account, the editor asserted that they would find in the book that the discovery of a Northwest Passage was held by 'the ablest judges' to be 'very probable'.

The effect that the apparent silence of the Spanish scholar had on at least one interested party was shown in a book published in London in 1768, *The Great Probability of a North West Passage: Deduced from Observations on the Letter of Admiral*

De Fonte. The book was the work of that elusive figure who, as T.S. Drage, had been the clerk of the *California* on the voyage to Hudson Bay of 1746–47, and, as Captain Charles Swaine, had commanded the *Argo* on the abortive discovery voyages of 1753 and 1754. Whatever the mystery surrounding him, the man with two names was no armchair explorer, for he had first-hand experience of the difficulties and dangers of northern voyaging. He had read Burriel's work only in its English edition, and so criticised the Spaniard for his failure even to mention the Fonte account. His explanation for the omission was that Burriel knew that the Spanish government preferred that the account 'should be continued in Oblivion than be revived'. Swaine scrutinised the latter with the microscopic attention normally reserved for a Biblical text, and concluded that it was not a forgery, but a careless and badly-printed translation of a Spanish document. Since he knew of William Christopher's explorations for the Hudson's Bay Company a few years earlier which had shown that Chesterfield Inlet was closed to the west, Swaine doubted whether there was any remaining hope of finding a passage through Hudson Bay. He maintained that Fonte's Strait of Ronquillo was the long-sought Strait of Anian, and that it probably had its outlet along the unexplored coastline between Hudson Bay and Baffin Bay. Interspersed with geographical arguments were anecdotes of doubtful reliability. So, the author during his researches in New England had met a merchant whose father was very old, and 'that when the dispute was between the late Governor Dobbs and Captain Middleton, he said, "Why do they make such a Fuzz about this Affair, our Old Nick (meaning Captain Shapley) was through there?" And this antient Gentleman had been an Intimate of Captain Shapley's.' Even so, the book attracted more attention than it might otherwise have done (its arguments were outlined, for example, in the *Monthly Review* of September 1768), because the map publisher and engraver, Thomas Jefferys, now bearing the honorary title of 'Geographer to the King', produced its maps; and since his was the only name on the title-page it was widely assumed that he was the book's author.

It was the more important that geographers and navigators should have been aware of Burriel's investigations because in Britain attention was turning to the prospect of searching for the entrance of a passage along the coastline of northwest America, encouraged by the supposed discoveries of Spanish expeditions sailing north of California. The change in direction was neatly marked by coincidental developments in 1764. In August, Moses Norton wrote from Churchill informing the Hudson's Bay Company that three years of exploration by the fort's sloops along the west coast of Hudson Bay had ended in failure. 'I am Certain and Shure,' he wrote, 'that there is no Pasage into the Western Ocan in this Hudsons Bay.' Just two months earlier a naval expedition had left Plymouth with instructions to find the Pacific entrance of the Northwest Passage which might lead to Hudson Bay. The orders given to Commodore John Byron in the summer of 1764 were a sign that the Admiralty, despite the disappointment of Middleton's voyage, was again preparing to take up the search.

Traditionally, Byron's voyage has been seen as the first in the series of Pacific-exploring voyages of George III's reign, followed by those of Wallis, Carteret and Cook. In reality, it was a throwback to an earlier period; it was the rumoured expedition of 1749 brought to life (see p.207 above). Byron had been on Anson's voyage round the world as a midshipman on the unlucky *Wager*, so it was appropriate that he commanded an expedition whose aims would be familiar to Anson and to Anson's generation; although the opening lines of Byron's instructions struck a new note as they proclaimed that 'nothing can redound more to the honor of this Nation as a Maritime Power, to the dignity of the Crown of Great Britain, and to the advancement of the Trade and Navigation thereof, than to make Discoveries of Countries hitherto unknown'. The sentiments were those of Arthur Dobbs and John Campbell, but they were now expressed by a minister of the crown. Maritime exploration had become a matter of national policy rather than the preserve of a few enthusiastic promoters. Although at the Treaty of Paris in 1763 Britain had gained huge overseas possessions in North America, the Caribbean and the East, and a period of assimilation might have been expected, the energies released in the war sought new outlets. In North America the conquest of Canada from the French slowed for the moment the process of western exploration, but by the mid-1760s the river routes west from Montreal were in use again, this time by traders whose resources were greater than those of their French predecessors. Supported by capital from Britain and the American colonies, the new breed of 'pedlars' soon formed the North West Company, and by their energetic domination of the fur trade pulled the Hudson's Bay Company inland in a rivalry that spread to the Rockies. The quest by French explorers such as La Vérendrye and his associates for a river-and-lake route to the western ocean was resumed, but now the names of the inland travellers had a different ring: Robert Rogers, Peter Pond, Alexander Mackenzie. Before the end of the century the overland thrust across the continent would meet the seaborne expeditions from Britain, France, Spain and Russia on the northwest coast of America.

As European interest in the Pacific increased, the Northwest Passage took on a new significance at the very time when the evidence of the old Spanish accounts, and the continuing Russian explorations, held out fresh hope that it might yet be found; and when advances in navigational science and shipboard health made voyages from Europe to the North Pacific more feasible. But in Britain, as elsewhere, other projects of oceanic discovery also engaged the attention of ministers, merchants and geographers; and whereas in the first half of the century the expeditions which sought the Northwest Passage represented virtually the only serious attempts at maritime exploration, after 1763 the discovery of a passage was one of a number of government objectives. Byron's instructions revealed two of these. In far southern waters he was to explore lands that included the Falkland Islands, whose position near the Strait of Magellan prompted First Lord of the Admiralty Egmont to describe them as 'the key to the whole Pacific Ocean'. After this, Byron was to pass into the Pacific and sail to the northwest coast of America, named New Albion by Drake in 1579 on his voyage round the world in the *Golden Hind*. 'The Countrey of New Albion in North America first discovered and taken possession of by Sir Francis Drake in the Year 1579', Byron was told, 'has never been examined with that care which it deserves, notwithstanding frequent recommendations of that Undertaking by the said Sir Frans Drake, Dampier, & many other Mariners of great Experience, who have thought it probable that a passage might be found between the Latitude of 38° and 54° from that Coast into Hudson's Bay'. The double task was one to stretch the resources of a more determined explorer than Byron. Even before struggling through the Strait of Magellan he decided that 'Our ships are too much disabled for the California voyage', and once in the Pacific he followed a diagonal track northwest across the ocean to the Marianas, and then to Batavia, and home.

The design revealed in Byron's instructions had origins, of a rather shadowy kind, in the reign of Elizabeth I. In 1574 a group of West Countrymen led by Richard Grenville obtained the sovereign's approval, later withdrawn, for an expedition to the Pacific that planned to fortify the Strait of Magellan and then, possibly, return to Europe through the Strait of Anian. In the event, the expedition was stillborn, and the first English expedition to reach the Pacific was that of Francis Drake, whose objectives had links with Grenville's proposals. Of all aspects of the *Golden Hind*'s dramatic voyage round the world in 1577–80, the events of the summer of 1579 after Drake had seized enormous amounts of Spanish silver in the South Sea are the most baffling. Off the coast of Mexico, Drake had to decide which route to take home. To sail back south along the coasts of Spanish America, now fully roused by his depredations, and then retrace his route through the tortuous twists and turns of the Strait of Magellan, was not an alluring prospect. Two other possibilities existed. One was to follow Magellan's track west across the Pacific, into the Indian Ocean, and so around the Cape of Good Hope and home. The other was to sail north in the hope of finding the Strait of Anian and a short route back to the Atlantic. The year before Drake sailed from England, Martin Frobisher was confident that he had found on the southeast coast of today's Baffin Island the entrance to 'the West Sea, whereby to pass to Cathay and to the East India'. In the end, Drake came home by the same route as Magellan, but not before sailing three thousand miles north. He may have been looking for the Strait of Anian or, less ambitiously, for favourable winds or currents to take him across the Pacific. How far north Drake sailed is uncertain, for his own journal and chart have disappeared. Accounts of the voyage give latitudes varying from 42°N. to 48°N., but Drake may have reached much farther north still, for the accounts for June and July describe 'extreme and nipping cold', fur-clad natives, and 'trees without leaves'. Such conditions have led some scholars to speculate that Drake was off the Alaskan coast, and the most recent interpretation has him entering Clarence Strait north of the Queen Charlotte Islands and sailing as far north as Chatham Strait in latitude 57°N. in search of entrance to the Strait of Anian or Northwest Passage. When Drake turned back south he careened at a harbour whose location has remained a matter of interminable dispute, the rival locations ranging from the great bay of San Francisco to Whale Cove, Oregon. Whichever harbour it was that Drake reached, he there took possession of the country in the name of the Queen, and his New Albion remained a standing challenge – if only on the maps – to Spanish claims of dominion over the entire Pacific seaboard of the Americas.

The reference to New Albion in Byron's instructions, and the reminder that it had been 'first discovered and taken possession of' by Drake, are clear indications of a revival of British interest in the region. Despite all the failures from Frobisher's day onwards to find an oceanic passage at the Atlantic end, New Albion retained its allure, and the possibility of a Pacific approach to the mystery of the Northwest Passage was not altogether forgotten. In 1603 on a voyage back to England from the Moluccas with East India Company ships Sir James Lancaster wrote a letter home to which he added an unexplained and cryptic postscript: 'The Passage to the East India lieth in 62.½ . . . degrees, by the North-west on the America side.' In 1625 Purchas printed Juan de Fuca's description of the strait the old pilot claimed to have found on the northwest coast of America between latitudes 47°N. and 48°N., approximately Drake's farthest north according to one account of his voyage. Then, towards the end of the seventeenth century, in a passage that Byron's instructions showed that the Lords of the Admiralty of 1764 had read, the buccaneer William Dampier argued in favour of finding the Pacific entrance of the Northwest Passage:

> If I was to go upon this Discovery, I would go first into the *South-Seas*, bend my course from thence along to *California*, and that way seek a Passage back into [the Atlantic]. For as others have spent the Summer, in first searching on this more known side nearer home, and so before they got through, the time of the Year obliged them to give over their Search, and provide for a long course back again, for fear of being left in the Winter; on the contrary, I would search first on the less known coast of the South-Sea-side, and then as the Year past away, I should need no retreat, for I should come farther into my Knowledge.

In 1750 Henry Ellis repeated these arguments, for the voyages of Knight, Middleton and Moor had confirmed the difficulties of finding the eastern entrance to the passage along the icebound shores of Hudson Bay. It was then that Anson and Sandwich at the Board of Admiralty were musing over the possibility of an expedition to the north Pacific, so it is not altogether surprising that when the first discovery voyage of George III's reign was planned a search for the Northwest Passage should be among Byron's instructions. By now Anson was dead and the originator of the scheme is not known, but it is perhaps significant that for six months in the summer of 1763 the Earl of Sandwich was once more First Lord of the Admiralty, and his later role in Cook's voyages was to show that his interest in Pacific exploration was a consistent one. What at first sight is surprising is that the Admiralty decided on another attempt to discover the Northwest Passage after repeated efforts to find its Atlantic entrance had failed. Even if some deep inlet was discovered on the Pacific coast of North America that led far into the interior, it was difficult to see where it might exit on the eastern side of the continent. It was a question of balancing the unpromising surveys of Hudson Bay by a succession of explorers against the conviction of some geographers and promoters that a passage existed, awaiting only the final effort of Dobbs's 'more happy Adventurer'. The odds are that someone at the Admiralty had been studying the maps of the speculative cartographers of this period, whose influence in determining the course of oceanic exploration should not be underestimated. The Pacific voyages soon to come – of Wallis and Carteret and Cook – owed much to the arguments of John Campbell, Charles de Brosses and Alexander Dalrymple that *Terra Australis Incognita* existed, while Philippe Buache was as energetic in showing that continent on his southern hemisphere maps as he was in depicting the discoveries of Juan de Fuca and Bartholomew de Fonte on his northern hemisphere maps. The detail of Byron's instructions strengthens the likelihood that the Admiralty was influenced by the Delisle/Buache maps despite the controversy surrounding them. Byron was ordered to explore the coast north from latitude 38°N., the supposed location of Drake's Californian landing place. Along those northern shores lay the entrances of the three rivers or straits thought to have been discovered by Spanish expeditions, by Fuca (1592), Aguilar (1603) and Fonte (1640). The farthest north of these openings, Fonte's Río los Reyes, lay in latitude 53°N.; Byron was ordered to explore as far north as 54°N., so his area of search included all the supposed Spanish discoveries.

However promising the Pacific approach might seem, it presented formidable diplomatic problems. To Spain, desperately trying to preserve its colonial monopoly, the Pacific was *mare clausum*, 'The Spanish Lake'. The depredations of the buccaneers in the seventeenth century had shown the fragility of that claim, but the Spanish government continued to regard foreign incursions into the Pacific with concern and indignation. British activities were regarded with particular suspicion; since Drake's time Spaniards had feared a surprise attack by way of that northern passage that the English were so determined to discover. Anson's destructive sweep through the South Sea in the 1740s had increased Spanish sensitivities, and these were reflected in Burriel's *Noticia de la California*. He saw ominous warnings in Anson's expedition and in his subsequent rise to high office in Britain; and pointed out that if the British ever found a Northwest Passage they would be able to raid Spanish territories in the South Sea at will, and eventually dominate its commerce. In this context, Byron's expedition was regarded as a threatening portent, and on its return the Spanish ambassador in London, Prince Fieschi de Masserano, persistently questioned ministers about its objectives. In one dispatch to Madrid he reported, erroneously, that Byron had reached New Albion, but had not been able to find a passage to Hudson Bay. In another, he reported a conversation with the Duke of Richmond, Secretary of State for the Southern Department. Richmond disclaimed all knowledge of

Byron's intentions in the Pacific, 'to which', Masserano wrote, 'I said that was a point about which I felt and ought to feel more curiosity, since all those countries are the King's and no one may settle in them. He asked me if the whole world was Spain's; and I replied that, as to that portion, yes'.

Spanish attempts at discouragement failed to prevent further voyages to the Pacific by both Britain and France. In the years after Byron's return the ships of Bougainville, Wallis, Carteret and Cook criss-crossed the Pacific. Their voyages represented a mix of scientific curiosity, national pride and commercial acquisitiveness. At a global level, the main quest was directed towards the great southern continent, at a more limited level the Falkland Islands or Malvinas represented a point of intense rivalry. The establishment of a British settlement at Port Egmont in the Falklands brought Britain and Spain close to war, but in 1774 the North government abandoned its post there, though it left the flag flying as a sign that it had not given up claims of possession. The same year, James Cook, far distant in Antarctic latitudes on his second Pacific voyage, was proving that the vision of a fertile southern continent had no substance, for he had found only 'a Country doomed by Nature never once to feel the warmth of the Suns rays, but to lie for ever buried under everlasting snow and ice'.

Even before these disappointments in the southern hemisphere, there were further signs in Britain of a revival of interest in exploration to the north. Since the end of 1772 a new generation of enthusiasts had been in contact with ministers with proposals for ventures to the north Pacific. They included John Blankett, a naval officer who had been interested in the Northwest Passage since his service in Canadian waters during the Seven Years War; John Hanson, a writer of long, Dobbs-like memorials on trade and exploration; the Anglophile Swiss geographer Samuel Engel; and Daines Barrington of the Royal Society. Their arguments were familiar: the benefits of new trade, the glory of making discoveries, and the danger that a foreign nation might anticipate Britain – this last a nod in the direction of France, where at this time there was much discussion, if not much action, in French ministerial and scientific circles about the possibility of an Arctic voyage. With the growing crisis in America dominating the attention of the British government, the response of ministers to these approaches was lukewarm. The files of the Earl of Dartmouth contain proposals for a whole array of northern expeditions, but since he was at this time Secretary of State for the American Colonies it is unlikely that he gave them more than a passing glance.

Requests and petitions from individuals were one thing, but an approach from the Royal Society was another, and weightier, matter altogether. The Society had a long tradition of interest in voyages and travels, and its influence both with the King and the Admiralty had recently been demonstrated by the central role it played in Cook's first voyage (whose original objective was to set up an astronomical station at Tahiti to observe the transit of Venus in 1769). President of the Society at this time was Sir John Pringle, author of a discourse on health at sea, and spokesman for a group of medical practitioners that had close links with the Admiralty. Pringle had long been interested in questions of exploration, had corresponded with Benjamin Franklin about the Fonte letter, and had sent him the unpublished observations on the Northwest Passage written by the Hudson's Bay Company captain William Coats. Among the Council members of the Royal Society was Daines Barrington: jurist, antiquarian, naturalist and a recent convert to the cause of northern exploration. One of his correspondents was Samuel Engel, who was convinced that the north polar sea was free from ice. His interest in the subject was picked up by Barrington, who proceeded to carry out enthusiastic if uncritical investigations as to whether ships could sail across the Pole, and so into the Pacific by way of the strait recently discovered by the Russians.

The idea of sailing from Europe to the East Indies across the Pole had been suggested as early as the 1520s, and in the seventeenth century several expeditions had tried the route, but ice prevented them from sailing beyond latitude 80°N. John Campbell and John Green had both argued in favour of an open polar sea, while Philippe Buache stated, rather plaintively, that a passage across the Pole was 'supported by every kind of proof . . . except the living testimony of mariners who have made the voyage'. Then in 1765 Engel published his weighty *Mémoires et Observations Géographiques et Critiques*, in which he advocated attempts to find an Atlantic-Pacific link across the Pole, or failing that a Northeast Passage along the coast of Siberia. Engel claimed that most of the ice encountered in high northern latitudes came from the rivers when they broke up in early summer, and so was thick only near land. In a series of tracts read to the Royal Society and then published, Barrington supported this theory with reports of scientific experiments that seemed to show that salt water could not freeze, and with examples of whalers who were alleged to have found an ice-free sea near the pole. The long list of sightings without dates and ships without names was impressive only to those who counted rather than weighed authorities. Barrington's varied and undiscriminating enthusiasms were a favourite subject of amusement among his contemporaries; so that when the sensational book of James Bruce's Abyssinian travels was published the rumour was that 'it will be dedicated to the Honourable Daines Barrington, with singular propriety, as he is the only one who possesses credulity enough of the author's purposes'. However, if only for a moment, Barrington played a role of some importance in national affairs, for in his capacity as a Council member of the Royal Society, and a friend of the Earl of Sandwich (once more First Lord of the Admiralty), he was the link between the Society and the Admiralty. In 1774 he was to help set in motion a plan for a voyage that was to lead five years later to the death on a distant Pacific beach of the leading explorer of the age.

First, though, there was the Pole and the ice-free sea. Early in 1773 Barrington raised the possibility of a polar voyage at a Council meeting, and stated that he had already discussed the matter with Sandwich. It was at about this time that Sandwich seems to have acquired Williams Coats's papers 'relative to Discoveries in the NorthWest', as well as his own copy of Christopher Middleton's journal of the *Furnace*. Encouraged by Barrington's report, the Secretary of the Royal Society, Dr Matthew Maty, wrote to the First Lord of the Admiralty, suggesting that a naval expedition should be sent to the East Indies by way of the North Pole. Such a voyage, Maty pointed out, would be 'of service to the promotion of Natural knowledge, the proper object of their [the Society's] institution'. After some hesitation, the Admiralty agreed, and chose two bomb-vessels, the *Racehorse* and *Carcass*. They were fitted with double bottoms, their bows fortified, and other alterations made to adapt them for work among ice. Pilots from the Greenland whale fishery were engaged to offset the lack of Arctic experience among regular naval officers, and at the beginning of June 1773 the expedition sailed under the command of Captain John Phipps (who was to become a Council member of the Royal Society on his return). Barrington was still busy collecting reports describing the ease with which whalers had reached high northern latitudes, but Phipps could not penetrate the ice-barrier that he found north of Spitzbergen in latitude 80°N. It was only with difficulty that he extricated his battered vessels from the ice and got them back to England. An account of the voyage was published the next year, with a series of scientific appendixes that made it a model of its kind, and certainly in the eyes of the Royal Society justified the decision to send out the vessels. At a different level, the voyage was remembered because on the *Carcass* was a young midshipman, Horatio Nelson, whose encounter with a polar bear was to become part of Nelsonian legend.

Barrington was not impressed by the pessimistic report brought back by the expedition. He thought that ice conditions changed from time to time, and that Phipps had been sent in a 'bad year'. This last explanation was to be heard many times during the Navy's dogged attempts to find a way through Arctic ice in the next century; but no further effort was made in the eighteenth century to put the idea of a transpolar route to practical test. Barrington, though still happily publishing pamphlets on the ease of navigation towards the pole, now turned his attention to the Northwest Passage, and the route he suggested was similar to that which Byron was instructed to follow in 1764. Once again, Barrington put his plan for a discovery expedition before the Council of the Royal Society, which approved it in meetings in February 1774. The sequence of events of the previous year was repeated as Maty represented the Council's views to the Admiralty, while Sandwich communicated privately with Barrington. Maty's letter proposed that a naval expedition should be sent to Canton. From there it would head across the Pacific towards North America, and 'proceed up the North western side of that continent, so as to discover whether there is a passage into the European seas'. If no passage was found, then the little-known coasts of Kamchatka and Korea should be explored.

It was a sign of the increasing interest in the north Pacific that several proposals along much the same lines reached the government at this time. There was now some urgency about the matter, for the London newspapers were reporting that the French were preparing one expedition to sail across the Pole, and another bound for the Pacific coast of North America to search for a Northwest Passage. This last, it was rumoured, would be commanded by the celebrated Louis-Antoine de Bougainville, whose Pacific voyage of 1766–69 had preceded Cook's first voyage. At about this time, a respected French academic periodical, the *Journal des Sçavans*, published in its November 1773 issue an account of yet another hoax voyage. A Danish navigator, Baron d'Ulfeld, who left Europe in 1769,

claimed to have found a Northwest Passage through Hudson
Bay, and to have sailed into the Pacific before returning home
by way of Cape Horn after a four-year absence. The *London
Chronicle* joined in the game with a report from Hamburg that
'The practicability of the North-west passage is not to be
disputed. A ship is now here, the Captain of which has produced his journals, and other testimonies of his having performed it.' Danes were one thing, the French quite another.
'Is it not very extraordinary,' the *Morning Chronicle* asked in
December 1773, 'that, though we are allowed to be the most
expert sailors in the world, that the French upon all occasions
excel us in their researches after countries?'

On this occasion, at least, the fears of the patriotic journal-
ist were not realised. There was to be no Bougainville voyage,
and it was the British Admiralty that was moving towards
approval of an ambitious discovery voyage to the North Pacific.
A memoir by John Hanson, dated 17 January 1774, among
the Dartmouth papers, proposed a voyage north of California
to determine the direction of the coast, and the existence or
otherwise of a Northwest Passage. The document concluded
that such a voyage 'will Crown great Britain with Never fading
Laurels, & Justly Entitle her; to the title of Empress of the
seas'. At the same time Samuel Engel wrote from Berne to
the government, enclosing a memorial for the attention of
the King concerning discovery and settlement in the region
between northeast Asia and northwest America. News of this
soon reached the East India Company, whose Palatine Agent
in London, Rudolph Valtravers, wrote to the Earl of Dartmouth asking whether the Company's directors might see
Engel's memoir since they were 'highly interested in a shorter
and safer passage to their present and future dominions'. Of
all the trading organizations of the period, the East India Company might be expected to benefit most from the discovery of
a navigable passage, for that would provide its ships with a
shorter route to Canton than the existing one from Europe
to the Cape of Good Hope, and then across the Indian Ocean

and North China Sea – the longest trade route in the world. The Company's China trade had increased spectacularly during the course of the century, with tea imports to London rising from less than 100,000 lbs in 1700 to 8 million lbs in 1770. Yet until this time the Company had shown little interest in the recent attempts to find a passage. There may have been good reasons for this cautious attitude. The Company's China trade was part of an intricate commercial network in the Eastern Seas, and the opening of an alternative route to Canton might not necessarily have worked to the Company's advantage. Its monopoly over British trading activities in the East applied only to goods shipped round the Cape of Good Hope, and in the Pacific stopped at a point three hundred leagues off the American coast (where it met the trading zone that had been awarded to the now-moribund South Sea Company in 1711). Valtravers was one of the group of advocates of northern exploration that included Engel and Barrington, but despite the wording of his letter to Dartmouth it is by no means certain that his enthusiasms were shared by the directors of the East India Company. They may well have been interested by the news that there were plans afoot to open up the dimly-known regions to the east of China, perhaps by way of a sea-passage from the Atlantic; but their main reaction would probably have been concern at the impact that such attempts by outsiders might have on its own trading position.

A third proposal, from a junior naval officer, for an expedition to the northwest coast was possibly more significant than Hanson's rhetorical outburst or Engel's learned treatise. Despite his lowly rank, Lieutenant John Blankett had received unofficial encouragement from Sandwich to visit St Petersburg and there obtain more details about the discoveries made by the Russians in the north Pacific. He also sent Sandwich schemes for opening trade in the seas between China, Korea and Japan. He was helped in all this, Blankett acknowledged, by Dr John Campbell – the same Campbell who had supported Dobbs's Northwest Passage schemes thirty years earlier. In a letter of 1780 to Lord Shelburne about Cook's third and final voyage, to discover the Northwest Passage, Blankett wrote: 'I must beg your Lordship if anything should arise of consequence from that Voyage to remember I was the proposer of it, Mr Daines Barrington having been the person who first laid my papers before the Royal Society, in consequence of which they applied to my Lord Sandwich to undertake the Expedition.'

What is without doubt is that in circles outside government, but close to ministers, several schemes were emerging at this time for a voyage to the north Pacific which would have among its objectives the search for a Northwest Passage. Although Sandwich's initial response to Maty's letter of 17 February 1774 was not promising – there were difficulties about costs, the current year's estimates and so on – a private letter that he sent Barrington was more reassuring. And after Barrington had 'a very full conversation' with Sandwich he was able to assure the Council of the Royal Society that once Cook had returned from the Pacific an expedition would be fitted out to make the discoveries suggested in Maty's letter. Amid the confusion of different schemes, what is clear is the decisive role played by Sandwich. Now in his third and longest spell as First Lord of the Admiralty, Sandwich had consistently shown support for exploration ventures. When in 1772 tension with Spain threatened to cancel Cook's second voyage, the venture was saved by what Cook called the 'perseverance' of Sandwich as First Lord and Hugh Palliser as Comptroller of the Navy. Now Sandwich had decided that the several discovery voyages to the south Pacific would be followed by a change of direction, and that once Cook and his ships had returned a new expedition would be fitted out to the north Pacific.

Cook was expected back in 1775, and evidence of the government's intention to send out a naval expedition to search for the Northwest Passage was shown by its support that year of a parliamentary bill offering a reward of £20,000 for the discovery of a passage. The bill was a revised version of the 1745 Act passed at Dobbs's instigation, and although the amount of the reward remained the same, other parts of the bill showed significant differences. The earlier Act had specified that the passage should run from Hudson Bay to the Pacific, limited the reward to private vessels, and referred to the discovery in terms of its advantage to 'the trade of this kingdom'. The 1775 version made no mention of Hudson Bay, but stipulated that the passage must lie north of latitude 52°N., opened the award to naval vessels, and referred to the 'many advantages both to commerce and science'. Much had changed in thirty years: the intervention of the Royal Society, attitudes at the Admiralty, and not least the influence of the Russian discoveries in the north Pacific. The Act also offered £5,000 to the crew of the first ship that approached within a degree of the North Pole – this a crumb thrown to Barrington who had hoped that the reward for this achievement would also be set at £20,000. Despite this setback, and though not a member of Parliament himself, Barrington worked diligently to get the bill through its several stages, and in December 1775 it received the royal assent.

Cook had returned in July 1775 with the *Resolution* after one of the most comprehensive of all seaborne voyages of exploration. His Whitby-built collier had served him well, and instead of being paid off the *Resolution* was put into dock at Deptford to be refitted for 'a voyage to remote parts'. Writers in the daily papers speculated widely and wildly about the destination of the rumoured new expedition, and whether Cook would again command it. Soon it was accepted that the *Resolution* would return to the south Pacific, and to Tahiti. What its precise objectives were was not clear, but there was a commitment to return to his home the young Polynesian, Omai (brought to England the year before by Captain Tobias Furneaux of the *Adventure*, consort vessel to the *Resolution*). In command of the new voyage, it seemed, would be Charles Clerke, who had been first lieutenant on the *Resolution*, though there were also rumours that the more junior John Blankett was being considered. Cook himself was moving in other directions, and in other circles. Soon after his return he was presented to the King, and promoted to post-captain. A few months later he was elected Fellow of the Royal Society, and presented with its Copley Gold Medal for his paper on the health of seamen – no theoretical discourse this, but the practical recommendations of a captain who in a three-year voyage had lost only one man through sickness. There were other forms of recognition, too. Cook was painted by Nathaniel Dance; his conversation was recorded by Boswell; he dined on easy terms with Sandwich, Pringle, Banks and other leading figures of London society. Cook was without doubt the 'first navigator in Europe', as Sandwich described him in a speech in the House of Lords, but his appointment in August to the post of captain at Greenwich Hospital seemed to signify his retirement from the sea.

Yet all was not quite as it seemed. The return of Omai might be a moral necessity, with royal weight behind it; but it could hardly justify an entire expedition. Nor was there a lack of wider objectives for another Pacific voyage, for the Act offering a reward for the discovery of a Northwest Passage was now on the statute book. At this point Cook comes to mind again, though according to his first biographer, his contemporary Andrew Kippis, neither Sandwich nor any other member of the Board of Admiralty was prepared to ask the explorer to serve again. This may be so, but there was no hesitation in drawing Cook into the arrangements for the new voyage. His advice was sought on the purchase of a consort vessel to the *Resolution*, and in the end it was Cook who selected the ship – not Clerke. Then there was the matter of the scope of the forthcoming voyage, and the instructions to be issued to its commander: routes, timing, ports of call. Kippis describes how these matters were discussed at a dinner party held in early February 1776 attended by Sandwich and Palliser, Philip

Stephens (the indispensable Secretary to the Admiralty) and Cook. Around the table, after animated discussion of the grand design, 'Captain Cook was so fired with the contemplation and representation of the object, that he started up, and declared that he himself would undertake the direction of the enterprise.' Biographers must be allowed dramatic licence, but the fact is that Cook was involved in the venture long before the celebrated dinner party. When he accepted the post at Greenwich Hospital from the Lords of the Admiralty, he did so on the understanding that 'they will allow me to quit it when either the call of my Country for more active Service, or that my endeavours in any shape can be essential to the publick'. There is no doubt that Cook appreciated the material benefits of his new post – 'a fine retreat and a pretty income' – but within a week of accepting (and long before there was any question of taking up actual residence at Greenwich) he wrote to his old master, John Walker of Whitby, in revealing terms: 'a few Months ago the whole Southern hemisphere was hardly big enough for me and now I am going to be confined within the limits of Greenwich Hospital'.

Had the proposed voyage been of a more routine nature, returning Omai, and then completing surveys of some of the Pacific island groups still imperfectly charted, then Cook would probably not have been tempted. The ships could have been entrusted to Clerke, or to Wallis. But the challenge of the Northwest Passage was different. It was as long-standing an objective of European ambition as that imagined southern continent that had dominated Cook's first two Pacific voyages. Furthermore, as events were to show, Cook was cautiously optimistic that he would finally solve the problem. His work in the south Pacific had been to eliminate *Terra Australis Incognita* from the world map, a substantial but essentially negative achievement. There had been much to balance the disappearance of the great southern continent – the revelation of the twin islands of New Zealand, the outlining of the east coast of Australia, the charting of a host of Polynesian islands – but there was a certain feeling of anti-climax at the end of it all. As Cook put it in his own prosaic words, 'If I have failed in discovering a Continent it is because it does not exist . . . and not for want of looking.' In contrast, what was held out to him now was the possibility of commanding the first ships to sail through the Northwest Passage, and with the fame and honour would come a substantial proportion of the £20,000 reward, a motive of some weight for one who did not possess any inherited wealth, but who was increasingly moving in circles of society well beyond the means of an ordinary naval officer. Four days after his appointment Cook wrote again to John Walker telling him about the new voyage, and adding, 'If I am fortunate enough to get safe home, theres no doubt but it will be greatly to my advantage.' The last words suggest a whole series of quiet commitments and pledges by those in authority. A glimpse of the explorer's eagerness and impatience to be away on the quest comes from Boswell, who wrote of a conversation he had with Cook in early April, 'I catched the enthusiasm of curiosity and adventure, and felt a strong inclination to go with him on his next voyage.'

With hindsight, knowing what was to happen on the voyage, and being more aware of the strains of command than perhaps our eighteenth-century predecessors were, we can argue that Cook should not have been approached, not been drawn into the planning process, not had the great prize dangled before him. For all but one of the previous seven years he had been away on voyages that were both physically gruelling and mentally exhausting. As he sailed into uncharted waters and confronted unknown coasts, he alone had taken all decisions; at no time was there a superior at hand to give counsel and support. During those years the sturdy physique and self-reliant disposition of the big Yorkshireman had borne the strain; but in the north Pacific he would be faced with new frustrations and dangers. They were met resolutely, and mostly overcome, but at a cost to Cook's sense of judgement that in the end resulted in violence and death.

9

The Puzzling Voyage of James Cook

*'We were upon a Coast where every step was to be con-
sidered, where no information could be had from Maps,
either modern or ancient: confiding too much in the former
we were frequently misled to our no small hindrance.'*

Captain James Cook to the Admiralty,
20 October 1778

IN HIS FIRST TWO Pacific voyages James Cook destroyed
the illusion fostered by the speculative geographers of his
and earlier times that a large temperate continent existed in
the southern hemisphere which offered untold opportunities
for European settlement and exploitation. Cook remained
sceptical about the entrancing hypotheses put forward by
geographers and projectors. Even before he sailed on his
second voyage he had written, 'as to a Southern Continent I
do not believe any such things exists unless in a high Latitude
. . . hanging clowds and a thick horizon are certainly no known
Signs of a Continent'; and on the voyage itself he sailed
through seas where cartographers had shown solid land. In
the precise impartiality of the detailed charts he brought back
with him, Cook demonstrated the reality of the south Pacific:
the great ice barrier of Antarctica; the coastal outlines of Australia, New Zealand and New Guinea; the position of many
other lesser island groups. The south Pacific emerged from
the haze which had allowed guesswork and fantasy to flourish,
and in Europe's eyes moved from the world of Gulliver to
that of James Cook, professional explorer.

The evidence that Cook provided in such abundance on his first two voyages of the unreliability of theoretical geography makes the events of his third voyage the more puzzling. It is true that the quest was different, and arguably more difficult; for instead of the looming haystack of a southern continent, Cook was searching for the slim needle of a Northwest Passage. It is true also that Cook was older (though still only forty-eight) and more tired, certainly more volatile and irascible, on his final voyage. But even before the ships sailed, Cook was in a sense behaving out of character. By now he virtually drew up his own instructions, and those instructions, dated 6 July 1776, reveal a reliance on speculative cartography that was to take months of frustrating exploration to dispel. There was enough of the old Cook to reject the fantasies of the French school of theorists about the geography of northwest America, but in following the interpretations of what may be called the German school the explorer sent himself in pursuit of a will-o'-the-wisp.

Cook's instructions show that he had set himself a tight timetable. After leaving the Cape of Good Hope, he intended to search for the islands in the Indian Ocean reported to have been sighted by the French in latitude 40°s. Then, after leaving Omai at the Society Islands he would head for the north Pacific and the coast of New Albion, which he expected to sight in the early summer of 1777. From there Cook was to sail more than fifteen hundred miles along the coast of Northwest America to latitude 65°N., 'taking care not to lose any time in exploring Rivers or Inlets. . . . When you get that Length, you are very carefully to search for, and to explore, such Rivers or Inlets as may appear to be of a considerable extent, and pointing towards Hudsons or Baffins Bay.' This directive was the most striking feature of Cook's instructions. Although he was free to take a running survey from shipboard as he kept north, there would be no detailed investigation of that unknown coastline where many geographers claimed that the straits of Fuca and Fonte lay, and where the Admiralty only a dozen years earlier had ordered Commodore Byron to search for a passage. There also, according to the old maps lay the Strait of Anian as well as the Mer de l'Ouest of Guillaume Delisle's invention; but however enticing an opening was sighted Cook was to ignore it. What on the face of it seemed a perverse limitation had its own logic, faulty though it proved to be. The explanation for the change in the direction of the search was to be found in the explorations for the Hudson's Bay Company of Samuel Hearne and William Christopher, the publication in England of a map supposedly based on the latest Russian discoveries, and the theories of Samuel Engel and others regarding the formation of sea ice.

Although Hearne's account of his journey to the Coppermine River was not published until 1795, a copy of his manuscript journal and three of his maps were loaned to the Admiralty before Cook sailed by Samuel Wegg, Deputy Governor of the Hudson's Bay Company. Wegg's attitude differed in many ways from that of his more secretive predecessors. He was a member of the Council of the Royal Society, and on good terms with Daines Barrington, Sir John Pringle and others interested in Arctic exploration. It was rough justice for Wegg that attacks on the Company for its allegedly non-cooperative attitude continued to appear in the press. So, the *Morning Post* of 5 January 1776 reported, wrongly and crassly, that 'It is determined in the cabinet not to renew the charter of that most impudent and pernicious monopoly of the Hudson's Bay Company, from the conviction that the act just passed, offering a reward for the discovery of the north-west passage can never have any effect while that company has the command of those regions.' Once they read Hearne's account, it became clear to Cook and the Board of Admiralty that whatever inlets were discovered on the northwest coast of America they could not stretch as far as Hudson Bay, because Hearne had crossed the northeast of the continent from Churchill to the shores of the Arctic Ocean without finding any strait or major river. This point was given added emphasis by the Admiralty's knowledge of the explorations made by the Company sloops along the west coast of Hudson Bay. Cook was a friend of the Company captain William Christopher, and since both men were in London during the winter before Cook sailed, it is reasonable to assume that they met and discussed Christopher's exploration of Chesterfield Inlet fifteen years earlier. Given all this, it is difficult to understand why Hudson Bay still featured in Cook's instructions as one of two possible exits for a strait running eastward from the Pacific coast.

If Hearne's explorations dispelled hopes of a passage through North America, his sighting of the Arctic Ocean at the mouth of the Coppermine River (though he placed it almost four degrees too far north in latitude 71°54'N.) raised the possibility that a route for ships might be found along the northern edge of the continent. Coincidentally, the publication in London in 1774 under the auspices of Dr Matthew Maty, Secretary of the Royal Society, of the English translation of a book issued the year before by his opposite number in Russia, Jacob von Stählin of the St Petersburg Academy of Sciences, raised the possibility that a short route might be discovered from the Pacific into the sea sighted by Hearne. On the face of it, Stählin's *Account of the New Northern Archipelago* offered a much-needed account of Russian explorations since Bering. The voyage of Bering and Chirikov in 1741 had been followed by private and often obscure trading ventures, for when the survivors from Bering's crew got back to Kamchatka in 1742 they brought with them nine hundred sea-otter pelts that fetched high prices at Canton. In the next decades the *promyshlenniki* or Russian fur traders moved from island to island in Alaskan waters in search of sea otters, but in ramshackle craft often held together by leather thongs they suffered heavy losses from storms, disease and native attacks, and had neither the instruments nor the competence to make accurate charts. A renewal of government interest led to some important survey work by Captain Petr Krenitsyn and Lieutenant Mikhail Leva-

shev in the years 1764 to 1769, and on one of their charts the
tip of the Alaskan peninsula, the Shumagin Islands, and the
large islands of Unimak and Unalaska were marked in a way
that showed the errors of Müller's map of 1758 (*Ill.29*). That
had implied that most of the landfalls made by Bering and
Chirikov were continental, an interpretation that led to a
bloated Alaskan peninsula which bulged far to the west to reach
within a few hundred miles of Kamchatka. Further surveys
of the islands between Kamchatka and Alaska were made by
Lieutenant Ivan Sindt who combined exploration and escort
work in those waters between 1764 and 1768.

None of the charts of these expeditions had been published, so the issue by Stählin in 1773 of what purported to
be an account and map of Sindt's voyages was an event of
some importance; and the co-operation of the secretaries of
the learned societies of St Petersburg and London in the book's
publication gave it added credibility. What Dr Maty presumably did not know was that there had been no collaboration
between the Russian Admiralty, which by now held a rich haul
of unpublished post-Bering surveys made by fur traders and
naval officers, and the St Petersburg Academy. Taken at face
value, Stählin's 'Map of the New Northern Archipelago' that
accompanied his book was dramatic and sensational (*Ill.30*),
for it shattered Müller's gigantic Alaskan peninsula. Set adrift
among the debris was 'Alaschka' or Alaska, not a peninsula at
all but a large island. Between it and the American continent
– which ended in 140°w., cut short at the northern end of the
Alaskan panhandle – lay a wide strait leading into the Arctic
Ocean in latitude 65°N. The detail of Cook's instructions, with
its emphasis on latitude 65°N., shows that he and the Admiralty
had accepted Stählin's account and map as authentic.

They were not alone in this, for the *American Atlas* issued
under Thomas Jefferys' name in 1776, and widely regarded as
authoritative, faithfully reproduced the outlines of Stählin's
'New Northern Archipelago'. What on the face of it was even
more surprising was that Robert de Vaugondy, so stern a critic

30. JACOB VON STÄHLIN. Section of 'A Map of the New Northern Archipelago'. 1774.

The tracks of Deshnev (1648). Bering (1728) and Sindt (1764-8), are marked; none approaches the wide strait between 'Alaschtia' and North America.

of Fonte-style geography in the 1750s, issued a memoir and map in 1774 that combined the waterways of the Fonte and Fuca accounts, Stählin's reconfiguration of Alaskan geography, and the route into the polar sea supposedly followed by the shadowy figure of Captain Cluny. Vaugondy presented copies of his map and memoir to the Royal Society in early 1775, and it seems likely that on one of his frequent visits to the Society's London premises during the following winter Cook saw the map. By now Vaugondy was collaborating with Samuel Engel in a *Supplément* to the first seventeen volumes of the prestigious *Encyclopédie*, whose publication under Diderot's editorship in the 1750s had been a landmark in the dissemination of the enlightened thought of the period. The original volumes had been criticised for their lack of attention to geography and exploration, a defect that the supplementary volumes were to put right. Engel provided the text for a section on the geography of the northern regions of the world, and Vaugondy supplied no fewer than ten maps. Among these were reissues of Guillaume Delisle's Sea of the West, the Fonte and Fuca discoveries of the Buache maps, and Alexander Cluny's chart. Like Vaugondy's map of 1774, those printed in the *Encyclopédie* were intended to illustrate the range of possible options for the geography of regions not yet properly explored. Vaugondy's personal opinions at this time seem to have been better represented in another map he published in 1774, 'Carte Polaire Arctique'. This had less of the elaborate theoretical geography of his *Nouvelle Systême*, and although there were still nods of recognition towards the Fonte and Cluny accounts, its most noticeable feature was an open polar sea which he thought offered the most practicable route between the Atlantic and Pacific oceans.

If the hypotheses of Engel and Barrington were correct, and the ice of the northern seas appeared when the rivers broke up in the summer, it would be limited in extent and short-lived. Certainly, ships should be able to sail through the wide strait marked on Stählin's map without obstruction. John

Hanson's memorial of 1774 in Lord Dartmouth's papers brought together the two strands of the argument as it insisted that 'to suppose that an immense body of ice can Exist in a compact, fix'd, and solid body, without being supported, by Land at its extreme Ends, or by a fix'd body at its Centre, is to suppose an impossibility', and then went on to speculate that between the various island groups lying in the space between America and Asia was a strait, at least sixty leagues across. Even if the ice field that had almost trapped Phipps in latitude 80°N. extended right across the polar regions, its southern edge would be several hundred miles north of the point where Hearne had reached the American coastline. Just when Hearne's overland journey showed that there could be no passage in temperate latitudes, there seemed to be evidence to show that the dreaded Arctic Ocean was for most of the year an open sea. On this assumption Cook's ships were not strengthened to meet ice.

Although Russian activity in the far north had not produced reliable charts, it was more than enough to provoke apprehension in Madrid and Mexico City. Anxious about possible incursions onto the northwest coast of America, a region claimed though neither settled nor explored by Spain, the Spanish government re-established diplomatic relations with Russia in 1760; and during the next fifteen years its ambassador in St Petersburg sent a stream of dispatches giving a remarkable amount of information (and some misinformation) about Russian expansion in the north Pacific. For a century and a half the Spaniards had made no sustained advance from Mexico along the Pacific coast to the north, but the alarmist dispatches arriving from St Petersburg helped to precipitate an expansion into Upper California. As Father Burriel had warned in his *Noticia de California*, foreign settlements there would endanger the silver mines of New Spain. The discovery of a navigable Northwest Passage farther north would turn the flank of the whole Spanish position, while Britain's dominant position in North America after the Treaty of Paris made more likely a strong overland thrust to the Pacific. In response to these fears, the Spaniards moved north, and by the end of the 1760s had reached San Diego, Monterey and San Francisco. Fear of foreign intrusion farther north remained, however, and the early 1770s saw a new crop of rumours. A squadron from Russia's Black Sea fleet was to be sent around the world to the northwest coast of America. An Englishman named Bings was sailing across the polar sea to California (this presumably a reference to the Phipps voyage). British fur traders had reached so far west from Hudson Bay that they had made contact with the Russians in Alaska. In Mexico City the Viceroy of New Spain, Antonio María Bucareli y Ursúa, was rightly sceptical of these reports, but they added to the general feeling of insecurity that led to the decision to send exploring expeditions far along the coast to the north.

In 1774 the veteran *piloto* (or master) Juan Pérez sailed in the *Santiago* from San Blas with sealed instructions to explore the coast as least as far as latitude 60°N. With him he had copies of Müller's map, though Bucareli warned him that it was based only 'on the alleged voyages of the Russians [and] may be of little use'. Pérez kept well out to sea until in latitude 55°N. he turned in towards the coast. There, at the northern end of the Queen Charlotte Islands the Spaniards encountered Haida Indians, who came out to the ship in large decorated canoes, beating drums and offering to trade furs and woollen blankets. Southerly winds (which threatened to make the homeward voyage difficult) and shortage of water persuaded Pérez that it was time to return, though he was still five degrees short of his objective. On the return voyage the *Santiago* ran south along the coast of Vancouver Island, and anchored off Nootka Sound where the crew traded with the local Indians but did not land. These were the first contacts between

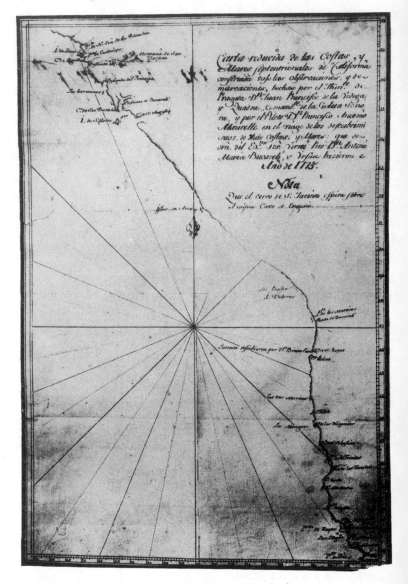

31. JUAN BODEGA Y QUADRA. 'Carta reducida de las costas y mares septentrionales de California'. 1779.
España. Ministerio de Educadión, Cultura y Deporte. Archivo General de Indias.

Europeans and Native Americans of the northwest coast, whose culture was different from any the Spaniards had encountered before. Some news of the Pérez voyage had reached England before Cook sailed in July 1776, for the *Madrid Gazette* of 24 March, rather surprisingly, had disclosed some brief details, and these were printed in the London newspapers in late May. Other information may also have leaked out from Spain, for the map of the northwest coast just published in Jefferys' *American Atlas* had two rather improbable notes that must refer to the voyage of the *Santiago* but were not included in the *Gazette*. One, placed in latitude 55°N., ran 'Here the Spaniards saw several White and Fair Indians in 1774'; the other, in latitude 50°N., noted 'Coast seen by the Spaniards in 1774 with inhabitants which go naked.'

The next year Bucareli sent the *Santiago* north again, commanded by Bruno de Hezeta, and accompanied by the schooner *Sonora* (*Ill.31*). Under the command of Juan Francisco de la Bodega y Quadra, the tiny *Sonora* made a heroic voyage north to 58°30'N., where Bodega became the first Spanish navigator to reach Alaska. He was also the first Spaniard to land on the northwest coast, at 'Puerto de Bucareli' (today's Bucareli Sound) on the west coast of Prince of Wales Island, where he searched for the strait that Bartholomew de Fonte was supposed to have passed through in 1640. Meanwhile, far to the south the *Santiago*, which had turned back because of sickness among the crew, sighted a large bay near latitude 46°N. through which 'the sea penetrates far into the land'. Hezeta reported that this might be the entrance of the strait discovered by Juan de Fuca; in reality he was off the

OPPOSITE: This manuscript map of the Spanish expeditions of 1775 covers fifteen hundred miles of coastline from Monterey in the south to the Alaskan coast in latitude 58°N., Bodega's farthest north. The lack of detail in the middle part of the map shows that Bodega y Quadra in the *Sonora* was out of sight of the coastline for most of the time. Near latitude 46°N. is marked the opening discovered by Bruno de Hezeta in the *Santiago*, which in fact was the mouth of the Columbia, named by Robert Gray after he entered the river in 1792.

mouth of one of North America's mightiest rivers, the Columbia, seventeen years before the American Robert Gray sighted and named it.

For the Spanish authorities the most reassuring aspect of these northern explorations was that no trace of foreign activity had been found. The reports from St Petersburg had exaggerated both the degree of official Russian interest in northwest America and the extent of Russian activity in an area many thousand miles distant from the seat of government. The *promyshlenniki* were operating only in the Aleutians and neighbouring islands. Not until 1784 was the first permanent Russian establishment set up in Alaska proper, and then on Kodiak Island and not on the mainland. But Spanish feelings of relief were short-lived, for during 1776 a stream of intelligence reports reached New Spain from Madrid warning that a British discovery expedition was about to leave for the northwest coast, commanded by the famous navigator, Captain James Cook. All officers in the Californias were ordered to be on the watch for the intruder, and although they were to avoid force, were to hinder his activities if possible. In July tougher instructions were sent out, and officials in New Spain were told to deny Cook access to their ports. Finally, in October yet another order from Madrid instructed Bucareli (who had already pointed out how ill prepared he was to resist Cook by force) to detain the explorer if and when his ships reached California.

This Spanish attitude of hostility raises the wider question of the motives behind Cook's final expedition. Those most immediately concerned with it in the Admiralty and other government departments left no written statements on the subject. In contrast, those who had a less official but more proprietorial interest in the voyage were only too ready to express a view. Daines Barrington was indignant that the Spaniards should regard the new venture with suspicion, and thought that they should 'be convinced that the English Nation is actuated merely by desiring to know as much as possible with regard to the planet which we inhabit'. In this he represented the attitude of the Royal Society and the new spirit of scientific investigation that was beginning to influence the course of maritime exploration, and which lies behind the Admiralty's decision to publish the accounts and charts of its Pacific explorers as soon after their return as possible. It explains the instructions issued by Benjamin Franklin in the midst of the War of American Independence on behalf of the United States Congress in 1779 to its naval vessels that if they encountered Cook they should give his ships and their crews free passage 'as common Friends to Mankind'. It was not an attitude shared by the Spaniards; from Drake to Anson, in times of peace as well as war, they had learned to fear English raiders in the Pacific. The French also had doubts about the real motives behind Cook's third voyage, and a memoir among French Foreign Office papers noted that its ostensible object of exploring the northwest coast of America was a blind, and that Cook was bound for Kamchatka where he was to combine with Russian forces to attack Japan!

There may well have been some justification for these suspicions, for even a passage far to the north would have some strategic significance. When hostilities with Spain threatened, the thoughts of British ministers invariably turned to the prospect of raiding Spanish commerce and settlements in the Pacific, but the long haul around Cape Horn that could devastate squadrons and give notice of their approach was a serious objection. A British naval force that entered the Pacific through a northern passage would arrive quickly and without warning. Even if the passage were navigable only for a limited season each year, this would not present the obstacle to naval raiders that it would to merchants seeking a regular trade route. The efforts by the government to establish a base in the Falklands had shown its eagerness to secure an entrance into the Pacific, and it may have been more than a coincidence that the decision to send a naval expedition to search for a Northwest Passage was made in the same year (1774) as the enforced abandonment of Port Egmont. The discovery of a northern route into the Pacific would more than compensate for loss of control over the longer southern one, and Cook received the customary order 'to take possession in the name of the King of Great Britain, of convenient situations in such countries as you may discover'. That his expedition was sent to sea at a time when war with the American colonies took on a new dimension and intensity suggests that it was something more than a voyage of scientific inquiry.

Nor should commercial considerations be entirely ignored. The Royal Society might have little interest in this mundane side of the voyages it urged on the Admiralty, but the desire to find new markets for the increasing range of British manufactures had played its part in the sending of previous expeditions to the Pacific. Traditionally, the Northwest Passage was of interest to Britain because its discovery was expected to stimulate trade; and only a few years before Cook's expedition the Board of Trade when examining Major Robert Rogers' plans for an overland expedition to find a way to the western ocean, reported that 'a passage by the North west to the great pacific Ocean, would doubtless be attended with many great national Advantages both in Commerce and Navigation'. For Lieutenant Blankett, who in his own view at least was the originator of Cook's third voyage, the unexploited trading potential of the north Pacific was the great incentive. Then there was the increasing importance of the East India Company's trade with China. A generation earlier the Company had shown no interest in Anson's project for a discovery expedition to the north Pacific, but in 1774 it asked Lord Dartmouth whether it might see a secret memoir on northern navigation sent to the government by Samuel Engel, since the directors were 'highly interested in a shorter and safer passage to their present and future settlements'. Despite these indications of commercial interest, the general lack of mercantile expectation at this time contrasted sharply with the surge of expectation that had accompanied earlier voyages to Hudson Bay. The disappointments of those voyages had brought caution; nor had Cook's demonstration of the non-existence of a southern continent induced any great confidence in the speculative geographers, some of whom had argued that there was a continent just as eloquently as they sought to prove the existence of a northern passage. The volumes of Campbell, Dobbs and Ellis were still on the shelves to be read, and if a passage were discovered their arguments might again be relevant; but most were prepared to await the outcome of Cook's investigations. Even those hopeful of finding some great strait along the unknown Pacific coast of North America could not shake off nagging doubts about where such a strait might come out on the Atlantic side.

For the Admiralty the whole matter was the more doubtful because it knew of Hearne's explorations. Hudson Bay, despite its mention in Cook's instructions, was no longer a realistic proposition; if a passage from the Pacific existed it must exit farther to the north, in or near Baffin Bay. If only to reassure themselves that Cook would not be trapped in an enclosed polar sea, the Lords of the Admiralty decided to send vessels to search the west coast of Baffin Bay at the same time that Cook was out. This huge inland sea of the north had not been explored since 1616, when that peerless navigator William Baffin had reached it through Davis Strait and had sailed as far as Smith Sound in latitude 78°N. before turning back. His report that none of the openings he had seen led into a Northwest Passage was accepted, and the area of Davis Strait was neglected except for the visits of whalers during the short summer seasons. In 1776 the Admiralty turned again to Baffin Bay, where according to Barrington whalers had often found ice-free water far to the north, and it decided to send expeditions there to search for the Atlantic entrance of the Northwest Passage. There would be a short preliminary voyage in 1776, followed by a second expedition the next year that would explore westward from Baffin Bay at the same time, it was hoped, as Cook was working his way east along the Arctic coast of North America. There was about this double-pronged effort the feel of a grand design, but one based on optimistic surmise rather than hard-headed realism.

Both Baffin Bay expeditions were to be entrusted to Lieutenant Richard Pickersgill, one of the Navy's most experienced junior officers as far as voyages of exploration were concerned. Still only twenty-seven years old, he had sailed as a youngster on Wallis's Pacific voyage, and then on Cook's first and second voyages. He seemed an ideal choice, though there was an ominous endpiece in a note on him by one of his shipboard companions on Cook's *Resolution*: 'a good officer and astronomer, but liking ye Grog'. In April 1776 he was appointed commander of the armed brig *Lyon*, and ordered to sail to Davis Strait. After driving off any American privateers that might be preying on British whalers near Disco, he was 'to proceed up Baffin's Bay and explore the Coasts thereof, as far as in your judgement can be done without apparent Risque'. Whether Pickersgill was given additional verbal orders is not known; but his journal shows that he knew he was to command another expedition the following year, and his task in 1776 was clear enough – to search the west coast of Baffin Bay and investigate any promising inlets. These would be explored further the next summer, so that if Cook's ships were encountered in polar waters they could be guided into Baffin Bay, and back to England. Pickersgill was supplied with accounts of the voyages of Frobisher, Davis and Baffin, and some more recent charts of the Davis Strait region (*Ill.32*). These were of little assistance because only Baffin had explored the bay which bore his name, and his chart had disappeared. The only reliable information available to Pickersgill was Baffin's brief account, which showed that in 1616 he had avoided the worst of the ice by keeping close to the east coast of the bay until he crossed into open water farther north.

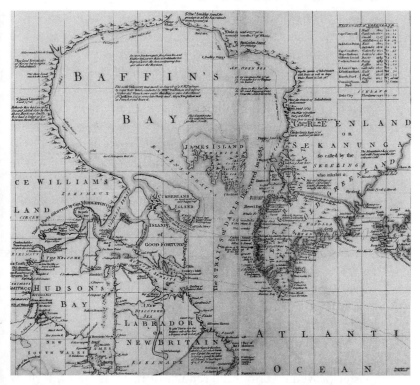

32. [THOMAS JEFFERYS]. Section of 'Chart comprising Greenland with the Countries and Islands about Baffins Bay and part of Hudsons Bay', 1775.
British Library

Jefferys' chart is representative of those supplied to Pickersgill and Young for their voyages to Baffin Bay in 1776 and 1777. Although clear in outline, it is sparse in geographical detail, and apart from some information obtained from whaling voyages along the west coast of Greenland, shows little that was not known after the voyages of Hudson and Baffin in the early seventeenth century.

It was the middle of May before the *Lyon* left Deptford, where Cook's two ships were being prepared for the Pacific, and at the end of the month Pickersgill was still sheltering in Torbay rather than face the attempts of his crew (over half of whom had never been to sea before) to handle sail in the Channel squalls. 'All the men', he wrote in his journal, 'tho' willing yet hardly knew a Rope in the Ship.' The brig was a poor sailor, and the passage northward was so slow that the southern tip of Greenland was not sighted until 7 July. Fog, sickness among the crew, and the collapse of the foremast had all delayed progress; and although spirits revived with the sight of land they were soon dampened again. Early the next morning Pickersgill entered in his journal: 'We saw a range of Field Ice, extending E.SW. which is almost beyond belief. What to do I know not the Water Smooth, no signs of an end to the field.' The vessel had reached only latitude 60°N.

Pickersgill directed his crew to hang spars and planks over the side to protect the hull, which had not been strengthened for the voyage, and with lookouts at the mastheads, and men at the sides to fend off ice, the *Lyon* penetrated six miles into the field. Despite Pickersgill's makeshift devices the vessel suffered severe blows from ice floes, and finally he took the brig out of the field and tried to find a way around it. On 10 July a Whitby whaler was sighted, and its master came on board with the news that the whaling fleet, which Pickersgill had been ordered to protect, had already left Disco for home. The master proved a veritable Jeremiah of the seas, and informed Pickersgill that the whalers, heavily strengthened though they were, never stayed at Disco after the beginning of July, since the weather then became thick and foggy, and great masses of ice drove down from the north. 'He wished me success but seemed to despair of our ever coming back . . . he told us that the Vessell, would be crush'd by the first Ice we came into.' It was effectively the end of the voyage, though Pickersgill kept edging north until he reached latitude 68° 26'N., still a hundred miles short of Disco. Now great icebergs were sighted, and with many of the crew sick and all lacking warm clothing, at the beginning of August, Pickersgill decided to head for home. Deptford was reached at the end of October, but his journal had come to an abrupt end a month earlier, 'Being now taken Ill', he wrote on 29 September.

The Admiralty rather than Pickersgill must bear the blame

for the failure of the expedition, for it sent him to Baffin Bay with an unstrengthened vessel, an inexperienced crew and vague instructions. Those instructions, moreover, were not given to Pickersgill until the middle of May, and consequently he was two months late reaching Davis Strait. As Cook's voyage was soon to show, the most determined explorer could do little if he reached the Arctic with the navigable season almost spent. For some time after the return of the *Lyon* Pickersgill was retained as commander, and his representations about the necessity for altering the brig so that it might carry more provisions, and supplying the crew with warm clothing for the 1777 voyage, were accepted. But in January the master of the *Lyon* made a number of allegations about Pickersgill's conduct during the previous year's voyage, and the Admiralty informed the lieutenant that he was to be court-martialled on the grounds that he had been 'frequently guilty of drunkenness and other irregularities . . . during the late Voyage to Davis's Streights and particularly that, for the latter part thereof, you were scarcely two days together sober'. At the court-martial several of the charges were found to be proved, and Pickersgill was dismissed the Navy.

The new commander of the *Lyon* was Lieutenant Walter Young, whose instructions revealed more clearly the connection between the brig's 1777 voyage to Davis Strait and the expedition under Cook, which by this time should be approaching the Pacific coast of North America. Young was given a copy of Cook's instructions, and told that he was to make every effort to find a passage from the Atlantic side along the west coast of Baffin Bay, even if he had to winter in the north. He was also given copies of Hearne's journal and maps, and ordered 'to discover whether the Sea mentioned by the said Mr. Hearne doth communicate with Baffin's Bay'. Young was not distracted by convoy duties, his men were supplied with adequate clothing, and an early start was made. Unfortunately, neither the ship nor its new commander was fitted for the task ahead. The *Lyon* sailed in the middle of March, and

by 5 June had reached Disco. Three days later the brig was
in latitude 72°42'N.; but Young was still on the east coast of
Davis Strait, and there he was confronted by ice just as Pickersgill had been. For a fortnight he tacked between the ice
and the shore in the company of the Disco whalers, and then,
on 22 June, long before Pickersgill the year before had sighted
Greenland, Young bore away for home. The *Lyon* was back at
its Deptford mooring by the first week of August.

    Young's journal, a sparse record, has no explanation for his
decision to leave Davis Strait so early. It has few observations of
interest, but one of its most frequent entries, 'exercised great
guns and small arms', hints at the reason for Young's failure.
Versed in the conventional naval tactics of the day, and later
to display great courage in the heat of battle, he was at a
loss when confronted with the problems of Arctic navigation.
Neither he nor Pickersgill was familiar with the specialist techniques used in ice navigation, for the ability to 'read' the ice
and to select the most promising leads was confined to the
experienced captains of the Hudson Bay and Greenland ships.
The Board of Admiralty, burdened with the heavy responsibilities of the American war, had not thought it necessary to
engage seasoned Greenland pilots as it had for the Phipps
expedition a few years earlier. Nor had it provided a suitable
ship. As Pickersgill and Young compared their unstrengthened
brig, in which they were expected to sail farther north in
Baffin Bay than any navigator since Baffin in 1616, with the
sturdy ships of the whalers (which invariably kept within sight
of each other when among ice), any enthusiasm they had for
their task must have vanished. The attempt to assist Cook by
discovering the eastern entrance of the Passage had ended in
total failure.

Cook had left Plymouth in the *Resolution* on 12 July 1776. His instructions allowed him less than twelve months to reach the northwest coast of America where he expected to be in latitude 65°N. by the following June; but he fell behind schedule almost from the beginning. He was already three weeks late when he left the Cape of Good Hope, where he had been joined by Charles Clerke in the *Discovery*. Cook's own ship was showing signs of poor workmanship at the Deptford yards, so much so that its first lieutenant, John Gore, wrote home from the Cape that if he ever got home 'the next Trip I may Safely Venture in a Ship Built of Ginger Bread'. In the Pacific unfavourable winds further delayed the expedition, and although the ships were expected to leave Tahiti for the North American coast in February 1777, they were still well short of the island in April, when Cook conceded that he would not be able to begin his major exploring effort until the next year. Visits to the Tongan group and other islands occupied the time, and led to a few new discoveries, but also to increasing problems for Cook, almost one might say of self-control. His patience, already strained by the failure to keep to his timetable, ran out in the face of persistent thieving by the islanders. Floggings, cropping of ears and slashing of arms, burnings of houses and canoes, reflected his exasperation. The problem was not new, but Cook's reaction was, at least in the scale and frequency of the punishments. For the crews, there were the usual island delights, and the usual attempts at desertion. By December, Cook was ready to leave the familiar setting of the Society Islands for the unknown waters and shores of the north Pacific. If he had lost his season in 1777, he had the consolation of knowing that in 1778 he should reach northwest America some weeks earlier in the year than anticipated. Not all on board shared their captain's sense of anticipation. Nineteen-year-old midshipman George Gilbert later recalled how 'We left these Islands with the greatest regret imaginable; as supposing all the pleasures of the voyage to be now at an end having nothing to expect in future but excess of cold, hunger, and every kind of hardship and distress.'

As the ships crossed the equator and sailed into the north Pacific their progress was interrupted by the unexpected sighting of land in mid-ocean in latitude 21°30'N. and 200°E. As island after island rose above the horizon Cook realised that he had found a group unmarked on any chart, whose inhabitants were undoubtedly Polynesian. As Cook asked: 'How shall we account for this Nation spreading it self so far over this Vast ocean . . . from New Zealand to the South, to these islands to the North?' Cook showed his opinion on the significance of his discovery by naming the group the Sandwich Islands after the First Lord of the Admiralty. For many, including Cook himself, the accidental discovery of these islands (soon to be known as the Hawaiian Islands) was to prove a fateful encounter, but he remained among the western islands of the group for only two weeks before resuming his course towards the distant coast of America. A month later, on 7 March 1778, with the ships in latitude 44°33'N, a shoreline was sighted thirty miles ahead. It was, in Cook's words, 'the long looked for Coast of new Albion', where Drake had been almost two hundred years earlier, and no Englishman since.

It said something about conditions that Cook's first place-name on the coast of present-day Oregon was Cape Foulweather, and the journals of his officers reflect their frustration as they strained for a glimpse through 'thick and hazey' weather of that mysterious shoreline claimed by Drake for his sovereign, where maps showed the entrances of great rivers or straits discovered by Aguilar, Fuca and Fonte. But as the ships veered first southwest and then north again, at one point being driven 180 miles off the coast, the weather continued misty and stormy, and only tantalising glimpses of the land could be caught. Cook's main concern was to find a harbour where he could repair the ships, and take on wood and water. He had hopes of finding one when an opening appeared on the far side of a headland in latitude 48°22'N., but as the ships approached he decided that it was too small for a harbour, and he named the headland Cape Flattery. In his journal he gave an unnecessary hostage to fortune when he wrote, 'It is in the very latitude we were now in where geographers have placed the pretended *Strait of Juan de Fuca*, but we saw nothing like it, nor is there the least probability that iver any such thing exhisted.' Although it was unusual for Cook to be dogmatic without good reason, the ships' logs show that he could not have seen enough of the coast as darkness fell to justify this pronouncement. Cape Flattery stands at the southern side of the entrance, fifteen miles wide, of the strait now named after Juan de Fuca. If Cook had entered it he would not have found the Northwest Passage, but he would have gained some sense of the complexity of the coastline, with inland waterways stretching south to Puget Sound and north to the Strait of Georgia – though only at the cost of ignoring his instructions to keep steadily north. Instead, during the night he headed out to sea, intending to close with the land at daybreak, but severe gales prevented him approaching the land again for nearly a week, and curiosity about possible openings in the coast was submerged by alarm lest the ships be driven on shore.

When the ships made land again a harbour was found, and Cook demonstrated the measure of his relief by naming it after his sovereign. King George's Sound later became known by what was thought to be its native name of Nootka, and subsequent events were to give it an international notoriety. Although Cook and his officers assumed that they were on the mainland, their harbour at Ship Cove was in fact on a small island which was situated off the oceanic coastline of Vancouver Island, with a rocky coastline and dense forests that extended to the water's edge. It was, Lieutenant James King thought, a melancholy, brooding landscape – 'as wild & savage a Country as one can well draw in so temperate a climate'. In comparison with the Polynesians of their recent experience, the crews found the Nootka (Nuu-chal-nulth) Indians physically unalluring with their faces and bodies painted, and smeared with grease. However, they were superbly skilled on

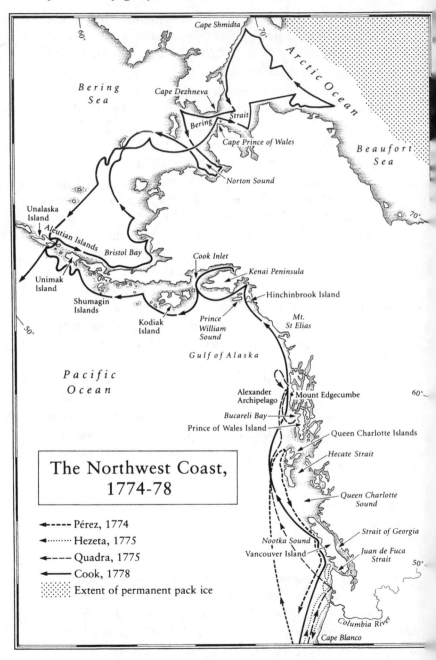

Cape Shmidta

A r c t i c O c e a n

*B e r i n g
S e a*

Cape Dezhneva

Bering Strait

Cape Prince of Wales

*B e a u f o r t
S e a*

Norton Sound

Unalaska
Island

Aleutian Islands

Bristol Bay

Unimak
Island

Shumagin
Islands

Kodiak
Island

Cook Inlet

Kenai Peninsula

Hinchinbrook Island

Prince
William
Sound

Mt.
St Elias

Gulf of Alaska

*P a c i f i c
O c e a n*

Alexander
Archipelago

Mount Edgecumbe

Bucareli Bay

Prince of Wales Island

Queen Charlotte Islands

Hecate Strait

*Queen Charlotte
Sound*

The Northwest Coast,
1774-78

◄----- Pérez, 1774
◄········· Hezeta, 1775
◄---- Quadra, 1775
◄——— Cook, 1778
⸬⸬⸬ Extent of permanent pack ice

Strait of Georgia

Nootka Sound

Vancouver Island

*Juan de Fuca
Strait*

Columbia River

Cape Blanco

the water in handling their canoes, and on land in building wooden dwellings with intricate totemic carvings which were to fascinate generations of visitors to the coast from Cook's time onwards. The expedition remained nearly a month in Ship Cove while the ships were rerigged, caulked and generally made trim. The discovery that the foremast of the *Resolution* was rotten, and the collapse of the mizenmast a few days later, meant that both masts had to be replaced, and the ships did not leave harbour until the end of April. On board was a collection of pelts, mostly sea otter, which had been traded from the Nootka. To their surprise the crews found some iron tools among the Indians, and even more surprisingly two silver table spoons which a man was wearing as an ornament around his neck. Cook guessed that the latter came from the Spanish ship (the *Santiago*) known to have been on the coast in 1774. The iron, on the other hand, had puzzled the Spaniards as much as it did Cook's men; for whether it came from the Russians in the north, Spanish settlements in Mexico, or the fur-traders of the interior, the distances involved seemed improbably great.

On 26 April Cook left Nootka in weather so bad that soon he could not see the length of the ship, but as he explained in his journal his anxiety to make up lost time outweighed any other consideration. Given the conditions he had no alternative but to keep well out to sea, and he did not sight land again until 1 May, when the ships were in latitude 55°20'N, the coast of Alaska. Cook noted that the entrance to Fonte's Río los Reyes was reputed to lie in latitude 53°N., and added that although 'I give no credet to such vague and improbable stories,' he regretted missing the opportunity to put the matter beyond all doubt. Cook's distrust of the theoretical geographers had led him into an error that was to take much subsequent exploration to put right. Even before leaving England he had rejected the the Delisle/Buache school which based its maps of the northwest coast on the supposed discoveries of Fuca and Fonte; so he assumed that the coastline north of

33. JOHN WEBBER. Mount Edgecumbe, May 1778.
British Library

Cape Flattery was mainland rather than a series of islands. This error is easy to understand by those familiar with that coast. From the vastness of Vancouver Island, with its snow-capped mountains rising in the interior, to the chain of offshore islands stretching from the Queen Charlottes to the Alexander Archipelago, intervening land screens the mainland coast from ships out to sea. Like the Spanish expeditions of 1774 and 1775 Cook laid down the general direction of the oceanic coast, but without any awareness of the maze of straits, islands and inland waterways that lay behind it.

As Cook reached Alaskan waters, passing and naming Cape Edgecumbe, Cross Sound and Cape Fairweather, so the shoreline, all dark green forest at Nootka, became bleaker. But the scenery, if stark, was dramatic, and the weather calm and bright. The snow-capped volcanic cone of Mount Edgecumbe was a notable landmark, the sight of which moved John Gore, first lieutenant of the *Resolution*, to name it 'Mount Beautifull' (*Ill.33*). However striking Mount Edgecumbe might be, it was dwarfed by the tremendous peak of Bering's Mount St Elias farther inland, 18,000 feet high, and visible 120 miles away. This, and a shoreline where, wrote Cook, 'we could perceive trees, as it were rising their heads out of the Sea', stood out sharp and clear. Whales, sea otters and seals surrounded the ships, and Charles Clerke, the experienced captain of the *Discovery*, now on his fourth Pacific voyage, was moved to enter in his journal that 'I never in my Life before, in any Climate whatever, saw for such a length of time, the Air so perfectly serene; the Sea so perfectly smooth, and the Weather altogether so perfectly pleasant ... the happy influence of the pure Atmosphere, was apparent in every Countenance.' Expectancy of some imminent discovery ran high. The journal of James King, second lieutenant of the *Resolution*, described how all the officers were on deck, constantly comparing the accounts and maps in Müller and Stählin with the actual coastline in sight, not always with reassuring results. By now the coast should be trending northward according to Stählin, but instead it steadily turned west. 'We are kept in a constant suspense', King added. Then, as the jagged outline of Kayak Island (Bering's landing-place on the coast) receded from view, and the land bore away in a westerly direction, a large inlet opened behind a point of land which Cook named Cape Hinchinbrook. It was, wrote the surgeon David Samwell, the first opening seen since the ships left Nootka, and revived 'Our Hopes of a Passage'. James Burney, first lieutenant of the *Discovery*, hoped that they had reached the western tip of America. John Rickman, the ship's second lieutenant, speculated that the long-lost Strait of Anian lay ahead. Even Cook, who had been grumbling in his journal about the inaccuracies of the Russian charts – 'very erroneous ... on too small a scale' and so on – was hopeful that the inlet would provide 'a passage to the North', and that the land glimpsed to the west consisted only of islands.

As the vessels anchored under Cape Hinchinbrook the first Alaskans seen by the expedition appeared, about twenty

34. JOHN WEBBER. A View of Snug Corner Cove, Prince William Sound, May 1778.
British Library

of them in two large canoes made of sealskin stretched over a wooden frame, resembling the *umiaks* of the Inuit, and dressed in skins. The ships' crews, having coasted some hundreds of miles of an increasingly barren shoreline for twelve days without sign of human habitation, were startled by the appearance of these ungainly craft. After gifts had been exchanged at a cautious distance, the ships beat through squalls under reefed topsails to anchor in Snug Corner Cove. Despite its homely name, John Webber's sketches of the anchorage show a forbidding scene in which the ships are dwarfed by snow-capped mountains (*Ill.34*). Now smaller one-and two-man *kayaks* came off to the vessels, and soon their occupants were on board trading their sea-otter skins, bartering for a few blue beads pelts that would fetch £40 apiece in Kamchatka, and more at Canton. There was much curiosity about the identity and origin of these 'Indians' (*Ill.35*), but of more immediate importance was whether the inlet opened north into an ice-free sea.

35. JOHN WEBBER. Man and Woman of Prince William Sound, May 1778.

Sign language persuaded some optimists to imagine that the local inhabitants were trying to indicate just that, though as David Samwell watched their gesticulations he thought 'tis ten to one that the Indians knew no more of what we were enquiring after than we knew of this supposed Passage'. As the ships sailed up the inlet (named Sandwich Sound by Cook, but later changed – at the First Lord of the Admiralty's own insistence – to Prince William Sound), it was worrying that the flood-tide entered by the same channel as the ships were passing through. However, the experience of earlier Hudson Bay expeditions had warned of the danger of relying on tidal observations to point the way to the passage, and Cook had already decided that he would not be influenced by them.

On 17 May the land seemed to be closing in to the north, and although Gore claimed that when he was sent ahead in a boat he had seen 'Deep Water and Bold Shores', Cook ordered the ships to head back down the sound and out to sea. As he explained, rather than get entangled in the shoals of a narrowing inlet, the expedition would do better to investigate farther west, where the Russian maps showed islands. The decision appears logical enough, but it was made only after some hesitation. Gore entered in his journal that when he reported to Cook on his return the captain ordered him to make a further examination of the inlet the next day, and this is confirmed by an entry in midshipman Edward Riou's log. He wrote that when Gore returned on the evening of the 17th with his report of a possible way through, Cook ordered the boats to be victualled for two days to investigate, but that when a fine breeze sprang up the next morning he cancelled the order. 'It is not to be presumed,' added Riou, 'that the Grand or N:W: passage is here meant ... but a shorter Way to the Northward.' Cook pointed out the same day that the ships were more than fifteen hundred miles west of Baffin Bay and Hudson Bay, and that there was no likelihood of finding a passage of that length. Rather, as the young midshipman appreciated, they were searching for a short strait that would take them into the sea sighted by Hearne, and then through it to Baffin Bay. Although Cook, most thorough of explorers, and one well aware of the ingenuity of mapmakers in turning partly-explored inlets into wide straits, was tempted to stay longer in Prince William Sound, the favourable breeze early the next morning settled the matter. It was a sign of how fleeting the expedition's contact with the land was that a year later a Spanish expedition commanded by Ignacio de Arteaga entered Prince William Sound, and reported that there was no sign that the English or Russians had ever been there.

The *Resolution*'s journals at this stage of the voyage reveal glimpses of tensions on board. Most of the officers had sailed with Cook before, and had assimilated much of his interest in geographical matters. All would have been aware of the reward of £20,000 promised for a successful discovery; at Tahiti the previous August, Cook and Clerke had explained to the crews the value of the reward, and how it would be divided. Even the humblest crew member could expect to get a sum equivalent to two or three years' wages. In their journals Cook's officers expressed their hopes and anxieties as they struggled to come to terms with the nature of the coastline coming into sight as the ships sailed steadily on. Some – Gore was certainly one – pressed Cook to stay longer, to investigate yet another opening, to give the Russian maps one more chance. It was not, one senses, a ship's company completely at ease with their situation.

When the ships reached open sea once more, they sailed southwest along the coast of the Kenai peninsula until a high point of land was sighted which Cook named Cape Elizabeth. At first, he thought that the headland might mark the limit of the North American continent, and although land soon appeared to the southwest, the sight of an unbroken horizon of sea and sky to the north as the ships stood off the cape 'inspired us', wrote Cook, 'with hopes of finding here a passage Northward'. On the *Discovery* Captain Clerke sympathised with the dilemma that now confronted Cook. Should he stop to examine this opening, with the risk that he might experience once again the time-wasting and frustrations of Sandwich Sound, or should he take advantage of the favourable wind and keep sailing west, ignoring what many on board thought was a promising opening? Neither Müller's map nor Stählin's helped: in Lieutenant King's words they were 'perfectly irre-concileable' with what could be seen from the ships. In reality, Cook had no alternative but to investigate. Memories of Arctic explorers from Martin Frobisher to Christopher Middleton who had been pilloried for failing to enter openings that might have led to a passage would not have been far distant. Within a day Cook suspected that he was engaged in a forlorn venture, for on the morning of 26 May as visibility improved to the north the distant 'islands' were found to be mountain tops pushing through the mist. He confided to his journal that there would be no passage this way, and that 'my persevering in it was more to satisfy other people than to confirm my own opinion'. This was not the decisive Cook of the first and second voyages, even though the journals of several of his officers show they were still hopeful that there was a way through to the north.

On the last day of the month as the channel began to divide, the water shoaled and freshened, and with 'low shores, very thick and Muddy water, large trees and all manner of dirt and rubbish' Cook was more than ever convinced that the ships were in a river. Urged on by one of his officers, probably Gore, Cook agreed to send boats into each channel, into the northern arm (past the location of present-day Anchorage), and also into the eastern arm. The tide proved too strong for the boats to get into the latter, which Cook named the Turnagain, and at last he ordered the ships to head back down what Clerke described as 'a fine spacious river, but a cursed unfortunate one to us'. Cook, still unaware that he was in an inlet, not a river, thought that it might well run deep into the interior, and was impressed enough to send a boat party ashore at Point Possession to display the flag and take possession of the surrounding country. As Cook described the standard rites of taking possession he remarked that whatever future advantages might be gained from the river, 'to us who had a much greater object in View it was an essential loss'. Hampered by adverse winds, the ships did not reach the sea until 6 June, and Cook reflected with some bitterness on the time spent in fruitless exploration. He had been persuaded 'very much against my own opinion and judgment, to pursue the Course I did' by the insistence of some of his officers that they were in a passage, and by 'the late pretended Discoveries' of the Russians. In a rather uncharacteristic remark for someone who prided himself on the comprehensiveness of his survey work, Cook complained that he had spent two weeks settling 'nothing but a triffling point of geography'. Caught between an increasingly uneasy reliance on the Russian maps, the unshakeable optimism of Gore and others, and his own realisation that the season was passing fast, Cook was showing increasing frustration.

At no time did Cook give the 'river' a name (*Ill.36*). For one normally so meticulous in naming natural features, Cook left an unusually large number unnamed in this area, but none of this importance. We can only speculate as to why this was, and it may be that Cook's frame of mind holds the explanation. Certainly there might be problems in choosing a name for a river that was at one and the same time a major geographical feature and yet a bitter disappointment. Cook simply referred to it as 'a River', and as late as October when he was reflecting about the season's explorations he left a blank space in his journal where normally the name would go – evidence of deliberate avoidance of the issue rather than an oversight. Others tried their hand. King, rather lamely, referred to 'the Great River'; Gore, characteristically, hit on the 'Gulf of Good Hope'; William Bayly, astronomer on the *Discovery*, thought 'Seduction River' an appropriate name. In London after the return of the ships, Sandwich ruled that the river should carry Cook's own name – appropriate in one sense, highly ironic in another. In the official account and charts published in 1784 'Cooks River' appears (*Ill.38*), and was to remain for ten years until Vancouver's definitive survey caused the name to be changed to Cook's Inlet (today, Cook Inlet).

Once out to sea, the vessels were again forced away in a southwesterly direction, edging their way along the tongue of the Alaskan peninsula, through the Shumagin Islands named by Bering. Near Unga Island came the first indication of a Russian presence, when natives paddled out to the *Discovery* and gave Captain Clerke a note in Russian. It is one of the oddities of Cook's third voyage that not a single person who could speak or read Russian was taken; this was an inconvenience that became increasingly serious in the weeks ahead. As the ships moved through the Sanak Islands just south of the tip of the Alaskan peninsula the appearance of the land to the north (the large island of Unimak) became ever more spectacular. Cook was vastly impressed by Shishaldin, more than 9000 feet high, 'a Volcano which continually threw out

36. [JAMES COOK?]. 'Chart of Cooks River in the NW part of America'. 1778.
British Library

'Cooks River' in the title was added for the 1784 publication.

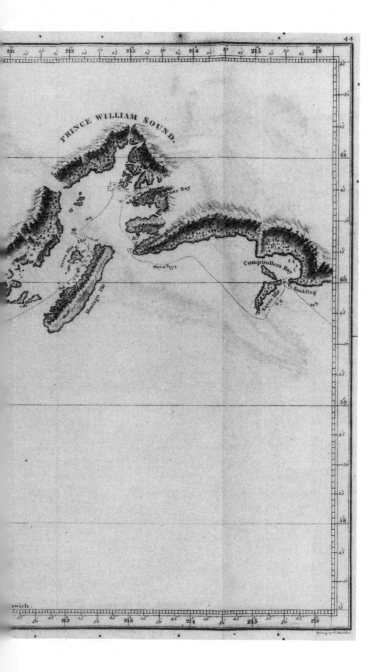

PRINCE WILLIAM SOUND.

Comptrollers Bay

C. Suckling

Montagu Ille

a vast column of black smoke'. Here were more traces of Russian influence – or so it was supposed – for an islander wearing a cloth jacket and breeches paddled out, bowed and doffed his cap. On 25 June the ships were at last able to turn north through a channel east of Unalaska Island, a short cut that saved the expedition from having to sail farther down the long tail of the Aleutians. In his haste to get round the continent, Cook was now taking risks that normally he would have avoided. On 26 June, on an uncharted coast, and with visibility less than a hundred yards, Cook let the ships run blindly before a moderate wind, and only hove to when the water shoaled suddenly and breakers could be heard. As the fog lifted, Cook found that the ships had run into a gap 'where I should not have ventured in a clear day', and had escaped disaster by the narrowest margin. Near here the crews met their first Aleuts, men who begged tobacco and repeated the word 'Russ'. Several notes in Russian were produced, but of the Russians themselves there was no sign, nor were they found at Samgunada harbour (English Bay) on Unalaska where the ships anchored for a few days.

From Unalaska the search for a passage to the north was resumed. The vessels tracked first into the blind alley of Bristol Bay and then out again, and on past Cape Newenham. Sometimes the fog was so thick that although the crews could hear the other vessel they could not see her. When the weather cleared, the land off the port side was uniformly depressing – as the ailing Clerke wrote, 'a damn'd unhappy part of the World, for the Country appears just as destitute as a Country can be, and the surrounding Seas are scarcely navigable for the numberless Shoals'. Finally, on 9 August the ships reached a strait of some kind just north of latitude 65°N., although identification was not easy. The eastern shore was presumably America, and Cook named the headland here Cape Prince of Wales, but he referred rather uncertainly to the coast in view on the opposite side of the strait as 'The Island of Alaschka or the Westland'. The strait fitted neither Müller's map nor

Stählin's. The first showed a strait more than a hundred miles across, while the second showed two straits, with 'Alaschka' lying between them. For many of the crews the issue was unimportant. Whether Müller or Stählin, or neither, was right seemed immaterial. As King wrote in his journal, 'we are in high spirits'; for as they sailed through the strait they could glimpse open sea ahead, 'free of land, and we hope ice'. At last the ships had reached latitude 65°N., and as the officers began to calculate the distance to Baffin Bay only the lateness of the season gave cause for concern.

A week later came the most dramatic moment of the voyage. Just before noon on 17 August an ominous brightness to the north reminded some on board of the 'ice blink' of the Greenland seas or the Antarctic Ocean, and within the hour their fears were realised as a great mass of ice slowly filled the northern horizon. This was not floe ice, but pack ice, compressed into a solid field that stretched as far as the eye could see, and was ten or twelve feet high at the water's edge. The ships were in latitude 70°41'N., and the shock and disappointment were the greater because five years earlier Phipps had sailed nearly ten degrees farther north before encountering the Spitzbergen ice-barrier. King noted that strengthened ships might have forced their way some distance through the broken pieces at the edge of the pack, but neither ship was equipped for work among ice, a further indication of the surprise at finding so formidable a barrier in this latitude. Engel and Barrington had argued that salt water did not freeze, and that the ice found in northern waters came from the rivers as they broke up each summer. Cook, despite all his experience of ice – the Baltic, Newfoundland and the St Lawrence, the Antarctic Ocean – seems to have accepted this, but now he pointed out that the sheer bulk of the slow-moving mass bearing down on the ships made nonsense of the assumption that it was the product of one season's break-up of the shallow rivers of the northern lands. Only 'Closet studdying Philosiphers' would maintain this, he wrote – a thinly-veiled reference

37. JOHN WEBBER. 'The *Resolution* beating through the Ice', August 1778
British Museum Department of Prints and Drawings

Webber's drawing may represent the moment near Icy Cape described by Cook in his journal for 18 August 1778: 'Our situation was now more and more critical, we were in shoald water upon a lee shore and the main body of ice in sight to windward driving upon us.'

to Barrington and his circle. With the ice still moving southward, Cook sighted and named Icy Cape on the American mainland before turning away southwest to prevent the ships being crushed between the shore and the oncoming ice (*Ill.37*).

The ships kept close to the ice as they steered towards the coast of Asia, but found no break in the great field. Near the end of August the Siberian coast was sighted at a point later named Cape North (today's Cape Otto Schimdta), and Cook followed it southeast until on 2 September he once more reached the strait he had passed through three weeks earlier. Its western shore, Cook now decided, must be the tip of Asia, sighted by Bering in 1728, less than thirteen leagues distant from Cape Prince of Wales on the American side. This settled, Cook was more than ever baffled by the Russian maps, and could only suppose that he had somehow sailed past the strait separating 'Alaschka' from the American mainland. The deep inlet of Norton Sound, missed on the northward leg, seemed to offer an answer, but by mid-September Cook found that it ended in a small river. Stählin's map, noted Cook, 'must be erroneous'. Later he would have more to say on the subject, but first he intended to pay a return visit to Unalaska to repair the leak in the *Resolution*, first sprung at Nootka, and a source of anxiety ever since, and to take on water. He would then winter at the Sandwich Islands, where he surely could 'make some improvement to Geography and Navigation' before returning to Bering's strait the following summer. It was a remarkable sign of intent at the end of an exhausting season of exploration.

The expedition spent more than three weeks at Samganuda, its longest stay in any part of Alaska, and more was learned about the region, its native inhabitants, and not least the Russians. The first direct contact with the Russians came on 10 October, when three seamen from their nearby trading factory accompanied Cook's American corporal of marines, John Ledyard, back to the ships. There, they were no doubt taken aback to be confronted by Cook brandishing Stählin's map at them: 'nor had they the least idea of what part of the World *Mr Staehlins* Map referd to when leid before them.' Before long Cook met the chief Russian factor in the area, Gregoriev Ismailov, a vigorous, intelligent man who had sailed with Sindt in the 1760s, and had a good knowledge of the Russian sphere of trading and exploring activities. 'I felt no small mortification', wrote Cook, 'in not being able to converse with him any other way then by signs.' It soon became obvious that for all the Russian references to Bering, and to later voyagers from Kamchatka, Cook knew more of the mainland, if not the islands, than the Russians. Ismailov produced his charts of the region, and although from Cook's description of them it seems that the island-strewn waters between Kamchatka and Alaska remained a scene of cartographical chaos, at least the confusion introduced by Stählin's insular 'Alaschka' was dispelled. As King put it, 'One of our first enquiries was the Situation of Alatska, & we were astonished to find it to be the Peninsula.' Having heard all this, Cook reverted to Stählin's map, that false guide which had beguiled and baffled them from May to September, and expressed his feelings in one breathless, furious sentence. 'If *Mr Staehlin* was not greatly imposed upon what could induce him to publish so erroneous a Map? in which many of these islands are jumbled in regular confusion, without the least regard to truth and yet he is pleased to call it a very accurate little Map? A Map that the most illiterate of his illiterate Sea-faring men would have been ashamed to put his name to.'

Cook's outburst was provoked by his realisation of how seriously he had been misled. His normal shrewd judgment of the works of theoretical geography had deserted him, with the result that the unremitting efforts of his crews had been guided in the wrong direction. He had set off on an expedition whose route had been largely determined by the accounts and maps of Müller and Stählin. The words of the journals of Cook's officers for the early summer of 1778 sound a continual refrain. 12 May: 'We have Dr Matys map of the N°ern Archipelago constantly in our hands.' 18 May: 'If the land on the west should prove to be islands agreable to the late Russian discoveries, we could not fail of getting far enough to the north.' 21 May: 'There is here a space where Behring is supposed to have seen no land; it also favoured the account published by Mtr Staehlin . . . so that everything inspired us with hopes of finding here a passage.' Yet by the time that Cook sailed there were scholars not only in Russia but in western Europe who were aware that Müller had retracted much of his map of 1758, and that Stählin's map was an absurdity.

Over the years Cook had developed a sense of the spurious and the exaggerated, and it did not need very close scrutiny to raise doubts about both the Russian maps he carried on board. Müller had described his efforts at cartography in self-deprecating terms: 'no more than to connect together according to probability, by points, the coast that had been seen in various places.' That Cook should have placed any trust in Stählin is even more puzzling. Stählin's account of Sindt's voyages in his book was vague to the point of meaninglessness, and his accompanying 'Map of the New Northern Archipelago' gave no indication as to why Alaska was shown as an island, with great straits to west and east. It marked Sindt's track only as far as the western coast of 'Alaschka', and neither Sindt nor any other navigator is shown actually reaching that strait between Alaska and America which promised a short cut into the polar sea. In 1774 Müller had written privately that Sindt 'knows nothing of a large island of Alashka'. In the same year Daines Barrington, not the most critical of men, concluded that Stählin's map was 'so unlike the notion Behring conveys of these straits, that no credit can be given to it', an opinion perhaps based on an account of the Russian discoveries sent to him by an Englishman who worked at the Russian naval dockyard at Kronstadt. Elsewhere in Britain scholars such as William Robertson and William Coxe were busy collecting information about the Russian voyages. Robertson had in his possession, probably before Cook sailed, a journal and map of the important expedition of Krenitsyn and Levashev of 1768 to the Aleutians. In Germany, scholars were receiving information from their colleagues in Russia, and were preparing books and articles for publication.

None of this seems to have been known to Cook and his superiors at the Admiralty. The weeks between his appointment to command the expedition in February 1776 and his sailing in July were crowded ones. The account of the second voyage had to be finished for publication; his family and a busy social and official life took up time; and there was the task of preparing ships and crews for the new voyage. All the signs are that there was little time and perhaps little inclination for thorough inquiry into the latest scholarly information on the Russian discoveries. The one man known to Cook who was thoroughly conversant with the world of continental, particularly German, scholarship was Johann Reinhold Forster, the naturalist of the second voyage, who was in London at this time. Unfortunately, he was at loggerheads with the Admiralty over the rights to the publication of Cook's second voyage, and in June 1776 he refused to meet Cook to discuss the dispute. Whatever information Forster, who was described (a little unfairly) by Sandwich as 'a violent and impracticable Man', had collected about the Russian voyages, was not likely to find its way to Cook.

Cook's instructions were based on two major fallacies: that there was a short strait east of Alaska to Hearne's sea, and that ice would not present a serious obstacle to navigation once he reached that sea. Cook had set himself an impossible task, and his journal and those of his officers reflect their frustration as this was realised. In planning the third voyage Cook lacked the professional detachment that had always been one of his strengths. Venturing into unfamiliar regions, he suspended critical judgment, took no Russian-speaking crew members, and relied on maps which even so credulous an enthusiast for 'easy' northern navigation as Barrington had dismissed. Cook's earlier experience in the south Pacific of some of the more eccentric cartographic products of the Academy of Sciences of Paris might have warned him that its counterpart in St Petersburg was no guarantor of the accuracy of the maps of Müller and Stählin. On his first voyage he had broken into a long complaint about the inaccuracy of existing charts, blaming navigators, cartographers and publishers in turn – 'so that between the one and the other we can hardly tell when we are possessed of a good sea Chart untill we our selves have proved it'. His vain efforts in 1778 to reconcile the Russian maps with the coastline revealed to the expedition led to a waste of time and energy that could be ill afforded. For the first time on his Pacific voyages Cook was haunted by the continual worry of all Arctic explorers, the shortness of the navigable season. Time and again he was faced with the problem of whether he should leave inlets and stretches of coastline unexplored in his haste to get to the north, or should stay to investigate, and perhaps arrive at a passage too late in the season. Caught between conflicting desires to satisfy the doubts of his officers on all points regarding a passage, to give the Russian maps every chance to prove their accuracy, and to push to the north, he arrived at the polar sea too late. For ten months of the year the ice-pack is locked tight to the American coast between Bering Strait and Point Barrow until in early July the seasonal southeasterlies push the ice away from the land, leaving a lane of open water. In August the wind changes to the northwest, and the pack returns, to rest in the shallow waters near the shore. By the time Cook reached Icy Cape in mid-August the pack was already grinding against the shoals, and blocking further progress to the east. Cook could have known nothing about this annual movement of the ice, and even if he had his unstrengthened ships, left him in no position to take advantage of it. If he had arrived earlier in the season, and been able to slip eastward past Point Barrow, it is unlikely that his ships would ever have returned.

The final word on the problem must be Cook's. In a letter written to the Admiralty at Unalaska in October 1778 he admitted: 'We were upon a Coast where every step was to be considered, where no information could be had from Maps, either modern or ancient: confiding too much in the former we were frequently misled to our no small hindrance.' If Cook had failed in his primary objective, he had discovered much. In a single season he had charted the American coastline from Mount St Elias to Bering Strait and beyond, determined the shape of the Alaskan peninsula, and farther south had touched at places along the coast from Oregon to British Columbia. He had closed the gap between the Spanish probes from the south and the Russian fur-trading activities in the north. The charts brought home by Cook's officers showed the extent of the achievement. Although the expedition's portable observatories had been taken ashore only twice, at Nootka Sound and Samgunada, Cook had used chronometers, sextants and lunar

38. Henry Roberts. Section of 'A General Chart exhibiting the Discoveries made by Capt. James Cook'. 1784.
British Library

The zig-zag tracks of Cook (in 1778) and Clerke in (1779) show the repeated attempts by the *Resolution* and *Discovery* to force their way through the ice north of Bering Strait. The outline of northwest America reveals that Cook thought that he was skirting the mainland on his long haul north along the coast from Nootka. The chart also demonstrates the relationship between the explorations of Cook and Hearne, though the latter's inland discoveries are placed too far north and west.

distances to make dozens of observations and calculations on shipboard in order to establish the latitudes and longitudes of salient features of the shoreline. In outline at least, the shape and position of the northwest coast of America were known at last. For the first time the region takes recognisable shape on the map (*Ill.38*), although it was not the shape that Cook had anticipated when he sailed from England in the summer of 1776.

Before leaving Unalaska, Cook entrusted Ismailov with his report to the Admiralty, together with a chart. A copy of the report reached the Admiralty on 10 January 1780, while Cook's original letter, and the chart, arrived in London two months later. Both had come by the long overland route from Kamchatka across Russia to St Petersburg, where the British ambassador, Sir James Harris, sent them by sea to England. This first-hand report had almost certainly been anticipated by local information about the expedition which was contained in a letter from Magnus Behm, Governor of Kamchatka, which was forwarded by Harris to London in late October or early November 1779. It has its own fascination, for it contains the first reference to Cook's expedition since the letters sent home by the discovery crews from the Cape of Good Hope in November 1776. From that point on, the ships had disappeared from European gaze. If by ill chance they had vanished in the ice north of Bering Strait in 1778 – and this was more than a remote possibility – the report from Behm would have offered the only clue as to what had happened, and indeed the only evidence that Cook's ships had reached the north Pacific. Behm reported to his superiors in St Petersburg

> that the Russians who go annually to hunt black Foxes in the *Insulae Aleutenses* [Aleutian Islands] were informed by the Inhabitants of these Islands, that towards the Autumn 1778, or in their own words, *before the Leaves were fallen, and while the Grass was still green*, there appeared on their Coasts Two Ships, one of Three, the other of Two Masts; That the Crews of these Ships

landed among them; They were dressed like Russians, but talked a Language they did not understand; That they behaved with the greatest civility, and were received with the greatest hospitality. They gave the Inhabitants Tobacco and Clasped Knives, and were offered in return several Things but would accept of nothing, but the Flesh of a young Whale. That after staying a short while, they sailed Northward, and were seen sometime afterwards by the *Tschuktskis* off the *Tschuktshotshev Nos*, or promontory of the North East Extremity of Asia; that however they did not proceed farther North, but returned by the same Track they went, and after again touching at the *Aleutensis* steered Southward.

From Unalaska the ships sailed south to the Hawaiian Islands to winter before returning to Bering Strait the next summer to resume the search for a passage, although Cook had already stated in his letter to the Admiralty that he had little hope of succeeding. The ships reached the islands in late November, but were unable to find a suitable harbour until mid-January. These final six weeks of frustration, with reduced allowances, had a depressing effect on the men, some of whom sent Cook 'a very mutinous letter'. Cook for his part stopped the men's grog ration, and wrote diatribes in his journal about his 'mutinous turbulent crew' and much else. Little of this was to be printed in the official account of the voyage, but there is no doubt that by the time the ships reached Kealakekua Bay on the southwest coast of the island of Hawaii, Cook was a weary, disappointed and possibly quite sick man. There is medical evidence to suggest that he was suffering from a parasitic infection of the intestine, whose effects would include irritability and loss of concentration. The extraordinary events during the ships' stay at Kealakekua Bay are still difficult to explain, and matters are not helped by the fact that Cook's own journal for those weeks has disappeared. After an ecstatic reception during which Cook seems to have been worshipped as the god Lono, the ships put to sea again, but were forced back by damage to the foremast of the *Resolution*. The expedition's return was met with open hostility, and in an atmosphere of mounting anger Cook was killed in a scuffle on 14 February 1779 during which he showed less than his usual judgement. The few words written by the German coxswain Heinrich Zimmermann reveal something of the effect Cook's death had on the crews: 'Everyone in the ships was stricken dumb, crushed, and felt as though he had lost his father.' The blow was the more severe because Charles Clerke, who had been with Cook on all his voyages, and who now took over command, was dying of consumption. It was a tribute to officers and men, and to naval discipline, that the expedition followed the orders of its captains – the one dead, the other incapacitated – and returned to the bleak Arctic seas in pursuit of its hopeless mission.

The ships left the Hawaiian Islands in the middle of March, and arrived at Kamchatka at the end of April. After a stay of six weeks, the ships sailed for Bering Strait. The strait was reached on 5 July, five weeks earlier than in the previous year, but the next day the familiar ice-barrier was sighted in latitude 67°N. The ships made repeated efforts to get through the drift-ice which lay off the pack, and received violent blows from loose floes. The farthest north that the ships reached was latitude 70°33'N., five leagues short of the year before. The *Discovery* was so badly battered by ice that she would need three weeks in port for repairs. In his last written instructions Clerke described 'the amazing mass of ice . . . an insurmountable barrier', and concluded that 'a passage, I fear, is totally out of the question'. As he lay dying, he ordered that the ships should make for Kamchatka to carry out repairs, and then return to England. John Gore, the *Resolution*'s first lieutenant, would take command. On the homeward voyage the ships called at Canton, where the sea-otter pelts casually collected along the American coast were sold for £2,000; and James King complained that 'the rage with which our Seamen were possessed to return to Cook's River and buy another cargo of skins to make their fortunes was at one time not far short of mutiny'.

The ships arrived home in October 1780 after what midshipman Gilbert described as 'a long, tedious, and disagreeable voyage, of four years, and three months'. It was all those things, but during that length of time only five men had died from sickness, and not one from scurvy. There were no celebrations to mark the ships' return to wartime Britain, for in the same package as the copy of Cook's last letter that had reached London in early January 1780 was one written by Clerke when he visited Kamchatka the previous summer, and it reported Cook's death at Hawaii. News of the disappointment and of the tragedy of the voyage reached London simultaneously. The Northwest Passage had not been found, and Captain Cook was dead.

10

Entering the Labyrinth

'In the afternoon, to our great astonishment, we arrived off a large opening extending to the eastward, the entrance of which appeared to be about four leagues wide, and remained about that width as far as the eye could see, with a clear easterly horizon, which my husband immediately recognized as the long lost strait of Juan de Fuca.'

Diary of Mrs Frances Barkley, *Imperial Eagle*,
June 1787

'We discovered that the straits of Adml. de font actually exist and I have but little doubt that they penetrate very far into the Continent.'

Log of Robert Haswell, *Columbia*, June 1789

As reports of Cook's voyage slowly crossed Russia and reached England the news of the explorer's death dominated all else. In St Petersburg the Empress Catherine II was 'greatly concern'd at the untimely death of Capt. Cooke', and hoped that it had not happened on Russian soil. When Captain Clerke's letter reporting Cook's death reached London on 10 January 1780 George III was said to have wept at the news, while the Earl of Sandwich wrote to Sir Joseph Banks that 'What is uppermost in our mind allways must come out first, poor captain Cooke is no more.' Later in the month newspapers printed more details about the other events of the voyage. The *London Chronicle* mentioned the stay at Nootka, the negotiating of Bering Strait, and the 'impenetrable mountains of ice' the ships encountered. Most of the newspapers noted that Clerke would be returning to Bering Strait for another attempt at the passage, and they wished him well. It was left to the *Gazeteer* to make the obvious point that if Clerke had found a passage in the summer of 1779 he should have been home well before January 1780.

Soon, those who were professionally interested in the geographical results of the voyage began to express opinions. Daines Barrington, who was given sight of Cook's journal and so should have known better, thought that the ships had reached the polar sea at the wrong time (late summer) when the river ice was floating out to form temporary fields of great extent near the land. Phipps, it will be remembered, had sailed north in 'a bad year'; for Barrington, it seems, there never would be a voyage that managed to get both the year and the month right. A different point of view was put forward by Jean-Nicolas Buache de la Neuville, nephew of the Philippe Buache whose maps of the 1750s had shaped the northwest coast after the narratives of Fuca and Fonte. Buache de la Neuville followed in his uncle's footsteps with a map and memoir in 1781 which showed Cook's explorations on the context of Admiral de Fonte's narrative. The map identified Sandwich Sound (Prince William Sound) as Fonte's celebrated Río los Reyes, while Cook's River led into a series of Fonte-style waterways to the north (*Ill.39*). Buache de la Neuville admitted that the voyages of Cook, Phipps and the Russians made less likely the possibility of a passage by way of the polar sea, but he was optimistic that Cook's discovery of openings along the coast north of Nootka would lead to a Northwest Passage through the continent. For the moment at least, the French geographer was in a small minority. As one London newspaper noted, 'the most sanguine, theoretical or practical navigators will give up, probably for ever, all hopes of finding out a passage'.

Such views were confirmed when the official three-volume account of Cook's voyage was published in June 1784. Lavishly illustrated, it was a costly buy at almost £5 the set, but one

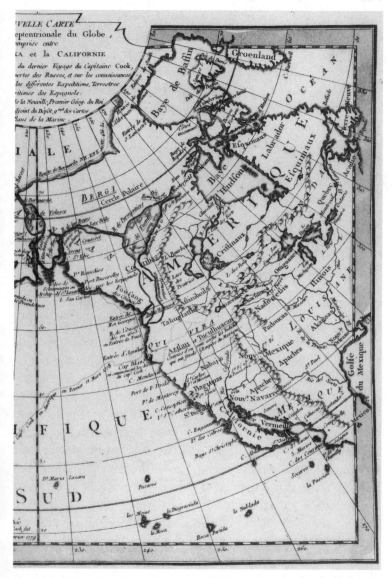

39. Jean-Nicolas Buache de la Neuville. Section of 'Nouvelle Carte de la Partie Septentrionale du Globe'. 1781.
British Library

London periodical noted: 'We remember not a circumstance like what has happened on this occasion. On the third day after publication, a copy was not to be met with in the hands of the bookseller; and to our certain knowledge, six, seven, eight, and even ten guineas, have since been offered for a sett.' Through the pages of the published account, which included a portfolio of charts and views, the dramatic scenery of the northwest coast and the startling appearance of its inhabitants became for the first time familiar sights to readers in Europe. The book's long introduction by the editor, Dr John Douglas, included the first description in print of Samuel Hearne's overland journey from Hudson Bay to the Arctic Ocean, so telling an argument against the existence of a Northwest Passage in temperate latitudes. Cook's forthright comments on the Fuca and Fonte fictions could now be read by all. To have instructed Cook to search for the reported straits, Douglas wrote in his introduction, would have been akin to directing him 'to trace the situation of Lilliput or Brobdignac'. Henry Roberts' map of northwest America which accompanied the official account showed an uncompromisingly solid coastline, although it revealed how far Cook was offshore for much of his zig-zag track north from Oregon (*Ill.38*). The map also marked Hearne's inland discoveries, although they were pushed too far north and west, and of the great barrier of the Rocky Mountains there was still no sign. Already on the market was Barrington's translation of the journal kept by Mourelle, the pilot on the Spanish voyage of 1775 along the northwest coast by Bodega y Quadra in the *Sonora*, which had searched in vain for the strait of Fonte. Although the journal had reached Barrington, not through official channels, but by way of Jean Hyacinthe de Magellan (a Fellow of the Royal Society living in London, and a descendant of the celebrated Portuguese navigator), there was no doubting its authenticity. Also recently in print was William Coxe's *Account of the Russian Discoveries between Asia and America* which replaced the imaginative maps of Müller and Stählin with more reliable charts.

All in all, as Johann Reinhold Forster remarked, it was difficult to see where there was room for the straits and rivers described in 'the narrative or rather reverie of de Fonte'.

If Cook's voyage seemed to have destroyed hopes of a navigable Northwest Passage, it drew attention to the commercial potentialities of Alaska, and especially to the ease with which sea-otter pelts could be obtained along the coast from Nootka northwards. Coxe's book described how since Bering's time Russian traders had reached the Aleutian and Fox islands, Kodiak and Unalaska, and although their losses were heavy, their profits were high. One of the first unofficial accounts of Cook's voyage, by William Ellis, surgeon's mate on the *Discovery*, claimed that pelts bought for a handful of beads in Prince William Sound fetched ninety or a hundred dollars apiece on the China market. This figure was confirmed in the official account, where Captain King noted that prime sea-otter skins had fetched as much as a hundred and twenty dollars at Canton, and suggested that the East India Company factors there might send ships to Cook's River to trade for furs. The account also included a drawing by John Webber of a young sea otter killed at Nootka Sound, with a description of how its fur was 'softer and finer' than that of any other known creature (*Ill.40*). The quest for beaver had lured the fur traders thousands of miles westward across the continent, and the maritime traders in their turn were quick to respond to the commercial opportunities offered by the lustrous sea-otter pelts of the north Pacific. By the mid-1780s British merchants in India and China were fitting out vessels for the northwest coast, and others from Europe and the United States soon followed. It was, a later writer remarked, as if a new gold coast had been discovered. Trade, not exploration, was the priority; but as these vessels entered bays and sailed through openings that Cook had never seen, their commanders (several of whom had sailed on the explorer's last voyage) began to question his conclusions about the geography of the northwest coast.

In 1785 the first trading vessel, commanded by James

40. JOHN WEBBER. 'A Sea Otter'. 1784.

The official account of Cook's voyage described how at Nootka Sound in 1778 a sea otter 'that had just been killed, was purchased from some strangers who came to barter; and of this Mr. Webber made a drawing. It was rather young, weighing only twenty-five pounds; of a shining or glossy black colour; but many of the hairs were tipt with white, gave it a greyish cast at first sight.'

Hanna and fitted out in India, reached Nootka. It was named the *Sea Otter*, indication enough of the purpose of the voyage. News of its successful trade encouraged further expeditions, for it was reported – with some exaggeration, it subsequently transpired – that the crew had received 50,000 dollars at Canton for 500 skins. The next year six trading ships were on the coast, together with an altogether more surprising arrival in the shape of two French naval frigates, the *Boussole* and the *Astrolabe*, commanded by Jean François Galaup de la Pérouse. The Comte de la Pérouse was one of France's most respected naval officers, and his expedition to the Pacific, which left Brest in August 1785, represented the French response to Cook's voyages. More than most other exploring voyages it reflected both the spirit of scientific enquiry of the Enlightenment and the great-power rivalries of the period. The first discussions of 1784 in French government circles seem to have envisaged the expedition as one intended to exploit those fur resources of the northwest coast that had been described in the accounts of Cook's last voyage; but with the encouragement of Louis XVI it soon turned into an ambitious voyage of exploration that aimed to complete the surveying of the Pacific that Cook had begun.

Among those involved in drawing up the instructions for La Pérouse was Buache de la Neuville, recently appointed *géographie du roi*. His 1781 map of the north Pacific had shown his ingenuity in trying to combine the recent explorations of Cook and the Russians with the old accounts of Fuca and Fonte; and later events were to suggest that the geographer retained his interest in the alleged discoveries of those and other early Spanish explorers. La Pérouse, on the other hand, was sceptical, and in one of his first letters home from the voyage made a scathing reference to the ignorance of 'Parisian geographers' (though he later named a prominent cape after Buache). His instructions reflected both the hopes of the geographer and the scepticism of the navigator. When La Pérouse reached the northwest coast of America he was to concentrate on exploring those stretches that Cook had not visited, including the 'Puerto de Bucareli' reached by Bodega's *Sonora* in 1775. Here and elsewhere La Pérouse was to 'investigate with the greatest care whether, in parts that are not yet known, there might not exist some river, or some narrow gulf, that communicates with some part of Hudson Bay by way of the interior lakes'. Another part of the instructions pointed out that Cook had been unable to examine the coast between latitudes 45°N. and 55°N., and that 'it is this gap that one can assume would be found the Entrance discovered in 1603 [sic] by Juan de Fuca, and the one of Martin d'Aguilar'. The King himself added an emphatic handwritten note here – 'This is the area that must be more carefully explored.' Of Bartholomew de Fonte and his voyage of 1640 there was no mention – this would come later.

La Pérouse reversed the order of priorities laid down in his instructions, which had directed him to carry out explorations in the south Pacific in 1786 before sailing north. Instead, once round Cape Horn he headed for Alaska, hoping to reach it near Bering's Mount St Elias. He then intended to turn south along the coast, so exploring in the opposite direction from Cook and the Spanish navigators. He explained the reason for this change in a letter to the relevant minister, the Count de Fleurieu, written on the outward voyage. Before he left Brest, he reminded Fleurieu, news had reached France that Captain John Gore, who had brought Cook's ships home in 1780, was preparing an expedition to the northwest coast. This was intended, La Pérouse wrote, 'to set up some establishment behind Hudson's Bay and I think it is good to get there before him'. For those familiar with the inner history of Cook's last voyage, there might have seemed some substance in this, for Gore had been the most persistent and optimistic advocate of a passage among the crew of the *Resolution*. All that one can say is that the rumoured voyage never occurred, and that Gore showed no sign of relinquishing his comfortable retirement post at Greenwich Hospital (the one left vacant by Cook's death). However, Gore's son is said to have sailed on the Portlock/Dixon expedition to the northwest coast that left England in 1785, and it may be that this had misled the French agents in London. Voyage or no voyage, La Pérouse's reference is evidence that if there were discoveries of commercial importance to be made in the north Pacific the French were anxious to be involved.

As the *Boussole* and *Astrolabe* sailed north from the Hawaiian Islands towards the northwest coast, La Pérouse's journal entries seemed deliberately to dampen expectation. He asked his readers to imagine the feelings of navigators, 'after a year at sea, struggling at the ends of the earth against fog, bad weather and scurvy along an unknown coast, which once upon a time was the setting for geographical tales that are too readily accepted by modern geographers'. In case the aforesaid readers needed guidance, La Pérouse added a footnote to the effect that he was referring to the supposed voyage of Bartholomew de Fonte and those of even earlier Chinese and Japanese navigators. When the fog cleared, and the distant mountain peaks of Alaska's coastal range were sighted, the commander's gloomy mood remained unchanged even after the identification of Bering's Mount St Elias, its great peak floating above the clouds: 'The sight of land, which ordinarily makes such a pleasing impression after such a long navigation, did not have that effect on us. The eye rested painfully upon all this snow covering a sterile and restless land.' Here La Pérouse turned south, for his instructions warned him against spending time in either Prince William Sound or Cook's River, which had already been explored by Cook.

After nine days he arrived off an inlet or bay in latitude 58°52'N. that seemed not to have been sighted either by Cook or by the Spaniards, and took his ships in after a hair-raising passage through tidal rips that led him to write that 'in the 30 years I have been sailing I have never seen two ships so close to destruction'. Despite the dangers of the entrance, La Pérouse named the inlet Port de Français (today's Lituya Bay), and suggested that if the French decided to establish a trading post on the coast this might be the spot. A battery of four cannon would be enough to make the entrance impassable to enemy ships, and the area lay strategically placed between the Russian and Spanish zones of influence. Although in his journal he expressed his disdain for the customary European acts of possession, La Pérouse nevertheless negotiated with a local chief the purchase for France of an island in the bay. The Tlingit inhabitants of the bay were both numerous and anxious to trade. They came alongside the ships in canoes loaded with sea-otter pelts, and the French thought it would be possible to collect ten thousand skins a year in the area. Intriguingly, the Tlingit possessed iron daggers, though whether the metal came from the Russians to the north, the Spaniards to the south, or from the fur traders of the interior, remained as

41. DUCHÉ DE VANCY. The ships of the La Pérouse expedition, the *Boussole* and *Astrolabe*, in Port de Français (Lituya Bay), July 1786. *Service Historique de la Marine, Paris*

As in Webber's drawing of Cook's ships in Prince William Sound (*Ill.34*), De Vancy's sketch shows the French ships dwarfed by their surroundings. An interesting feature of this drawing is the way in which the trees on both sides of the inlet are separated from the water by bare slopes. This lends support to the findings of geologists that during the eighteenth century a *tsunami* or volcanic tidal wave swept through the inlet and sheered off the trees for several hundred feet above the water's edge.

much a puzzle to them as to Cook's crews at Nootka Sound in 1778.

Investigation of the inlet revealed that what appeared to be its end opened into two great channels, and even La Pérouse was tempted to muse on the possibility that one or other of these might penetrate deep into the interior. The impressive setting, well represented in Duché de Vancy's drawing from one of the cliffs (*Ill.41*), encouraged thoughts of some signifi-

cant discovery – perhaps even the long-sought entrance of the Northwest Passage. The end of the bay, La Pérouse wrote,

> is perhaps the most extraordinary place on earth. Imagine a vast basin, whose depth in the centre is impossible to estimate, edged by great, steep, snow-covered mountains; not a single blade of grass can be seen on this immense rocky mass which nature has condemned to perpetual sterility. I have never seen a single breath of wind disturb

the surface of this water which is affected only by the enormous blocks of ice that fall quite frequently from five different glaciers, making as they drop a sound that echoes far into the mountains. The air is so clear and the silence so deep that the voice of one man can be heard half a league away, as can the sound of birds which have laid their eggs in the hollows formed by the rocks. This is the channel by which we planned to enter into the heart of America; we thought that it might lead to a great river running between the mountains, which had its source in one of the great rivers in northern Canada. Such was our dream . . .

The reality was that both channels ran into abrupt dead-ends, sealed with huge blocks of ice. Disconsolate, the boats' crews returned to the ships, 'having completed in a few hours', La Pérouse added wryly, 'our voyage into the interior of America'. As on Cook's last voyage, there seems to have been a difference in outlook between commander and some of his officers, although the disappearance of La Pérouse's ships in the South Pacific two years later meant that the only journal to survive for this part of the voyage was the commander's, sent with his dispatches and other mail overland from Kamchatka to France.

To disappointment was now added tragedy when two of the ships' boats capsized near the entrance with the loss of all their crews – six officers and fifteen men. Not a single body was recovered. All La Pérouse's instincts were to leave this place of death and disappointment, but contrary winds and a lingering hope that some survivors might yet appear, kept the expedition in the bay until the end of July. As the ships finally sailed southward, La Pérouse realised that the three months set aside for the exploration of the coast was totally inadequate. Given the intricate nature of the shoreline, the frequent fogs and the hazards of tide and current, a proper survey would take several seasons. He was, he reflected, in as much of a hurry as Cook had been, and could hope to record only the main features of the coast. On 4 August 1786 the ships passed Cross Sound, seen and named by Cook eight years earlier, and then sailed outside a string of islands (today's Alexander Archipelago). Could this be Admiral de Fonte's Archipelago of San Lazarus, La Pérouse wondered. Although he doubted the very existence of the Spanish admiral, he thought it possible that some early Spanish navigator had sailed into an inlet in this region, and that this discovery was the basis for 'the ridiculous tale of Fuentes and Barnarda'. Even if he came across such an opening, La Pérouse would not follow it inland in search of the Northwest Passage, for he more than most realised that 'this passage is a dream'. Four years earlier during the War of American Independence, La Pérouse had commanded a squadron which raided British posts in Hudson Bay. Among the prisoners taken by the French was Samuel Hearne, the explorer who in 1771–72 had crossed overland from Hudson Bay to the shores of the polar sea. Hearne still had in his possession a copy of his journal of that momentous journey, and this also fell into French hands. On board ship back to Europe La Pérouse treated Hearne well, and even returned his journal, but not before reading it. It convinced the French commander that there could be no transcontinental strait. In any case, he went on to ask, what use would any such communication be to his country now that France had lost the territories it once possessed in the eastern half of the American continent?

As he kept south along the outer coast of the Queen Charlotte Islands, La Pérouse struggled to place the bays and capes of 'this labyrinth' on his chart. Sometimes the fog was so thick that although the *Boussole* was within hailing distance of the *Astrolabe* its crew could see nothing of the other vessel. On 19 August came a dramatic moment when they 'sighted a cape which seemed to end the coast of America'. La Pérouse went on to explain what he meant. Cape Hector (now Cape St James), in latitude 51°56'N., marked the end of the coast he had been following for six hundred miles, and since he could see no land to the east he thought that the islands he had been following were separated from the mainland by a great channel which stretched all the way back to latitude 57°N. Cape Hector marked the southernmost limit of the Queen Charlotte Islands, and La Pérouse was correct in appreciating its significance. He had realised what had eluded Cook, that the outer coast of the Alaskan panhandle was insular, and that a series of straits – today's Inland Passage – separated the outer barrier of the Alexander Archipelago and the Queen Charlotte Islands from the unseen mainland. The need to hurry south, and persistent fog, hampered the expedition's attempts to identify prominent landmarks along the coast. Nootka Sound and the entrance of the Strait of Juan de Fuca were both passed unseen in thick weather, and La Pérouse bore away for California scribbling journal entries which reflected his scepticism and irritation. Fonte had never existed but was the invention of the English; and the idea of a Northwest Passage was as 'absurd' as those 'pious frauds' of a more credulous age which all good rationalists had rejected.

The six trading vessels that were on the northwest coast in 1786 were all British-owned, and operated under licence from the East India Company. Two had been fitted out in India, two sailed came from Canton, while the remaining two had made the long, fourteen-thousand mile voyage from England. First to reach the coast were the two ships fitted out in Bombay, and sailing under the command of James Strange. They found conditions hard and trade poor. Their scurvy-ridden crews reached Canton with a disappointing cargo of a few hundred pelts for which the Chinese merchants offered only a fraction of the price that Cook's crews had obtained for their furs. In terms of exploration, however, Strange's voyage opened up intriguing possibilities, for he had entered a great

gulf that he named Queen Charlotte's Sound at the northern
tip of what would later be called Vancouver Island. The opening had not been seen by Cook in 1778, for he was well
offshore, and realisation was dawning among his successors on
the coast that his dismissal of the inland channels reported to
have been entered by Juan de Fuca in 1592 and Bartholomew
de Fonte in 1640 might have been premature. Although the
location of the sound in latitude 51°N. placed it a full two-
degrees south of the latitude given to the Río los Reyes in the
printed account of Fonte's voyage, Strange believed that it
might be Fonte's entrance (see map on p.391).

The 1787 season brought further exciting discoveries. The
two ships on the coast which had made the year-long voyage
from England were the *King George* and *Queen Charlotte*, commanded by Nathaniel Portlock and George Dixon. Both commanders had been with Cook on his last voyage, and their ships
were well-equipped with navigational instruments: sextants,
copies of the *Nautical Almanac* so that longitude could be
obtained by lunar distances, and (on Dixon's ship) a pocket
chronometer. They left England with high expectations of
commercial gain, as shown by a newspaper article published
as they prepared for departure.

> The North West Continent discovered by Captain Cook,
> is upwards of 1600 miles extent of coast; the bays, sounds,
> harbours, and rivers, are as noble as any in the world,
> and abound with that most valuable of all land or marine
> animals, the sea otter; the skins of which the natives wear
> for clothing, the fur of which is the most beautiful and
> rich of any ever met with, and is held in the highest
> estimation by the Japanese, the Chinese, and at all the
> Courts of Asia. This valuable branch of Commerce hath
> hitherto been totally engrossed by the Russians.

In the event, the voyage was more notable for exploration
than for trade. As Dixon sailed north along the American
shoreline between latitudes 51°N. and 55°N. he soon realised

that the land in sight to starboard was a group of islands, not a continuous stretch of coastline, and not the mainland, as Cook had assumed. In late July 1787, in the passage inside the islands (today's Hecate Strait) floating debris 'made us conclude, that there is a large river setting out from that part of the coast'. The latitude was 53°N., that of Fonte's Río los Reyes, and in his published account Dixon wrote that this location 'evidently shows' that the islands were 'the Archipelago of St Lazarus, and consequently near the Straight of De Fonte'.

An even more intriguing discovery had been made farther south the month before as William Barkley, in the *Imperial Eagle*, sailed south along the coast from Nootka to Cape Flattery. Unusually, the master's wife was on board, and Frances Barkley's later recollections describe how 'In the afternoon, to our great astonishment, we arrived off a large opening extending to the eastward, the entrance of which appeared to be about four leagues wide, and remained about that width as far as the eye could see, with a clear easterly horizon, which my husband immediately recognized as the long lost strait of Juan de Fuca, and to which he gave the name of the original discoverer.'

Exploration of the strait soon followed. In August 1788 the tiny 65-ton *Princess Royal*, commanded by Charles Duncan, anchored just inside the entrance off the Indian village of Claaset. Duncan's sketch of the opening was published early in 1790 (*Ill.42*), with Pinnacle Rock shown near Cape Claaset (Cape Flattery), a reminder of that 'exceeding high Pinacle' which two centuries earlier Fuca had reported in the entrance of his strait, though he had placed it on its *northern* side. The chart showed the tide setting out of the inlet, and an accompanying note stated that 'the Indians of Claaset said that they knew not of any land to the Eastward; and that it was A'ass toopulse, which signifies a Great Sea'. In March 1789 the American trading sloop *Lady Washington*, commanded by Robert Gray, sailed into the strait for twenty-five miles before bad weather forced it back. To the east the strait broadened to form 'a Large sea stretching to the east and no land to obstruct the view as far as the eye could reach'. The logs kept on board the *Columbia*, the *Lady Washington*'s consort vessel, show that the ship's crew had the accounts of Fuca and Fonte to hand, and in June 1789 first mate Robert Haswell concluded that farther north in Clarence Strait they had discovered Fonte's famous opening, and that it extended far into the interior. In the same area James Colnett, master of another trading vessel, the *Prince of Wales*, who had sailed with Cook on his second voyage, thought that a navigable strait 'might not improperly be conjectured to run to Hudson's Bay from the Depth of water, width of the Channel and tending to the NE as far as the Eye could reach'.

As reports of new discoveries came in thick and fast, it became increasingly clear that Cook's assumption that in 1778 he was sailing along the mainland coast between Nootka and Cape Edgecumbe was wrong. The masters of the trading vessels sailing in and out of the numerous inlets and channels in that region realised that most of the time they were among islands. After spending two seasons on the coast Colnett wrote, 'It's a doubt with me if ever I have seen the Coast of America at all.' Did the straits of Fuca and Fonte lie somewhere in this labyrinth? The most recent signs were hopeful. The Queen Charlotte Islands stretched across the latitude of Fonte's Archipelago of St Lazarus, and near the mainland coast there were indications of a large river. Farther south Fuca was supposed to have discovered a strait between latitudes 47°N. and 48°N., and now Barkley, Duncan and Gray had found an opening only one degree off this latitude which seemed to run into a great inland sea, perhaps the Mer de l'Ouest of the French geographers. On one point the traders were agreed. On board the *Lady Washington*, Haswell reflected in his log: 'to survey this coast would be an allmost endless task . . . trading vessels to this coast will make considerable advances toward this but it never can be thuroughly done intill it is done at

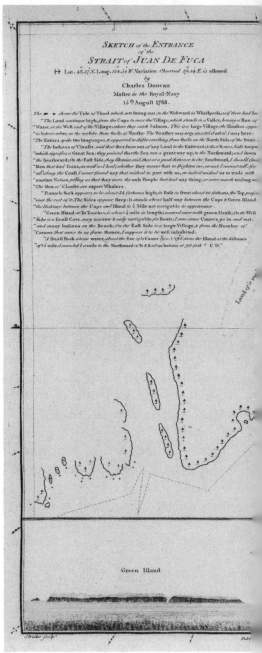

42. CHARLES DUNCAN,
'Sketch of the Entrance
of the Strait of Juan de
Fuca . . . 15 August
1788'.
British Library

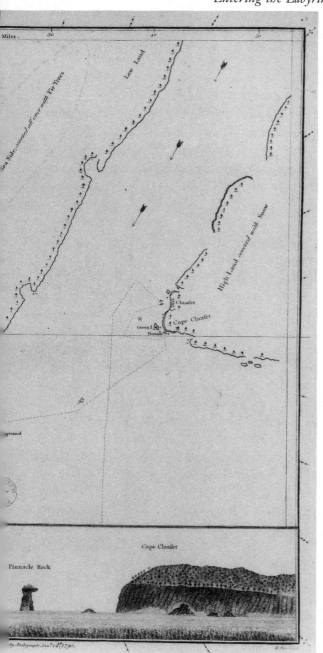

some national expense whose Commanders are uninterested by commerce.'

The lead in this task was to be shared by Spain and Britain, although the difference in attitude between their respective governments towards the publication of explorers' journals meant that most of the credit for the surveys of the next few years would go to the British. Spanish policy still tended towards the defensive and the fearful. Holding a claim to the whole of the northwest coast that was looking flimsier by the year, Spain's anxiety about foreign incursions prompted reconnaissance voyages to the north, but not any willingness to publish their surveys. New Spain's northern frontiers were protected by their inaccessibility, and for long it had been a set Spanish assumption that the less knowledge about them that reached foreign powers the better. After two centuries state secrecy died hard. In Britain, on the other hand, from the time of Cook's first voyage the Admiralty had recognised the advantages both to science and to the national interest that prompt publication would bring. At the end of the journal of his first voyage Cook had urged that it should be 'published by Authority to fix the prior right of discovery beyond dispute'. In his introduction to Cook's journal of his last voyage Dr John Douglas represented an expansionist and self-confident national outlook when he remarked of this and other published accounts that 'Every nation that sends a ship to sea will partake of the benefit; but Great Britain herself, whose commerce is boundless, must take the lead in reaping the full advantage of her own discoveries.' Within three years of the book's publication in 1784 such a process was under way. A fleet sailed for New South Wales to establish the first European settlement in Australia, albeit a convict one; William Bligh, master of the *Resolution* on Cook's last voyage, left for Tahiti in the *Bounty* to collect breadfruit for the Caribbean plantations; and British vessels, some commanded by men who had sailed with Cook, were on the northwest coast, trading and, almost incidentally, exploring. As their journals and charts reached England, several were published: those of Dixon and Portlock in 1789, of Meares and Duncan the next year.

In England, the most important supporters of trade and exploration on the northwest coast were Sir Joseph Banks and Alexander Dalrymple, who had known each other for more than twenty years. Banks had come far since the days when as a young botanist he had sailed with Cook on his first Pacific voyage. He was now President of the Royal Society, adviser to cabinet ministers, and patron of the sciences on an international scale. He was interested from the beginning in the trading voyages to the northwest coast, primarily through his support of a new enterprise, the King George's Sound Company, headed by Richard Cadman Etches. Banks was, in the words of Richard's brother, John, a leading patron of schemes 'for prosecuting and converting to national utility the discoveries of the late Captain Cook'. When the expedition of Portlock and Dixon was fitting out, Banks had visited the ships, christened one of them the *Queen Charlotte*, and loaned Portlock a copy of one of Cook's logs. The ships of Colnett and Duncan also belonged to Etches' company, whose name was that given by Cook to Nootka Sound in April 1778; and all four of them bore names of members of the royal family: *King George, Queen Charlotte, Prince of Wales, Princess Royal*. In a quite deliberate way the Etches brothers were linking their activities in the North Pacific with royalty, with Banks and Cook, and with the pursuit of 'national utility'. Sir Joseph kept closely in touch with the activities of the Etches ships on the northwest coast, and also heard from Richard Etches about William Barkley's discovery of an opening south of Nootka. There is 'evident probability', Etches told Banks, 'that this is the strait laid down by Juan de Fuca and from the depth of water, bredth, strong tide and the trending to the N.E. we may presume that the

Western Sea laid down by de Fuca, de Fonte, and Aguilar hath an existence.' Then, when Dixon returned home he described to Banks the archipelago of islands that he had discovered, and stressed how closely it resembled Fonte's Archipelago of St Lazarus.

If Banks was the most prestigious figure involved in the voyages to the north Pacific, undoubtedly the most tireless was Alexander Dalrymple, hydrographer to the East India Company, and an indefatigable publisher of charts and memoirs. On his return to Britain in 1765 after thirteen years' service in the East, Dalrymple became the leading advocate of the case for a great southern continent. In 1768 he had hoped to command the *Endeavour* on its voyage to find the unknown continent, but the Admiralty preferred to appoint the little-known James Cook rather than a non-Navy man. While Cook was away in the Pacific, Dalrymple continued to argue the case for a great southern continent, only to find his theories destroyed by the surveys of Cook's first two voyages. Although Dalrymple continued to publish charts on many parts of the world, the connection of the East India Company and its Canton establishment with the new trading operations on the northwest coast of America helped to turn his attention to that region. The fact that Cook's interpretation of the geography of the northwest coast now seemed likely to be proved faulty was no doubt an incentive. Like Banks, Dalrymple began receiving journals, reports and charts from the returning maritime fur traders, and established a close relationship with George Dixon whose practical seamanship and knowledge of the coast proved invaluable.

In 1789 and 1790 Dalrymple published pamphlets, and a series of sketches and charts drawn by traders on the coast, and began an intensive lobby of government ministers. Never a man to think small – it was Dalrymple after all who had argued that the southern continent was five thousand miles across and contained fifty million inhabitants – he proposed a union of the East India Company and the Hudson's Bay

Company. With government support, and using a Northwest Passage to link operations in America and the Pacific, this giant organisation would dominate Europe's trade across a region stretching from the Canadian North to Canton and Bombay. Dalrymple pointed out that China offered a vast market for furs, and that the experience of the Hudson Bay traders in collecting furs could be combined with the facilities the East India factors in Canton possessed for selling them. There is no indication that this grand design met with much interest from the East India Company, and in February 1791 Dalrymple was complaining to the Court of Directors that 'unless we profit by the advantage of our possessions in Hudson's Bay, the Americans will certainly beat us out'. Under his scheme, the East India ships trading to Canton would, after unloading there, sail to the northwest coast and return to Canton with furs collected at a Hudson's Bay Company factory at Nootka or some other location on that coast. If necessary, the route could be used in reverse, and furs from the northwest coast sent to Hudson Bay for shipment to Europe. All depended on the discovery of a safe, navigable route through the continent. Cook, it was true, had denied that such a passage existed, but one man's opinion was simply that – 'I cannot admit of a Pope in Geography or Navigation,' was Dalrymple's way of putting it. His friendship with Samuel Wegg, now Governor of the Hudson's Bay Company, gave him access to the maps and journals in the Company's archives, and he used his unique position to link the explorations on the east and west sides of the continent.

Dalrymple found much of interest in the Northern Indian maps of Hudson Bay brought to London by Moses Norton in the 1760s (*Ills.20, 22*). To Dalrymple, they indicated that Repulse Bay did not block the way to the north, and that a channel led from it to the polar sea. He therefore omitted Christopher Middleton's Frozen Strait – cause of so much dispute forty years earlier – from his 'Map of the Lands around the North-Pole'. Dalrymple then turned to Samuel Hearne's journals and maps, and estimated (correctly) that the polar shore reached by Hearne lay in latitude 68°N., not in 72°N. as the explorer had claimed. This shift made the chances of a navigable passage not quite as remote as they had appeared immediately after Cook's last voyage. Alternatively, a route might yet be found through rather than round the continent. Dalrymple's study of the Northern Indian maps suggested that Chesterfield Inlet, or one of the other openings on the west coast of Hudson Bay, communicated with the lakes of the interior. The largest of these marked on the maps was shown connecting with Hudson Bay, and Dalrymple thought that this might be the Lake de Fonte reached by the Spanish admiral on 6 July 1640, little more than three weeks sailing time from the Pacific. This interior route was similar in some respects to the waterway sought by the Canadian fur traders who were struggling westward across the continent, but whereas they were looking for a river, lake and portage route for their canoes, Dalrymple was still hoping for the discovery of a coast-to-coast waterway navigable by seagoing vessels. Time was short, he insisted, for while the Russians were establishing themselves at Cook's River and Prince William Sound, the Spaniards were extending their activities northward.

Dramatic confirmation of the urgency of the situation came with the Nootka Sound 'incident' in the summer of 1789, when Spanish forces from San Blas seized British-owned ships and a shanty trading hut at Nootka built by John Meares, master of a trading vessel and a half-pay lieutenant in the Royal Navy. This seizure, though not specifically authorised by Madrid, marked the climax of the Spanish claim to the entire Pacific coast of America. When Meares reached England in 1790, he found that the dispute had not yet been made public, although the British and Spanish governments had been negotiating for several months; but a series of tendentious memorials composed by Meares with the intention of extracting the maximum advantage to his owners from the dispute led to a hardening of attitude by the Pitt cabinet, and to the flaring of anti-Spanish feelings in the country. At the end of the year, after the two nations had come near war before reaching agreement in October, Meares' account of his voyages was published, and was widely read. It was prefaced by 'Observations on the Probable Existence of a North West Passage', and this once more raised the question of the significance of the discoveries being made on the north-west coast.

In the summer of 1788 Meares had sailed south from Nootka in the *Felice Adventurer* with, it seems, William Barkley's journal and charts in his possession. At the end of June he arrived off a 'great inlet' that he supposed was the Strait of Juan de Fuca, complete with 'a very remarkable rock, that wore the form of an obelisk' near its southern shore. On his return northward in July, Meares sent his first mate, Robert Duffin, in the ship's longboat to investigate the opening. An accompanying engraving shows the scene, with the boat flying the British flag (*Ill.43*), though in fact Meares was sailing under Portuguese colours to avoid the monopoly rights of the British East India Company. According to Meares, the longboat sailed thirty leagues into the strait, and when a native attack forced them back its crew could see a clear horizon stretching another fifteen leagues to the east. 'Such an extraordinary circumstance filled us with strange conjectures as to the extremity of this strait, which we concluded, at all events, could not be at any great distance from Hudson's Bay.' There is much nonsense and exaggeration here. The mate's journal shows that the long-boat sailed eleven, not thirty, leagues into the strait; and even if the strait did extend forty-five leagues, the nearest part of Hudson Bay would still be more than a thousand miles distant. In his account of the voyage of the American trader, Robert Gray, in the *Lady Washington* Meares further distorted the evidence. He first mentioned the *Lady Washington* in July 1790, when he stated that the vessel 'went up de Fonti's Strait and passing thro' a Sea came out at the Strait of Juan de Fuca'; but in a memorial written at the end of the month Meares

43. 'Entrance of the Strait of Juan de Fuca', July 1788. John Meares, *Voyages* (1790).
British Library

reversed the track of the vessel, and had it sailing south to north. Finally, in his book Meares claimed that Gray had heard about Fuca's strait from him, and that the American skipper had passed through the strait into a sea 'of great extent' to the eastward before returning to the Pacific through a passage farther north along the coast.

It was little wonder that reviewers adopted a generally

critical stance to Meares' volume, and George Dixon in particular published detailed refutations of several of his claims. Nevertheless, Dixon agreed that east of Nootka and the Fuca strait stretched a sea of unknown extent, and he argued that this should be explored by a British naval expedition. Among private ruminations on the significance of it all sounded a voice from the past, that of Henry Ellis. More than forty years after sailing on the *Dobbs Galley* in search of the Northwest Passage, he found in Meares' discoveries evidence that a passage indeed existed. As a friend responded to Ellis's remarks on the subject:

'your grounds and reasons for the North West passage are still intact and are stronger now than before. Capt.Cook did not explore enough the coast . . .'

By 1790, then, there were hopes that a passage to the Pacific might be found by two possible routes. One would take ships through an opening on the west coast of Hudson Bay into Hearne's polar sea. They would sail along the northern shores of the continent until they reached Bering Strait, or before that find an opening into the Pacific through Cook's River. A more southerly route, ice-free but tortuous, extended from Hudson Bay along the rivers and lakes of the interior to Cook's River or into the great inland sea thought to lie east of the Strait of Juan de Fuca. How Hearne had failed to notice this as he journeyed northwest from Churchill was nowhere explained. On the Pacific coast Cook's River was an especially inviting objective, for in June 1778 Cook had turned back before reaching its end, and speculated that it might lead to 'a very extensive inland communication'. This was consistent with the reports now reaching London about the discoveries of the overland fur traders. The most enterprising and combative of these was Peter Pond, a New Englander working for the Montreal-based North West Company. Like Dalrymple, who seized eagerly on his maps while distrusting the man and his nationality ('by encouraging him we may be fostering a viper in our bosom'), Pond was prone to global thoughts. He had canoed and portaged as far west as Great Slave Lake, but his eyes were fixed on more distant horizons. By the end of 1787 he had constructed a map that showed a vast region stretching for thousands of miles from Hudson Bay to Kamchatka. This was to be presented to Catherine II, Empress of Russia, by the first explorer to follow the waterways of North America to the Pacific coast, and then trek across Russia to

44. PETER POND. 'A Map . . .' *Gentleman's Magazine*, March 1790. *British Library*

This simplified version of one of Pond's large manuscript maps shows one river flowing north from Great Slave Lake ('Slave Lake') to the Arctic (Mackenzie's discovery of 1789), and another running from the western end of Great Slave Lake to the Pacific coast at Cook Inlet and Prince William Sound. For this part of his map Pond was dependent on Indian information, for he was turned back by 'Falls said to be the Largest in the known world.' As in his earlier maps, Pond's longitudes are hugely in error, so that here Great Slave Lake is shown six or seven hundred miles nearer the Pacific than it actually is, thus increasing hopes that an inland passage of rivers and lakes might exist between the Great Lakes of Canada and the Pacific coast.

St Petersburg. Today it is in the Public Record Office at Kew, a melancholy relic of thwarted hopes.

In his accompanying notes Pond claimed to have met Indians at Great Slave Lake who had seen Cook's ships on the

Pacific coast, and he estimated that at his farthest west he was only six days' travel from the ocean. In other reports this became three days' travel, and the Indians were said to have produced an actual blanket traded from Cook's crews in 1778. All Pond's maps from this period were dominated by a gigantic Great Slave Lake, shown seven hundred miles west of its true position, and with an unexplored river flowing from its western end. Cook's track along the Pacific coast was also marked, with less than three hundred miles between the farthest point his ships reached in Cook's River and the open end of Pond's river running out of Great Slave Lake. The inference was clear: the two rivers were one and the same, and the fur traders were at last within reach of the Pacific coast. At the same time as Dalrymple, Banks and others in London were studying these maps and accounts, in North America another North West Company servant, Alexander Mackenzie, was discovering that the river (soon to be named after him) which flowed out of Great Slave Lake led north to the Arctic Ocean and not west to the Pacific. By the end of 1790 the first rumours of this discovery reached England, where Dalrymple and Barrington mulled over the disconcerting news. The fact was that Pond, tough in body and mind, lacked surveying skills and instruments. He knew the routes of the Canadian northwest better than any other non-Native, but as one contemporary put it, his longitudes 'seemed to be guesswork'. And longitudes were not the only problem. None of the land explorers realised that between the fur-trade country of the Canadian interior and the Pacific lay the mighty barrier of the northern Rockies. Pond had a clearer idea of the geography of the northwest than most, but he assumed that 'the great chain of mountains that extend from Mexico' stopped short of his river of the north (*Ill.44*).

In a long memorandum to the government in February 1790 Dalrymple argued that the case for a Northwest Passage had been 'strongly confirmed' by the Indian maps and by the reports of those on the northwest coast. The only 'allegations' to the contrary came from Middleton and Cook. Bering Strait was the long-sought Strait of Anian, and the field of ice that had stopped Cook's ships north of the strait in 1778 had dissolved a month later. Three times in the eighteenth century the government sent expeditions to find the Northwest Passage, and each time the driving force came from an enthusiast who had contacts with navigators, geographers and ministers: Dobbs in the 1740s, Barrington in the 1770s and now Dalrymple. He collected and collated reports on the northwest coast of America from every possible source, and then presented his conclusions to the government and to the chartered companies. The rough charts drawn by captains of vessels trading for furs along the northwest coast; the visionary maps of Pond away in the far north; the forgotten Chipewyan sketches of Hudson Bay brought home by Moses Norton many years earlier: all found their way to Dalrymple in his hydrographer's office in the East India Company's headquarters in London. There he pored over the maps, studied the journals of the explorers, and talked to the men recently returned from Hudson Bay and the northwest coast, and always with the thought in mind that if his fellow countrymen discovered a passage from the east to west coast, then Britain would dominate the trade of the northern half of the continent and the seas beyond.

With information reaching him every month reporting the discovery of great lakes and rivers in the interior, identifying areas of the northwest coast as those described in the accounts of Fuca and Fonte, and testifying to the growing interest of foreign powers in the Pacific northwest, Dalrymple put growing pressure on both the government and the Hudson's Bay Company to act. Adding his considerable weight to Dalrymple's efforts was Joseph Banks, who was pursuing his own scheme for establishing a trading base on the northwest coast, preferably in the Queen Charlotte Islands. The combination of Dalrymple and Banks was an effective one, and by the spring of 1790 William Wyndham Grenville, Secretary of State in the Pitt administration, was contemplating the dispatch of a naval expedition to the northwest coast under the command of Henry Roberts, who had been with Cook on his last voyage. Its draft instructions reveal the various motives at work. Roberts was to investigate the events at Nootka in 1789 (the government's priority), explore the coast (as Dalrymple was urging), and establish a trading settlement in the Queen Charlotte Islands (the scheme promoted by Banks and Etches). At the same time, the Hudson's Bay Company agreed to Dalrymple's urgent request that it should send a sloop from Churchill to examine the west coast of Hudson Bay for a passage into the interior. For Dalrymple, time was of the essence; whereas Roberts' ships could not reach the northwest coast until 1791, the Hudson's Bay Company sloop should be able to carry out its surveys in the summer of 1790.

In the event, neither 1790 nor 1791 saw any exploration. As the crisis with Spain worsened during the spring and summer of 1790 to the point where war seemed likely, the Roberts expedition was shelved. When in October Britain and Spain signed the Nootka Sound Convention the expedition was reinstated, but with a different commander and different instructions. George Vancouver, chosen as first lieutenant on the original expedition, was appointed captain of the *Discovery*, with the *Chatham* under Lieutenant William Broughton serving as a tender. Vancouver had sailed as a midshipman with Cook on both his second and third voyages, and so had first-hand experience of the northwest coast. He was given two tasks: to receive restitution of the land and buildings at Nootka seized by Spain in 1789, and to explore the coast as far north as latitude 60°N. for a waterway through the continent. That it was to be a route open to ocean-going vessels is clear from the instruction not 'to pursue any inlet or river further than it shall appear to be navigable by vessels of such burden as might safely navigate the Pacific Ocean'. Vancouver's survey would be the more important because, by the terms of the Nootka Sound Convention, Spain had abandoned its exclusive claim to the northwest coast. Two stretches of coast were singled out for special attention. First, Vancouver was to explore 'the supposed straits of Juan de Fuca' and then Cook's River, since there was 'the greatest probability' that it rose in one of the interior lakes. There was no mention of Mackenzie's recent disappointing discovery that Pond's river out of Great Slave Lake flowed to the Arctic, not the Pacific.

While the delayed naval expedition was fitting out for the Pacific, the Dalrymple-inspired venture to Hudson Bay was running into difficulties. When the Hudson's Bay Company agreed to Dalrymple's proposal it added a rider that echoed its painful experiences during the Dobbs crisis, for it was insistent that the government should choose the sloop's commander so that 'the Publick may be assured of every thing being done to effect the desired Purpose'. The man selected was Charles Duncan, who had proved his seamanship by his voyage in the diminutive *Princess Royal* to the northwest coast, where he had charted the entrance of the Strait of Juan de Fuca. His instructions of May 1790 ordered him to investigate once more those inlets on the west coast of Hudson Bay that had been the scene of so much fruitless effort in the middle decades of the century, and to find a way through one of them to the interior lakes seen by Hearne on his overland journey thirty years earlier. The Company directors had scrutinised Henry Ellis's published chart of Hudson Bay of 1748 (which had been recently reprinted), and the manuscript surveys of its own seamen, William Christopher and Magnus Johnston, and realised that no two charts seemed to agree on the precise location and name of inlets along the west coast of the Bay. Several inlets were shown on different charts either slightly north or south of Chesterfield Inlet, but there was no certainty as to their navigability or even existence. If Duncan failed to find a previously unknown inlet, then he was to sail up Chesterfield Inlet, and cross from its head to the Yathked and Dobaunt lakes shown on Hearne's map. With him would sail another ex-navy man, George Dixon, who at this point would leave the vessel to prospect an overland route to the Pacific. If Duncan found a passage through the continent he was to follow it to that inland sea described to him two years earlier by the natives he had met at the entrance of the Strait of Juan de Fuca. He could then either return eastwards or sail to China, and with him he carried a letter from the Company directors to the East India Company factors at Canton.

It is difficult to take this project seriously. Hearne's explorations had shown that there could be no passage south of the polar sea, and Dalrymple had accepted that the most hopeful route was to sail through Repulse Bay into that sea; but Duncan was only to go farther north after he had finished his survey of the Yathked and Dobaunt lakes, almost an impossible extra task given the shortness of the navigable season. News of Alexander Mackenzie's discovery that the river running out of Great Slave Lake flowed north, not west, further diminished expectations. As Barrington glumly remarked, where Duncan 'is to navigate in a N: W: inland passage seems to be rather a difficult problem'. Dixon's proposed land trip across the continent was an even more improbable venture for a seaman who had no experience of the Canadian north, and it was his good fortune that this part of the plan was dropped. The likeliest explanation for the Company's involvement in this madcap scheme was its eagerness, in an era of growing rivalry with the more flamboyant North West Company, to rebut the continuing criticism that it had no interest in exploration, for there were those who still suspected that 'the Governors and Directors of the Hudson's Bay Company were desirous of withholding from the public the probability of a North West Passage'. Its use of warrant officers from the Royal Navy to carry out this project revealed its anxiety to create a good impression on government and public alike. There was nothing reprehensible about this desire for favourable publicity. For too long the Company's explorations of the second half of the century had been carried on in undeserved obscurity; and the release of Hearne's journal to the Admiralty before Cook sailed, the permission to Dalrymple to inspect the maps in the Company's archives, and the co-operation with the cartographer Aaron Arrowsmith that was to see many of its surveys published in the following years, were evidence of the change in Company policy that followed Wegg's appointment as Governor. It was now essential, not only that exploration should be done, but that it should be seen to be done, and the Company accordingly made arrangements for Duncan's journal to be published after his return.

The year 1790 saw a false start by Duncan. The Company ship taking him to Hudson Bay did not arrive at Churchill until the middle of September, and there he found the sloop falling to pieces, its crew unenthusiastic, and the factor obstructive. In London the Company was sufficiently concerned about Duncan's outraged return to purchase a strong brig, the *Beaver*, for his use the next year. Duncan made an early start from England, sailing ahead of the regular Company ships; but to little purpose, because ice delayed him in Hudson Strait for seven weeks, and he lost the remainder of the brief navigable season weatherbound at Marble Island. After wintering at Churchill, Duncan sailed north in July 1792, but made no discoveries of any consequence along the coast. At the beginning of August he reached Chesterfield Inlet, and had little alternative but to enter an inlet that had already been explored three times. At its head in Baker Lake, Duncan and his mate George Taylor went up the same small river that Moses Norton had reached in 1762. Four miles from its mouth the river was no more than a stream, with only three feet of water, and it soon shallowed to a series of dry ridges that not even a canoe could cross. It was a predictable end to a hopeless venture.

The voyage had been altogether devoid of interest, but a Company document relates how Duncan, who before sailing, 'entertained the most positive Assurances that he should discover the often sought for North West Passage . . . felt the disappointment so severely, that whilst on his Voyage home he was attack'd by a Brain Fever'. Taylor's journal relates the story of the homeward voyage in clinical detail. After Duncan made several attempts to commit suicide the crew tied him to his bunk, until he was transferred in mid-ocean to one of the Company's ships, which brought him back to England. Whether it was Dalrymple who encouraged him with 'most positive Assurances' is not clear; but certainly the geographer had suggested Duncan for the expedition, and when Duncan wrote to the Company from Churchill in September 1791 he asked specifically that news of his progress should be passed on to Dalrymple. Duncan clearly made some sort of recovery, for he later held a post at Chatham dockyard, and a year after his return he explained to William Goldson, a Portsmouth surgeon much enamoured of theoretical geography, why he had failed to find a strait on the west coast of Hudson Bay. Duncan remained convinced that Fonte's account was authentic, but believed that since 1640 the sea had retreated so that the route described in the account was now impassable. It is true that isostatic lift was slowly altering sea levels, but not even the most extravagant estimates of its effect would justify a claim that the Northwest Passage of one century was dry land the next. A more realistic viewpoint was that of a disgruntled director of the Hudson's Bay Company, who complained that the expedition had cost £3,000, and had accomplished nothing. Duncan's explorations served only to confirm the opinion of Middleton, Norton and Hearne that no passage existed in Hudson Bay – but on the other side of the continent the final act in the drama was still being played.

11

Last Hopes

'Such a great readiness on the part of geographers to continue to espouse outdated opinions whatever their foundations . . .'

ALEJANDRO MALASPINA, *Diario General*, 1792

'I trust the precision with which the survey of the coast of North West America has been carried into effect, will remove every doubt, and set aside every opinion of a northwest passage.'

CAPTAIN GEORGE VANCOUVER, *A Voyage of Discovery*,
August 1794

THE EXPEDITION OF George Vancouver left England on 1 April 1791, a date which Vancouver would later recall as having a wry significance. The *Discovery* and the *Chatham* took more than a year to reach their destination, described by Vancouver in his journal as 'the remote and barbarous regions' of the northwest coast of America, and by then Spanish vessels had finished much of the task entrusted to him. As British ministers suspected when they added to Vancouver's instructions a clause ordering him to co-operate with any Spanish vessels which he found engaged in survey work, the Spaniards were busy exploring those stretches of the coast where they thought that the entrance of the Northwest Passage might lie. Among the ships taking part were the *Descubierta* and *Atrevida* of one of the best-equipped discovery expeditions ever to leave Europe, that of Alejandro Malaspina. This had been diverted from its comprehensive survey of Spain's overseas empire by the decision of the Spanish government to investigate yet another account of an apocryphal voyage through the Northwest Passage.

First, however, the Spaniards relied on surveys by local-based ships. The officer responsible for seizing British vessels at Nootka in 1789 was Estéban José Martínez, who the year before had commanded an expedition north to the Alaskan coast, where he encountered Russian traders. In 1774 Martínez had accompanied Juan Pérez in the *Santiago* on the first Spanish reconnaissance voyage along the northwest coast, and, if his own later claim is to be believed, on that voyage he had urged Pérez, without success, to enter an opening in latitude 48°20′N. From his new establishment at Nootka, Martínez was now in a good position to determine the existence of a strait, rumoured to have been recently discovered by British trading vessels, in that location. He sent José María Narváez to investigate who returned with the news that he had found the entrance of the Strait of Juan de Fuca, twenty-one miles wide, just where Martínez had indicated it would be. The latter reacted triumphantly: 'If Captain Cook had lived to the present time, there is no doubt he would have been undeceived about the existence of these straits, as all Europe will be made to see within a short time.' Martínez, an erratic and unstable character who had done much to provoke the clash at Nootka, saw the Spanish rediscovery and control of the straits of Fuca and Fonte as part of a grand scheme to dominate the entire northwest coast and beyond. At Mexico City his superiors were of a different cast of mind, and although the new Viceroy, the Conde de Revillagigedo, ordered that the strait entered by Narváez south of Nootka should be investigated his attitude was sombre and pessimistic. The claims and projects of Martínez, he pronounced, existed only in a 'sphere of dreams'.

In the event, Spanish survey vessels took three seasons to explore the complicated waterways that lay inside the Strait of Juan de Fuca. In 1790 Manuel Quimper charted the strait's north and south shores. His voyage brought into view Haro

Strait, although he did not follow it into the Strait of Georgia, nor did he explore the inlets in the southeast corner of the Fuca strait which lead into Puget Sound. In the same year, another expedition commanded by Salvador Fidalgo sailed north to Prince William Sound and Cook Inlet. Unaware of diplomatic agreements being made in Europe, Fidalgo not only carried out useful survey work but took possession of several Alaskan locations in the name of the Spanish Crown. In 1791 Francisco de Eliza resumed the investigation of the Strait of Juan de Fuca. He sailed up the Strait of Georgia as far as latitude 50°N., about halfway along the eastern side of Vancouver Island, and reported that if there was a Northwest Passage it must be in that area.

It was at this point that events took an unexpected turn with the arrival on the northwest coast of the prestigious 'politico-scientific' expedition of Alejandro Malaspina. This had left Spain in 1789 on an ambitious mission of survey and inspection that was to last more than five years, and before its end had visited the coasts of Spanish America and the Philippines, Macao, New South Wales and Tonga. The ships, the *Descubierta* and the *Atrevida*, had been specially built for the voyage, and carried the latest navigational and hydrographical instruments. The scientists and artists on board had been carefully chosen by Malaspina, who at the age of thirty-five had already completed one circumnavigation. Italian-born, he was a man of wide reading, whose political and economic opinions were much influenced by the Enlightenment. The initiative for the voyage came from him and his fellow commander, José Bustamante, rather than from the Spanish government, and the expedition as a whole was seen by Malaspina as part of an ambitious project of imperial reorganisation and regeneration. Although he was careful not to compare his proposed voyage with those of Cook, there is no doubt that it was as much a response to the voyages of the English navigator as that of La Pérouse had been a few years earlier.

By the end of March 1791, almost two years into the

45. ALEJANDRO MALASPINA. Portrait by José Galván based on a drawing by Juan Ravenet made on the voyage, January 1794.
Museo Naval, Madrid

voyage, Malaspina in the *Descubierta* had reached Acapulco, while Bustamante in the *Atrevida* was farther north at San Blas. After visiting the Viceroy in Mexico City, Malaspina intended to rejoin Bustamante, and sail to the Hawaiian Islands. At that point everything changed, as instructions from Madrid ordered the expedition to sail immediately along the northwest coast to latitude 60°N. in search of the passage between the Pacific and the Atlantic claimed to have been discovered by Lorenzo Ferrer Maldonado in 1588. Much remains unclear about the events that led to these unexpected new instructions. In the original plan for the voyage put forward in September 1788 by Malaspina and Bustamante, the northwest coast featured only in the vaguest of terms: 'After following the coast of California northward the voyage will continue northward between Asia and America as far as the snows will allow.' There was no mention of exploration in any general way, though this could be assumed, nor of a specific search for a Northwest Passage. On the other hand, before he sailed Malaspina had been at pains to collect all available journals and reports about the Russian voyages to Alaska, and had also obtained a summary of the journal of La Pérouse's explorations on the northwest coast which had reached Paris overland from Kamchatka. Then in June 1789, only weeks before the expedition was due to leave Cádiz, José Espinosa, a young naval officer who had been sent to the Archive of the Indies in Seville to copy journals that might prove useful to the expedition, found a curious document that he drew to Malaspina's attention. It described a voyage said to have been made by Lorenzo Ferrer Maldonado in 1588 through the Strait of Anian. The provenance of this particular document is far from certain, but it seems to have been one of several copies of the memorial which Maldonado had presented to the Spanish Crown in 1609, more than twenty years after his supposed voyage. One copy had come to light in 1781, when an investigating scholar, Juan Bautista Muñoz, discovered it in a private collection and made a copy for the Real Academia de la Historia in Madrid, together with Maldonado's accompanying sketch maps of the Strait of Anian.

Even by the standards of the Fuca and Fonte accounts Ferrer Maldonado's story was extraordinary (see pp.423–30 below). He claimed to have embarked on a voyage from Spain

46. LORENZO FERRER MALDONADO. View of the Strait of Anian, 1609
British Library

This was one of several views and maps with which Maldonado accompanied
his memorial of 1609. They were copied by Juan Bautista Muñoz when he
found the memorial and maps in 1781, and were subsequently printed by,
among others, Carlo Amoretti in his *Viaggio dal Mare Atlantico al Pacifico per
le Via del Nord-Ouest* (1811), as shown here. The capital letters represent
A – north entrance of the Strait, B – south entrance of the Strait, C – port,
D – river of pure water, E – place for a fort, F – canebrake, G – lookouts,
H – bastions, L – part of Asia, M – part of America.

in 1588 during which he entered 'the Strait of Labrador' or Davis Strait. This was 290 leagues long, and took the vessel almost as far north as latitude 75°N. Although this part of the voyage was made in February, when 'the cold [was] so great that the sea water which dashed against the sides of the ship froze, so that the ship seemed to be made of crystal,' the sea itself never froze. From this farthest point north the vessel sailed southwest and westsouthwest for 770 leagues. There, in latitude 60°N. Maldonado reached the entrance of the fabled Strait of Anian, separating Asia from America. The strait was fifteen leagues long, with high, mountainous sides. Near its outlet into the Pacific was a harbour capable of holding five hundred ships, and while his vessel was anchored there Maldonado encountered a large, 800-ton merchantman entering the strait which carried a rich cargo of pearls, gold, brocades, silks and porcelain. Its crew were Hanseatic Lutherans with whom Maldonado conversed in Latin. In June his ship left the harbour on its return voyage, finding temperatures north of the Arctic Circle warmer than those 'in the hottest place in Spain'. The Strait of Anian, with its narrow entrances and high sides, could be easily defended, Maldonado thought, so that 'only the Spaniards can navigate it with entire security and enjoy the great utilities which it promises', and he drew sketch maps showing how it could be fortified (*Ill.46*).

The lack of interest in Spain of Ferrer Maldonado's presentation in 1609 of his alleged discovery of 1588 is entirely understandable. Why he waited more than twenty years before revealing his sensational news has never been explained, though a reference in his memorial to the discoveries of Quiros might hold a key to the mystery. The year 1609 was the one in which the Portuguese navigator Pedro de Quiros published his celebrated 'Eighth Memorial' in which he inflated his discovery of the island of Espiritu Santo (Vanuatu in the southwest Pacific) to epic and mystical proportions. It covered, he told Philip III of Spain, 'the fifth part of the Terrestrial Globe', and was more than twice the size of all Spain's existing territories. Maldonado's memorial can be seen as the northern counterpart of Quiros's, a rival bid to attract attention and patronage. What is more difficult to explain is its reception two hundred years later, in a climate of opinion generally regarded as altogether more critical and less credulous; and after the failure of repeated attempts to find a navigable passage from both the Atlantic and Pacific sides.

The sequence of events is puzzling. On 24 April 1789 Malaspina asked Antonio Valdés, the Navy Minister, whether when on the coast north of California he should look for the Northwest Passage 'according to the well-known but very imprecise manuscript of Ferrer Maldonado'. This was presumably a reference to an examination of Maldonado's voyage that had appeared the year before in the fourth volume of the monumental *Historia política de los establecimientos ultramarinos de las Naciones Europeas* compiled by the Duque de Almodóvar, who wrote under the pseudonym of Eduardo Malo de Luque. Almodóvar found difficulties in relating Maldonado's discoveries to those of Cook and other recent navigators, and apologised for leaving his readers 'immersed in doubts', but he concluded that the account of the voyage of 1588 bore 'all the hallmarks of authenticity'. On 9 June 1789, Malaspina wrote again to Valdés on the matter, informing him that Espinosa had just found a copy of the Maldonado account. This, Malaspina added in a phrase which showed that he had read Almodóvar's remarks, had 'all the hallmarks of authenticity'. Although both Cook and La Pérouse had searched for the Northwest Passage, Malaspina thought there was now 'scope for a new exploration'. He concluded by asking whether he should send copies of Maldonado's memorial to the learned societies of Paris and London. In a reply that reached Malaspina on the day he sailed, 29 July 1789, Valdés authorised him to search for the passage 'according to circumstances', but ordered that nothing about Maldonado's account should be communicated to foreign nations until the expedition returned.

Like most other objectives of the expedition, the matter was left to Malaspina's discretion. When the lateness of his arrival at Acapulco at the end of March 1791 made it impossible to carry out his planned visits to both the northwest coast and the Hawaiian Islands that year, Malaspina decided that the survey of Hawaii should have priority, and that he would abandon the Alaskan stage of his voyage. This decision was overturned when Malaspina arrived in Mexico and received news from Bustamante at San Blas that a letter from Valdés had arrived which contained new orders from King Carlos IV. The expedition was to sail north in search of the Strait of Anian, guided by an assessment of the Maldonado voyage which had just appeared in France. This was a memoir which had been presented to the Paris Academy of Sciences on 13 November 1790 by Jean-Nicolas Buache de la Neuville. Forty years earlier his uncle, Philippe Buache, had collaborated with Joseph Nicolas Delisle in offering the same institution his celebrated paper on Admiral Fonte's account, and the new presentation followed the family tradition of hypothetical and controversial geography as it sought to link Maldonado's voyage with the explorations along the northwest coast of America by the Russians and James Cook. Buache de la Neuville had obtained a copy of the Maldonado account from José de Mendoza y Ríos, a naval officer who travelled from Spain to Paris soon after Espinosa's retrieval of the Maldonado document in June 1789, and who may have been unaware that a few weeks after its discovery Valdés had expressly prohibited its showing to foreigners. Who exactly in Spain was impressed by Buache's attempts to prove the authenticity of the Maldonado narrative is not clear. His paper of November 1790 consisted of an abbreviated account of Maldonado's voyage, supported by a list of outdated references to the fanciful explorations of Captain Cluny, Lieutenant Sindt and Baron d' Ulfeld. Of the recent surveys by the navigators who had followed Cook to the northwest coast Buache made no mention. A more realistic comment on the Maldonado account came from Juan Bautista Muñoz, who had first discovered the memorial in 1781. Writing in the same month that Malaspina was on the Alaskan coast searching for the strait described in the memorial, Muñoz called Maldonado 'a greedy and vainglorious charlatan', whose alleged voyage had no foundation in fact.

Malaspina's reaction to his new instructions confirms the impression given by his decision of a few weeks earlier to abandon the Alaskan leg of his voyage, that his doubts about the Maldonado account had increased during the voyage, though there were moments when he thought the reported passage was not 'altogether improbable'. In his journal Bustamante was more forthright, and listed the many inconsistencies in the narrative that Espinosa had found. He stressed the differences between Maldonado's description of the northwest coast in 1588 and the recent surveys of Spanish and British vessels along that coast, but reserved his main criticism for Buache's memoir. This was, in Bustamante's view, 'a very poorly digested work, intended, in fact, to delude Europe ... rather than to serve that love of truth which should be the principal rule in an Academy of Sciences'. Whatever their reservations, Malaspina and Bustamante joined forces once more at Acapulco, and prepared for their unexpected voyage to the north. They had gathered much valuable information, not least from Bodega y Quadra, now in command at San Blas, about the Spanish exploring ventures that had followed his voyage to Alaska in 1775, and these surveys can only have increased Malaspina's doubts about the task ahead. In a long letter Bodega gave Malaspina detailed advice on the course his ships should follow, and the dangers to be anticipated. While the vessels were preparing for sea at Acapulco a dozen seamen attempted to desert on hearing that they were bound for the far north.

Following Bodega's advice, Malaspina took his ships on a long curving track well out to sea before heading in towards the Alaskan coast in about latitude 57°N. which he reached in late June near Cook's Cape Edgecumbe. The snow-covered mountains awed the journal-keepers, and the cold was so intense that the artist Suria was unable to sketch on deck and had to retreat below to complete his drawings. From this landfall the ships sailed north towards the location of Maldonado's supposed strait in latitude 60°N., and on 27 June were off Yakutat Bay, visited by George Dixon four years earlier, when he named it Port Mulgrave. Although Dixon had stayed there for ten days, he had not made a complete survey, and admitted in his journal that 'How extensive the sound is, I cannot say.' On board the *Descubierta* and *Atrevida* excitement grew as the ships steered towards a deep cleft in the coastal range in latitude 59°15'N. Its appearance, Lieutenant Tova Arredondo wrote, 'had the most exact conformity' with the opening described by Maldonado two hundred years earlier. Suria took up the story in his journal: 'Great was the joy of the commander and of all the officers because they believed, and with some foundation, that this might be the so much desired and sought-for strait . . . Transported with joy, our commander steered towards the opening.' Suria's reaction could perhaps be discounted as the excitable reaction of an artist and a landsman, but the captains' journals confirm the air of expectancy on the ships. Malaspina confessed that his imagination supplied a thousand reasons why the entrance slowly coming into view might be Maldonado's. Like others on board he seems to have been impressed by the majestic grandeur of the landscape, which made so appropriate a setting for some grand discovery that for the time being all doubts were laid aside. By nightfall the ships were at anchorage inside Yakutat Bay, close to a beach and a Tlingit village. The expedition's portable observatory was set up, the artists made their drawings of people and places, wood and water were collected, and the customary trade for sea-otter pelts took place.

By 2 July, Malaspina was ready to explore the inner reaches of the inlet in search of Maldonado's strait, sailing with two launches and fifteen days' provisions, and leaving Bustamante in charge of the ships. It took only a few hours to dispel

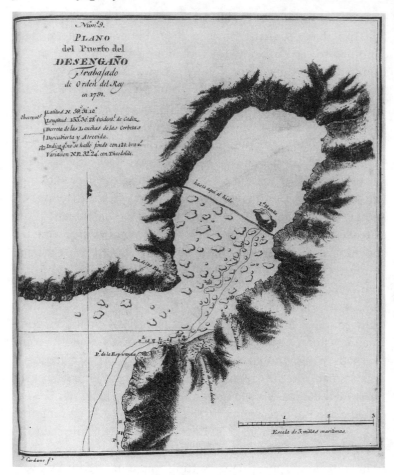

47. ALEJANDRO MALASPINA. 'Plano del Puerto del Desengaño . . . 1791'
British Library

This chart, printed in *Relación del Viaje hecho por las Goletas Sutil y Mexicana*
(1802) shows Malaspina's survey by boat inside Yakutat Bay in July 1791.
With his way blocked by the ice shown here (Hubbard Glacier), Malaspina
turned back and named the inlet Disenchantment Bay.

their hopes, for soon after mid-day the water shoaled and the
thunderous sound of large chunks of ice calving from a glacier
could be heard. Then the bottom of the inlet came in sight,
its low shore ending in a glacier (today's Hubbard Glacier)

behind which rose the great wall of the coastal range (*Ill.47*). It was the same sight that had disheartened La Pérouse and his crews in Lituya Bay five years earlier, and was one that was becoming depressingly familiar to navigators entering the ice-bound fiords of the Alaskan coastline. Malaspina named the spot Puerto del Desengaño (Disenchantment Bay), and the outer entrance of the bay Ferrer, 'after the ancient navigator'. The juxtaposition of the two names was probably not accidental. After taking possession of the area, Malaspina prepared to head out to sea. Much had been accomplished in the week's stay. The scientists on board had gathered a rich harvest of ethnographic and natural history material, and the artists had made some superb sketches and paintings; but the over-riding fact was that there was no strait leading deep into the interior.

The disappointment showed in the events of the following weeks, as the ships first headed for Prince William Sound, more to satisfy Malaspina's superiors that the expedition had reached as far as the latitude of Maldonado's supposed strait in 60°N. than to carry out further exploration. In the event, strong winds kept the ships from entering the sound, and without attempting to reach Cook Inlet they bore away back down the coast on their way to Nootka. Several openings were sighted and named, but none was investigated, despite the opinion of some on board that Maldonado's strait might yet be discovered along this stretch of coast. As Suria put it: 'Even if we were not successful in finding it there would at least be left the complete satisfaction that no-one in the future could carry off this glory. Such considerations brought much grief to the pilots and some of the officers, among whom there exists a true appreciation of the honour and glory of the nation.' For his part Malaspina had lost all faith in Maldonado's account. The hypothesis advanced by Buache de la Neuville on the basis of that account, Malaspina reflected a year later, was another example of the damage done by the splitting of geography between scholars and navigators, and the 'great readiness on the part of geographers to continue to espouse outdated opinions whatever their foundation'. By now Malaspina had identified a dozen inconsistencies in Maldonado's account, and to these he added others that stemmed from the glosses of Buache. The encounter with the Hanseatic ship whose crew spoke Latin, the hot weather in high northern latitudes, the ease with which Maldonado sailed far to the north in midwinter, all this and much else gave cause for doubt. A reader in the 21st century, he concluded, would be amazed to see how seriously the stories of Fuca, Fonte and Maldonado had been taken in an age that called itself scientific and enlightened.

After his return to Acapulco, Malaspina detached two of his officers, Dionisio Alcalá Galiano and Cayetano Valdés, to carry out the third and final season of exploration in the Strait of Juan de Fuca in 1792. They were to give priority to inlets leading eastward 'to decide once and for all the excessively confused and complicated questions of the communication or proximity of the Pacific Ocean and the Atlantic in this latitude'. In two small, locally-built vessels, the *Sutil* and *Mexicana*, Galiano and Valdés spent almost four months investigating the farthest recesses of the Strait of Juan de Fuca, paying special attention, as their instructions directed, to the mainland shore. While engaged on their survey, the Spaniards encountered Vancouver's ships, recently arrived on the coast, and after exclamations of mutual surprise there was an interchange of information and courtesies. Painstaking work in boats failed to reveal any way through to the east, though of openings and bays there were more than enough. By late August the Spanish vessels had sailed along the entire east coast of Vancouver Island, and rounded its northern extremity to gain the open ocean. On 31 August they arrived back at Nootka. The expedition had completed the first continuous circumnavigation of Vancouver Island, but the reaction on board the two vessels was far from euphoric. An anonymous journal keeper on the expedition referred to their work as serving 'only to satisfy curiosity and draw philosophical conclusions, but in no way of use to navigators'.

This journal of the surveys inside the Strait of Juan de Fuca was the only documentation associated with the Malaspina expedition to be published during the navigator's lifetime. Malaspina's plans for a comprehensive eight-volume publication of his voyage were shattered when, soon after his return to Spain in late 1794, he unwisely became involved in political intrigue directed against young chief minister, Manuel Godoy. Malaspina's downfall was sudden and catastrophic. In March 1795 he was received at court by King Carlos IV and Queen María Luisa, and promoted to *brigadier* (admiral). In November of the same year, after a summer spent in political and possibly conspiratorial activities, he was arrested. After a hurried trial he was stripped of his rank, and sentenced to life imprisonment (conventionally, ten years and a day). Although he was released in 1803, Malaspina was forced to spend the remaining seven years of his life in obscure retirement in Italy. Among the sad details of his last years is a document dated September 1806 noting that he had sold his sextant, that most personal and treasured of a sea-officer's possessions. There was no rehabilitation, no restoration of his naval rank, and no resumption by him of the ambitious edition of his voyage that he had planned. In 1802 the journal of the voyage of the *Sutil* and *Mexicana* was printed in Madrid, together with a handsome atlas and an introductory essay that summarised Spanish voyages to the northwest coast; but all mention of Malaspina's name was deleted. It was as stealthy, and effective, a removal of a personality from the historical record as any more recent authoritarian regime could wish for. Malaspina's own journal of the main voyage of the *Descubierta* and *Atrevida* was not published in Spain until 1885, and for long he was the forgotten man among the Pacific navigators of the eighteenth century.

By the late summer of 1792, before Vancouver's ships had been on the coast more than a few months, the Spaniards had satisfied themselves that the wondrous straits of the old accounts – of Fuca, Fonte and Maldonado – did not exist. Jacinto Caamaño, who had spent dangerous weeks on the Alaskan coast that summer searching for Fonte's strait, pronounced that such accounts had no foundation other 'than the madness or ignorance of some one devoid of all knowledge of either navigation or geography'. Vancouver did not allow these conclusions to deter him from making his own detailed surveys of the mainland coast, but inevitably his expedition's work was tinged by scepticism and pessimism. The *Discovery* and *Chatham* had left the Hawaiian Islands in mid-March 1792, and after an uneventful passage sighted the Oregon coast a month later. The long voyage from England by way of the Cape of Good Hope had revealed how ill-matched Vancouver's two vessels were. The *Discovery* was a 330-ton merchant ship, purchased new from its Thameside builders, 'not a pretty ship' a Spanish observer had remarked of it, but commodious and with decent sailing qualities. The *Chatham* was a small brig-rigged tender of 131 tons, crank and a slow sailor, and much disliked by her crew – 'our Dung Barge', one of them called her. It seemed unlikely that she would cope with the inshore surveys that were expected of her.

As the two ships followed the American coast north from their landfall they came within a few miles of what appeared to be a bar across the mouth of a large river near latitude 46°N., but Vancouver refused to be distracted from his main task and kept steadily north. On 29 April the ships drew near Cape Flattery at the southern entrance of the Strait of Juan de Fuca, and sighted a ship flying American colours. The sight of any vessel was a novelty, for the expedition had not seen another sail for eight months, and excitement rose when the ship, the *Columbia* of Boston, was found to be commanded by Robert Gray. This was the navigator who, according to John Meares, had two years earlier taken the *Lady Washington* sloop

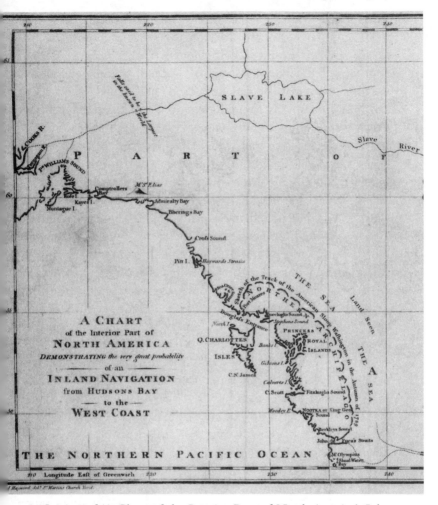

48. Section of 'A Chart of the Interior Part of North America'. John Meares, *Voyages* (1790).
British Library

The most striking feature of the chart is the track of the *Lady Washington*, commander Robert Gray, shown sailing in 1789 through a huge inland sea that stretched from the Strait of Juan de Fuca almost four hundred miles north.

through the strait of Fuca into an inland sea, and back into the Pacific farther north through the strait of Fonte (*Ill.48*). It was an extraordinary coincidence that as the expedition approached the famous strait of Fuca, it should encounter the one man who, it was supposed, had sailed through it. Disillusionment was immediate, for when Lieutenant Peter Puget went on board the *Columbia* Gray told him that he had indeed entered the strait, but had sailed in it less than fifty miles. Gray still thought that the strait was the one discovered by Fuca, but on Vancouver's ships confidence was sadly shaken, and was not restored when the crews had difficulty picking out the high pinnacle rock that according to the original account in Purchas marked the entrance of the strait. For his part Gray sailed south, entered the great river half-sighted by Vancouver's men, and named it the Columbia after his ship. Thirteen years later discovery by sea and discovery by land were to be linked, for in November 1805 Lewis and Clark came downstream to the mouth of the Columbia after their epic journey overland from the Missouri.

After parting company with Gray, the *Discovery* and *Chatham* sailed into the strait reputed to have been discovered by Juan de Fuca exactly two hundred years earlier. On 30 April Vancouver, who had no inkling of the Spanish explorations of the previous two years, wrote that they were now in waters never before seen by Europeans. While he and his officers explored the deep inlets of Puget Sound and Hood Canal to the south, Broughton in the *Chatham* was sent north, and on his return he reported that an extensive sound filled with islands stretched in several branches from the northwest to the northeast. This was the southern entrance of the Strait of Georgia. Broughton's report, and the intricate nature of the coastline revealed to the *Discovery*'s surveying parties, forced Vancouver to reconsider his instructions. These stressed that in his quest for straits or rivers navigable for ocean-going vessels he was not to concern himself with 'too minute and particular an examination of the detail of the different parts of the coast'. After less than a month Vancouver saw that this policy of doing things by halves was not satisfactory. To produce charts that would settle once and for all the question of a Northwest Passage through the continent, he needed to survey every mile of the fractured mainland coast. Since the *Chatham*, as predicted, proved too clumsy for inshore work, and the *Discovery* was far too large, this meant working from the ships' boats most of the time. In all, there were forty-six boat excursions during the three years of the survey, some of them lasting weeks at a time, and usually under the command of the expedition's two masters, Joseph Whidbey of the *Discovery* and James Johnstone of the *Chatham*.

The change of method condemned officers and men alike to grinding, tiring work, especially as they moved farther north. There, it seemed, it was invariably raining, food often ran short, the canoes looming out of the mist might or might not be friendly. As Vancouver's officers set up their instruments, carried out observations, took soundings, and filled their notebooks, the next group of Indians was never far away. The crews encountered the coastal peoples in all their variety: Salish, Kwakiutl, Haida and Tlingit among them. In contrast to Cook, Vancouver seems to have had little interest in their customs, and when his brother John tried to supplement the journal for publication with the captain's notes on the subject he found them 'too concise and too unconnected' to be of use. For Vancouver's men the Indians were an ever-present but unpredictable accompaniment to the business of surveying, often a distraction and an irritant, sometimes a threat. How their own activities appeared to the local inhabitants rarely seems to have been taken into account. There can be no doubt that the investigatory nature of the survey work, with the boats prying into every inlet, and landing men near dwellings and families, led to uneasiness and resentment. As Vancouver put it in his journal, the crews in their open boats would be exposed 'to numberless dangers and unpleasant situations, that might occasionally produce great fatigue'. When the ships headed up the Strait of Georgia the mountains began to press in so close to the shoreline that the boat parties often found it difficult to spot any level ground where they could land for the night. Puget's description of one day's experience can stand for many. It was eleven o' clock at night before they landed, 'after a most disagreeable & laborious Row, the Boats and their Furniture were all wet nor was there a Spot to shelter us from the Inclemency of the Weather, & as it was equally uncomfortable either remaining in the Water afloat or on Shore most of us preferred the Ground & Fire for the Remainder of the Night'. Their number included Vancouver, whose own stoical journal entry simply recorded that it was 'a tolerably comfortable situation'. Yet for all the hardship and danger, the observations were taken and the surveys made – and the crews kept fit. Of the six deaths on the long voyage, only one was from illness, and none from scurvy. It was a remarkable record that rivalled Cook's.

Vancouver's survey of the continental shore was carried out, step by step, according to the best practice of the day. When in harbour, Vancouver proceeded by land-based triangulation surveys, and the portable observatory was set up on shore to obtain an exact geographical position. Latitude was obtained by observing the meridian altitude of the sun, and longitude by means of several hundred sets of lunar distances, which involved three observers and a great deal of complicated mathematics. Inside the shelter of the observatory tent, the performance of the expedition's chronometers, one of which had been with Cook on his last voyage, was checked by astronomical observations; but the instruments' main use was to carry forward longitude between observation spots. The landing places afforded the fixed points on the grid on which the details of the survey were plotted. For reasons of time and practicability most of these came from running surveys, sometimes made from the ships, often from the boats. From the ship azimuth compass bearings were taken to headlands and other prominent features, soundings and shoals were

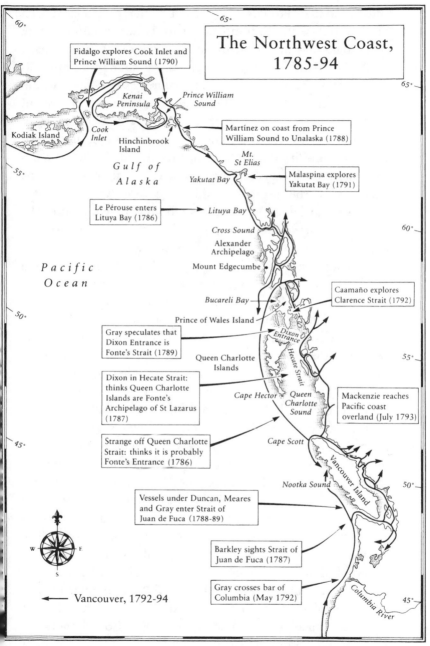

The Northwest Coast, 1785-94

Fidalgo explores Cook Inlet and Prince William Sound (1790)

Martínez on coast from Prince William Sound to Unalaska (1788)

Malaspina explores Yakutat Bay (1791)

Le Pérouse enters Lituya Bay (1786)

Caamaño explores Clarence Strait (1792)

Gray speculates that Dixon Entrance is Fonte's Strait (1789)

Dixon in Hecate Strait: thinks Queen Charlotte Islands are Fonte's Archipelago of St Lazarus (1787)

Mackenzie reaches Pacific coast overland (July 1793)

Strange off Queen Charlotte Strait: thinks it is probably Fonte's Entrance (1786)

Vessels under Duncan, Meares and Gray enter Strait of Juan de Fuca (1788-89)

Barkley sights Strait of Juan de Fuca (1787)

Gray crosses bar of Columbia (May 1792)

Kenai Peninsula

Prince William Sound

Kodiak Island

Cook Inlet

Hinchinbrook Island

Gulf of Alaska

Mt. St Elias

Yakutat Bay

Pacific Ocean

Lituya Bay

Cross Sound

Alexander Archipelago

Mount Edgecumbe

Bucareli Bay

Prince of Wales Island

Dixon Entrance

Queen Charlotte Islands

Hecate Strait

Cape Hector

Queen Charlotte Sound

Cape Scott

Vancouver Island

Nootka Sound

Columbia River

← Vancouver, 1792-94

60°   65°   55°   60°   55°   50°   45°   50°   45°

added, and then a rough sketch drawn of that particular stretch of coast before the ship moved on to its next position. At all times allowance had to be made for variation of the compass. When boats were used close inshore, the same procedure was followed, but with the added aid to accuracy that officers would land as often as possible to take angles to and from prominent landmarks with sextants or theodolites. Profiles were drawn from the sea of parts of the coastline that held special interest. Back on the ship, the outlines of the pencilled field sketches and charts were transferred to the grid of the master charts, which after the return of the expedition were redrawn, engraved and published. This task, both during and after the voyage, was undertaken by Joseph Baker, third lieutenant of the *Discovery* at the beginning of the voyage. The survey work was intricate and time-consuming, and it was the beginning of June before the survey of the southeast corner of the Fuca strait completed. The length of time this survey of a limited area had taken was an indication, Vancouver realised, that to survey the coast to latitude 60°N. would be accomplished only by 'very slow degrees', and Puget forecast (correctly) that the expedition would take three years to complete its task.

On 4 June, the King's birthday, Vancouver took possession for the Crown of the entire region from his landfall of 39° 20'N. on the Oregon coast (New Albion in Vancouver's journal) to the Strait of Juan de Fuca. There was nothing in Vancouver's instructions about carrying out such acts, and his journal simply said that he had 'long since designed to take formal possession' of the country. Nor was there any mention of negotiation or consent. For Vancouver the region offered a tempting prospect, and his literary abilities were strained to the utmost as he described 'a landscape, almost as enchantingly beautiful as the most elegantly finished pleasure grounds in Europe . . . I could not possibly believe that any uncultivated country had ever been discovered exhibiting so rich a picture.' From the pleasant surroundings of Puget Sound the ships headed up the Strait of Georgia, anchoring at intervals to allow the boat parties to explore each of the long, narrow inlets that could extend a hundred miles or more inland. Returning to the *Discovery* at the end of June after surveying Burrard Inlet, where the great city named after him now stands, Vancouver was astonished to find two small Spanish vessels lying at anchor off Point Grey. They were the *Sutil* and the *Mexicana*, engaged on completing the survey of the Strait of Juan de Fuca begun by Quimper two years before. To Vancouver, convinced that he was the first European to explore these waterways, this was mortifying news, but relations between the two groups were good, and for some weeks they worked together. They were not able to give each other information of any great value since their surveys had covered the same areas, and they were using much the same instruments and methods. Nor did the expeditions gain the knowledge they expected from the other about earlier voyages. The only account that the Spaniards possessed of voyages through the Fuca strait came from John Meares' book – not the most reliable of sources – and, as Vancouver noted, 'so far were those gentlemen from being better acquainted with the discoveries of De Fuca or De Fonte than ourselves, that, from us, they expected much information as to the truth of such reports'.

So Vancouver carried on the interminable survey of the inlets along the eastern shores of the Strait of Georgia. On more than one occasion officers commanding the boats became optimistic that the channel they were following deep into the mountains might pass through the deep range towering over them; but none did. A Spanish journal described the deceptive appearance of these inland waterways. They were so deep that no soundings could be taken from the boat, but just when the officer in charge hoped for some spectacular breakthrough, 'without having seen any sign that the channel is coming to an end, he will find on turning a bend that the mountains have closed up on both sides and form an arc, leaving usually a narrow beach, on which a few steps may be taken'. In July one of Vancouver's boat parties found that a channel connected

49. ZACHARIAH MUDGE. 'The *Discovery* on the Rocks in Queen Charlotte's Sound'.
Hydrographic Office Taunton

Vancouver's journal for 6 August 1792 noted that after the *Discovery* ran aground at 4 o'clock in the afternoon the crew took down topmasts and yards, and threw overboard ballast, wood and water. Even so, 'Soon after the ship was aground, the tide took her on the starboard quarter; and as she was afloat abaft it caused her to take a sudden swing, and made her heel so very considerably on the starboard side, which was from the rocks, that her situation, for a few seconds, was alarming to the highest degree . . . by the time it was low water, the starboard main chains were within three inches of the surface of the sea.'

the northern end of the Strait of Georgia with the Pacific, and so confirmed that the region around Nootka was part of a large island. On 9 August the ships reached the ocean through Queen Charlotte Strait, where first the *Discovery* and then the *Chatham* ran aground on underwater reefs as their survey work took them dangerously close to the northern shore (*Ill.49*). As Vancouver extricated the ships and turned south along the oceanic coast of what would later be named Vancouver Island he was on a part of the coast already visited by British traders.

Among these had been Charles Duncan, who in this same month was seeking a way from Hudson Bay to the northwest coast through Chesterfield Inlet, but whose doomed attempt left him fifteen hundred miles short of his destination. In Vancouver's mind the season had been well spent, for the three months of survey work had proved that even if Juan de Fuca had discovered the great gulf named after him he had never made the voyage recounted by Michael Lok. This result Vancouver had expected, but the coast to the north, where many maps placed the entrance of Fonte's strait, remained to be explored.

For Vancouver and his crews, life followed an annual cycle: winter at Hawaii; summer spent in arduous small boat work along the northwest coast; and a call at Nootka for the promised further instructions that would guide Vancouver in his negotiations with the Spanish commandant there. The instructions never came, but the survey continued. In May 1793 Vancouver's ships returned to the northernmost point of their explorations of the previous year. This part of the coast, from latitude 52°N. northward, was even more intricate than the eastern shore of the Strait of Georgia, and it was often difficult to tell mainland from island; but it was in latitude 53°N. that the maps showed Fonte's Río los Reyes entering the sea. Parts of the coast had been visited the year before by Caamaño (and a copy of his chart had been given to Vancouver) as well as by British trading vessels, but Vancouver was insistent that his boat parties must continue to chart the coastline mile by mile, regardless of surveys made by other expeditions. By now the boats had been much improved, with canvas awnings and covers, and bags and lockers to keep the men's clothes dry. Even so, as Thomas Manby put it in his journal, the cold, wet weather 'gave the Blue Devils to everyone on board'. Vancouver's 388 place-names allocated during the voyage mostly follow conventional forms – royalty, the peerage, ministers and patrons, officers (and the occasional crew member from below decks) – but a few hint at something more heartfelt. There is Desolation Sound, Foulweather Bluff, Traitors Cove, Escape Island, Deception Passage, Destruction Island, Poison Cove, all of them reminders of dangers and hardships. One name never found its way onto the charts. Starve-Gut Cove was the unofficial name given by the crew of the *Chatham* to an anchorage in the elegantly-named Princess Royal Channel, a miserable spot marked by 'a constant torrent of Rain – Neither Fish nor Fowl, could be procured, or even a Nettle top gather'd to eat, with our salt Beef'.

As the season's work began in the Inside Passage, the mouth of a small river was passed just north of latitude 52°N. It was the Bella Coola, down which seven weeks later Alexander Mackenzie of the North West Company reached the coast after a dramatic overland journey from the interior. It was his second attempt to reach the Pacific, mounted after his earlier effort had taken him to the Arctic Ocean. Mackenzie and his party of *voyageurs* and Indians had wintered on the Peace River, and in the spring of 1793 became the first Europeans to reach the northern Rockies from the east. Men and canoe received a terrible battering from the seething waters and jagged rocks of Peace River Canyon, and although they managed to cross the continental divide a tangle of rivers, mountains and forests almost brought them to a halt. At the beginning of July they abandoned their canoe, and with 90lb packs on their backs, struggled towards the ocean on foot. Passed from one Indian guide to another they were brought down the Bella Coola River by canoe to the sea at a point in Dean Channel that Vancouver had reached on 5 June. By this time, Vancouver's ships had moved north, and he knew nothing of Mackenzie's arrival on the coast. The fur trader for his part heard from the local Indians about the recent visit of 'Macubah' in 'a large canoe', but was in no position to connect this sighting with

Vancouver's visit in the *Discovery*. Mackenzie was the first non-Native to cross the American continent north of Mexico, but he had come not by the navigable waterway envisaged by Pond, Dalrymple and others, but along perilous streams and difficult portages. As Mackenzie simply inscribed on a rock on the shoreline on 22 July 1793, he had come 'from Canada, by land'. It would be five hundred miles farther south, by way of the Columbia River, that the fur traders eventually found their route to the Pacific. For projectors dreaming of easy ways across the continent Mackenzie's hazardous journey was as disillusioning as Vancouver's meticulous surveys. As the navigator closed the last gaps in the coastline, so the fur trader experienced the difficulties of the overland approach, established the true distance between the Athabaska region and the Pacific, and revealed the harsh reality of the northern Rockies.

The latitude of Fonte's Río los Reyes was crossed by Vancouver's surveying parties without any sign of a river, and by the end of the season they had reached latitude 56°N. The season had been a hard one, with the boat crews suffering from exposure and hunger. As they inched their way north, so the mountain sides became more precipitous, and the fiords deeper and at times so narrow that the pines clinging to the cliffs brushed the sails of the ships. Much of the work was done in drenching rain, and Vancouver himself was ill for long stretches at a time, but his determination to carry on the survey with the same detailed accuracy with which he had begun it never faltered. Along one especially fractured stretch of coast the boat was away from the ship for twenty-three days, and charted seven hundred miles of shoreline – all this to advance knowledge of the mainland coast by a mere sixty miles. During the entire season the survey parties had advanced north by only three hundred miles, but for Vancouver the most important aspect of their work was that it had destroyed the credibility of the Fonte account, for they had found no river that corresponded in size or location with the description of Fonte's Río los Reyes. 'Unfortunately for the great ingenuity of its

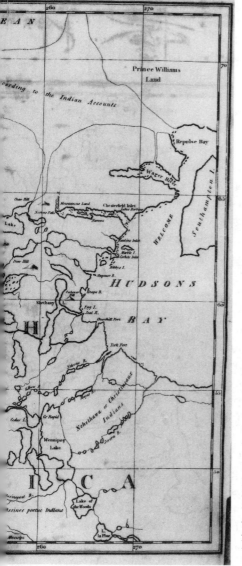

50. WILLIAM GOLDSON.
'Chart exhibiting the
Tracks of Maldonado and
De Fonte . . . compared
with the modern discover-
ies'. 1793.
British Library

This concoction showed a
colossal sea of Juan de Fuca
covering most of the pre-
sent-day state of Washington and the province of
British Columbia, linked
Fonte's rivers and lakes with
the discoveries of Hearne
and Pond, marked a huge
sea from 'the Indian
Accounts' which ran from
the northwest of Hudson
Bay to Hearne's Cop-
permine River, and finally
identified Prince William
Sound as the Strait of
Anian, sailed through by
Maldonado in 1588 and by
Fonte's Captain Barnarda in
1640.

hypothetical projectors', he wrote of the system of geography based on the Fonte account, 'our practical labours have thus far made it totter ... should the information we had thus obtained reached Europe, there would no longer remain a doubt as to the extent or the fallacy of the pretended discoveries'. One enthusiast in England, William Goldson, had not waited for news of Vancouver's findings before publishing in 1793 his *Observations on the Passage between the Atlantic and Pacific Oceans*. Together with its accompanying chart this was an example of speculative geography to end all speculative geography as it juggled the Indian reports of James Knight's day with the accounts of Fuca, Fonte and Maldonado (*Ill.50*).

Not all on the *Discovery* shared their commander's contempt for old accounts and theoretical geography. Archibald Menzies, the botanist, wished that one 'rivulet' (Vancouver's term for the Nass River) had been properly investigated because even if it were not the River Parmentier described by Fonte, Indian reports suggested that it extended far inland and Menzies thought that it 'might in the end turn out of the greatest utility to the commercial interest of our Colonies on the opposite side'. There was nothing in this, but the one serious blemish on Vancouver's survey was that he missed altogether, or failed to appreciate the importance of, the major rivers of the region: the Columbia, Fraser, Skeena and Stikine. His response, no doubt, would have been that his instructions forbade him from pursuing any inlet beyond the point where it was navigable for ocean-going ships. The botanist was prudent enough to confine his observations to the privacy of his journal (which he refused to hand to Vancouver at the end of the voyage), and there was no repetition of the events of Cook's last voyage, when the attention Cook paid to the differing opinions of his officers delayed his attempt to get north. Vancouver had been a midshipman on that voyage, and it may be that his witnessing of arguments on board the *Resolution* explains the inflexibility of his attitude once he was in command. In his published journal Vancouver paid tribute to the work of his officers; on the actual voyage relations were often strained. Vancouver was in failing health, for much of the time under stress through the responsibility of representing his country in the difficult negotiations at Nootka as well as conducting his meticulous survey. Men such as Whidbey, Johnstone and Menzies were as devoted as Vancouver to their particular tasks, whether it was surveying or collecting specimens, but they felt the rough edge of their captain's tongue when things went wrong. Cook had also shouted and stamped, but he was able to inspire loyalty, even affection, in a way that seemed to lie beyond Vancouver's reach.

The third season of the survey began with Cook's River, where Vancouver had been on Cook's *Resolution* sixteen years earlier. By late April 1794 in freezing weather the *Discovery* reached the point where Cook had turned back, hinting as he did so at the probability of a considerable inland navigation. Whidbey in the cutter made his way up the Turnagain and found it to be, not a river as Cook had supposed, but an inlet ending in a basin surrounded by snow-capped mountains. Vancouver himself explored the northern branch (Knik Arm). It was the last boat expedition that his health allowed him to make, and it ended almost as soon as it began when it became clear that this branch also was an inlet, not a river. Renaming this deep arm of the sea Cook's Inlet, Vancouver reflected that if Cook had spent one more day there he would have realised this for himself – and so 'spared the theoretical navigators, who have followed him in their closets, the task of ingeniously ascribing to this arm of the ocean . . . a north-west passage'. From there Prince William Sound was surveyed, not for the first time, for as well as Cook in 1778, Salvador Fidalgo's Spanish expedition had spent six weeks there in 1790. Then Yakutat Bay, Cross Sound and the coastline back to latitude 56°N. were charted. Deep in the recesses of Cross Sound the boat parties negotiated a channel that took them closer to the lakes of the interior than any other stretch of water, and Vancouver named it Lynn Canal after his birthplace of King's

Lynn. But this arm of the sea also ended in the towering range of mountains that had baulked all efforts to reach inland. As Vancouver explained to the Admiralty in words that for the first time revealed the extent of the Rocky Mountains: 'We have never been able to penetrate beyond the barrier of the lofty mountains, which, covered with eternal frost and snow, extend nearly in a connected chain, along the western border of the continent I believe, to its utmost Northern limits.' On 19 August 1794 the boats returned from their final survey, and an extra allowance of grog was served. Among the celebrations Vancouver wrote that 'no small portion of facetious mirth passed amongst the seamen, in consequence of our having sailed from old England on the *first of April*, for the purpose of discovering a north-west passage, by following up the discoveries of De Fuca, De Fonte, and a numerous train of hypothetical navigators'.

Three years of dogged survey work had seen little of the drama of Cook's season on the coast in 1778, when hopes of finding a passage into an open polar sea rose and fell almost from day to day. From the beginning of his own voyage, Vancouver seems to have been convinced that the reports of a great strait were groundless – probably invented by the Spaniards, he remarked more than once, so that they could claim the credit if a passage were ever found. His view was echoed in a sentence (later deleted) in the first draft of his official instructions: 'The discoveries of Captain Cook & of the later Navigators seem to prove that any actual Communication by Sea, such as has commonly been understood by the name of a North West passage cannot be looked for with any probability of success.' Vancouver saw his mission, not as an attempt to discover the passage but as one to prove, once and for all, that it did not exist. He found his satisfaction in carrying out a detailed survey of unprecedented extent, so accurate that many of his charts were still in use a century later (*Ill. 51*). More immediately, they enabled Vancouver to controvert and humiliate those who in their eagerness to find a northwest passage had belittled the achievements of his old commander. Triumph rather than dejection was the note struck in Vancouver's report from Nootka on the results of his three-year survey as he wrote that he and his crews were all in high spirits, 'having *finally determined* the nonexistence of any water communication between this & the opposite side of America'.

As was now its custom, the Admiralty made it clear to Vancouver on his return in October 1795 that it wished the events of his voyage to be made available 'for Publick information'. In wretched health, beset with money worries, harassed by an obnoxious but well-connected midshipman with whom he had fallen out on the voyage, Vancouver found the task of preparing his journal for publication a heavy burden, and in the end his brother John saw the final sections through the press. Vancouver died in May 1798, a few months before his published journal appeared. It was an impressive three-volume work containing half a million words of text, and was accompanied by a folio atlas of charts and views. By contrast, most of the surveys carried out by the Spanish expeditions on the northwest coast remained buried in the archives; so that it was Vancouver's charts, Vancouver's place-names and Vancouver's conclusions, that dominated public awareness in Europe of this phase of exploration.

Sailing twice with Cook, Vancouver had graduated in the most demanding of training schools. Like Cook, Vancouver treated the 'impediments' of ice, fog, tempest and reef with a seaman's respect, but they were not allowed to distract from the relentless determination to explore, survey and chart. The insistence on accuracy can be taken for granted, but there was more to the surveys than this. Several of those who had sailed with Cook inherited from him a sense of working and writing for posterity. At the end of his first voyage Cook, still only a

51. JOSEPH BAKER. 'A Chart showing part of the Coast of N.W. America'. 1798
Hydrographic Office

This chart showing the northwest coast from the Columbia River to the region north of Vancouver Island (here 'Quadra' and Vancouver's Island) is an example of the meticulous nature of the surveys carried out by the Vancouver expedition. Joseph Baker, who finished the voyage as first lieutenant on the *Discovery*, was responsible for preparing most of the charts on the voyage.

junior officer, proclaimed, 'I have exploard more of the Great South Sea than any that have gone before me, so much that little remains now to be done.' More than twenty years later, Vancouver showed similar self-confidence. As he sailed for the last time from Nootka, he summed up the results of his voyage with uncompromising, almost legalistic, finality:

> I trust the precision with which the survey of the coast of North West America has been carried into effect, will remove every doubt, and set aside every opinion of a north-west passage, or any water communication navigable for shipping, existing between the North Pacific, and the interior of the American continent, within the limits of our researches. The discovery that no such communication does exist has been zealously pursued, and with a degree of minuteness far exceeding the letter of my commission or instructions.

CONCLUSION

The surveys of the 1790s marked the end of an era; for after three centuries it was at last clear that no Northwest Passage existed that could provide a practicable route for sailing ships. Explorers had not found a passage because none existed in temperate latitudes, and this despite the imaginative efforts of geographers who had filled the unmapped spaces of the North American continent with an array of straits and inland seas. There is a rancorous edge to the satisfaction with which Vancouver and Malaspina disproved these fabrications of the 'closet navigators', the 'speculative fabricators', the 'purveyors of vague and improbable stories'. The role of geographers in stimulating interest in distant regions was ignored in the face of complaints about their uncritical approach, their lack of practical experience, their casual misdirection of explorers. Such strictures underestimated the importance of promotional geography in securing support for discovery ventures, and the difficulties under which cartographers laboured as they tried to make sense of the journals and charts in front of them. It is entirely understandable that navigators such as Cook, La Pérouse, Vancouver and Malaspina, with their insistence on making precise observations, often under the most adverse conditions, were outraged by the fanciful outlines of speculative geography; but not all possessed their regard for accuracy. Cook himself criticised fellow seamen who 'lay down the line of a Coast they have never seen and put down soundings where they have never sounded'. The emphasis on conflict between explorers and geographers has tended to obscure the other side of their relationship, that of mutual dependence and shared interests.

The explorers of the eighteenth century who searched for a navigable Northwest Passage were pursuing a phantom, but during their quest they uncovered much. Hopes of an open waterway to the north drew discovery ships to remote and inaccessible regions of North America, and when the search moved to the Pacific side of the continent long stretches of coastline from California to the Arctic were charted. As these seaborne surveys met the probes of overland explorers coming west across the continent, the way was opened to trade and settlement – and international rivalry. By the end of the eighteenth century it was clear that more than the sea-otter trade was at stake as the nationals of Spain, Russia, Britain and the United States jostled each other along the northwest coast. As a British cabinet minister explained to Parliament at the time of the Nootka Sound crisis in 1790, the contest was not 'for a few miles, but a large world'. There would be no Northwest Passage to provide easy access to that world, but explorers searching for it had revealed, for better or for worse, much of the North American continent to outside gaze.

The most daunting implication of the failure to find a passage in the eighteenth century was the realisation that if one existed it must lie far to the north among the ice-choked channels of the Arctic Ocean. After the ending of the Napoleonic Wars in 1815 Britain took up the quest again, for as John Barrow at the Admiralty put it, 'the discovery of a north-west passage to India and China has always been considered as an object peculiarly British'. Soon the search turned into a grim and protracted business, with ships wintering in the Arctic for two, three, even four, years. It was a matter of inching forward, of false leads, dead ends and ceaseless frustration. Despite all the dispiriting revelations, all the hardships and the deaths in long Arctic winters, the Northwest Passage still cast its spell. The quest became almost mystical in nature, beyond reasonable explanation. In 1850 Captain Robert McClure of the Royal Navy, who was searching for the lost Franklin expedition, reached by sledge Banks Island on the western edge of the Arctic Archipelago, and saw to the east the frozen surface of Melville Sound. McClure's ship the *Investigator* had come through Bering Strait from the Pacific; Melville Sound had been discovered by navigators pushing west from Baffin Bay. It was a crucial link in the chain of discovery. McClure had found the Northwest Passage, or at least *a* Northwest Passage, for time was to show that there was more than one tortuous route through the frozen archipelago of the north. It is a sign of how redundant the quest had now become in practical terms that although McClure could indicate a passage on his charts he and his contemporaries were unable to enter it. After three years trapped in the ice the *Investigator* was abandoned in 1853, and it was another year before her survivors reached England. The short cut between oceans had turned into a nightmarish labyrinth where men and ships might disappear without trace.

The first continuous navigation of the Northwest Passage was not accomplished for another half-century; and the route which Roald Amundsen followed in 1903–6 in the tiny *Gjøa* was a different one from that glimpsed by McClure. Nor was the Norwegian's four-year endurance test among Arctic ice what the eighteenth-century navigators, from James Knight to James Cook, had in mind when they sailed in search of the Northwest Passage. The prize they hoped to gain was the discovery of a practicable route for shipping which would change their own fortunes and those of their nation. It was their Philosopher's Stone, and in the end it proved just as elusive as that magic formula which had been sought in vain by generations of alchemists and speculators.

APPENDIX I

Voyages of the Imagination

=====

A. THE VOYAGE OF JUAN DE FUCA

B. THE VOYAGE OF BARTHOLOMEW
DE FONTE

C. THE VOYAGE OF LORENZO
FERRER MALDONADO

A. THE VOYAGE OF
JUAN DE FUCA

Michael Lok's account of the voyage of Juan de Fuca first appeared in Samuel Purchas, *Hakluytus Posthumus, or Purchas His Pilgrimes* (1625). This part of the text is taken from the 1906 Glasgow reprint, XIV, pp. 415–18. The second half of Lok's account, dealing with his unsuccessful efforts to bring Fuca to England, has been omitted.

A note made by me Michael Lok the elder, touching the Strait of Sea, commonly called Fretum Anian, in the South Sea, through the North-west passage of Meta Incognita.

When I was at Venice, in April 1596, happily arrived there an old man, about three-score yeares of age, called commonly Juan de Fuca, but named properly Apostolos Valerianos, of Nation a Greeke, borne in the Iland Cefalonia, of profession a Mariner, and an ancient Pilot of Shippes. This man being come lately out of Spaine, arrived first at Ligorno, and went thence to Florence in Italie, where he found one John Dowglas [Douglas], an Englishman, a famous Mariner, ready comming for Venice, to be Pilot of a Venetian Ship, named Ragasona for England, in whose company they came both together to Venice. And John Dowglas being well acquainted with me before, he gave me knowledge of this Greeke Pilot, and brought him to my speech: and in long talke and conference betweene us, in presence of John Dowglas: this Greeke Pilot declared in the Italian and Spanish languages, thus much in effect as followeth.

First he said, that he had bin the West Indies of Spaine by

the space of fortie yeeres, and had sailed to and from many places thereof, as Mariner and Pilot, in the service of the Spaniards.

Also he said, that he was in the Spanish Shippe, which in returning from the Ilands, Philippinas and China, towards Nova Spania, was robbed and taken at the Cape California, by Captain Candish [Cavendish] Englishman, whereby he lost sixtie thousand Duckets, of his owne goods.

Also he said, that he was Pilot of three small Ships which the Viceroy of Mexico sent from Mexico, armed with one hundred men, Souldiers, under a Captain, Spaniards, to discover the Straits of Anian, along the coast of the South-Sea, and to fortifie in that Strait, to resist the passage and proceedings of the English Nation, which were feared to passe through those Straits into the South Sea. And that by reason of a Mutinie which happened among the Souldiers, for the Sodomie of their Captaine, that Voyage was overthrown, and the Ships returned backe from California coast to Nova Spania, without any effect of thing done in that Voyage. And that after their returne, the Captaine was at Mexico punished by justice.

Also he said, that shortly after the said Voyage was so ill ended, the said Viceroy of Mexico, sent him out again Anno 1592. with a small Caravela, and a Pinnace, armed with Mariners onely, to follow the said Voyage, for discovery of the same Straits of Anian, and the passage thereof, into the Sea which they call the North Sea, which is our North-west Sea. And that he followed his course in that Voyage West and North-west in the South Sea, all alongst the coast of Nova Spania, and California, and the Indies, now called North America (all which Voyage hee signified to me in a great Map, and a Sea-card of mine owne, which I laied before him) untill hee came to the Latitude of fortie seven degrees, and that there finding that the Land trended North and North-east, with a broad Inlet of Sea, betweene 47. and 48. degrees of Latitude: hee entred thereinto, sayling therein more than twentie dayes, and found that Land trending still sometime North-west and North-east, and North, and also East and South-eastward, and very much broader Sea then was at the said entrance, and that hee passed by divers Ilands in that sayling. And that at the entrance of this said Strait, there is on the North-west coast thereof, a great Hedland or Iland, with an exceeding high Pinacle, or spired Rocke, like a piller thereupon.

Also he said, that he went on Land in divers places, and that he saw some people on Land, clad in Beasts skins; and that the Land is very fruitfull, and rich of gold, Silver, Pearle, and other things, like Nova Spania.

And also he said, that he being entred thus farre into the said Strait, and being come into the North Sea already, and finding the Sea wide enough every where, and to be about thirtie or fortie leagues wide in the mouth of the Straits, where hee entred; he thought he had now well discharged his office, and done the thing which he was sent to doe: and that he not being armed to resist the force of the Salvage people that might happen, hee therefore set sayle and returned homeward again towards Nova Spania, where hee arrived at Acapulco, Anno 1592. hoping to be rewarded greatly of the Viceroy, for this service done in this said Voyage.

Also he said, that after his comming to Mexico, hee was greatly welcomed by the Viceroy, and had great promises of great reward, but having sued there two yeares time, and obtained nothing to his content, the Viceroy told him, that he should be rewarded in Spaine of the King himself very greatly, and willed him therefore to goe into Spaine, which Voyage he did performe.

Also he said, that when he was come into Spaine, he was greatly welcomed there at the Kings Court, in wordes after the Spanish manner, but after long time of suite there also, hee could not get any reward there neither to his content. And that therefore at the length he stole out of Spaine, and came into Italie, to goe home againe and live among his owne Kindred and Countrimen, he being very old.

Also he said, that hee thought the cause of his ill reward had of the Spaniards, to bee for that they did understand very well, that the English Nation had now given over all their voyages for discoverie of the North-west passage, wherefore they need not feare them any more to come that way into the South Sea, and therefore they needed not his service therein any more.

Also he said, that in regard of this ill reward had of the

Spaniards, and understanding of the noble minde of the Queene of England, and of her warres maintayned so valiantly against the Spaniards, and hoping that her Majestie would doe him justice for his goods lost by Captaine Candish, he would be content to goe into England, and serve her Majestie in that voyage for the discoveries perfectly of the North-west passage into the South Sea, and would put his life into her Majesties hands to perform the same, if shee would furnish him with onely one ship of fortie tunnes burden and a Pinnasse, and that he would performe it in thirtie dayes time, from one end to the other of the Streights. And he willed me so to write into England . . .

B. THE VOYAGE OF
BARTHOLOMEW DE FONTE

The Fonte letter first appeared in two parts in *The Monthly Miscellany or Memoirs for the Curious* for April and June 1708, pp. 123–6 and pp. 183–6. *The Monthly Miscellany* was a short-lived periodical of serious intent edited by James Petiver, whose library included books of voyages and travels, but whose main interest was botany. No indication was given of the letter's provenance, and 'the Chart' to which readers were referred at the end of the account was not included. From Arthur Dobbs's *Account of Hudson's Bay* in 1744 onwards, the letter was reprinted, in whole or in part, and in several languages, at least nine times during the course of the century. About one-sixth of the text, dealing with the voyage from Lima to California, is omitted here. What appear to be editorial explanations, placed in the margin of the 1708 publication, are shown here inside square brackets.

A Letter from Admiral Bartholomew de Fonte, then Admiral of New Spain and Peru, and now Prince of Chili; giving an Account of the most material Transactions in a Journal of his from the Calo of Lima in Peru, on his Discoveries to find out if there was any North West Passage from the Atlantick Ocean into the South and Tartarian Sea.

The Viceroys of New Spain and Peru, having advice from the Court of Spain, that the several Attempts of the English, both in the Reigns of Queen Elizabeth, King James, and of Capt. Hudson and Capt. James, in the 2nd, 3rd and 4th Years of King Charles, was in the 14th Year of the said King Charles, A.D.1639, undertaken from some Industrious Navigators from Boston in New England, upon which I Admiral de Fonte received Orders from Spain and the Viceroys to Equip four Ships of Force, and being ready we put to Sea the 3rd of April 1640, from the Calo of Lima, I Admiral Bartholomew de Fonte in the Ship St. Spiritus, the Vice-Admiral Don Diego Pennelossa, in the Ship St. Lucia, Pedro de Bonardae, in the Ship Rosario, Philip de Ronquillo in the King Philip ... Admiral de Fonte with the other 3 Ships sailed from them within the Islands Chamily the 10th of May 1640. and having the length of Cape Abel, on the w.s.w. side of California in 26 Degrees of N.Latitude, 160 Leagues N.W. and W. from the Isles of Chamily; the Wind sprung up at S.S.E. a steady Gale, that from the 26th of May to the 14th of June, he had sail'd to the River los Reyes in 53 Degrees of N.Latitude, not having occasion to lower a Topsail, in sailing 866 Leagues N.N.W. 410 Leagues from Port Abel to Cape Blanco, 456 Leagues to Riolos Reyes, all the time most pleasant weather, and sailed about 260 Leagues in crooked Channels, amongst Islands named the Archipelago de St. Lazarus [So named by de Fonte, he being the first that made that Discovery]; where his Ships Boats always sail'd a mile a head, sounding to see what Water, Rocks and Sands there was.

The 22nd of June, Admiral Fonte dispatch'd one of his Captains Pedro de Barnarda to sail up a fair River, a gentle Stream and deep Water, went first N. and then N.E.N. and N.W. into a large Lake full of Islands, and one very large Peninsula full of Inhabitants, a Friendly honest People in this Lake; he named Lake Valasco, where Capt. Barnarda left his Ship; nor all up the River was less than 4, 5, 6, 7 and 8 fathom Water, both the Rivers and Lakes abounding with Salmon Trouts, and very large white Pearch, some of them two foot long; and with 3 large Indian Boats, by them called Periagos, made of two large Trees 50 and 60 foot long, Capt. Barnarda first sailed from his Ships in the Lake Velasco, one hundred and forty Leagues West, and then 436 E.N.E. to 77 Degrees of Latitude.

Admiral de Fonte, after he had dispatch'd Captain Barnarda on the Discovery of the North and East part of the Tartarian Sea, the Admiral sail'd up a very Navigable River, which he named Riolos Reyes, that run nearest North East, but on several Points of the Compass 60 Leagues at low Water, in a fair Navigable Channel, not less than 4 or 5 Fathoms Water. It flow'd in both Rivers near the same Water, in the River los Reyes, 24 foot Full and Change of the Moon; a s.s.e. Moon made high Water. It flow'd in the River de Haro 22 foot and a half Full and Change. They had two Jesuits [One of those that went with Capt. Barnarda on his Discovery] with them that had been on their Mission to the 66 Degrees of North Latitude, and had made curious Observations. The Admiral de Fonte received a Letter from Captain Barnarda, dated the 27th of June, 1640. that he had left his Ship in the Lake Valasco, betwixt the Island Barnarda and the Peninsula Conihasset, a very safe Port; it went down a River from the Lake, 3 Falls, 80 Leagues, and fell into the Tartarian Sea in 61 Degrees, with the Pater Jesuits and 36 Natives in three of their Boats, and 20 of his Spanish Seamen; that the Land trended a way North East; that they should want no Provisions, the Country abounding with Venison of 3 sorts, and the Sea and Rivers with excellent Fish (Bread, Salt, Oyl and Brandy they carry'd with them) that he should do what was possible. The Admiral, when he received the Letter from Captain Barnarda, was arrived at an Indian Town called Conosset, on the South-side the Lake Belle, where the two Pater Jesuits on their Mission had been two Years; a p[l]easant Place. The Admiral with his two Ships, enter'd the Lake the 22nd of June, an Hour before high Water, and there was no Fall or Catract, and 4 or 5 Fathom Water, and 6 or 7 generally in the Lake Belle, there is a little fall of Water till half Flood, and an Hour and a quarter before high Water the Flood begins to set gently into the Lake Belle; the River is fresh at 20 Leagues distance from the Mouth, or Entrance of the River los Reyes. The River and Lake abounds with Salmon, Salmon-Trouts, Pikes, Perch and Mullets, and two other sorts of Fish peculiar to that River, admirable good, and Lake Belle; also abounds with all those sorts of Fish large and delicate; and Admiral de Fonte says, the

Mullets catch'd in Rios Reyes and Lake Belle, are much delicate than are to be found, he believes, in any part of the World.

JUNE

We concluded with giving an Account of a Letter from Capt. Barnarda, dated the 27th of June, 1640. on his Discovery in the Lake Valasco. The first of July 1640, Admiral de Fonte sailed from the rest of his Ships in the Lake Belle, in a good Port cover'd by a fine Island before the Town Conosset from thence to a River I named Parmentiers, in honour of my Industrious Judicious Comrade, Mr Parmentiers, who had most exactly mark'd every thing in and about that River; we pass'd 8 Falls, in all 32 foot, perpendicular from its Sourse out of Belle; it falls into the large Lake I named Lake de Fonte, at which place we arrived the 6th of July. This Lake is 160 Leagues long and 60 broad, the Length is E.N.E. and W.S.W. to 20 or 30, in some places 60 Fathom deep; the Lake abounds with excellent Cod and Ling, very large and well fed, there are several very large Islands and 10 small ones; they are covered with shrubby Woods, the Moss grows 6 or 7 foot long, with which the Moose, a very large sort of Deer, are fat with in the Winter, and other lesser Deer, as Fallow, &c. There are abundance of wild Cherries, Strawberries, Hurtle-berries, and wild Currants, and also of wild Fowl, Heath Cocks and Hens, likewise Partridges and Turkeys, and Sea Fowl in great plenty on the South side; the Lake is a very large fruitful Island, had a great many Inhabitants, a very excellent Timber, as Oaks, Ashes, Elms and Fur-Trees, very large and tall.

The 14th of July we sailed out of the E.N.E. end of the Lake de Fonte, and pass'd a Lake I named Estricho de Ronquillo, 34 Leagues long, 2 or 3 Leagues broad, 20, 26, and 28 Fathom of Water; we pass'd this strait in 10 hours, having a stout Gale of Wind and whole Ebb. As we sailed more Easterly, the Country grew very sensibly worse, as it is in the North and South parts of America, from [latitude] 36 to the extream Parts North and South, the West differs not only in Fertility but in Temperature of Air, at least 10 Degrees, and it is warmer on the West side than on the East, as the best Spanish Discoverers found it, whose business it was in the time of the Emperor Charles the V. to Phillip the III. as is noted by Aloares and a Costa and Mariana, &c.

The 17ᵗʰ we came to an Indian Town, and the Indians told our Interpreter Mr Parmentiers, that a little way from us lay a great Ship where there had never been one before; we sailed to them, and found only one Man advanced in years, and a Youth; the Man was the greatest Man in the Mechanical Parts of the Mathematicks I had ever met with; my second Mate was an English Man, an excellent Seaman, as was my Gunner, who had been taken Prisoners at Campechy, as well as the Master's Son; they told me the Ship was of New England, from a Town called Boston. The Owner and the whole Ships Company came on board the 30ᵗʰ, and the Navigator of the Ship, Capt. Shapley, told me, his Owner was a fine Gentleman, and Major General of the largest Colony in New England, called the Mastechusets; so I received him like a Gentleman, and told him, my Commission was to make Prize of any People seeking a North West or West Passage into the South Sea, but I would look upon them as Merchants trading with the Natives for Bevers, Otters, and other Furs and Skins, and so for a small Present of Provisions I had no need of, I gave him my Diamond Ring, which cost me 1200 Pieces of Eight, (which the modest Gentleman received with difficulty) and having given the brave Navigator, Capt. Shapley for his fine Charts and Journals, 1000 Pieces of Eight, and the Owner of the Ship, Scimor Gibbons a quarter Cask of good Peruan Wine, and the 10 Seamen each 20 Pieces of Eight, the 6ᵗʰ of August, with as much Wind as we could fly before, and a Currant, we arrived at the first Fall of the River Parmentiers, the 11ᵗʰ of August, 86 Leagues, and was on the South Side of the Lake Belle on board our Ships the 16ᵗʰ of August, before the fine Town Conosset, where we found all things well; and the honest Natives of Conosett had in our absence treated our People with great humanity, and Capt. de Ronquillo answer'd their Civility and Justice.

The 20ᵗʰ of August an Indian brought me a Letter to Conosset on the Lake Belle, from Capt. Barnarda, dated the 11ᵗʰ of August, where he sent me word he was returned from his Cold Expedition, and did assure me there was no Communication out of the Spanish or Atlantick Sea, by Davis Strait; for the Natives had conducted one of his Seamen to the head of Davis Strait, which terminated in a fresh Lake of about 30 Miles in circumference, in the 80ᵗʰ Degree of North Latitude; and that there was prodigious Mountains North of it, besides the North West from that Lake, the Ice was so fix'd, that from the Shore to 100 Fathom Water, for ought he knew from the Creation; for Mankind knew little of the wonderful Works of God, especially near the North and South Poles; he writ further, that he had sailed from Basset Island North East, and East North East, and North East and by East, to the 79ᵗʰ Degree of Latitude, and then the Land trended North, and the Ice rested on the Land. I received afterwards a second Letter from Capt. Barnarda, dated from Minhanset, informing me, that he made the Port of Arena, 20 Leagues up the River los Reyes the 29ᵗʰ of August, where he waited my Commands. I having a store of good Salt Provisions, of Venison and Fish, that Capt. de Ronquillo had salted (by my order) in my absence, and 100 Hogsheads of Indian Wheat or Mais, sailed the 2ⁿᵈ of September 1640. accompanied with many of the honest Natives of Conosset, and the 5ᵗʰ of September in the Morning about 8, was at an Anchor betwixt Arena and Mynhanset, in the River los Reyes, sailing down that River to the North East part of the South Sea; after that returned home, having found that there was no Passage into the South Sea by that they call the North West Passage. The Chart will make this much more demonstrable.

Tho the Style of the foregoing Peice is not altogether so Polite, (being writ like a Man, whose livelihood depended on another way) but with abundance of Experience and a Traveller, yet there are so many Curious, and hitherto unknown Discoveries, that it was thought worthy of a place in these Memoirs; and 'tis humbly presum'd it will not be unacceptable to those who have either been in those Parts, or will give themselves the trouble of reviewing the Chart.

END

C. THE VOYAGE OF
LORENZO FERRER MALDONADO

The Maldonado account first appeared in the form of a memorial to the Spanish crown in 1609. A version was found in the collection of the Duque de Infantado in Spain in 1781, and a copy made for the Real Academia de la Historia. In 1788 this was examined by the Duque de Almodóvar in his *Historia política delos establecimientos ultramarinos de las Naciones Europeas*, IV (Madrid, 1788). The following year another copy of the memorial was found in the Archive of the Indies in Seville by José Espinosa, who passed it on to Malaspina. It seems to have been this version that found its way to Paris, where it became the subject of a paper presented to the Académie des Sciences by Philippe Buache de la Neuville in November 1790. A copy of this was sent by the Spanish government to Malaspina with orders to search for the entrance of Maldonado's strait along the Alaskan coast. The most reliable English translation of the account is by Henry Raup Wagner, published in 'Apocryphal Voyages to the Northwest Coast of America', *Proceedings of the American Antiquarian Society*, New Series, XLI (1931), pp.219–28. The text below is a shortened version of Wagner's, with some of the preliminary and other material omitted.

Account of the discovery of the Strait of Anian made by me Captain Lorenzo Ferrer Maldonado in 1588, and in which he sets forth the course of the voyage, the disposition of the site, the method of fortifying it, the benefits of this navigation, and the resulting harm if it be not followed.

You leave from Spain, let us suppose from Lisbon. From there it is advisable to steer northwest for 450 leagues until you reach 60° north latitude where the island of Frislandia [Iceland], anciently known as Tyle or Tule, will come into sight. It is an island but little smaller than Ireland. From there you take a westerly course running along the sixtieth parallel for 180 leagues until you reach Labrador, where the Strait of Labrador or Davis Strait commences . . . you must steer northwest, entering by this strait for eighty leagues until you reach a short 64° of latitude. There the strait takes another bend to the north for 120 leagues until it reaches 72° of latitude. It then turns and makes another bend to the northwest. Through this you have to sail ninety leagues until you reach a little short of 75°. At the end of this you have passed the Strait of Labrador, which commences at 60° and ends at 75°, and is 290 leagues long . . .

Having emerged from the Strait of Labrador you commence to fall down from that latitude and, sailing west a quarter southwest for 350 leagues, you will reach 71°. This is where we discovered a very high land on our return voyage without being able to ascertain whether it was mainland or island. However, if it was mainland, it must be the opposite coast of New Spain. From this land, seen in 71°, you have to sail westsouthwest for 440 leagues to fall down to 60° where the Strait of Anian is to be found . . . According to the account just given it seems to be 450 leagues from Spain to Frislandia, from there to Labrador 180, to the exit of the strait of that name 290, or altogether 920 leagues. These added to the 790 which we found from the northern exit of the Strait of Labrador to the Strait of Anian make 1710 leagues, that is, the distance from Spain to the Strait of Anian.

The weather was very severe when we made our exit from the Strait of Labrador, as it was the beginning of March, having navigated the strait for part of February. Thus we endured the greatest hardships of darkness, cold and storm. The day was short during all that period and the cold so great that the sea water which dashed against the sides of the ship froze, so that the ship seemed to be made of crystal and made it necessary to chop off the ice, which was growing to such an extent that at times we found it to be more than a palm thick . . . When, however, we returned through the Strait of Labrador in the month of June and part of July we always enjoyed continued light, so much so that when we reached the Arctic Circle in 66° we commenced to have permanent sun. This was never covered by the horizon until we again cut the Circle in the middle of the Strait of Labrador. Thus the continuance of the sun above the horizon heated the air so that it gave us more heat than is to be found in the hottest part of Spain, although this was not because the rays of the sun were burdensome when we exposed ourselves to them. We always had free winds from the north with which exit from the Strait of Labrador was effected easily and quickly. True it is that the great currents there of flux and reflux give much aid in entering and leaving, although the winds may be contrary. On the journey from Spain to Anian it is necessary to take advantage of the tide, because the winds from the north are very continuous. With this account, that of the courses in this navigation and of the methods of conducting it, is concluded.

The strait we discovered in 60° of latitude, 1710 leagues from Spain, appears, according to ancient tradition to be the one the cosmographers name 'Anian' on their maps. If this be true it follows necessarily that the strait is formed on one side by Asia and on the other by America. This seems to be the case from the following array of facts. After we had disembogued in the Great [South] Sea we went coasting along the American side southeast for more than 100 leagues until we reached 55°. On this coast no settlement was found nor any inlet from the sea, thus furnishing an indication that there was not another strait which could isolate that part by connecting the South Sea with the North Sea [Atlantic]. It was therefore concluded that all that coast was America, and that by following along it one could shortly reach Quivira and Cabo Mendocino. We left this part which, as just stated, we understood carried on, and turning towards the west sailed four days with a wind estimated to carry us thirty leagues in a day's journey. Having sailed 120 leagues according to this reckoning and to our estimated positions on the map (although we did not have any of that sea), we discovered a very great country and grand sierras with a long continuous coastline. We kept away from this, as was advisable in view of our purposes, always giving ourselves plenty of sea room and steering at times northeast at others north-northeast and at others north. From this it seemed to us that the coast on the whole ran northeast-southwest. We were not able to obtain any particular information about it as we were giving it so much room, and therefore I can simply affirm that it contains some settlements to very near the strait, because many smokes were seen to rise in many parts. Thus according to good cosmography it seemed to us to be the country of the Tartars, or Catai, and that a few leagues from the coast must be the great city of Cambalu, the metropolis of the great Tartar. Finally, following along this coast, we found ourselves at the entrance of the Strait of Anian itself, from which fifteen days previously we had made our exit into the Great Sea, which we recognized as that of the South Sea, in which are located Japan, China, the Malucas, India and New Guinea with the discovery of Captain Quiros, and all the coast of New Spain and Peru.

There is a port at the outlet of the strait into the South Sea on the American side capable of holding 500 ships, although in a certain part it is rough and the anchorage is bad, because of the currents which enter the mouth of it during the tide, which runs from north to south ... although this country is in 59° of latitude it has a very mild climate, as all that part on the south side, and which is sheltered and defended by the mountains to the north of it, is very temperate. The cold in winter is not excessive but very moderate, as it is always open to the rays of the sun and free from the north wind. When the winds blow they are only from the south. These are always mild and the more so because they come across the sea which is what customarily warms the air ... The part on the side of Asia and Tartary fronting this contains some very high mountains, so high that in some places at their greatest elevation they carry snow all the year, particularly those which face the north. They are so mountainous, rough and cragged that it seems impossible to traverse them. The greater part of the trees are very high pine trees which grow even down to the banks of the sea. On the same side of Asia in front of the entrance to the port there is a quiet place of sea water where there is a large marsh of reeds which grow out of the water. Near this we found the best fishing in all these parts. Many fish were caught there, some well known, such as sea-bass, conger-eels, sole and other similar fish, although larger than are found here. At times very large fish were seen passing on their way from the South Sea to the North Sea; among them whales, *buffadores*, and other very large monsters were recognized. It appeared that the reason for their making this journey was that they were leaving the warm waters of the South Sea, as it was now the beginning of summer, to enjoy the fresh waters of the North Sea.

The Strait of Anian is fifteen leagues long and you can easily pass through it with a tide, which lasts for six hours, as these tides are exceptionally strong there. In this length it has six bends, and its two mouths of entrance and exit look the one to the other on a north-south line, I mean, one is north-south of the other. The mouth on the north side, which is the one by which we entered, is less than a quarter of a league wide and on each side has two steep rocks. The one on the side of Asia is higher and steeper than the other, so much so, that it furnishes beneath it such shelter that nothing that falls from the top could strike the foot of it. The outlet to the South Sea close to the port is more than a quarter of a league wide and from there on both the coasts keep on widening and opening out. In the middle of the strait at the end of the third bend there is a great *peñon*, or island or steep rock, three *estados* high, more or less, and, as it is of a round shape, shows it diameter to be about 200 paces. Looking at it from a distance it seems to be but little removed from the mainland of Asia but everything is shoals and reefs and cannot be navigated except with boats. That part, however, from the island to the mainland in front of it on the American side is less than one-half of a quarter of a league wide. Although the channel is so deep that two vessels and even three can pass through it together, towards the banks it has shoals over which two bastions can easily be raised and built, thus narrowing the channel to the width of a musket shot. On the island, or over the shoals which can be raised, and on the coast opposite two bastions can be made as stated, which with artillery can guard and defend the strait very securely. If the currents were not so strong a chain might be put across which would be of great service, although now one could be made with such industry that it could sustain and resist the currents.

The strait is so disposed that with three lookouts which can see each other, thirty leagues in the North Sea can be overlooked. If they discover ships they can give notice to the bastions and to the fort at the port with smokes so as to prevent their passage if they should be hostile. Two ships kept ready in the port for similar needs could lie to between the two bastions (for all of which there would be time on the supposition that whoever wished to enter would have to await the tide), and there entertain and embarrass the enemies' ships, while the bastions cannonaded them and sent them to the bottom, because it is to be understood, as stated, that although many enemy vessels may come, no more than two or three can pass through the channel [together]. If it should be thought advisable to keep a watch on the South Sea, (although I do not think this necessary at present), the strait has two high mountains, one on the side of Asia and one on the side of America which face each other and both face the fort and the sentinels. These overlook both coasts, each the opposite one, and can give notice of all the vessels sighted in the South Sea, so as to enable the precautions mentioned to be taken. Thus this strait will be defended and only the Spaniards can navigate it with entire security and enjoy the great utilities which it promises. Truly, I do not know what place there is in all the discovered world which like this has connection with almost all the lands in the world, as from here you can sail to all of them. It may therefore be presumed that the time will come to make there a very large and rich settlement.

The entrance to the strait on the north side is difficult to recognize because of the coast which trends from east to west, and because one of the two sides which form it covers the other. The entrance and the first bend trend northeast-southwest and cannot be seen from the sea outside. For this reason it is not to be wondered at that those who have searched for it have not found it. When we reached it we did not recognize it for some days and were tacking along the coast, although we had a very good account of Juan Martinez, my pilot, a Portuguese, native of Algarve, a very old man of great experience. The landmarks of those mountains, which I took and have painted in order to make a second voyage, if offered me as I thought it would be, were however lacking. Although we knew we had to find it in 60° of latitude we were in such doubts about it, as that coast extends a long distance from east to west, that it seemed to the pilot that we had not come within 100 leagues of it according to the reckoning of his course. To me it seemed that we were already off it. Such was the case because, embarking in a shallop to follow the shore, the current itself carried me into the strait and thus it was recognized . . .

In the port where our ship anchored (which is the one stated to have been at the mouth of the strait on the south side) we remained from the beginning of April to the beginning of June. During this time a great ship of more than 800 tons came to pass from the side of the South Sea into the strait. This caused us to put ourselves under arms, but each party taking on a peaceful attitude their people took pleasure in giving us some of the things they carried for cargo and for trade. This was much; all, or the greater part of it, consisted of things known to be similar to those of China, such as brocades, silks, porcelains, feathers, boxes, stones, pearls and gold. The men appeared to be Hanseatic, those inhabiting the Bahia de San Nicolas or the Puerto de San Miguel. In order to understand them better it was necessary for us to talk Latin, that is those who knew it, as many of them knew how to speak it. They did not seem to be Catholics but Lutherans. They said they came from a large city a little more than 100 leagues from the strait. Although I do not remember its name well, it seems to me they called it "Roba" or some name like that. They said it was a very large port and there was a navigable river, subject to the Great Khan (since they said it was of Tartary), and that they had left another vessel of their own country in the port. We could obtain no more information about these people as they always acted with caution and displayed little confidence, being afraid of our men. For this reason we separated and having left them near the strait in the North Sea we came back in the direction of Spain. It is greatly to be believed that they were Hanseatics, because as these live in 72° of latitude it is easy and fitting for them to make use of this strait and navigation.

APPENDIX II

Sources

ABBREVIATIONS

Adm	Admiralty Records, PRO
ADM	Admiralty Records, NMM
AMAE	Archives du Ministère des Affaires Etrangères, Paris
BL	British Library
Burney	Burney Newspaper Collection, BL
CO	Colonial Office Records, PRO
DCB	*Dictionary of Canadian Biography*
HBC	Hudson's Bay Company Archives (Provincial Archives of Manitoba), Winnipeg
IOR	India Office Records, BL
MN	Museo Naval, Madrid
NMM	National Maritime Museum, Greenwich
PRO	Public Record Office, Kew
PRONI	Public Record Office of Northern Ireland, Belfast
RS	Royal Society, London
SP	State Papers, PRO
WSL	William Salt Library, Stafford

For printed books the place of publication is London unless otherwise stated.

GENERAL

The subject of the Northwest Passage has produced a literature overwhelming in quantity and variable in quality. Two essential reference works are Alan Cooke and Clive Holland, *The Exploration of Northern Canada 500 to 1920: A Chronology* (Toronto, 1978), which lists all known voyages in search of the Northwest Passage, and Clive Holland, *Arctic Exploration and Development, c.500 xb.c. to 1915: An Encyclopedia* (New York, 1994), which takes a wider approach, both regionally and in subject-matter. Most of the accounts of the sixteenth- and early seventeenth-century voyages have been published by the Hakluyt Society: among those most relevant to this book are G.M. Asher, ed., *Henry Hudson the Navigator* (1860); C.R. Markham, ed., *The Voyages of William Baffin 1612–1627* (1881); and Miller Christy, ed., *The Voyages of Captain Luke Foxe of Hull, and Captain Thomas James of Bristol* (1894). A splendid essay on the search in this early period is by D.B. Quinn, 'The Northwest Passage in Theory and Practice', in J.L. Allen, ed., *North American Exploration*, I, *A New World Disclosed* (Lincoln, Nebraska, 1997), pp.292–343. Extensive documentary selections are contained in D.B. Quinn, Alison Quinn and Susan Hillier, eds, *New American World: A Documentary History of North America to 1612* (5 vols., 1979). For a good balance of text and commentary, supplemented by numerous illustrations and maps, which sets the search for a northern passage in the context of North American exploration more generally, W.P. Cumming *et al.*, *The Discovery of North America* (1971), and *The Exploration of North America* (1974), take the story to the late eighteenth century. William Goetzmann and Glyndwr Williams, *The Atlas of North American Exploration: From the Norse Voyages to the Race to the Pole* (1992, 1998, Norman, Oklahoma) uses both contemporary and modern maps to illustrate its subject-matter. The standard work on the Hudson's Bay Company, whose activities loom large in the story of the Northwest Passage in the eighteenth century, remains E.E. Rich, *The History of the Hudson's Bay Company 1670–1870* (2 vols, 1958, 1961). Glyndwr Williams, *The British Search for the Northwest Passage in the Eighteenth Century* (1962) was among the first to make full use of the Company's records in this context, and to bring together explorations both in Hudson Bay and along the Pacific coast of North America. A recent collection of essays that covers the exploration of the continent from the late seventeenth century to the end of the eighteenth century, and is especially strong on the French explorers, is J.L. Allen, ed., *North American Exploration*, II, *A Continent Defined* (Lincoln, Nebraska, 1997). Finally, there are two excellent single-volume works on the Northwest Passage which concentrate on the search in the nineteenth century, Pierre Berton, *The Arctic Grail: The Quest for the Northwest Passage and the North Pole 1818–1909* (Toronto, 1988), and Ann Savours, *The Search for the North West Passage* (1999), which has three introductory chapters on the search from the sixteenth to the eighteenth centuries.

CHAPTER 1: *Dead Man's Island: The Doomed Voyage of James Knight*

There are short but authoritative biographies of the main personalities who feature in this chapter – James Knight, Henry Kelsey, William Stuart, Thanadelthur, George Barlow (Berley), David Vaughan, William Scroggs – in DCB, II, 1701–1740 (Toronto and Quebec, 1969). The French stay at York Factory is described in Nicolas Jérémie, *Twenty Years of York Factory 1694–1714*, translated from the French edition of 1720 with notes and introduction by R. Douglas and J.N. Wallace (Ottawa, 1926). Knight's voluminous journals during his years as Governor at York Factory have never been published: they are in HBC B 239/a/1–5. His letters and those of his successor, Kelsey, are in HBC B 239/b/1–3. Minutes of the London Committee of the Hudson's Bay Company relating to the Knight expedition are in HBC A 1/117, fos.12v, 17v, 24v; other material is in HBC A 15/6, pp.183–98; HBC A 15/7, p.34; HBC A 14/7, p.110. The map drawn by Knight from Northern Indian information is classified as HBC G 1/19; an analysis of it is included in Richard I. Ruggles, *A Country So Interesting: The Hudson's Bay Company and Two Centuries of Mapping 1670–1870* (Montreal & Kingston, 1991), pp.30–1.

Sailing orders for the expedition of 1719 and other references to it are in HBC A 6/4, fos.32v, 38v, 49v. A short account of the disastrous voyage of Jens Munk was in print during Knight's lifetime in Awnsham and John Churchill, *A Collection of Voyages and Travels*, Vol II (1704), pp. 472–6. Scroggs's manuscript journal has disappeared, but there is a long extract from it in Clerk of the *California, An Account of a Voyage for the Discovery of a North-West Passage by Hudson's Streights*, Vol II (1749), pp. 174–80. A shorter version is in Arthur Dobbs, *Remarks upon Capt.Middleton's Defence* (1744), pp.112–18, reprinted in William Barr and Glyndwr Williams, *Voyages to Hudson Bay in Search of a Northwest Passage 1741–1747*, Vol I, *The Voyage of Christopher Middleton 1741–1742* (1994), pp. 58–62. This version includes Middleton's recollections of the Scroggs voyage. A slightly different account of the Scroggs voyage, and of the relics he found on Marble Island, is in an anonymous pamphlet in the British Library (10460 d.26), *A Description of the Coast, Tides, and Currents, in Button's Bay* [1745]. Newspaper entries on Knight and his plans are in *Saturday's Post*, 22 November, 20 December 1718, 6 June 1719 (Burney). Other references to the voyage are in a book, highly critical of the Hudson's Bay Company, Joseph Robson, *An Account of Six Years Residence in Hudson's-Bay* (1752), p.15, and Appendix, p.37. The journals of Luke Foxe and Thomas James have been printed in Christy, *Voyages of Foxe and James*.

Details of the discovery of the wreck site on Marble Island are given in Joseph Stevens' log of the *Success* sloop for 1767, HBC 42/a/69, and in Magnus Johnston's log of the *Churchill* sloop, HBC 42/a/68. Hearne's later recollections were contained in the Introduction to his journal, *A Journey from Prince of Wales's Fort in Hudson's Bay to the Northern Ocean* (1795). Ian S. Maclaren has scrutinised the reliability of Hearne's published journal in 'Samuel Hearne's Accounts of the Massacre at Bloody Fall, 17 July 1771', in *A Review of International English Literature*, 22 (1991), pp. 25–51. There are details of the investigations carried out at Marble Island in 1970 and 1971 in a series of articles in *The Musk-Ox*: Ralph Smith and William Barr, 'Marble Island: a search for the Knight expedition', No. 8 (1971); Ralph Smith, 'Discovery of one of James Knight's ships at Marble Island', No. 9 (1971); W. Gillies Ross and William Barr, 'Voyages in Northwestern Hudson Bay (1720–1771) and discovery of the Knight relics on Marble Island', No.11 (1972); and in *The Beaver*: Ralph Smith, 'Relics of James Knight', *The Beaver* (Spring 1972), pp.36–41, and Walter Zacharchuk, 'The House that Knight Built', *The Beaver* (Autumn 1973), pp. 12–15. John Geiger and Owen Beattie describe their field work on Marble Island in their important study of the Knight expedition and its fate, *Dead Silence: the Greatest Mystery in Arctic Discovery* (1993). Thomas James's description of winter conditions is contained in Christy, *The Voyages of Foxe and James*. Richard Norton's journal entry of 13 June 1725 on the sighting of a ship's boat is in HBC B 42/a/5, fo.24d.-25; I owe this reference to the researches of O.J.Luchak, William Barr and Judith Beattie. James Walker's journal of the *Churchill* sloop for 1753 is in HBC 42/a/41. Moses Norton's journal at Prince of Wales Fort, Churchill, for 1765, containing references to the testimony of the two Inuit youths, is in HBC 42/a/64. Nineteenth-century Inuit memories of Frobisher's expeditions are scattered through Charles Francis Hall, *Life with the Esquimaux* (2 vols, 1864). The reference by Francis Smith to a possible son of one of Knight's crew living among the Inuit, and descriptions by Henry Ellis and the clerk of the *California* of the two non-Inuit men they saw at Wager Bay, are printed in Barr and Williams, *Voyages*, II, pp. 115–16, 271, 291.

CHAPTER 2: *A Passage to California*

Desmond Clarke, *Arthur Dobbs Esquire 1689–1765: Surveyor General of Ireland, Prospector and Governor of North Carolina* (1958) sets Dobbs's interest in the Northwest Passage in the context of his general political career. Several manuscript copies exist of Dobbs's Memorial of 1731: one in PRONI: D.O.D. 162/25; one addressed to Frederick, Prince of Wales, in the Library of the Hunterian Museum, Glasgow (MS Hunter 434); a slightly shorter and earlier version in the John Carter Brown Library (Codex Eng 15); and two in the Archives of the Hudson's Bay Company (HBC E 18/1). Substantial extracts from the latter are printed in Barr and Williams, *Voyages*, Vol. I, pp.9–36. PRONI D.2092 contains eighteen private (and revealing) letters written by Dobbs to Judge Michael Ward between 1734 and 1748, most of which contain references to the Northwest Passage campaign. Dobbs's first encounters with the Hudson's Bay Company, his negotiations with Christopher Middleton and Sir Charles Wager, and Middleton's encounters with government ministers are covered in Arthur Dobbs, *Remarks upon Capt. Middleton's Defence* (1744), mostly in the form of exchanges of letters. Examples of the Company's policy of secrecy are to be found in HBC A 6/5, fo.56 and HBC A 6/6, fos.83, 110 (restrictions on correspondence by Company servants); HBC A 1/33, fo.77d. (Company's charter not to be disclosed); *A Compleat Guide to London* (1740) (lists Lake only as director of the Royal African Company). A copy of the charter of the Hudson's Bay Company was printed in *Report from the Committee Appointed to Inquire into the State and Conditions of the Countries Adjoining to Hudson's Bay, and of the Trade carried on there* (1749), Appendix I. Richard Norton's instructions of 1736 are in HBC A 6/5, fos.108–9; his account of the disappointing voyage of 1737 is in HBC A 11/13, fos.35, 40. For the voyage of Captain William Coats that same year see HBC A 6/5, fos. 109, 129.

There are biographical sketches of Christopher Middleton, Richard Norton and William Coats in *DCB*, III, 1741–1770 (Toronto and Quebec, 1974); and of Sir Charles Wager by Daniel A. Baugh in Peter Le Fevre and Richard Harding, eds, *Precursors of Nelson: British Admirals of the Eighteenth Century* (2000), pp. 101–26. Editions of the voyages of Edmond Halley and William Dampier that deal both with their achievements and their problems are by Norman J.W.Thrower, ed., *The Three Voyages of Edmond Halley* (1981); and John Masefield, ed., *Dampier's Voyages* (1906).

The Admiralty records have much material on the outfitting of Middleton's expedition between March and June 1741: Middleton's letters and lists in the file under his name in Adm 1/2099; letters to him and other papers in Adm 2/202, p.276, Adm 2/473, 11, 14 Mar 1741, 6 May 1741, 25 May 1741, 29 May 1741 and Adm 3/45, 5, 9 Mar 1741. Middleton's instructions are in Adm 2/57, pp. 98–100, 116. For Dobbs's part in drawing them up see Christopher Middleton, *A Vindication of the Conduct of Captain Christopher Middleton* (1743), pp. 6, 67; Dobbs, *Remarks*, p.12. The reference in the instructions to Coxton's voyage can be traced back to Daniel Coxe, *A Description of the English Province of Carolana* (1722), pp. 63–4. ADM B/114, 17 Mar 1741, 23 Apr 1741 has the Navy Board's correspondence relating to preparations for the expedition. Documents on the negotiations between the government and the Hudson's Bay Company are in SP Dom.42/81 and SP Dom.43/103. The reactions of the Hudson's Bay Company to the expedition can be followed in HBC A 1/35, A 2/1, and A 6/6. An important letter from Dobbs to Judge Ward on the attitude of the Company to the expedition is in PRONI: D 2092/1/5/131.

For details of the navigational and astronomical instruments taken by Middleton on the voyage see E.G.R.Taylor, *The Mathematical Practitioners of Hanoverian England* (Cambridge, 1966), pp. 186, 192, and W.E. May, *A History of Marine Navigation* (Henley-on-Thames, 1973), pp.67, 145–6. References to pressgang activities in the spring of 1741 are in Lieut. John Rankin's log of the *Furnace* (ADM L/F/109), and in the *London Evening Post*, 3 Mar 1741 (Burney). Evidence of the trade goods taken on the *Furnace* is in Christopher Middleton, *A Reply to the Remarks of Arthur Dobbs* (1744), Appendix, p.3. Peter Goodwin, *The Bomb Vessel Granado 1742* (Annapolis, 1989) has detailed descriptions and plans of a bomb vessel similar to the *Furnace*.

CHAPTER 3: *The Controversial Voyage of Christopher Middleton*

Middleton's log/journal of the *Furnace* is in Adm 51/379, I–III. under the title of 'A Journal of the Proceedings on board his Majesty's Ship Furnace Under my Command in a Voyage for the Discovery of a Passage thro' Hudsons Bay to the South Sea.' The right-hand page journal entries have been printed in Barr and Williams, *Voyages*, I, pp.111–216, except for those dealing with the outward voyage to Hudson Strait and the return voyage from Marble Island. William Moor's log/journal of the *Discovery* is in Adm 51/290, X; Rankin's log of the *Furnace* in ADM L/F/ 109. William Coats's description of the dangers of ice navigation is taken from John Barrow, ed., *The Geography of Hudson's Bay: Being the Remarks of Captain W.Coats in many voyages to that locality, between the years 1727 and 1751* (1852), pp. 90–1. Norton's building work on Fort Prince of Wales is criticised in Robson, *Account of Six Years' Residence*, and assessed more dispassionately, in Rich, *History of the Hudson's Bay Company*, I, pp. 533–5; Norton's demolition of the Old Factory can be followed in his Churchill journal for 1740–1 in HBC B 42/a/22. James Isham's Churchill journal for 1741–2, which is an invaluable source for the expedition's wintering at Churchill, is in HBC B 42/a/23. Details of clothing and other items supplied by Isham to Middleton's men are in HBC A 1/35, p.344. The 'Observations' that Isham began writing this winter are printed in E.E. Rich and A.M. Johnson, eds., *James Isham's Observations on Hudsons Bay* (Toronto and London, 1949); they have much detail on conditions at Churchill, the routine of the garrison, the importance of the Home Indians, and the construction of log tents. Middleton's scientific observations were published in 'Captain Middleton's Account of the Extraordinary Degrees and Surprising Effects of COLD in *Hudson's-Bay, North America*', *Philosophical Transactions*, XLII, pp.157–71 (1742–3). Dobbs's accusations about conditions at Churchill were made in his *Remarks*, p.50. Middleton's letter to Sir Charles Wager of 28 June 1742, describing the winter's events, is in Adm 1/2099; Isham's equivalent letter to the London Committee, dated July 1742, is in HBC A 11/13, fos.75–6.

Daily records of the explorations of the summer of 1742 are contained in the journals of Middleton, Moor and Rankin listed above. Middleton's several reports to the Admiralty about the voyage, written after he reached home waters, are in Adm 1/2099 (19 Sep., 2 Oct., 16 Oct., 28 Oct., 24 Nov 1742). John Lanrick's letter, dated 19 Sep 1742, was printed in the *Gentleman's Magazine*, XII (Nov 1742), pp. 586–7.

The central document in the controversy between Middleton and Dobbs is in Adm 1/2099 under the title 'Objections of Mr.Arthur Dobbs to the Conduct of Capt. Christopher Middleton, in a late Voyage for a Discovery of a North-West Passage: Together with Capt. Christopher Middleton's Defence of his Conduct, in Answer to the Objections of Mr. Arthur Dobbs'. It was printed in Middleton, *A Vindication of the Conduct of Captain Christopher Middleton* ... (1743), and has been reprinted in Barr and Williams, *Voyages*, I, pp.273–310. In order of publication, other books and pamphlets issued by the two protagonists are Dobbs, *Remarks upon Capt.Middleton's Defence* ... (1744); Middleton, *A Reply to the Remarks of Arthur Dobbs* ... (1744) and *Forgery Detected* ... (1744); Dobbs, *A Reply to Capt.Middleton's Answer* ... (London, 1745); Middleton, *A Reply to Mr.Dobbs's Answer* ... (1745) and *A Rejoinder to Mr.Dobbs's Reply* ... (1745). The brusque return by the Admiralty to Bulkeley of his journal of the *Wager* is mentioned in John Bulkeley and

John Cummins, *A Voyage to the South Seas, in the Years 1740–1* (2nd edn, Philadelphia, 1757), p.157.

Most of the letters exchanged between Middleton and Dobbs were printed in Middleton, *Vindication* (also Rankin's letter of 12 Feb 1742, p.155) or in Dobbs, *Remarks* (also the letters from 'Brook and Cobham', pp.142–4). Among other key documents Moor's letters of April and May supporting Middleton are in Middleton, *Rejoinder*, pp.149–50, his undated letter of 1745 attacking Middleton and denying any interest in a command is in Dobbs, *Reply*, pp.121–8, and evidence that he was in fact hoping for a command is in Dobbs to Ward, 31 March 1744: PRONI: D 2092/1/6/100. Axx's report and sketch-map of Frozen Strait were printed by Dobbs in his *Remarks*, pp.35, 144–5; Axx's denial of their authenticity is in Middleton, *Forgery Detected*, pp.5, 19–20, which also has Hodgson's sketch-map of Frozen Strait (p.15). Narratives of later voyages to Frozen Strait that confirmed Middleton's findings are in W.E. Parry, *Journal of a Second Voyage for the Discovery of a North-West Passage* (1824), and George Back, *Narrative of An Expedition in H.M.S.Terror* (1838).

Middleton's petition to the Admiralty (undated, but received 3 Jan 1745), and Dobbs's refusal to take out a private prosecution, 11 Jan 1745, are both in Adm 1/2099 (filed under date).

CHAPTER 4: *The Maritime Philosopher's Stone*

Many of the documents consulted for this chapter are printed, in whole or in part, in William Barr and Glyndwr Williams, eds, *Voyages to Hudson Bay in Search of a Northwest Passage 1741–1747*, Vol II, *The Voyage of William Moor and Francis Smith 1746–1747* (1995). Dobbs's petition to the Privy Council of March 1744 is in *Acts of the Privy Council of England: Colonial Series*, III, 1720–1745 (Hereford, 1910), p.776. His letters to Judge Ward are a valuable source of information for the events of 1744–6, especially those contained in PRONI: D2092/1/6/85, 86, 95, 100, 105. Arthur Dobbs, *An Account of the Countries adjoining to Hudson's Bay* (1744), among much else, contains the relation of Joseph la France (p. 44) and the letter of Admiral de Fonte (pp.123–8). A contemporary description of the way in which Joseph la France's map was constructed is quoted in Christian Brun, 'Dobbs and the Passage', *The Beaver* (Autumn 1958), p.29. For the Earl of Granard's interest in the Northwest Passage, his discovery of the Fonte account, and Wager's inquiries about Captain Shapley see Philippe Buache, *Considérations géographiques et physiques sur les nouvelles découvertes au nord de la Grande Mer* (Paris, 1753), p. 6; Wager to Dobbs, 4 Mar 1738, printed in Dobbs, *Remarks*, pp.100–2; and Dobbs, *Account of Hudson's Bay*, p.128. The first account of Bering's 1741–2 voyage to reach England was published in the *Gentleman's Magazine*, XIII (1743), p. 552. The comments by Coats, Isham and Oldmixon are in Coats, *Geography of Hudson's Bay*, p.2; *Isham's Observations*, pp.235, 237; John Oldmixon, *The British Empire in America* (2nd edn, 1741), I, pp.566–7.

The merchants' petition of January 1745 is printed in *Journals of the House of Commons*, XXIV, p.720; and the report and decision of the Commons on the petition in Sheila Lambert, ed., *House of Commons Sessional Papers of the 18th Century* (Wilmington, 1975), XVIII, pp.167–9, XXIV, p.805. The Act stipulating a reward for the discovery of a Northwest Passage is CAP.XVII (1745) in *The Statutes at Large* (1765). A printed copy of the Articles of Agreement of the subscribers to the new discovery expedition, dated 30 March 1745, is in BL 10460 b.38. The list of subscribers appears in Henry Ellis, *A Voyage to Hudson's Bay by the Dobbs Galley and California* (1748), pp. xxiii–v. The report of the French agent in London on the expedition is in AMAE: Correspondance Politique, Angleterre/419, fos.297v, 306v. A rough draft of the warning letter from the Hudson's Bay Company to its factors in the Bay is in HBC B 135/C/1, fos.5, 9; the reaction of the factor at Moose to the report of a shipwreck is in HBC B 135/a/16, fo.20. The sailing instructions to Captains Moor and Smith are printed in Ellis, *Voyage*, pp. 106–19. The letter from the 'Clerk of the *California*' to the Earl of Hillsborough is printed in Howard N. Eavenson, *Swaine and Drage: A Sequel to Map Maker and Indian Traders* (Pittsburgh, 1950).

The exchanges between Dobbs and Leonhard Euler are in *Philosophical Transactions*, No. 482 (1746), p. 422 and No. 483 (1747), pp. 471–6; they are summarised in the *Gentleman's Magazine*, XIX (June 1749), pp. 255–8. William Coats's views on the Northwest Passage are in his *Geography of Hudson's Bay*, p.26; Stephen Whatley's in *A Complete System of Geography* (1747), II, p.799; and John Campbell's in John Harris, ed., *Navigantium atque Itinerantium Bibliotheca: or, a compleat Collection of Voyages and Travels*, revised and enlarged by John Campbell (1744–48), II, pp.399–404, 1039–41.

CHAPTER 5: *The Disputatious Voyage of William Moor and Francis Smith*

Three accounts of the voyage survive: Henry Ellis, *A Voyage to Hudson's Bay by the Dobbs Galley and California, In the years 1746 and 1747, for Discovering a North West Passage* (1748); Clerk of the *California* [T.S. Drage], *An Account of a Voyage for the Discovery of a North-West Passage by Hudson's Streights*, 2 vols (1748–49); and Francis Smith's journal of the *California* among the Dobbs Papers in PRONI: T.416/2, with a copy in HBC E 18/2. The expedition's encounter with the Inuit in Hudson Strait is set in context in William Barr, 'The Eighteenth Century Trade between the Ships of the Hudson's Bay Company and the Hudson Strait Inuit', *Arctic*, 47 (1994), pp. 236–46. Isham's day-by-day version of the events of the winter of 1746–47 at York, including copies of the letters between him and the discovery expedition, is contained in his post journal, HBC B 239/a/29, with further comments in his 'Notes and Observations on a book *entitled* A VOYAGE TO HUDSONS BAY IN THE DOBBS GALLEY &c 1746 & 1747 *Wrote by* HENRY ELLIS's'; these are printed in Rich and Johnson, *Isham's Observations*, pp. 241–308 and pp. 197–238. Extracts from these accounts are printed in Barr and Williams, *Voyages*, II. Joseph Robson's criticism of the construction of York Fort is in his *Account of Six Years Residence*, p.30. Isham's letter home about the events of the winter is in HBC A 11/114, fo.125. Other material concerning the wintering is in *Report from the Committee Appointed to Inquire into the State and Conditions of the Countries Adjoining to Hudson's Bay, and of the Trade carried on there* (1749), especially pp.23, 29, 42, 283. Details of the explorations of the 1747 season are in the accounts of Ellis, Drage and Smith listed above.

CHAPTER 6: *A Parliamentary Inquriy and its Aftermath*

Letters from Dobbs and Samuel Smith to Judge Ward – of 26 Dec 1747, 8 Feb, 19 Apr, 26 Sep 1748 in PRONI: D 2092/1/6/42, 144, 145, and D 2092/1/7/60 – have many details not available elsewhere. Extracts from these, and from other documents used in this chapter are printed in Barr and Williams, *Voyages*, II, pp.321ff. A draft of North West Committee's petition of 26 Jan 1747, together with the responses of the Hudson's Bay Company, is in HBC E 18/1, fos. 112–15. The newspaper advertisements for the books of Drage and Ellis are in the *General Advertiser* for 27 Jan and 5 Feb 1748 (Burney). Ellis's account of the voyage was published as *A Voyage to Hudson's-Bay, by the Dobbs Galley and California In the Years 1746 and 1747* (1748). A recent biography of Ellis is Edward J. Cashin, *Governor Henry Ellis and the Transformation of British North America* (Athens, Ga., 1993). Isham's comments on Ellis's book are in *Isham's Observations*, p.199.

The campaign against the Hudson's Bay Company is covered in Glyndwr Williams, 'The Hudson's Bay Company and its Critics in the Eighteenth Century', *Transactions of the Royal Historical Society*, 5th Series, XX (1970), pp.157–63. The report of the Law Officers on the North West Committee's petition was printed in *Papers Presented to the Committee Appointed to Inquire into the State and Conditions of the Countries Adjoining to Hudson's Bay, and of the Trade carried on there* (1749), pp.74–9. For the merchants' petitions see *Journals of the House of Commons*, XXV, pp. 810–52. The evidence on the Northwest Passage given to the Parliamentary Committee of 1749 is contained in *Report from the Committee Appointed to Inquire into the State and Conditions of the Countries Adjoining to Hudson's Bay, and of the Trade carried on there* (1749), pp.27, 30, 45, 48, 53, 55, 57–8; the evidence of James Isham and George Spurrell is in HBC E.18/1, fos.197, 199. The rival submissions of the North West Committee and the Hudson's Bay Company were issued in printed form as [Arthur Dobbs], *A Short Narrative and Justification* (1749) and *A Short State of the Countries and Trade of North America. Claimed by the Hudson's Bay Company* (1749); [Joshua Sharpe], *The Case of the Hudson's-Bay Company* (1749), and *A Short View of the Countries and Trade carried on by the Company in Hudson's-Bay* (1749). The second volume of Drage's account was published as 'Clerk of the *California*', *An Account of a Voyage for the Discovery of a North-West Passage by Hudson's Streights*, II (1749). His version of the Fonte map is discussed in Warren Heckrotte and Edward H. Dahl, 'George Le Rouge, Vitus Bering, and Admiral de Fonte: a Cautionary Tale about "Cartographic Firsts"', *The Map Collector*, 64 (Autumn 1993), pp. 18–23. The location of the Strait of Anian is given in Pascoe Thomas, *A True and Impartial Journal of a Voyage to the South Sea* (1745), Appendix, p. 36. The poem on Dobbs and the Northwest Passage was published as *An Epistle to the Hon. Arthur Dobbs from a Clergyman in America* (1752). Comments on the Parliamentary outcome of the matter are in E. 18/1, f.203v. and the *London Magazine* (1749), XVIII, p.411. Henry Ellis's pamphlet was printed as *Considerations on the Great Advantages that would arise from the Discovery of the North West Passage* (1750). The reports of his approaches to the Admiralty in 1749 are contained in the *London Evening Post*, 12–14, 14–16, 26–28 Dec 1749 (Burney), and in the *Gentleman's Magazine*, 19 (1749), pp. 570–1; see also Alan Frost and Glyndwr Williams, 'The Beginnings of Britain's

Exploration of the Pacific Ocean in the Eighteenth Century', *Mariner's Mirror*, 83 (1997), p.416.

Documents relating to Middleton's last years in the Navy are in Adm 1/2105–6; Adm 2/479; Adm 3/47. His letters of 1751–2 to the Hudson's Bay Company are noted in HBC A 1/35, A 2/1. For evidence of his circumstances at the time of his death see the *Monthly Review*, LXX (1784), p. 469. His will is in PRO, Prob.11/963. Isham's career with the Hudson's Bay Company is described in an editorial appendix to *Isham's Observations*, pp. 318–25. Dobbs's career as Governor of North Carolina is assessed in Desmond Clarke, *Arthur Dobbs Esquire* (1958). His letters of 1763 and 1765 on the Northwest Passage are in CO 5/310, fos.27v, 33v. Ellis's later career is traced in Cashin, *Governor Henry Ellis*. The tangled matter of the identity of the 'Clerk of the *California*' can be followed in Howard N. Eavenson, *Map Maker and Indian Traders* (Pittsburg, 1949) and *Swaine and Drage – a Sequel to Map Maker and Indian Traders* (Pittsburg, 1950); and Percy G. Adams, 'The Case of Swaine Versus Drage: An Eighteenth-Century Publishing Mystery Solved', in Heinz Buhm, ed., *Essays in History and Literature* (Chicago, 1985), pp.157–68.

CHAPTER 7: *The Edge of a Frozen Sea*

The hostile comments of the 1750s on the Hudson's Bay Company are to be found in Josiah Tucker, *A Brief Essay . . . with regard to Trade* (2nd edn.,1750), p. 41, and R.L. Schuyler, ed., *Josiah Tucker: A Selection from his Economic and Political Writings* (New York, 1931), pp. 166–79; Joseph Robson, *An Account of Six Years Residence in Hudson's-Bay* (1752), p.6, but see also Glyndwr Williams, 'Arthur Dobbs and Joseph Robson: New Light on the Relationship between Two Early Critics of the Hudson's Bay Company', *Canadian Historical Review*, XL (1959), pp. 132–6, and Isham's views in HBC 42/b/1a, fos.3, 6v. The remark of the director of the Hudson's Bay Company on its policy of secrecy is in the copy of *A Short State* in the HBC Archives, handwritten annotation on p.5.

The journals of James Walker for the slooping voyages of 1750–4 are in HBC B 42/a/35, 37, 39, 41; his instructions and other material relating to the voyages are in HBC A 6/8, fos.17v-18, 46, 71. John Bean's sloop journals are in HBC B 42/a/45, 47. The 'Draught' taken to London by Moses Norton in 1760 is in HBC H 2/8. Details of William Christopher's voyage of 1761 are in HBC A 11/13, fo.165, B 42/b/8, fo.4; A 6/10, fo.31v. William Christopher's sloop journals for 1762 and 1763 are in HBC B 42/a/57, 58; Magnus Johnston's for 1764 in B 42/a/61. The chart showing the explorations of these voyages is HBC G 2/9; for its possible authorship see Richard I.Ruggles, *A Country So Interesting: The Hudson's Bay Company and Two Centuries of Mapping 1670–1870* (Montreal & Kingston, 1991), p. 42. Norton's conclusions are in HBC A 11/ 14, fo.3v. Joseph Robson's proposals are in his *The British Mars. Containing several Schemes and Inventions, To be Practised by Land or Sea against the Enemies of Great-Britain* (1763), pp.198–9.

Moses Norton's plans for an overland expedition to the river of copper are set out in HBC A 11/14, fo.78v, 131v; A 1/43, fo.78. 'Matonabee's and Idotlyazee's Draught' of 1767 is in HBC G 2/27. For analyses and explanations of the map see John Warkentin and Richard Ruggles, eds, *Manitoba Historical Atlas* (Winnipeg, 1970), p. 90; June Helm, 'Matonabee's Map', *Arctic Anthropology*, 26 (1989), pp. 28–47; Malcolm Lewis, 'Maps, Mapmaking and Map Use by Native North Americans', in David Woodward and G. Malcolm Lewis, eds., *The History of Cartography*, Vol II, Bk 3, *Cartography in the Traditional African, American, Arctic, Australian, and Pacific Societies* (Chicago, 1998), pp. 140–51. Alexander Cluny's book was published as *The American Traveller . . . By an old and experienced Trader* (1769); pre-publication newspaper references to it are in *Lloyd's Evening Post*, 27–29 Mar, 31 Mar-3 Apr 1769. Andrew Graham's comments on Cluny are in Glyndwr Williams, ed., *Andrew Graham's Observations on Hudson's Bay 1767–91* (1969), pp.324–30. For the manuscript copy of Cluny's book, together with a letter from the author, sent to the Earl of Dartmouth, 13 Apr 1769, see *Historical Manuscripts Commission*, 14th Report (1895), Appendix Part x, p. 67. Cluny's response to questions about his supposed explorations is in [Daines Barrington], *Summary Observations and Facts . . .* (1776), pp.18–19. Samuel Hearne's journal, together with his instructions from the Company, was published after his death as *A Journey from Prince of Wales's Fort in Hudson's Bay to the Northern Ocean* (1795). His manuscript map of his journey is in HBC G 2/10.

CHAPTER 8: *Maps, Hoaxes and Projects*

H.R.Wagner, *A Cartography of the Northwest Coast of America to the Year 1800* (Berkeley, 1937) remains indispensable; it can now be supplemented by the shorter but well-illustrated Derek Hayes, *Historical Atlas of the Pacific Northwest* (Seattle, 1999). Spanish knowledge of the American coast north of California is assessed in Dora Beale Polk, *The Island of California: A History of the Myth* (Spokane, 1991). The 'Bering phase' of Russian voyages to America has produced a considerable body of scholarly work, of which the following are available in English: Evgenii G. Kushnarev, edited and translated by E.A.P. Crownhart-Vaughan, *Bering's Search for the Strait: the First Kamchatka Expedition 1725–1730* (Portland, Oregon, 1990); Raymond H. Fisher, *Bering's Voyages: Whither and Why* (Seattle, 1997); Georg Wilhelm Steller, *Journal of a Voyage with Bering 1741–1742*, edited with an introduction by O.W. Frost (Stanford, 1988); Sven Waxell, *The American Expedition*, translated by M.A. Michael (1952); *Russian Penetration of the North Pacific Ocean*, II, *A Documentary Record 1700–1797*, edited and translated by Basil Dmytryshyn, E.A.P. Crownhart-Vaughan and Thomas Vaughan (Portland, Oregon, 1988); *Bering's Voyages: The Reports from Russia by Gerhard Friedrich Müller*, translated with commentary by Carol Urness (Fairbanks, 1986); O.W. Frost, ed., *Bering and Chirikov: The American Voyages and their Impact* (Anchorage, 1992). The earliest report of Bering's first voyage to reach England was printed in the *Historical Register*, XV (1730), p.60; and of his second voyage in the *Gentleman's Magazine*, XIII (1743), p.552. J.B.du Halde, *Histoire de la Chine*, was published in Paris in 1735, with an English edition, *The General History of China*, published in London the next year which contained the Bering narrative in Vol IV, pp.429–40. For the debate between Dobbs, Campbell and Euler see Sources for Chapter 4 above.

The speculative geography of northwest America based on the Fuca and Fonte accounts was outlined in J.N. Delisle, *Explication de la Carte des Nouvelles Découvertes au Nord de la Mer du Sud* (Paris, 1752) and Philippe Buache, *Considerations Géographiques et Physiques sur les Nouvelles Découvertes au Nord de la Grande Mer* (Paris, 1753); and criticised in John Green, *Remarks in Support of the New Chart of North and South America* (1753), Robert de Vaugondy, *Essai sur l'Histoire de la Géographie* (Paris, 1755); J.N. Bellin, *Remarques sur la Carte de l'Amérique Septentrionale* (Paris, 1755). For illuminating comment on the role of geographers in France at this time see Mary Spanberg Pedley, *Bel et Utile: the Work of the Robert de Vaugondy Family of Mapmakers* (Tring, 1992), especially Ch 4, 'Patrons, Politics, and Polar Exploration'. J.N. Delisle's interview with Charles de Brosses is described in A.C.Taylor, *Le Président De Brosses et l'Australie* (Paris, 1937), p.53. The volume containing Dobbs's reaction to the Fonte controversy, together with translations of Delisle's memoir of 1750 and of Müller's *Lettre* was published in 1754 under the title, *Observations on the Russian Discoveries, etc. by Governor Dobbs*. The *Gentleman's Magazine*, XXIV (1754), pp. 123–8, 166–7, printed a summary of the whole matter, together with Delisle's map of September 1752. An earlier description of Buache's map was printed in *London Daily Advertiser*, 16 Jul 1752 (Burney). Collinson's letter to Franklin is in Bertha Solis-

Cohen, 'Philadelphia's Expeditions to Labrador', *Pennsylvania History*, XIX (1952), p. 159; Franklin's opinion on the Fonte account is in *Notes and Queries*, 4th Series, IV (1869), pp.406–7. An English translation of the third volume of G.F. Müller's *Sammlung Russischer Geschicte* (St Petersburg, 1758) was published in 1761 under the title, *Voyages from Asia to America, for Completing the Discoveries of the North West Coast of America*. *Noticia de la California* (Madrid, 1757) by Andrés Marcos Burriel was published in English as *A Natural and Civil History of California* (1759). The reaction of T.S. Drage/Charles Swaine to the Fonte letter fills the pages of *The Great Probability of a North West Passage: Deduced from Observations on the Letter of Admiral De Fonte* (1768). For evaluations of the Fonte controversy see H.R. Wagner, 'Apocryphal Voyages to the Northwest Coast of America', *Proceedings of the American Antiquarian Society*, XLI (1931), pp.179–234; Numa Broc, *La Géographie des Philosophes: Géographes et Voyageurs Français au XVIIIe-Siècle* (Paris, 1974); Lucie Lagarde, 'Le Passage du Nord-Ouest et la Mer de l'Ouest dans la Cartographie Française du 18e Siècle', *Imago Mundi*, 41 (1989), pp.19–43; Glyndwr Williams, 'An Eighteenth-Century Spanish Investigation into the Apocryphal Voyage of Admiral Fonte', *Pacific Historical Review*, 30 (1961), pp.319–27. Many of the speculative maps of North America in this period are reproduced in 'The Apocryphal De Fonte Maps', in Kenneth A. Kershaw, ed., *Early Printed Maps of Canada*, Vol IV, *1703–1799* (Ancaster, Ont., 1998), pp.171–206.

For Byron's voyage, his instructions, and the Spanish reaction see Robert E. Gallagher, ed., *Byron's Journal of his Circumnavigation 1764–1766* (Cambridge, 1964). Much scholarship on Drake's voyage is gathered together in Norman J.W.Thrower, ed., *Sir Francis Drake and the Famous Voyage, 1577–1580* (Berkeley and Los Angeles, 1984). A radically new interpretation of Drake's 'farthest north' is presented in Samuel Bawlf, *Sir Francis Drake's Secret Voyage to the Northwest Coast of America AD 1579* (Salt Spring Island, BC, 2001). Lancaster's mysterious reference to the Northwest Passage first appeared in Samuel Purchas, *Pilgrimes* (Glasgow, 1905–6 edn), XIV, p. 435. William Dampier, *A New Voyage Round the World* (1697) has been reprinted many times from 1729 onwards. The authoritative edition of Cook's second voyage is J.C. Beaglehole, ed., *The Voyage of the Resolution and Adventure 1772–1775* (Cambridge, 1961); Cook's comments on his failure to find the southern continent are printed on p. 693. Proposals to the Earl of Dartmouth from Engel, Hanson and others regarding northern exploration are in WSL: Dartmouth MSS. D 1778; those from Barrington, Blankett, Engel and others to the Earl of Sandwich are scattered through NMM: Sandwich Papers, especially F/5/1 (Engel), F 36/13, 15, 16, 22, 29, 32 (Barrington),

F 5/38 and F 6/29 (Blankett). For Blankett's proposals see also Howard Fry, 'The Commercial Ambitions behind Captain Cook's Last Voyage', *New Zealand Journal of History*, 7 (1973), p.189. French interest in mounting a northern voyage in 1772–4 is described in Jean-Etienne Martin-Allanic, *Bougainville Navigateur et les Découvertes de son Temps* (Paris, 1964), II, especially Ch.XLIV. For London newspaper worries about such a voyage see the *Morning Chronicle*, 4 Dec 1773, and the *London Chronicle*, 28–30 Dec 1773; the report on Baron d'Ulfeld's voyage is in the *London Chronicle*, 15–18 Jan 1774 (all Burney). The Royal Society's role in northern exploration can be followed in its Minute Book, VI. Among relevant publications are Philippe Buache, 'Observations upon the North Sea, commonly called the Ice Sea', *Gentleman's Magazine*, 30 (1760), pp.284–6; Daines Barrington, *The Probability of Reaching the North Pole Discussed* (1775) and *Summary Observations and Facts* (1776); Samuel Engel, *Mémoires et Observations Géographiques et Critiques sur la Situation des Pays Septentrionaux de l'Asie et l'Amérique* (Lausanne, 1765). There is evidence of the East India Company's interest in Engel's theories in a letter from Rudolph Valtravers to the Earl of Dartmouth, 30 Dec 1774, printed in *Historical Manuscripts Commission*, 15th Report (London, 1896), Appendix, Pt I, p.212. John Constantine Phipps' account of his attempt to sail near the North Pole was published as *A Voyage towards the North Pole* (1774). The Act of 1775 is contained in *The Statutes at Large*, XXXI, pp. 155–7. The description of the dinner party at which Cook volunteered his services is in Andrew Kippis, *The Life of Captain James Cook* (1788), pp.324–5. Cook's letter to John Walker is printed in J.C. Beaglehole, ed., *The Voyage of the Resolution and Discovery* (Cambridge, 1967), p.1488, while Boswell's comment is in G.B. Hill, ed., *Boswell's Life of Johnson* (Oxford, 1934–50), III, p.7.

CHAPTER 9: *The Puzzling Voyage of James Cook*

The main source for Cook's last voyage is the comprehensive two-volume work edited by J.C. Beaglehole, *The Voyage of the Resolution and Discovery* (1967). This contains Cook's instructions, his journal, and extracts from several other journals kept on the expedition, and can be supplemented by J.C. Beaglehole, *The Life of Captain James Cook* (1974). For the background to the voyage see Glyndwr Williams, 'Myth and Reality: James Cook and the Theoretical Geography of Northwest America', in Robin Fisher and Hugh Johnston, eds, *Captain James Cook and His Times* (Vancouver, 1979), pp.59–80. Details of the assistance given by the Hudson's Bay Company to the Admiralty are contained in the introduction by

John Douglas to the official account of the voyage by James Cook and James King, *A Voyage to the Pacific Ocean . . . for Making Discoveries in the Northern Hemisphere* (1784), I; and notes on the friendship of Cook and William Christopher in A.C.S. Christopher, *The Family of Christopher and Some Others* (privately printed 1933, copy in HBC Archives).

The English edition of Jacob von Stählin's work was published as *An Account of the New Northern Archipelago, Lately Discovered by the Russians* (1774). Robert de Vaugondy's map, 'Nouveau Système Géographique', is contained in his *Mémoire sur les Pays de l'Asie et de l'Amérique* (Paris, 1774). Hanson's memorial is in WSL: Dartmouth MSS, D 1778, v.286. Russian trading and other voyages to Alaska after Bering are covered in James R. Masterton and Helen Brower, *Bering's Successors 1745–1780* (Seattle, 1948); and in Stuart R.Tompkins and Max L.Moorhead, 'Russia's Approach to America. Part I – From Russian Sources, 1741–1761. Part II – From Spanish Sources, 1761–1775', *British Columbia Historical Quarterly*, XIII (1949), pp. 55–66, 231–55. General accounts of Spanish activity on the northwest coast in the 1770s are Warren L.Cook, *Flood Tide of Empire: Spain and the Pacific Northwest, 1543–1819* (New Haven, 1973), John Kendrick, *The Men with Wooden Feet: The Spanish Exploration of the Pacific Northwest* (Toronto, 1986) and Christon I.Archer, 'The Spanish Reaction to Cook's Third Voyage', in Fisher and Johnston, *Captain James Cook and His Times*, pp. 99–120. Accounts of the first two Spanish voyages along the coast have been edited by Herbert K.Beals, *Juan Pérez on the Northwest Coast* (Portland, Oregon, 1989) and *For Honor & Country: The Diary of Bruno de Hezeta* (Portland, Oregon, 1985). Daines Barrington's response to Spanish suspicions about Cook's third voyage is to be found in his *Miscellanies* (1781), p.472; French suspicions are set out in a memorandum in AMAE: Mémoires et Documents, Angleterre/6. fos.156–61. The Board of Trade's opinion on Robert Rogers' plans is in C.O. 324/18, p. 411. For the East India Company's interest in Engel's memoir see *Historical Manuscripts Commission*, 15th Report (1896), Appendix, Part I, p.212.

Lieut Pickersgill's instructions are in Adm 2/101, 14 May 1776; his journal for 1776 is in Adm 51/540, Part VII. Letters from the Admiralty after his return are in Adm 2/736, pp.38–9, 57, 123; the minutes of his court-martial in Adm 1/5308. On his personality see Beaglehole, *Voyage of the Resolution and Endeavour*, p.975; Johan Reinhold Forster, *History of the Voyages and Discoveries made in the North* (1786), p.408. Lieut Young's instructions are in Adm 2/1132, 13 Mar 1777; his journal is in Adm 51/540, Part VIII.

The quotations from the journals kept on Cook's third voyage by Cook and other officers are taken from Beaglehole, *Voyage of the Resolution and Discovery*, supplemented by extracts from Christine Holmes, ed., *Captain Cook's Final Voyage: the Journal of Midshipman George Gilbert* (Horsham, 1982), pp. 60, 157; log of Lieut James King, Adm 55/122; [John Rickman], *Journal of Captain Cook's Last Voyage to the Pacific Ocean, on Discovery* (1781); David Samwell, BL Eg.MS.2591; James Burney, *A Chronological History of North-Eastern Voyages of Discovery . . .* (1819); log of Lieut John Gore, Adm 55/120; log of midshipman Edward Riou, Adm 51/4529, Part III; log of midshipman Henry Martin, Adm 51/4531, Part I. The report of the Spanish voyage of 1774 to the northwest coast appeared in the *London Evening Post*, 29 May 1776. The charts made by Cook and his officers on the voyage have been printed in Andrew David, ed., *The Charts and Coastal Views of Captain Cook's Voyages*, Vol III, *The Voyage of the Resolution and Discovery 1776–1780* (1997). Helpful line maps of the tracks of Cook's ships throughout the voyage appear in John Robson, *Captain Cook's World: Maps of the Life and Voyages of James Cook R.N.* (Auckland, 2000). For Cook's behaviour on the voyage, especially in Hawaii, see the contrasting views in Gananath Obeyesekere, *The Apotheosis of Captain Cook: European Mythmaking in the Pacific* (2nd edn, Princeton, 1997) and Marshall Sahlins, *How "Natives" Think: About Captain Cook, For Example* (Chicago, 1995). There is interesting comment on Cook's health during the voyage in James Watt, 'Medical Aspects and Consequences of Cook's Voyages', in Fisher and Johnston, *Captain James Cook and His Times*, especially pp.152–7.

For information on the Russian discoveries and charts, including Müller's opinions, see William Coxe, *An Account of the Russian Discoveries between Asia and America* (1780); also William Robertson, *The History of America*, Vol I (1777). More recent evaluations of the Russian accounts and charts are in A.I. Andreyev, 'Trudy G.F.Millera o vtoroi Kamchatskoi ekspeditsii', *Izvestiia Vsesoiuznogo Geograficheskogo Obshchestva*, XCI (1959), pp.1–16, kindly translated for the present writer by the late Professor Raymond H. Fisher; O.M. Medushevskaya, 'Cartographical Sources for the history of Russian geographical discoveries in the Pacific Ocean in the second half of the 18th century', transl. J.R. Gibson, *Cartographica*, Monograph No.13 (Toronto, 1975), pp. 67–89. Sandwich's comment on Forster is in NMM Sandwich Papers: v/12, p.336. Cook's letter to the Admiralty of 20 October 1778 and Governor Behm's report on the sighting of Cook's ships are printed in Beaglehole, *Voyage of the Resolution and Discovery*, pp.1530–32, 1547.

CHAPTER 10: *Entering the Labyrinth*

For news of Cook's death see the *London Gazette*, 11 Jan 1780; Beagle-hole, *Voyage of the Resolution and Discovery*, pp.1552, 1554; Beaglehole, *Life of Cook*, p.689 (for reactions of Sandwich, Catherine II, and George III). Comments on the geographical significance of his voyage are in the *London Chronicle*, 12 , 22 and 28 Jan 1780; the *Gazeteer*, 17 Jan and 17 Oct 1780; the *London Magazine*, XLIX (Jul 1780), pp.307–12; Barrington, *Miscellanies*, preface; Samuel Engel, *Remarques sur la Partie de la Relation du Capitaine Cook, qui concerne de Détroit entre l'Asie et l'Amérique* (Berne, 1781); William Coxe, *An Account of the Russian Discoveries between Asia and America* (2nd edn, 1787), pp. 441–3; John Reinhold Forster, *History of the Voyages and Discoveries made in the North* (1786), p. 454.

For the burgeoning maritime fur trade on the northwest coast see William Ellis, *An Authentic Narrative of a Voyage . . . in search of a North-West Passage* (1782); Thomas Vaughan and Bill Holm, *Soft Gold: The Fur Trade & Cultural Exchange on the Northwest Coast of America* (2nd edn, Portland, Oregon, 1990); James R.Gibson, *Otter Skins, Boston Ships, and China Goods: the Maritime Fur Trade of the Northwest Coast, 1785–1841* (Seattle, 1992), especially Chapter I. The voyage of La Pérouse can be followed in Catherine Gaziello, *L'Expedition de Lapérouse 1785–1788* (Paris, 1984) while the extracts from his journal are taken from John Dunmore, ed. and transl., *The Journal of Jean-François de Galaup de la Pérouse 1785–1788* (1994). For first-hand accounts of the voyages of the maritime fur traders see [James Strange], *James Strange's Journal and Narrative* (Madras, 1928); [William Beresford], *A Voyage round the World 1785–1788 by Captain George Dixon* (1789); Nathaniel Portlock, *A Voyage Round the World* (1789); James Colnett, 'A Voyage to the N.W. Side of America by J.Colnett', Adm 55/146; F.W. Howay, ed., *The Journal of Captain James Colnett aboard the Argonaut 1789–1791* (Toronto, 1940); W. Kaye Lamb, 'The Mystery of Mrs.Barkley's Diary', *British Columbia Historical Quarterly*, VI (1942), pp. 31–59; F.W.Howay, *Voyages of the "Columbia" to the Northwest Coast 1787–1790 and 1790–1793* (repr. Portland, Oregon, 1990), for Robert Haswell's log. Many of the traders' charts of the northwest coast are reproduced (with explanatory text) in Derek Hayes, *Historical Atlas of the Pacific Northwest: Maps of Exploration and Discovery* (Seattle, 1999).

Evidence that the Mourelle journal was brought to England by J.H. Magellan is in NMM: Sandwich Papers F 65, 66, 67. For Joseph Banks's interest in the northwest coast see David Mackay, *In the Wake of Cook: Exploration, Science & Empire 1780–1801* (1985), especially

Chapters 3, 4; F.W. Howay, 'Four Letters from Richard Cadman Etches to Sir Joseph Banks, 1788–1792', *British Columbia Historical Quarterly* VI (1942), pp.125–39. There is information about the northwest coast voyages in the Banks Papers at the Sutro Library, San Francisco, copies of which are held at the Banks Archive, Natural History Museum, London: PNI: 3A (James Hanna); 19A, 19B, 21 (James Strange); 8 (William Barkley); 1 (Charles Duncan), 18C (Peter Pond). Extracts from these have been printed in Glyndwr Williams, '"The Common Center of We Discoverers": Sir Joseph Banks, Exploration and Empire in the Late 18th Century', R.E.R.Banks and others, *Sir Joseph Banks: A Global Perspective* (Kew, 1994), pp. 177–191. On Dalrymple and the northwest coast see Howard Fry, *Alexander Dalrymple and the Expansion of British Trade* (1970), especially Chapter 8; and a series of pamphlets and memoranda written by Dalrymple at this time: *A Plan for Promoting the Fur-Trade, and Securing it to This Country, by Uniting the Operations of the East-India and Hudson's Bay Companys* (1789); *Memoir of a Map of the Lands around the North-Pole* (1789); memoranda, n.d. and 23 Feb 1791, IOR: Home Series, Misc.494/5, pp. 429, 445–6; memorandum [Sep 1789?], CO 42/21, fos.56–62; memoranda to Evan Nepean, 2 , 11 Feb 1790, CO 42/72 (p.501 of this file has Dalrymple's refusal to admit of 'a Pope in Geography'). On the voyages and projects of John Meares see his *Voyages made in the Years 1788 and 1789, from China to the North West Coast of America* (1790); George Dixon, *Remarks on the Voyages of John Meares* (1790); F.W. Howay, ed., *The Dixon-Meares Controversy* (Toronto, 1929); and a recent biography which makes the best of a poor case, J.Richard Nokes, *Almost a Hero: The Voyages of John Meares, R.N., to China, Hawaii and the Northwest Coast* (Pullman, WA, 1998). Critical comments on Meares' book are in the *Monthly Review*, N.S. (Mar 1791), p.257 and the *Critical Review*, N.S., I (Jan 1791), p.4. Henry Ellis's support for Meares is shown by a letter of 6 Aug 1789 in the Whewell Papers (Add MS a 81) in the Wren Library, Trinity College, Cambridge. On Peter Pond see H.R. Wagner, *Peter Pond, Fur Trader and Explorer* (New Haven, 1955); R.H. Dillon, 'Peter Pond and the Overland Route to Cook's Inlet', *Pacific North West Quarterly*, XLII (1951) (which also contains the critical comment, by J.M. Nooth, on Pond's longitudes); Barry Gough, 'Peter Pond', DCB, V (1983), 681–6. Pond's prototype map of the Northwest, dated 6 December 1787 (and at 50 x 24 inches too large to reproduce here) is in PRO: CO 700/America 49. There is a recent biography of Mackenzie by Barry Gough, *First Across the Continent: Sir Alexander Mackenzie* (Norman, Oklahoma, 1997). For the reaction of Barrington and Dalrymple to reports of Mackenzie's journey to the Arctic Ocean see BL Eg.MSS. 2186, fo.18.

A summary of the plans for a naval expedition to the northwest coast, and Vancouver's instructions are contained in W.Kaye Lamb, ed., *The Voyage of George Vancouver 1791–1795* (1984), I, pp.21–7, 283–6. The voyage of Charles Duncan to Hudson Bay can be followed in HBC C 7/175, fo.4v (Duncan's instructions), fos.10–11 (George Dixon's instructions); HBC C 1/204, 205 (journals of the *Beaver* kept by its mate, George Taylor); HBC C 7/13 (Duncan's illness). Duncan's explanation of his failure is in William Goldson, *Observations on the Passage between the Atlantic and Pacific Oceans* (Portsmouth, 1793). For the complaint of the Hudson's Bay Company director about the expense of the voyage see BL Eg.MSS.2186, fo.73.

CHAPTER 11: *Last Hopes*

The best English-language survey of the Spanish voyages on the northwest coast and their diplomatic background remains Cook, *Flood Tide of Empire*. The expedition of Alejandro Malaspina has given rise to a great deal of recent scholarship, much of it in Spanish, although there is now a good, short biography in English: John Kendrick, *Alejandro Malaspina: Portrait of a Visionary* (Montreal/Kingston, London, and Ithica, 1999). Correspondence between Malaspina and the Navy Minister, Antonio Valdés, is in the Museo Naval, Madrid. Letters which discuss Malaspina's route and the alleged voyage of Ferrer Maldonado, are in MN: MS 1826, fos.1–5v, MS 278, fos.6v, 53, 109–11, MS 2296, fos.36–8, MS 583, fos.46–8, 86–7v, 88v-9v. The journals of Malaspina and of José Bustamante, recently published in Spain as part of a multi-volume edition of the more important documents from the expedition, have much detail on the expedition's diversion to Alaska to search for Maldonado's strait: Ricardo Cerezo Martínez, ed., *La Expedición Malaspina 1789–1794*, Vol II (in 2 parts), *Diario General del Viaje por Alejandro Malaspina* (Madrid, 1990) especially pp.279–85 for Malaspina's comments on the Maldonado account, written during the summer of 1792, and pp.285–323 on the explorations of the Alaskan coast the previous summer; and Dolores Higueras Rodríguez, ed., *La Expedición Malaspina 1789–1794*, Vol IX, *Diario General del Viaje Corbeta Atrevida por José Bustamante y Guerra* (Madrid, 1999), especially pp.231–56 for Bustamante's assessment of the Maldonado account. The quotations from Suria are taken from Donald C. Cutter, ed., *Journal of Tomás de Suria of his Voyage with Malaspina to the North-West Coast of America* (Fairfield, Washington, 1980), pp.35, 58. Among many stimulating essays in Robin Inglis, ed., *Spain and the Northwest Coast* (Vancouver, 1992), Dario Manfredi, 'An unknown episode behind the Northwest Coast campaign of Malaspina's expedition', takes a fresh look at the influence of Maldonado's supposed voyage. I am indebted to Carlos Novi for the critical reference to Maldonado by Juan Bautista Muñoz (Colección Muñoz, Indias – Viajes (9/4802), I, fos. 18–21, 31 Jul 1791, Real Academia de la Historia, Madrid), as well as for much help generally on the rediscovery of Maldonado's account. George Dixon's description and chart of Port Mulgrave are in [William Beresford], *A Voyage Round the World ... by Captain George Dixon* (1789), especially p.170. For the Spanish surveys of the Strait of Juan de Fuca in 1790–2 see H.R. Wagner, *Spanish Explorations in the Strait of Juan de Fuca* (Santa Ana, 1933), and John Kendrick, ed., *The Voyage of the Sutil and Mexicana 1792: The last Spanish exploration of the northwest coast of America* (Spokane, 1991). Caamaño's comment on the apocryphal voyages is in H.R. Wagner and W.A. Newcombe, eds, 'The Journal of Jacinto Caamaño', *British Columbia Historical Quarterly*, II (1938), p.299.

The standard source for Vancouver's voyage is the magnificent edition by W. Kaye Lamb, *Voyage of George Vancouver*, whose four volumes not only contain Vancouver's own journal and letters, but also substantial extracts from the journals kept by other officers and crew members as well as by the naturalist, Archibald Menzies. Recent scholarship is represented in essays on various aspects of the voyage in Robin Fisher and Hugh Johnston, *From Maps to Metaphors: the Pacific World of George Vancouver* (Vancouver, 1993), and Stephen Haycox et al., *Enlightenment and Exploration in the North Pacific 1741–1805* (Seattle and London, 1997). Those interested in Vancouver's survey methods will find much expert guidance in the essays in those volumes by Andrew David ('Vancouver's Survey Methods and Surveys', *Maps to Metaphors*, pp. 51–69 and 'From Cook to Vancouver: The British Contribution to the Cartography of Alaska', *Enlightenment and Exploration*, pp.116–31). John M.Naish, *The Interwoven Lives of George Vancouver, Archibald Menzies, Joseph Whidbey, and Peter Puget: Exploring the Pacific Northwest Coast* (Lewiston/Queenston/Lampeter, 1996), pays tribute to the collaborative nature of Vancouver's great survey. The Spanish description of a 'dead-end' channel in the Strait of Juan de Fuca comes from Wagner, *Spanish Explorations*, pp. 264–5. Howay, *Voyages of the "Columbia"*, gives the American side of the encounter with Vancouver near the entrance of the Strait of Juan de Fuca. Gough, *First Across the Continent*, has a hair-raising account of Mackenzie's descent of the Bella Coola River. Robin Fisher, *Vancouver's Voyage: Charting the Northwest Coast, 1791–1795* (Vancouver, Toronto and Seattle, 1992) combines a scholarly text with photographs of the coastline surveyed by Vancouver two hundred years earlier.

CONCLUSION

Cook's criticism of other seamen's surveys is in Beaglehole, *Voyage of the Endeavour*, p. 413. The speech (by Henry Dundas) on the wider implications of the Nootka Sound crisis is printed in *Parliamentary History*, XXVIII, p. 979. John Barrow's claim was made in his *Chronological History of Voyages into the Arctic Regions* (1818), p.364.

INDEX